B73:17

THE PEOPLE
LOOK AT
TELEVISION

THE PEOPLE LOOK AT TELEVISION

A Study of Audience Attitudes

BY

GARY·A·STEINER

A Report of a Study at the

Bureau of Applied Social Research

Columbia University

ALFRED·A·KNOPF

New York　:　1 9 6 3

L. C. catalog card number: 63-9124

THIS IS A BORZOI BOOK

PUBLISHED BY ALFRED A. KNOPF, INC.

FIRST EDITION

To **B.B.** *and* **J.H.L.**

for the best of reasons

Foreword

FOR ABOUT fifteen years now, television has been at, or close to, the center of attention in America. The people have been watching television, and the critics, commentators, and educators have been watching the people watching television. On the whole, the one has liked what it saw; the other, not.

Anything attracting so much attention and taking up so much time is bound to come in for close scrutiny in a society as open and as self-conscious as ours. So it is no wonder that, just as it has taken over their audiences, television has taken over from radio and the movies as a subject of controversy and debate: Is it good? Is it good enough? Can it be better? Should it be better? How should it be run? Who is responsible? Is it ruining American taste, morality, values? Is it sufficiently uplifting or only Playtime U.S.A.?

This running debate has been especially intense over the past few years, since the quiz scandals and the charges about "the vast waste-land." In the main, it has rested on two differing approaches: differing judgments about the proper values to be used in appraising television, and their appropriate weights; and differing assumptions about the facts.

As for the values: To what extent should television be judged as an educational medium or an entertainment medium? How much should audience preferences be taken into account in determining what is on? How can we adjudicate among the preferences of audiences of different composition and size? What public ends should television be asked to serve? Such questions are not only complicated but are invested with ethical and aesthetic, economic and political, considerations; in the end, they represent personal judgments of taste and social values. It is impor-tant to clarify such issues and, if not build agreement, as least know where the disagreements lie and what they are based on. As anyone who has ever been involved in this debate knows, such issues are not easy to discuss constructively even among men of good will and selfless interest. In any case, this book does not address itself directly to such matters—though it has an indirect contribution to make that is, in my view, of considerable substance.

What this book does deal with directly is the second source of difference: the facts of the matter. It sets forth an important set of facts about the public's reaction to, feelings about, and uses of television. To the extent that the protagonists make assumptions about these facts—and various sides do make opposing assumptions, each to its own ben-efit—to that extent this volume does speak directly to the case. For it sets down, in my judgment, an important set of findings about audience response that are supported by scientific evidence rather than personal preference. The findings are relevant to the great public issues involved, and they should be taken into account by the debaters of all sides, regardless of how congenial they may be to a particular position. There may be no disputing tastes, in the sense that partisans cannot easily be brought to change their minds, but there is no disputing facts except with better facts. That seems to me the contribution of this book: it presents an array of facts about people's use of television that re-moves some aspects of the debate from further controversy. It provides a factual platform from which the debate must subsequently go forward.

I say "must" because I believe that until better or full evidence is produced, the protagonists have to accept Dr. Steiner's determination of the answers to such questions as these: How devoted are the people to television? To what extent do they think they are dependent on it? How guilty do they feel about how much or what they watch? What are their real concerns about their children's viewing? How selective in their watching are people of different educational levels? How do their attitudes toward particular programs relate to their feelings about viewing in general? How much satisfaction is there with television programming in general, and with one's own favorite programs? How fully or consistently do the rank-and-file critics of television practice what they preach? How do the viewing practices of the critics differ from those of the criticized, if at all?

Unless one takes the position that how the audience feels has nothing to do with what television ought to be, it seems to me that one test of the seriousness of the debaters' intentions is the degree to which these facts are considered—all of them, and not simply those that happen to support any particular position. For some findings of this study can be taken to support or oppose practically every position taken in the current discussion over the state of television. Both those who believe that the present system is the best of all possible systems and those who believe it the worst will find things in this study to please and to displease them. The study will have served one of its purposes—and it is an important social purpose—if its results are accepted for what they are and, in time to come, constitute an agreed-upon foundation for the continuing discussion of what the facts "mean." Certainly nothing in this book will settle any of the important issues revolving around American television, but everything in it is aimed at clarifying, verifying, discriminating, the facts about the audience.

In my view, Dr. Steiner has done as good a study of the audience, of this kind, as exists in the literature of communications research. The inquiry was carefully planned and skillfully carried out. Dr. Steiner has added a number of ingenious innovations to such inquiries—for example, in his application of projective devices to a mass survey and his use of word lists. Furthermore, and perhaps even more important, he developed a quasi-experimental test of the correspondence between what people say about television and what they do about it, in a supplementary study of the responses of a special sample on whose viewing habits he has independent data. In such respects, he shows the distinctive contributions the professional psychologist can bring to a field usually investigated from the standpoint of public opinion.

A few years ago I had occasion to make some critical remarks about the present state of communications research. Had this study been available then, I would have had to qualify a part of what I said. Accordingly, it is a matter of professional as well as personal gratification that this study was done under the sponsorship of the Bureau of Applied Social Research, Columbia University, when I was its Director. The Bureau has a tradition of research in this field, and in my view Dr. Steiner has added to it a most worthy study.

This inquiry was first proposed in 1955 by Dr. Frank Stanton, president of the Columbia Broadcasting System and himself a pioneer in communications research. Dr. Stanton urges, as he later told the F.C.C., that "we embark on a comprehensive, impartial nationwide study of what the public wants from television and what it means to the public. We need the answer to the most difficult and vexing questions, on which public opinion of all degrees should be solicited, as to the role of television in our society." I am grateful to Dr. Stanton and his colleagues at the Columbia Broadcasting System for recognizing the need for this study, providing the financial support, and allowing the Bureau full freedom in its planning and execution. I am also grateful to the University of Chicago for enabling Dr. Steiner, a member of the faculty of the Graduate School of Business there, to conduct this inquiry.

I can only hope that the research community, the broadcasting industry, the government officers involved, the critics and the commentators, and all other parties interested in the present and the future of this most powerful of communications media—that each will see in this study of television, as I do, a large body of informed findings for their consideration and their reflection.

BERNARD BERELSON

August 15, 1962
Irvington-on-Hudson, New York

Acknowledgments

THIS STUDY was initiated and supported by a grant from the Columbia Broadcasting System to the Bureau of Applied Social Research, for the purpose of developing comprehensive data on the present place of television in the minds of its public. The findings were to provide a base-line from which trends could be measured, and to form a background for further investigation of the medium's potential.

Such an investigation was first proposed in 1955 by the President of the Columbia Broadcasting System, Dr. Frank Stanton; in 1960 he summarized its purpose as follows: ". . . we owe it to our audience as well as ourselves to establish some systematic method of inviting the public to participate in shaping what we do. Such a thoughtful and conscientious probing could well provide a newer and far better set of navigation charts than anyone in the broadcasting industry—or in any area in the mass communications—has ever had."

First, then, I am indebted to Dr. Stanton, whose continued and objective interest in the role of the mass media and in communications research made this book possible.

Bernard Berelson, as Director of the Bureau, was responsible for my affiliation with the project, and bore the consequences with patience. I thank him for the opportunity to carry out this interesting study, for the help and advice he provided throughout, and for editorial polish on the manuscript.

Deans W. Allen Wallis and James H. Lorie, of the Graduate School of Business, the University of Chicago, kindly permitted and encouraged my participation in the enterprise. The School also made substantial contributions of physical and administrative resources.

The survey itself had at least as many benefactors as respondents; but I should like, specifically, to mention just a few of those to whom I owe special gratitude. My thanks to:

Jay Eliasberg and Phil Luttinger, of CBS, for technical advice and resources throughout the investigation;

The field supervisors, Selma Monsky and Carolyn Crusius, and their respective organizations, NORC and Elmo Roper and Associates, for excellent interviews with an unusually long and complicated questionnaire;

Barbara McAllister and Ruth Campbell, who supervised the elaborate coding operation with great skill and perseverance;

Helmut Guttenberg, for getting the mass of data onto the cards and off again and making it intelligible in the process—his analytic ability was a source of continuous clarity;

Nan Reiss, much more than secretary, who saw me through this and several concurrent crises with efficient equanimity;

My research assistant, Peter Scalise, whose contributions defy description;

Clara Shapiro, who kept tabs on a bewildering collection of administrative and personal matters, with good humor and careful consideration;

Harry Roberts, for his always ready and helpful statistical advice, with the clear understanding that he bears no responsibility for the specific treatments;

For most helpful readings of the manuscript, Professors Sam Becker, Edmund DeS. Brunner, Paul Lazarsfeld, Kurt Lange, Bill McPhee, Ithiel Pool, and Wilbur Schramm;

John Cowden, of CBS, who facilitated and expedited the project in any number of ways, and Herbert Roan, who styled the charts that make the survey data not only clear but attractive.

Finally, few of my colleagues at Chicago or at the Bureau escaped involvement in some aspect of design or interpretation; I acknowledge them collectively, but appreciate them singly.

G. A. S.

Contents

Contents

THE PEOPLE
LOOK AT
TELEVISION

Introduction

TELEVISION, like most matters invested with the public interest, has had more critics and supporters than scholars; and those who view with alarm, as well as those who take pride in its nightly audience assume an enormous if unspecified impact on America, its families, and its future.

The hopes and fears have often been boundless, and long-lived. As early as 1938, over a decade before the real beginning of home television, a distinguished commentator on the American scene wrote:

> I believe TV is going to be the test of the modern world, and that in this new opportunity to see beyond the range of our vision we shall discover either a new and unbearable disturbance of the general peace or a saving radiance in the sky. We shall stand or fall by TV—of that I am quite sure.[1]

[1] E. B. White: "Removal," July 1938, quoted in *Harper's Magazine,* September 1960.

Twelve years later, in 1950, the great test began in earnest. The number of television homes had risen from 1 million to nearly 4 million during the previous year alone, leading a contemporary reviewer to conclude:

> It may be a reflection on our sense of values, but the sundered atom is far behind the TV tube as the greatest technological influence on the daily lives of millions of Americans.[2]

And this at a time when coverage was still confined to one home in ten.

The growth continued at a phenomenal rate. By the end of 1950 there were 9 million TV homes; the next year, 15; then 20; and so on until, in January 1961, 47 of our 53 million homes had one or more sets. And throughout this time, the average daily use, calculated on 365 days a year, rises from four and a half to five hours. During the winter it approaches, and in some months exceeds, six hours per day per set. That bears repeating: if we count every home with television and every day of the week, the average during the peak season comes to six hours of use per day per set.[3] The sheer arithmetic weight of the fact that 90 per cent of our homes average over one third of each waking day with the television set on is at the core of the issue, however drawn. Most of the things that are true of television are true either because of or in spite of this statistic; it is at the base of much of today's concern with the medium, and implicit in most of the rest.

In the public forum the focus of discussion has now shifted, understandably, from initial awe with the technical scope, growth, and potential of the medium, to its content and use. But the public discussion still runs to superlatives: the implications are rarely less than "far-reaching."

The major issues seem to lie in the nature of programming, the degree of public consumption, and the projected personal and national consequences. Much interest focuses on the relationship between entertainment and information—the relative amounts wanted by the public, needed by the nation, provided by the broadcasters—as well as the aesthetic level of television fare—what it is, what it should be, who is to say.[4]

---

[2] M. C. Faught: "Television—An Interim Summing Up." *Saturday Review of Literature,* August 26, 1950.

[3] What "use" means, we shall come to. Technically, it means only that the set is turned on and drawing electricity. What else it consumes and produces is one of the questions of this study.

[4] For a discussion of the major positions on these issues, see Bernard Berelson: "The Great Debate on Cultural Democracy," pp. 147-68 in Donald N. Barrett

The Present Purpose

Thus, from its inception through its growth (and no doubt into the future), television, its programs, and its public have been subjects of widespread interest and speculation. Our purpose is to pause at this point in the life of the medium and take empirical stock—to formulate some of the major questions in fairly precise and hopefully objective terms and to supply, if not answers, at least substantial clues.

The emphasis in this study is on the attitudes and feelings associated with the television set and what is on it. We accept the general findings of the rating services with respect to the incidence of viewing and its temporal and geographic distribution.[5] By and large, this study speaks not to such specific, of who, when, and how much, but to underlying questions of *why*. To list just a few of these:

> In their own eyes, what does the phenomenon of television mean to the American people? What place has it come to occupy in their lives and how does it relate to other things they do —for amusement, for relaxation, for information, for a living? In short, what kind of activity *is* watching television?
>
> And how do people feel about the industry and the job it is doing? Are they happy with the present program level and mix? Is the public aware of any imbalance, of needs and desires served inadequately or not at all? Are there recognized or implied areas of untapped potential?
>
> More specifically, how do viewers react to various types of programs and commercials? How does their chosen diet relate to the proportions offered on the menu; how and to what extent do they actually select? Which specific entries are favorites, or especially memorable, or notorious? Can the underlying elements that seem to attract, repel, or bore the audience be isolated?

(ed.): *Values in America* (University of Notre Dame Press, 1961); abridged version in *Studies in Public Communication,* No. 3, 1961 (University of Chicago). A symposium on the topic with contributions by Hannah Arendt, Ernest van der Haag, Edward Shils, Frank Stanton, *et al.* appears in *Daedalus,* Vol. 89 (Spring 1960).

[5] Not without reservation, and not to the last percentage point, but certainly in the broad picture they present. How much difference does it make, in the consideration of television *in toto*, if the ratings are reduced by 20 or even 40 per cent?

Finally, and perhaps of greatest importance, we consider all such questions against two touchstones:

First, how does the abstract and general "Viewing Public" divide into real and distinct viewing publics? What are the areas of general agreement, and where are people of clearly divided or opposing frames of mind? And when there is more than one point of view, how many people adhere to each, and who are they?

Second, how do their expressed attitudes and feelings relate to their actual behavior with respect to the television set? Is there a simple equation between what they say and what they do, or are there discrepancies of practical as well as academic concern?

Our Point of View

By inquiring into such questions, we inevitably deal with issues related to the current debate about television in particular and "cultural democracy" in general. Even the largest set of objective-scientific blinders cannot obscure implications of questions so intimately tied to controversies of policy. That findings from this and other serious studies are germane to the dialectic is proper, and intended. But we trust that our position is self-evident; namely, to report relevant data, and all of it—neither in support of nor in answer to any particular camp, but hopefully interesting and important to all.

If this book speaks *for* anyone, we would like to think that it speaks for the audience(s)—not on behalf of, but in echo to. To the extent that we have measured what we set out to measure, these pages should reflect the point of view of the viewer. It is *his* responses that constitute the data.

In attempting to measure and describe the public's reactions to television, we do not mean to condone or condemn. We believe simply that an empirical reading on such feelings and attitudes is of intrinsic interest to the student of mass communications, and certainly relevant to informed and productive discussion of the issues.

The Design of the Study

Our information comes primarily from two sources:

The National Survey   In March and April of 1960, we completed personal interviews with a national sample of 2498 adults, aged eighteen to over seventy, in as many homes. Both the sampling procedure and the results we obtained on such factors of known distribution as age and education indicate that findings can be generalized to the population with confidence. (Details of the sample design appear in the Appendix.)

Two hundred seven of the interviews occurred in homes that had no television set at the time; 71 of the respondents in no-TV homes said they "never watch," while the remainder reported viewing elsewhere. So 2427 viewers are our principal informants.

The field work was conducted by two organizations: The National Opinion Research Center at the University of Chicago and Elmo Roper and Associates. Each was to provide an independently selected and administered national sample of 1250.

There were two main reasons for this split in interviewing: to get the field work done as quickly as possible and to provide the various methodological and statistical safeguards inherent in two independent samples. (The replication may also be of technical interest to survey researchers.)

Comparison revealed small and mostly mechanical differences in the two sets of results. The substantive findings were almost always the same, so the findings throughout the book are presented for the total sample, undifferentiated by interviewing organization. Appendix tables showing responses for the major questions divided by interviewing service document the degree of consistency between the two samples.

Interviewing was concentrated in the evening and on weekends in order to avoid a heavy proportion of daytime stay-at-homes. On the assumption that there would probably be a strong relationship between attitudes toward television and the amount of time spent at home, we restricted all interviews with men, and half of those with women, to hours when a large percentage of the population is normally at home.[6]

This plan still did not completely avoid selective sampling, as it obviously underrepresents people who tend to go out evenings and weekends. To the extent that the tendency to spend evenings and weekends at home is related to TV use and to feelings about the medium, our results will be somewhat affected by this sampling influence.

---

[6] Men found at home on weekdays would be atypical, probably especially so when it comes to television. And, in general, the amount of time people spend at home—by choice or by necessity—probably has a lot to do with how they feel about television. Homebodies have more occasion and use for watching and, conversely, people who like TV more are more apt to stay home in order to watch it.

The Interview Itself: The interview was solicited on the doorstep, and conducted immediately in the respondent's home.[7] Interviewers introduced themselves and the study with as little specific information as the respondent would allow. In no case did they indicate that the interview dealt with television, since the questionnaire was designed to secure some responses before that focus became apparent. When pressed for the subject of the interview, they said something vague about "how people spend their time" and then led directly into the first question: "For example, think of the way you spend an ordinary day . . . what part of the day do you enjoy most?" It was important to avoid any mention of television or other mass media at this point, since the early questions depended on respondent naïveté in this respect.

If questioned regarding sponsorship, the interviewers were instructed to mention, in all cases, the three affiliations: The Bureau of Applied Social Research, Columbia University; Elmo Roper and Associates, and NORC. We thought that perhaps the sole mention of a university, of a well-known polling organization, or of an academic research center might produce different types of response bias, so rather than have various interviews differentially affected, we decided to introduce the same, mixed effects in all cases. If answers in such interviews do indeed tend to gravitate toward the "interests" of the sponsoring organization as seen by the respondent, our "sponsorship bias," if any, is probably toward "intellectual criticism" of television.

Interviews were conducted according to the questionnaire shown in the Appendix.[8] It proceeds from general to specific issues, by means of "open-ended" and "pre-coded" questions, a variety of rating scales, word lists, and other instruments. In open-ended questions, respondents are entirely free to answer in their own words; e.g.: "How do you feel about television in general?" Interviewers record the answer verbatim, or as faithfully as possible, and we later classify, or "code," responses into what appear to be meaningful categories. In "pre-coded" questions, re-

---

[7] One modification was introduced by Roper only: after the initial portion of the interview, respondents were given their choice of completing the interview on the spot or arranging a future date. (Details in Appendix.)

[8] As elaborated in the Appendix, several questions were asked in various forms of different subsamples. In order to equalize the alternate forms, there were sixteen versions of the questionnaire in all, with a common core of questions, but in various combinations of additional and alternative queries.

spondents select from a list of alternative replies provided by the interviewer; e.g.: "Would you say there are enough, not enough, or too many
educational programs?"

The average interview lasted about two hours, far beyond the
typical in-the-house interview without an appointment; this in itself is
testimony to the intrinsic interest of the subject matter. The order of
areas probed in the interview (*not* the specific questions asked) is as
follows:

General evaluation
> how important is television?
> how good or bad a job is the industry doing?

Television in context
> other leisure activities
> other mass media

Watching television
> reasons for watching
> satisfactions and frustrations

The programs
> general level of satisfaction
> specific favorites, disliked programs

Children
> advantages and disadvantages of TV

Commercials
> general reaction
> specific likes and dislikes

Miscellaneous
> pay TV, quiz scandals, channel or network images

Classification data
> personal and demographic characteristics

The interested reader may take a few minutes at this point to glance
through the questionnaire, but it is not necessary in order to follow the
discussion.

Timing: Finally, a few words are needed about the choice and the
implications of the April–May 1960 interviewing period.

First, with respect to the general TV climate at that time, we inherited, for better or for worse (probably the latter), whatever changes in public response were produced by the notoriety of the quiz scandals that reached their climax with Charles Van Doren's confession in November 1959.

We assume that whatever influences persisted until April are regarded more accurately as "real" or lasting effects of the scandals than as temporary response biases reflecting an unusual situation then in the limelight. If some temporary effects did in fact persist throughout April, then our results are biased in a negative direction, since few people were more favorably disposed toward the medium as a result of the disclosures.

In other respects, 1959–60 was a "normal" season for TV—devoid of the problems and the opportunities created for the medium and its viewers in times of extraordinary coverage. There were no national elections or conventions; no wars or police actions started or ended; no McCarthy or Kefauver hearings and no space flights. The major special coverage of the season was the Winter Olympics. There were no important technical innovations in the medium itself. And of course, these interviews preceded and therefore fail to measure the effects of two major events on the television scene: the Kennedy-Nixon debates and Newton Minow.[9]

With regard to the specific dates of the field work, several considerations dictated an early spring survey. We had postponed the interviewing from January to April in order to avoid an overriding preoccupation with the quiz issue, since our goal was to accumulate comprehensive base-line data on television, not reactions to that particular crisis.

Moreover, April is late enough in the year for viewers to have full acquaintance with the season's offerings and still not far enough into spring for outdoor interests and fill-in programming to have cut into regular TV habits and attitudes. Finally, April is sufficiently removed from the holiday season to avoid the influence of whatever special reactions to the medium or to being interviewed arise at that time.

This completes our description of the first, and major, source of our data. Now for the second, which gives us an important check on these survey responses.

[9] For detailed reference, the three network schedules during the interviewing period appear in Appendix B.

The American Research Bureau (ARB) Sample The practical as well as the theoretical significance of expressed attitudes depends largely on how they relate to actual behavior, yet it is virtually impossible to develop a single test or interview that yields both pieces of information without bias. If evaluations of the medium are elicited first, that may influence subsequent reports of viewing, and vice versa. Once people report watching a certain program regularly, they are likely to find some good things to say about it. Or, conversely, if a respondent begins by describing programming as trash aimed at five-year-old intellects, he may underestimate the extent of his own viewing in subsequent questions. The ARB analysis represents our approach to this problem.

ARB provides a rating service based on the diary method: people keep a detailed record of what they watch on TV. We followed up 300 people who had participated in such an ARB television rating panel three to six months previously, so that we had diaries reporting their complete viewing for a one-week period. We now interviewed them with essentially the same questionnaire used in the national survey, in an independent study unrelated to their previous ARB participation so far as the respondents knew.

The objective was to get some idea of how to interpret verbal responses of the type collected in our survey, by comparing them with independently assessed viewing patterns of the respondent. Is a respondent who says there should be more informational programming more likely to watch a documentary than somebody who says there is already enough or too much enlightenment on the air? When opera and horse-opera compete, how do viewers' *actual* selections relate to their *stated* preferences? In short, as gauged by their own viewing behavior, how much do the various factions mean what they say?

The ARB respondents were all in the New York City metropolitan area, because that was, at the time, the only market with enough available diaries recording viewing by individuals, not merely by household. They were interviewed from the middle to the end of May, or about one month after the national survey.

The delay was not part of the design, but a practical necessity. Slight changes in attitudes toward the medium may have intervened, but they would be of no real concern to the major purpose of the analysis. The object of the ARB study is not to generalize the questionnaire results *per se,* but only something of the *relationship* between interview results

and actual viewing. For example: the number of people who agree that
there is "not enough information" may change by a few percentage points;
but that should not affect the essential comparison between the viewing
habits of those who agree and those who disagree.

At any rate, a more serious limitation may exist in the geographic
restriction of the ARB sample. The extent of consistency or inconsistency
between New Yorkers' expressed attitudes and viewing behavior may be
greater, less, or of a different type than that, say, of Nebraskans. At the
same time, the more varied New York TV menu—then seven channels,
all commercial—offers some interesting choices not found in Nebraska,
and this allows us to put these viewers to a more sensitive test.

We take the ARB sample as an interesting and important first step
toward the ultimately necessary behavioral validation of verbal reports
regarding TV, or for that matter, any other "socially loaded" issue.

The Nature of the Report

It remains to say something of the nature and organization of
the book.

First, a sweeping hedge: the major portion of this report is devoted
to a presentation and discussion of the key findings—and only the key
findings—of the two studies. The technical appendix includes some more-
detailed survey results and the methodological specifics of sampling,
interviewing procedure, and so on.

The technical reader will quickly realize that we touch on the high
points and not much more. The data we collected allow a great many
more intensive, sophisticated, and possibly significant analyses not under-
taken in this report. This arises partly out of the interests of time and
timeliness, and partly out of the belief that the general reader's concern
is chiefly with the main-line findings, and not equally with the various
special issues on which the data may bear.

At any rate, the results are in, the IBM cards are punched, and
further, more specific analyses will follow. This overview not only stands
on its own as a report on the central findings; in addition, it can serve as
a starting point for later, intensive investigation of particular issues.

As for organization, we divide "television" into three closely related
but distinct sets of considerations:

Part I: Overview—Television as a Medium   To begin, we hear the
viewer on the subject of "television in general." Here we deal with the

public's over-all response to this relatively new and ubiquitous part of the American scene. How does the medium as such rate—in absolute terms and in comparison with other developments and services?

Part II: Television as Viewing Next we turn to viewing as an activity. What is it like to watch television; what satisfactions and frustrations are involved beyond reactions to specific programs? Each medium of communication—books, car radio, legitimate stage—offers and demands certain things of its audience. What are the personal and social rewards of televiewing? What are the costs?

Part III: Television as Content Finally, there is the content itself, the programs and commercials—past, present, and potential. Here we focus on viewer response to programming and advertising—*in toto,* by category or type, and by some specifics.

Each of these Parts builds on what has gone before, and the analysis becomes more complex and detailed as we go along.

Finally, for the technical reader, a word about statistical tests of significance—or rather, about their absence. Because survey data yielding innumerable and unenumerated comparisons are difficult to treat within the classical statistical framework, and because our purpose was point estimation and not hypothesis testing, we made no attempt to apply standard "significance" models. Further, we have in this case an empirical answer to one of the conceptual foundations of the significance question: to what extent would another sample have yielded similar results? That information appears, directly, in the NORC-Roper comparisons. (For a more detailed discussion, see Technical Note on Statistical Inference in Appendix D.)

PART I

Overview: Television As a Medium

"TV is wonderful—just wonderful. Why, TV has brought me the whole world. I just love it. I love everything. I love to see our President, that's something I could never do. And I love the stories and the westerns. I just love every minute. It's the most thrilling thing of my life."

"TV engineers are going to roast in hell till eternity as a result of what they have done."

AT THE START of 1946, about as many homes had television sets as had newborn triplets: there are no precise figures on either frequency, but each is estimated below 5000. Today, 90 per cent of our households have their own sets, and use them an average of five to six hours a day. So the overt acceptance of the medium has been obvious and virtually universal. How do people feel about this change in their lives?

Our concern in this section is with the general public's over-all response to the medium. In subsequent chapters we divide and analyze. We distinguish viewing as such from programming; westerns from public affairs, and even westerns from other westerns. But to start the story, it helps to stake out the general place accorded television by the public. When the people look at television over-all, what do they see?

The appraisal proceeds along two lines:

First, how *important* is television to its audience; how much do people care, one way or another?

Second, how *satisfied* is the public with television? How does the medium rate, by whatever criteria the viewers themselves choose to apply?

All of the questions designed to bear on these issues occurred at the beginning of the interview, before interest was focused on television. This makes it possible to assess the spontaneous level of awareness and concern with the medium, and it also insures a certain objectivity in evaluative responses.

Chapter 1

IMPORTANCE:
THE DAILY SIGNIFICANCE
OF THE SET

As AN EASY introduction to the interview, and in order to get some indication of the importance of television in the daily routine, we began with this open-ended question:

Q. 1A   *"First, think of the way you spend an ordinary day—just a typical weekday when nothing special is happening. What part of the day do you enjoy most?"*

	SET OWNERS		NON-OWNERS	
	Men	Women	Men	Women
Evening*	62%	44%	41%	29%
Afternoon	8	25	13	24
Morning	12	17	21	37
Noon, Mid-day	7	7	11	5
Bedtime	1	1	4	0
Don't enjoy anything	0	0	0	2
NA, DK	10	6	10	3
Base: 100% =	1099	1189	111	96

*In this and subsequent tables, headings in *italics* indicate pre-coded alternatives. Categories of answers to open-ended questions such as these are shown in this type.

The difference between the general population of set owners and the 207 non-owners (9 per cent of the sample) seems striking. Fewer of the latter find the evening the most enjoyable part of the day; more of them mention the morning, and they cite more "active" sources of enjoyment in general. But subtle causal or psychological interpretations are precluded by important demographic differences between the two groups (see Appendix Table 2). Our non-owners are concentrated in the lower-educated, lower-income, laboring and rural groups. Thus, most of them appear to be without TV mainly on economic or situational grounds.

But the general pattern is clear. Taking it easy after work or when the chores are done is the favorite part of the ordinary day for most people. Some women get time to relax a little earlier than most men, but both sexes concentrate responses on the later hours, and chiefly because they provide leisure:[1]

Q. 1B   "What makes that part of the day particularly enjoyable?"

	SET OWNERS	NON-OWNERS
Work done, relax	54%	42%
Watch television	25	3
Be with family	18	10
Kids out of the way	10	5
Read	9	13
Gardening, outdoor	8	13
Hobbies, crafts	7	7
Work, housework	7	8
Feel fresh	6	18
Visit, talk to friends	6	6
Outside activities	4	2
Eat	4	2
Radio	1	5
Music	1	2
Other	5	9
NA, DK	6	7
Base: 100% =	2291	207

NOTE: Percentages add to more than 100% because of multiple responses.

[1] The full breakdown of what is enjoyed, according to the time of day mentioned, appears in Appendix Table 1. The pattern is as expected: "feeling fresh," "outdoor" and "work" satisfactions are referred to the earlier hours; "relaxing" and the leisure pursuits are concentrated in the later parts of the day.

Incidentally, these reasons are generally similar for men and women within each group—except for one category: "Kids out of the way," which is mentioned by about 15 per cent of the women as against only 1 per cent of the men!

At any rate, among those who have sets at home, watching television is the single specific activity (beyond just "taking it easy") most frequently named in connection with the most enjoyed part of the day. The association is somewhat stronger among women, and it rises steadily as the day progresses:

Of the men who most enjoy:		This percentage mention TV as reason *	Of the women who most enjoy:		This percentage mention TV as reason *
	Base: 100%			Base: 100%	
Morning	129	5%	Morning	198	10%
Mid-day	73	5	Mid-day	81	21
Afternoon	89	13	Afternoon	293	30
Evening	685	31	Evening	521	38
ALL	1099	22%	ALL	1189	28%

* Each percentage is based on those naming that time of day.

So among men who say they prefer the evening—as most of them do—the mention of TV rises to 31%, and the figure is still higher for women. Afternoons gain in popularity among women, and they mention television almost as frequently in this connection.

To what extent is television *the* activity that underlies the indicated preference? Of all those who referred to the medium at all, just over a third named it as the primary source of enjoyment: as *the* reason for designating that particular part of the day:

"Every night I watch TV and that's my pleasure. In fact, I'd say it's my hobby. I'm truly for TV."

The rest associate it with other pleasures, or see it as part of the larger scene:

"That's when I can be with my family and watch TV."

In either case, television is directly associated with everyday gratifications, and a good share of our respondents recall and report this fact in our initial probe—before the interview itself gets onto the subject.

This may be part of the explanation behind the rather dramatic results of our next index of the personal importance of TV:

Q. 2   *"Considering all the new inventions, new products and new developments of the past 25 years or so, which—if any—have done the most to make* your *life more enjoyable, pleasant, or interesting?"*

VIEWERS*

Men		Women	
television	62%	television	61%
cars	37	home laundry equipment	51
miscellaneous "appliances"	14	freezer, refrigerator	24
freezer, refrigerator	13	cars	15
basic utilities	13	miscellaneous "appliances"	15
radio	13	cooking appliances	14
home laundry equipment	7	cleaning appliances	11
farm machinery	7	basic utilities	10
cooking appliances	4	radio	9
hi-fi, stereo	4	misc. products	6
other	23	hi-fi, stereo	4
DK, NA	5	telephone	4
		other	7
		DK, NA	2

Base: 100% = 1177   1246

*We include, as "viewers," the 136 non-owners who view elsewhere, and exclude only the 71 non-owners who report they "never watch." This yields the basic sample of 2427 viewers, used in most of the analyses from this point on.

NOTE: Percentages add to more than 100% because of multiple responses.

The vote for television may not be quite so impressive as first appears, on the ground that there are not many other major developments that qualify if the question is interpreted literally, except for home appliances. And they, as a group, do outscore TV among women: in all, 76 per cent of the women named one or another appliance.

Yet the degree of consensus is impressive enough, and in some ways no less significant for reflecting a limited field of choice. The fact is that, in their free responses, over 60 per cent of both sexes designate television as a development that has made their lives "more enjoyable, pleasant, or interesting." By contrast, 1 per cent took the trouble to state, explicitly, that TV does *not* qualify. Again, this response appeared before the interviewers revealed any particular interest in television—in fact, before they so much as mentioned the word.

The order of response is also indicative. As is clear in the above tabulation, most people cited more than one development; those who mention television divide as follows:

Mention only television	11%
Mention TV first of two	12
Mention TV first of three or more	13
Mention TV, but not first	25
ALL	61%

So 61 per cent of all respondents refer to TV, and for a majority of them it constitutes the primary or principal response to the question.

To test the limits—to see just how far people are willing to go in acknowledging or denying the subjective importance of the medium—we asked these two loaded[2] questions, each of half the sample:

Q. 5B   *"Here are some things that many people take for granted today. But suppose the clock were suddenly turned back and all of these things were gone. Which do you think you personally would miss most?"*

	Men	Women
Television	40%	28%
Home freezer	24	19
Frozen foods	9	8
Power steering, brakes	6	3
Air conditioning	6	3
Miracle fabrics	6	11
Vacuum cleaners	5	23
Hi-fi	2	3
DK, NA	2	2
Base: 100% =	598	623

Q. 5A   *"Here are some things that many people take for granted today. But imagine, if you can, that for 2 or 3 months you could have only one of these and you'd have to do without the rest. Which one would you choose?"*

2 Question 5B obviously favors TV. Most people in the sample have a television set; most people do not have each of the other items, so they would be less likely to miss them if gone. Question 5A leans in the other direction by placing TV

	Men	Women
Automobile	42%	21%
Refrigerator	29	56
Newspaper	14	7
Telephone	9	11
Television	5	5
DK, NA	1	0
Base: 100% =	579	623

The responses are clear-cut, discriminating, and "rational." The general public clearly says that television has come to mean more than any single development we named in the convenience-luxury area, though the margin is much greater among men than for women, where vacuum cleaners and freezers are in close pursuit.

Just as clearly, people say they would not or could not sacrifice their cars or refrigerators (which, depending on sex) in favor of television, the newspaper, or the telephone.[3] In fact, TV finishes dead last against these more utilitarian "necessities"—though the vote for all three losers is small, and probably subject to some bias toward the more "sensible" choice.[4]

Real life rarely approaches the horrors of fantasy, but most television homes have experienced a situation that actually embodies some of the deprivation we tried to hypothesize in our Question 5B. At a subsequent point in the interview we asked people what happened the last time their television set broke down.

The results are discussed in detail later, but we can anticipate one aspect of the findings at this point since it provides concrete behavioral support for the more abstract indications of the daily importance of the television set:

---

against items considered absolutely essential by most people. There are also other differences in wording—"all gone" vs. "have only one for 2 or 3 months"—which keep the questions from being directly comparable. But they do tend to isolate respondents who are extremely favorably or unfavorably disposed to the medium.

[3] This assumes that everyone has all of these things to give up. But the vote for automobiles, for example, is probably swollen by at least some people who don't own a car but would like to for three months.

[4] Question 5A, incidentally, provides indirect evidence of the absence of any overriding response bias in favor of TV, such as might result if respondents somehow thought of the interviewers as pro-TV. In this sense, it increases our confidence in other results.

Q. 37D *"Altogether, about how long were you without a television set?"*

Set repaired or
replaced within:

Half a day	26%
One day	47
Three days	67
One week	82
Three weeks	92

Base: 100% = 1592

The urgency with which viewers cope with the problem testifies to its seriousness. One quarter report restoring the set within a few hours, nearly half have it working the same day, and so on. But numbers, no matter how impressive, can hardly communicate the desperation that often attends what has been called "the new American tragedy." Here are some extremes, selected to illustrate the extent to which self-acknowledged dependence on daily viewing can go:

"When it is out of order I feel like someone is dead."

"We went crazy. My husband said, 'What did I do before TV?' We're sitting here. The children say, 'Please get it fixed.' We couldn't do anything. Didn't even try to read a paper. Just walked around brooding."

"I nearly lost my mind. The days were so long, and I just couldn't stand to miss my continued stories."

"I went from house to house to watch TV, or to the filling station, or went to bed early because I was lost for something to do."

So these preliminary queries suggest that television has achieved great importance in the average household as an enjoyable part of the ordinary day; and that it is clearly considered among the most personally significant of recent developments. The TV set is not, for most people, quite in the category of "basic essentials," but its temporary loss does seem to be among the most critical of everyday crises.

As we shall see, dependence on the medium is probably most extreme among those restricted in interests and activities—the aged, the shut-ins, the lonely:

> "I'm an old man and all alone, and the TV brings people and music and talk into my life. Maybe without TV I would be ready to die; but this TV gives me life. It gives me what to look forward to—that tomorrow, if I live, I'll watch this and that program."

But commitment to routine daily viewing is the rule, not the exception, in the nation's television homes.

These findings reflect and add substance to the basic statistic with which we began: five to six hours of set-use per home per day—not just an electronic fact, but a recognized and important part of contemporary life.

Chapter 2

SATISFACTION:
THE DEGREE AND NATURE
OF PUBLIC ACCEPTANCE

Most people, then, watch a good deal of television; they know it, and many of them consider it an important part of daily existence. But that in itself, of course, does not demonstrate how satisfied they are—with what they see, with what they do, with the job the industry is doing. Some things, like smog or public transportation, are widely consumed over long periods of time despite overt unhappiness with the "product" and the people responsible. Other things—the second cup of coffee—may be accepted simply because they are available and apparently "free" once the initial investment has been made. Or an evening with television, like a political candidate, can be elected merely because it seems the less unfortunate alternative.

In the following pages we hope to specify the general level of satisfaction with television today; what viewers like most and dislike most about it; and how different kinds of people differ on this issue. First, we shall look at the industry vis-à-vis other enterprises that strive to appeal to or influence popular tastes. Next we focus on television in the context of other mass media. Finally, we elicit reactions to television in general, allowing the viewer to choose the setting and apply any criteria he feels appropriate.

TV and the Public "Taste"

The television industry, like several others, produces a product in the public eye that is subject to aesthetic and other highly subjective evaluations by its consumers. Accordingly, we asked viewers to compare TV programs with some other products designed to achieve general appeal. First they told us how satisfied they think "most people" are.

Speaking for "people" in general, our respondents give television programming a solid second place behind automobiles, while they tend to reject popular music, movies, and women's fashions. (Except for the obvious difference in response to women's fashions, men and women are in close agreement on all counts.)

Q. 3   "Here is a list of five different products and services designed to please the general public."

	3A "Generally speaking, which of these do you think people are most satisfied with today?"	3B "Which does the next best job of satisfying most people?"	3C "And which, if any, don't seem to be designed with people's real interests and tastes in mind?"
Today's:			
Automobiles	57%	25%	3%
TV programs	28	42	7
Popular music	5	10	27
Movies	2	7	18
Women's fashions	6	12	21
None of them	0	0	8
NA, DK	2	4	16
Base: 100% =	2427	2427	2427

Then, more directly:

	4A "And which are you personally most satisfied with?"			4B "And which is next best in your opinion?"		
	Men	Women	All*	Men	Women	All
Automobiles	57%	38%	48%	20%	27%	24%
TV programs	27	32	29	42	29	36
Popular music	7	8	7	12	11	11
Movies	3	2	2	10	7	8
Women's fashions	3	18	11	7	19	13
NA, DK	3	2	3	9	7	8
Base: 100% =	1177	1246	2427	1177	1246	2427

NOTE: There was no personal equivalent of 3C, on the grounds that it would be largely redundant.

* Includes 4 cases unclassified as to sex.

Their personal opinions retain the general pattern, except that the gap between cars and TV nearly closes among women. The over-all verdict seems to be something like this: automobiles and TV programming satisfy "most people" and they satisfy me, while popular music, movies, and women's fashions "don't seem to be [as well] designed with people's real interests and tastes in mind."

These results are comparative, and the responses have meaning principally in terms of the specific alternatives we provide.[1] But the very least we can say is that there is no evidence of widespread personal dissatisfaction with the industry's performance, nor even of the belief that general dissatisfaction exists.

[1] If the list seems loaded with some industries that appear to do a particularly bad job, that in itself is interesting. We included literally every enterprise we could think of (except other mass media) that:

   a) provides a product or service for the public at large, which
   b) caters to public tastes—i.e., depends economically on aesthetic acceptance by most of the American people.

Try to think of another, especially one of whose products you find more acceptable than these.

TV and Other Mass Media

Now, more specifically, we turn to television as an instrument for the mass dissemination of information and entertainment. How do viewers compare TV with the other major media? The basic data appear in the facing chart.

To begin with, note the high discrimination, low "halo-effect" in these judgments. The public does not praise or damn any medium *in toto:* "It all depends." Television, for example, runs from a high of 68 per cent (most entertaining) to a low of 13 per cent (does least for the public); and each of the others shows a similar range.

The pattern is clearly one of differential comparative advantages, and it implies a division of labor in what the audience expects and/or gets from the four sources.

As many as ten of the sixteen comparatives are assigned to one or another of the four media by a decisive plurality. Thus, in the total sample there is substantial agreement that:

Television		Radio	
Is the most entertaining	68%	*Brings you the latest news*	
Creates the most interest		*most quickly*	57%
in new things going on	56		
Seems to be getting better		**Newspapers**	
all the time	49	*Gives the most complete*	
Has the hardest job to do	45	*news coverage*	59%
		Does the most for the	
Magazines		*public*	44
Is the least important			
to you	49%	**None**	
Does the least for the		*Seems to be getting worse*	
public	47	*all the time*	35%

As for the remainder, TV and newspapers run a close race with each other, but clearly surpass radio and magazines on these counts:

	Television	Newspapers
Gives you the clearest understanding of		
*candidates and issues in national elections**	42%	36%
Presents things most intelligently	27	33
Is the most educational	32	31
Presents the fairest, most unbiased news	29	31
Is doing its job best	29	33
Is the most important to you	37	38

* Recall that this is before coverage of the 1960 presidential elections, and does not reflect any changes that may have occurred then.

QUESTION 7 *"Now I would like to get your opinions about how radio, newspapers, television and magazines compare. Generally speaking, which of these would you say ..."*

TELEVISION

RADIO

NONE OR DK

MAGAZINES

NEWSPAPERS

Is the most entertaining?"

| 68% | 9% | 9% | 13% |

Base: 100% = 2427

Which gives the most complete news coverage?"

| 19 | 18 | 3 | 59 |

Presents things most intelligently?"

| 27 | 8 | 5 | 27 | 33 |

Is the most educational?"

| 32 | 3 | 3 | 31 | 31 |

Brings you the latest news most quickly?"

| 36 | 57 | 5 |

Does the most for the public?"

| 34 | 11 | 9 | 3 | 44 |

Seems to be getting worse all the time?"

| 24 | 14 | 35 | 17 | 10 |

Presents the fairest, most unbiased news?"

| 29 | 22 | 9 | 9 | 31 |

Is doing its job best?"

| 29 | 14 | 15 | 9 | 33 |

Is the most important to you?"

| 37 | 15 | 4 | 6 | 38 |

Is the least important to you?"

| 15 | 22 | 7 | 49 | 7 |

Creates the most interest in new things going on?"

| 56 | 4 | 4 | 18 | 18 |

Does the least for the public?"

| 13 | 12 | 23 | 47 | 5 |

Seems to be getting better all the time?"

| 49 | 10 | 19 | 11 | 11 |

Gives clearest understanding of candidates and issues in national elections?"†

| 42 | 5 | 7 | 10 | 36 |

And which has the hardest job to do?"

| 45 | 7 | 13 | 5 | 30 |

*Entries smaller than 3% not shown numerically

† *Which of these gives you the clearest understanding of the candidates and issues in national elections?*

So for the public at large, newspapers provide the most comprehensive news, and radio the fastest news; magazines are less important altogether; television offers the most entertaining and stimulating fare.

That is the picture for the total, undifferentiated "public," and to the extent that a medium aims at all the people, these figures are paramount. But they override and mask distinct differences among various segments of the population. Minority opinion remains on each of the comparisons, and on several we saw people almost equally divided between newspapers and TV. What, if anything, decides the vote?

This chart divides the sample into seven groups according to their level of formal education—the factor that makes the greatest single difference in the relative capacities and limitations attributed to the four media:[2]

First, across the entire range, education seems to have its greatest effects on attitudes toward magazines and television—and in opposite directions. As education increases, magazines gain and television loses in general acceptance—and especially so among those with education beyond college.

More specifically still, as education increases, respondents turn from television to newspapers or magazines for "intelligent," "educational" material (items A, B, C, G). And the more education, the more likely it will be magazines rather than newspapers. For example: on "Which gives you the clearest understanding of the candidates and issues in national elections?" TV drops from 47 per cent to 18 per cent across the educational spectrum, while magazines show a concomitant increase from 1 per cent to 41 per cent. The higher-educated are also much less inclined to praise TV generally (items D, E, J), and much more likely to disavow its personal or social importance (items F, K, L). Again, the converse is true for magazines.

On the other hand, television remains "most entertaining" for all groups, with almost as high a vote among college people as among those with only a grade-school education (item N). The bulk of each educational group also thinks TV has the "hardest job" (item P); and save for those with education beyond college, people in each category divide about the same on which medium has the fairest news (item M) and

[2] We analyzed this matter by such other characteristics as age, sex, family composition, urban-rural residence, and income. Where differences do exist, they are less pronounced and always in a direction consistent with educational differences among the groups. See Appendix Table 3.

QUESTION 7 Comparison of Four Media by Seven Educational Groups

TELEVISION

EDUCATION
1. **0-6 Years Grade School/Base:** 100% = 203
2. **7-8 Years Grade School/Base:** 100% = 424
3. **1-3 Years High School/Base:** 100% = 531
4. **4 Years High School/Base:** 100% = 683
5. **1-2 Years College/Base:** 100% = 208
6. **3-4 Years College/Base:** 100% = 194
7. **Education Beyond College/Base:** 100% = 114

RADIO

NONE OR DON'T KNOW

MAGAZINES

NEWSPAPERS

A . . . most complete news coverage?

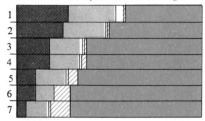

E . . . doing its job best?

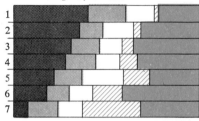

B–Presents things most intelligently?

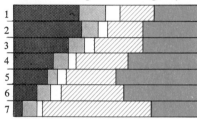

F . . . the most important to you?

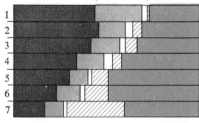

C . . . the most educational?

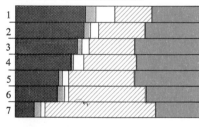

G . . . understanding of national elections? *

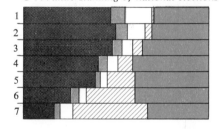

D . . . getting better all the time?

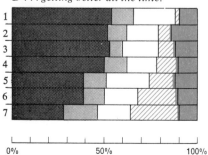

H–Creates . . . interest in new things . . .†

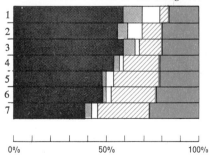

0%   50%   100%

0%   50%   100%

. . . gives you the clearest understanding of the candidates and issues in national elections?
†*Creates the most interest in new things going on?*

continued next page

EDUCATION
1. 0-6 Years Grade School/**Base:** 100% = 203
2. 7-8 Years Grade School/**Base:** 100% = 424
3. 1-3 Years High School/**Base:** 100% = 531
4. 4 Years High School/**Base:** 100% = 683
5. 1-2 Years College/**Base:** 100% = 208
6. 3-4 Years College/**Base:** 100% = 194
7. Education Beyond College/**Base:** 100% = 114

TELEVISION

RADIO

NONE OR DON'T KNOW

MAGAZINES

NEWSPAPERS

I . . . the latest news most quickly?

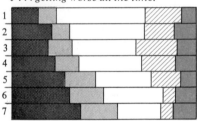

M . . . the fairest, most unbiased news?

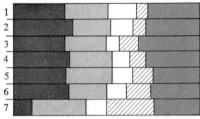

J . . . getting worse all the time?

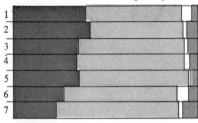

N . . . the most entertaining?

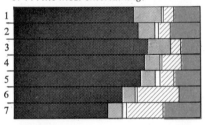

K–Does the least for the public?

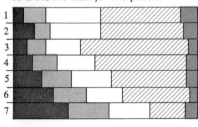

O–Does the most for the public?

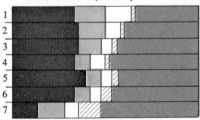

L . . . the least important to you?

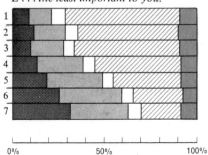

P . . . has the hardest job to do?

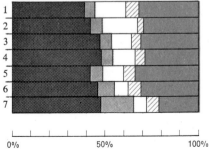

0%   50%   100%

0%   50%   100%

"does the most for the public" (item O). On the remaining item (I), radio, the leader in many categories only fifteen years before,[3] wins its only victory, for speed in newscasting.

So, over-all, the analysis reflects a pattern often found in communication research: increasing acceptance of print vs. broadcast media with increasing formal education.[4] But the relationship holds mainly with respect to the media as sources of comprehensive information. For fast information, or for entertainment, even the intellectual elite most often say they turn to the air waves.

These differences are worth some speculation and interpretation. This is our first evidence of serious differences of opinion within our sample, and among groups that will turn out to differ on many of the issues we take up with them.

The rapid rise of magazines at the very top of the educational ladder is particularly interesting and revealing. It probably stems from at least two facts: first, more people in this category read magazines regularly; and secondly, they read different ones. When 56 per cent of our beyond-college respondents say that magazines "present things most intelligently," as against 18 per cent at the other end of the educational scale, they are not talking about *True Confessions* and probably not even *The Saturday Evening Post*.

We did not ask them which ones they had in mind, but the following simplification probably is not too far wrong: the higher the education, the more "serious" and "editorial" (vs. entertaining) content in the magazines behind these responses. All in all, the word "magazines" probably has less *common* meaning across educational strata than any of the other three labels.

In this sense, magazines as such are the least "mass" of these media; and highbrow magazines, of course, are the least "mass" of magazines. *Harper's,* for example, has a monthly national circulation of a quarter of a million—about the same as the number of homes tuned to the only Green Bay, Wisconsin, TV channel in the course of an ordinary week. Mostly for economic reasons, there simply are no comparable newspapers or commercially supported TV stations catering to and supported by 2 or 3 per cent of the community. Newspapers

[3] Cf. Paul Lazarsfeld: *The People Look at Radio* (University of North Carolina Press, 1946).

[4] Cf. Paul Lazarsfeld and Patricia L. Kendall: *Radio Listening in America* (Prentice-Hall, Inc., 1948).

in a given city may differ somewhat in level of sophistication and cover-age, but each aims to sell to almost everybody, or at least to a very sub-stantial segment of the population. The same is true of TV, but to a lesser degree of radio stations.[5]

So the sophisticates must take their daily news and commercial television from the same few sources available to the general public and designed for widespread appeal.[6] But they can choose magazines from among thousands of independent publications—some aimed at a general market, others catering to the most highly specialized interests. A pro-fessional can often discuss the morning comics or last night's television with his elevator operator, but rarely the lead article in his favorite magazine.

This difference is an important factor behind reactions to the media *per se,* and it becomes crucial in understanding the response in one of the most important, if least typical, segments of society—the highly educated. The amount of selectivity the viewer can and does exercise will be at the root of many of his attitudes. For the time being, what is clear is that as education increases, so does dissatisfaction with many, though by no means all aspects of American television.

TV in General

We have so far talked to people about modern developments, about "taste" industries, and about mass media. Now, for the first time in the interview, we single out television itself with a deliberately broad, open-ended question:

Q. 8   "Now let's just consider television. How do you feel about tele-vision in general?"

In many ways, this produces the most meaningful data on the ques-tion of evaluation. At this point, respondents still did not know that the remainder of the interview dealt with TV; and the question itself gives no clues as to what aspect of television we want evaluated. We hope that

---

[5] There are many more AM radio than TV stations; and in addition, there is FM. A higher degree of radio specialization is evident in the foreign-language, jazz, Bible, and other special stations supported by small audiences in major met-ropolitan areas.

[6] True, each *program* (or news story) does not necessarily try for a general, undifferentiated audience. But programs are not independent of each other—the station thrives or perishes on its total performance, and each hour's rating affects the next. Hence, from an economic point of view, the individual station is more comparable to the individual magazine; the individual program, to the individual article.

it brings to the fore those feelings about television that are uppermost in the viewers' minds.

We went through the verbatim responses twice, coding independently for:

a) *general evaluation:* how favorable or unfavorable is the tone of the answer?

b) *content:* what specific aspects of television are discussed?

First, here are the five categories we used on the matter of *evaluation.* The illustrative responses are typical of those coded in the various categories. As is apparent, there was little question about the coding at the extremes; as to the middle categories, the examples illustrate our somewhat "conservative" policy on evaluational questions—when in doubt, lean toward the negative:

Categories with Examples

POSITIVE—extreme, unqualified *"I'd about as soon have my throat cut as not have a TV set." "I couldn't live without it. I enjoy the shows so much, they hold my interest so much. I think all the shows that I watch are so good. They are fun to watch—interesting . . ." "I love it—it moves me just like a woman."*

POSITIVE—less extreme, or qualified *"I'd like it, I enjoy it, it's entertaining for the children and me too. It keeps me company." "I find it fascinating and find myself watching when I shouldn't be."*

50-50—positive *and* negative, or noncommittal *"Well, I don't know. Sometimes they have good programs and sometimes poor ones." "Oh, I'm pretty satisfied with it. I don't care for fights or soap operas, but then I don't watch them." "Well, it's OK. I think it's progress. I don't know."*

NEGATIVE—less extreme, or qualified *"I think the number of worthwhile programs on TV are quite limited. But there are some fine programs. I don't enjoy TV as much as good reading."*

NEGATIVE—extreme, unqualified *"I think they ought to drop an atom bomb and wipe it all out. I would say that TV has smashed home life. It has not brought us closer together, it has separated us." "It comes from the devil." "I think it's one of the worst things the South ever had. I think it's ruining the younger generation. The way kids don't do nothing but sit and wait on their programs to come on. And TV is mostly to blame for all this race trouble. Ed Sullivan hugging the niggers and I suspect that TV people started half this trouble just so they'd have something to show on TV. I believe half of these lunch room sit down strikes are deliberately staged by TV stations."*

Here are the over-all results:

QUESTION 8 *"How do you feel about television in general?"*

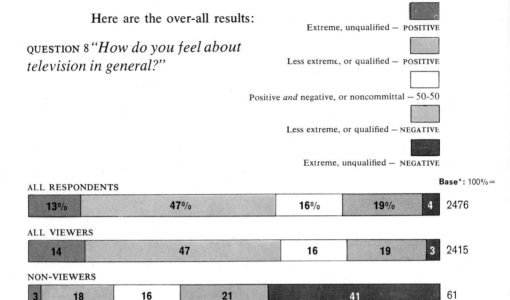

ALL RESPONDENTS — Base*: 100% =

| 13% | 47% | 16% | 19% | 4 | 2476 |

ALL VIEWERS

| 14 | 47 | 16 | 19 | 3 | 2415 |

NON-VIEWERS

| 3 | 18 | 16 | 21 | 41 | 61 |

*Excludes NA

The general public feels generally good about television in general! In the sample at large, predominantly favorable reactions outnumber unfavorable ones by 2½ to 1; and there are three times as many un-qualified enthusiasts as unqualified critics. The only strongly negative pattern comes from the non-set owners who never watch.

But again the various publics differ. Different subgroups respond with distributions that range from heavily positive to somewhat critical, as indicated in the detailed chart on the following pages.

1. Education matters for critical tone, but not substantially until after high school. From then on, each successive group is less favorably disposed toward TV until those with education beyond college become the only viewing segment, in *any* such analysis, with a predominantly critical set of responses.

2. Religion also makes a difference: Jews appear to be significantly more critical than Protestants or Catholics (as Appendix Table 4 shows, this is true beyond the effects of education or urban residence). We shall return to this difference later, with more detailed data, and we reserve interpretations at this point.

3. Since income is closely related to formal education, the relation-ship here is in the same direction, though not so strong. But as we shall

QUESTION 8 *"How do you feel about television in general?"*

BY VIEWER CHARACTERISTICS

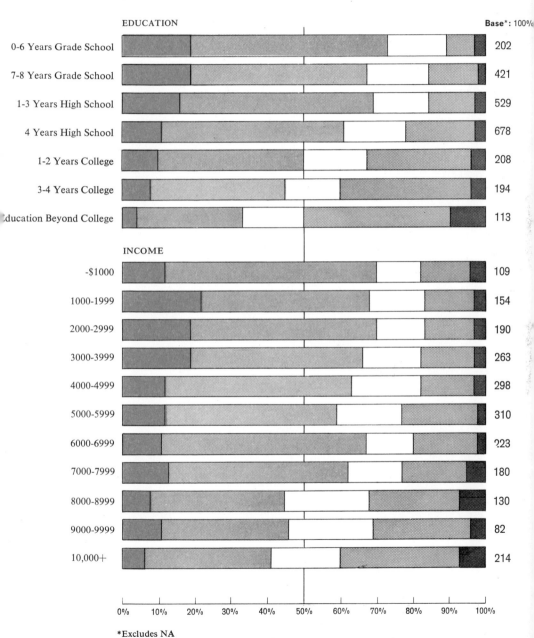

EDUCATION

Base*: 100%

0-6 Years Grade School	202
7-8 Years Grade School	421
1-3 Years High School	529
4 Years High School	678
1-2 Years College	208
3-4 Years College	194
Education Beyond College	113

INCOME

-$1000	109
1000-1999	154
2000-2999	190
3000-3999	263
4000-4999	298
5000-5999	310
6000-6999	223
7000-7999	180
8000-8999	130
9000-9999	82
10,000+	214

0%   10%   20%   30%   40%   50%   60%   70%   80%   90%   100%

*Excludes NA

continued next page

QUESTION 8 *"How do you feel about television in general?"*

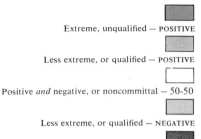

Extreme, unqualified — POSITIVE

Less extreme, or qualified — POSITIVE

Positive *and* negative, or noncommittal — 50-50

Less extreme, or qualified — NEGATIVE

Extreme, unqualified — NEGATIVE

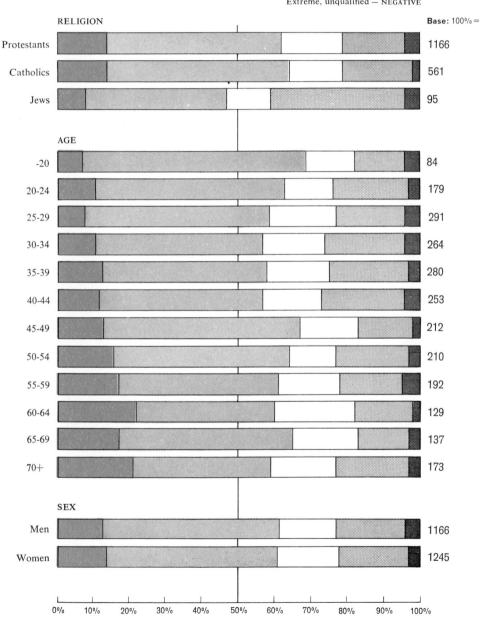

RELIGION

Base: 100% =

Protestants	1166
Catholics	561
Jews	95

AGE

-20	84
20-24	179
25-29	291
30-34	264
35-39	280
40-44	253
45-49	212
50-54	210
55-59	192
60-64	129
65-69	137
70+	173

SEX

| Men | 1166 |
| Women | 1245 |

0%   10%   20%   30%   40%   50%   60%   70%   80%   90%   100%

*Excludes NA

see, financial status probably also exerts some slight independent influence on attitudes toward TV.

4. Advancing age is not particularly associated with a larger total proportion of favorable vs. critical reactions, but it does seem to produce more *extreme* positive reactions. This probably reflects the increasing dependence on television for diversion and company that reaches its peak in some otherwise isolated oldsters. (Recall: "Maybe without TV I would be ready to die . . . ," page 26.)

5. Men and women do not differ at all in their over-all evaluations. Here, where we do not ask them to compare television with other products that have differential utility for the sexes, their responses are indistinguishable as to general level of acceptance. In fact, except for specifics obviously related to differences between male and female life patterns and tastes, we shall find very few differences in their attitudes toward television throughout this report.

All of these leads are pursued and elaborated later. Here we note mainly that:

—The audience as a whole has predominantly favorable feelings about "television in general," but

—Different segments of the population have different opinions on the matter. And, among them,

—Those who are most favorably disposed toward the medium come from the most numerous segments of society.

As the analysis by education and the analysis by income both illustrate, those groups who make up the largest share of the community and the audience are the most satisfied, thus making for the over-all score. The critics tend to come from a small but influential minority[7]—and that sets the stage for one of television's major policy dilemmas.

So much, for the moment, for general evaluation. Let us turn now to the other major analysis of the answers to that question: their specific *content*. What do people think about when asked about "television in general"?

Following are the results in terms of the broad categories that emerged in the coding. We show figures for the sample as a whole, as well as according to the over-all tone of the response as independently judged.

---

[7] Also one which some critics believe has more "right" to an opinion on grounds of greater sophistication.

QUESTION 8 *"Now let's just consider television. How do you feel about television in general?"*

		Over-all Response				
Respondents: ALL		Extremely Positive	Positive	50-50	Negative	Extremely Negative
Base*: 100% = 2416		328	1145	397	465	81
ASPECTS OF TV MENTIONED						
PROGRAMMING	**58%**	**32%**	**57%**	**70%**	**73%**	**42%**
praise	39	31	48	38	39	7
criticism	29	1	20	46	64	38
some good, some bad	6	0	3	21	4	0
VIEWING-Personal relationship	**30**	**47**	**24**	**35**	**31**	**26**
dependence: I couldn't live without it	9	36	7	2	1	0
independence: I could live without it	8	1	2	19	18	19
it's good "company"	6	14	8	2	1	1
I'm selective	7	2	6	12	7	4
I feel guilty about it	4	2	4	3	6	5
VIEWING-Effects	**21**	**25**	**28**	**14**	**9**	**23**
relaxing	8	10	13	5	0	1
waste of time	8	5	8	7	8	22
educational	8	13	12	4	1	0
VIEWING-Family, Social	**9**	**16**	**10**	**5**	**5**	**7**
makes for togetherness, home life	6	15	8	1	1	0
interferes with home life, visiting	3	1	2	4	4	7
CHILDREN	**19**	**14**	**17**	**22**	**26**	**21**
good for children (or helps parents)	9	13	11	6	3	0
bad for children (or makes it tough for parents)	12	1	6	19	23	21
COMMERCIALS	**7**	**1**	**6**	**8**	**15**	**6**
praise	1	1	1	1	0	0
criticism	7	1	5	7	15	6
TECHNICAL-Mechanical great invention, etc.	**10**	**25**	**10**	**4**	**5**	**2**
SPECIFIC CHANNELS, networks	**2**	**0**	**1**	**1**	**5**	**7**
GENERAL POSITIVE -it's great	**53**	**74**	**73**	**35**	**11**	**11**
GENERAL NEGATIVE-it's awful	**8**	**0**	**0**	**6**	**27**	**65**

*Excludes NA

Multiple responses: The detailed percentages within major categories do not necessarily add to the category totals, which show % of respondents mentioning any (one or more) of the subordinate categories

Speaking in their own words, the viewers raise all of these issues, and in substantial numbers: the programs; how they, the viewers, feel about and during viewing; what television does for or against home life; and how children (or parents) are affected. Commercials also come up, but less frequently and mostly in the negative. Beyond these specifics, there is an abundance of sweeping, unspecified praise; and some general damnation.

Within each of these major categories, people note the particular advantages and disadvantages, benefits gained and costs assessed. In fact, the respondents anticipate here almost every line of inquiry we later take up with them in detail. The table, taken as a whole, virtually serves as an outline for the organization of the specific sections that follow.

Perhaps the most significant thing to note at the outset, then, is the very range of responses—the simple fact that the viewers themselves think about such a variety of matters. Their mentions are not confined to programming or commercials. The viewer's own relation to the television set also appears as a primary concern, and in this sense respondents support our own emphasis on this consideration in the design of the study and in these pages.

We should make it quite clear that these coding categories denote explicit statements, not our interpretations of the psychological significance behind responses. That is, 9 per cent actually *say* "I couldn't live without it," or the equivalent; 4 per cent *state* "I feel guilty;" 8 per cent specifically assert that they *"could* do without television." Some interpreters might conclude that the last-mentioned are people who really can *not* do without it. But at this point, we are not concerned with the "true, deep meanings" behind the reactions, just the reactions themselves.

All of the specific responses naturally correlate with the over-all code assigned to the answers. Programs, viewing, children and TV, commercials—all tend to be discussed in more favorable terms by those giving the generally more favorable responses. But a look at the extreme cases reveals some interesting sidelights.

Those who feel most strongly about television—pro or con— are less likely to mention programming at all than the more moderate respondents. Only 32 per cent of the enthusiasts and 42 per cent of the unqualified critics refer to programming, as against 57 per cent, 70 per cent, and 73 per cent in the middle categories. To put it the other way, responses in terms of programming are less likely to be extreme than reactions to certain other aspects of TV.

In fact, fewer of the extreme critics have something bad to say about programs than either the "qualified-negative" or "50-50" groups. And the converse is true of the unqualified enthusiasts: fewer of them say something favorable about TV content than the three adjacent groups.

But on other items—especially on "viewing"—the two extreme groups are most apt to mention the pros and cons, respectively. The answers that most clearly characterize and distinguish the extreme, unqualified respondents—from each other and from the moderates—are these:

"pros": "I couldn't live without it" (36%)

"cons": "TV is a waste of time" (22%)

These considerations recall the composition of the two groups—the concentration of education and income among the critics; and the opposite, plus advancing age, in the enthusiast group. We shall hear a great deal more of the reasons behind these feelings in Part II.

Our final and most graphic look at television in general comes from a series of bipolar, or "opposite," rating scales.[8] Each respondent was handed a sheet, much like the one illustrated, and asked to ". . . read each pair quickly and put a check mark someplace between them, wherever you think it belongs, to describe television. Just your off-hand impression . . . ")

This device demands fast, spontaneous answers, so it reduces some of the bias associated with replies carefully weighed to be "right." And it provides a simple, quantitative measure on each of the evaluative items included so as to allow ready comparisons between various groups of respondents.[9] The numerical entries show the percentage who checked in each of the six possible positions; and for a quick overview, the shaded boxes show the single, most frequent response for the total sample. The general verdict is clear.

1. On most of the clearly positive-negative items, more people check in the *most* favorable position than in any other box; and on all of the good-bad scales, the majority is heavily on the positive side.

Ranking the good-bad scales by the proportion who mark the extreme favorable position produces the following picture:

---

[8] This format, though not these specific phrases, is adapted from the "semantic differential" developed by Charles Osgood. See C. Osgood, G. Suci, and P. Tannenbaum: *Measurement of Meaning* (University of Illinois Press, 1957).

[9] Notice that the instrument sometimes places the positive alternative on the

QUESTION 9 Put a check (✓) between each pair – wherever you think it belongs – to describe television.

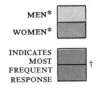

MEN*

WOMEN*

INDICATES MOST FREQUENT RESPONSE †

TELEVISION IS GENERALLY:

Left	1	2	3	4	5	6	Right
EXCITING (Men)	31%	20%	26%	12%	6%	5%	DULL
EXCITING (Women)	30%	17%	31%	14%	4%	4%	DULL
IN GOOD TASTE (Men)	25	22	29	24	6	4	IN BAD TASTE
IN GOOD TASTE (Women)	24	20	32	14	6	4	IN BAD TASTE
IMPORTANT (Men)	39	16	20	11	7	7	UNIMPORTANT
IMPORTANT (Women)	39	18	21	10	6	6	UNIMPORTANT
GENERALLY BAD (Men)	5	6	16	31	20	22	GENERALLY EXCELLENT
GENERALLY BAD (Women)	4	5	19	32	18	22	GENERALLY EXCELLENT
LOTS OF VARIETY (Men)	33	17	18	13	11	8	ALL THE SAME
LOTS OF VARIETY (Women)	36	15	19	12	10	8	ALL THE SAME
UPSETTING (Men)	4	4	8	18	23	43	RELAXING
UPSETTING (Women)	4	3	10	20	20	43	RELAXING
INTERESTING (Men)	43	22	17	10	5	3	UNINTERESTING
INTERESTING (Women)	41	21	21	9	4	4	UNINTERESTING
WONDERFUL (Men)	27	17	32	17	4	3	TERRIBLE
WONDERFUL (Women)	28	15	34	16	4	3	TERRIBLE
NOBODY CARES MUCH (Men)	4	4	13	25	23	31	ON EVERYONE'S MIND
NOBODY CARES MUCH (Women)	2	4	16	24	20	34	ON EVERYONE'S MIND
FOR ME (Men)	41	17	18	10	7	7	NOT FOR ME
FOR ME (Women)	41	16	19	10	5	9	NOT FOR ME
TOO "SIMPLE-MINDED" (Men)	11	12	39	30	4	4	TOO "HIGH-BROW"
TOO "SIMPLE-MINDED" (Women)	8	11	45	29	3	4	TOO "HIGH-BROW"
GETTING WORSE (Men)	8	8	13	25	20	26	GETTING BETTER
GETTING WORSE (Women)	9	8	18	23	18	24	GETTING BETTER
STAYS THE SAME (Men)	8	9	18	24	17	24	KEEPS CHANGING
STAYS THE SAME (Women)	10	11	18	21	17	23	KEEPS CHANGING
INFORMATIVE (Men)	38	25	20	9	4	4	NOT INFORMATIVE
INFORMATIVE (Women)	40	25	20	8	5	2	NOT INFORMATIVE
LOTS OF FUN (Men)	32	22	24	10	7	5	NOT MUCH FUN
LOTS OF FUN (Women)	32	18	25	14	5	6	NOT MUCH FUN
SERIOUS (Men)	9	9	28	30	11	13	PLAYFUL
SERIOUS (Women)	7	8	34	29	12	10	PLAYFUL
IMAGINATIVE (Men)	26	23	26	13	7	5	NO IMAGINATION
IMAGINATIVE (Women)	26	20	29	15	5	5	NO IMAGINATION

†Most frequent response (combined)
*Entries exclude NA which varies from item to item
Bases: Men, varies from 1094 to 1159; Women, varies from 1169 to 1232

Television is generally:

	Men	Women
Relaxing	43%	43%
Interesting	43	41
For me	41	41
Informative	38	40
Important	39	39
Lots of variety	33	36
On everyone's mind	31	34
Lots of fun	32	32
Exciting	31	30
Wonderful	27	28
Imaginative	26	26
Getting better	26	24
In good taste	25	24
Generally excellent	22	22

"Relaxing" and "interesting" turn up as the two adjectives most applicable to television as such—here and wherever else we ask a similar question. Unqualified praise ("wonderful," "generally excellent") is less frequently lavished on TV in general; and "imaginative" and "good taste" are also relatively low in order.

2. On the two scales where either extreme might represent the criticism that TV is "one-sided," responses cluster in the middle. There seems to be no widespread feeling that TV is either too heavy ("serious," "highbrow") or too light ("playful," "simple-minded"). This, in itself, does not warrant the conclusion that people feel TV fare to be properly balanced, or at an appropriate compromise in presentation. Middle-checking means only that neither extreme is widely recognized as descriptive of television in general.

3. The remaining scale ("changing") has no clear-cut evaluative interpretation; especially in view of the generally favorable response on the other items. "Stays the same" may well be an equally or more desirable alternative for many. But whichever way most people want it, most of them think it does keep changing.

4. Finally, note again the remarkable similarity between the sexes. The two sets of results are almost closer to each other than would be expected of the same group tested on two different occasions, or of one

___

right, and other times in the left-hand position. This discourages a simple "response set," or tendency to check one or the other side, by attempting to force individual judgments on each scale—though of course some halo-effects remain.

group randomly divided in half. Men and women may turn out to differ in some specific program preferences or in viewing hours, but their over-all evaluation of television appears to be basically the same.

The profiles produced by the three major educational groups appear in Appendix Table 5. Wherever they diverge they display the now fa-miliar pattern—less positive as education increases, with somewhat larger differences between those with high-school education, and the college-educated. The difference contracts on some of the scales: the college-educated are in closer agreement with the others on how "relaxing" TV is; and interestingly enough, they are not much more likely to describe it as "too simple-minded" or "too playful." Perhaps this reflects selective viewing, or some feeling that television in general isn't *supposed* to be "high brow" or "serious."

In any case, the pattern again suggests that the higher-educated are much less favorably impressed with the informational significance of the medium in general as compared with its capacity to provide relaxation.

Similarly, the analysis by income again finds that that factor makes less difference than formal schooling. The greatest difference occurs for those who report annual incomes above $8,000. This discontinuity suggests that the $8,000 level may reflect the cut-off point between those with sufficient disposable income to provide for a variety of alternative outside interests and recreational activities, and those eco-nomically more dependent on the "free" entertainment supplied by home TV.

These different life situations, incidentally, are nicely summarized in two responses to a later question: "What kind of people do you feel most of the programs on the air today are designed for?"

Looking down: "People that don't have time to live. People who just go to work, come home, and vege-tate."

Looking up: "The working class of people. The high 'mucky-mucks' are out on parties. It's the laboring class that gets the good out of it."

An Overview of the Overview

All of these preliminary probes—diverse as they are in form and content—produce much the same picture of how television rates with the people today.

1. The public at large, accustomed to spending several hours a day

relaxing with television, likes it and is generally satisfied with the job the industry is doing. The average viewer is by no means overwhelmed with its general excellence, but he certainly gives no indication of general dissatisfaction. All in all, a rough grade given TV by the public would be B plus, 85 per cent, three stars.

2. At the very top of the educational ladder, people are considerably less impressed. There are no doubt several reasons:

First, they probably impress less easily on any score. Education and the related financial means develop discrimination and critical standards, both real and verbal. The man with a professional or graduate education has more stringent criteria for excellence in the first place, and he also feels more need to demonstrate critical reactions as opposed to blanket praise.[1]

Next, they have less need and use for television; they have other interests and things to do, and the money to do them with.

Finally, television in general is not designed for their specialized tastes in the same sense as are their magazines, their music, their sports, or even their advertising campaigns. Quite the opposite: based on the extent and popular distribution of viewing, TV is the least specialized, the most "mass," of all the media.

3. At present, the appeals most frequently associated with the television set by its public are its ability to provide interesting and entertaining relaxation. And while the average viewer is also dependent on his television screen for the important news of the world—more so than his highly educated counterpart—all segments seem to regard the mass media largely in a context of complementary, not competing, functions. In this complex, TV as such is clearly *the* entertainment-relaxation medium—for everyone, including the highbrows.

But these are generalized statements about generalized reactions, on a topic where specific attitudes toward specific issues may be the most revealing. We begin with the study of viewing itself.

[1] This relates, incidentally, to a current upheaval in the field of personality testing. Many tests or inventories previously thought to distinguish between people who agree or disagree with *certain ideas,* now appear to distinguish in large part between people who simply tend to agree or disagree with anything—including the direct opposite of the statement they have apparently taken a position on. For example, the same people who "strongly agree" that "All X are Y" will also tend to "strongly agree" with the statement "No X are Y." And the general tendency to accept or reject strongly worded statements has been shown to correlate with formal schooling: the more training, the less "acquiescent" to extremes.

PART II

Television
As Viewing

SOME FUNDAMENTALIST sects prohibit movie-going, but their members feel quite comfortable watching movies at home on *The Late Show*. The same intellectuals who hurry to the art theater or the supper club for *Bitter Rice, Macbeth,* or Nichols and May may ignore them on TV, or find them inadequate there as commercialized for the masses. Communications researchers know that the same message is more persuasive in printed than in mimeographed form. So the medium, as such, clearly makes a difference; and people's reactions stem from more than the specific content transmitted.

Communications channels impose conditions on the audience—by their physical demands and by the social situations they encourage or preclude. Theater films are presented to large numbers of people sitting together quietly in the dark. Novels are usually read alone, with little distraction, and at a time, place, and pace selected by the reader. Television is most often watched after the evening meal, in a particular room of the home, and by several family members at once. The media also vary in the size of their audiences, simultaneous and accumulative. Over time, such concomitants give rise to important and persistent generalized associations. As a result, significant aspects of attitudes and feelings toward the various media relate not only to *what* is seen or heard or read, but to theater-*going,* or novel-*reading,* or tele*viewing*—in and of itself.

This Part is concerned with such considerations: What kind of activity is watching television? What part does it play in people's lives and how do they feel about it? How significant a part of people's attitudes toward television itself are their feelings about the act of watching?

In Chapter 3 we begin by comparing viewing with several other pastimes. What feelings are associated with watching TV, as compared with playing golf, reading a book, visiting with friends, etc.? Then we concentrate in greater detail on televiewing itself. What is it like, and what should it be like? What reasons do people give for watching, and how acceptable do they themselves think the reasons are?

Chapter 4 considers viewing in its most frequent setting—the home, with others present. The two major concerns here are how parents think it involves the children, for better or worse, and how it affects home life in general.

Chapter 3

TELEVISION AND LEISURE:
A BASIC CONFLICT

"I am really relaxed when I watch TV. In fact, it's the most enjoyable part of the day to me."

"It's a darn good medium if you have nothing better to do. It's something that I couldn't do without and yet sometimes I sure wonder. So often it seems like such a waste of time. I always feel like I should be reading or sewing or something like that. In general, I like it though."

TV vs. Other Pastimes

Early in the interview, before we had singled out television, we showed the pictures reduced on the top of page 55 and gave these instructions:

"I'm going to read some thoughts this man (woman) might be having, and I'd like you to tell me which picture each thought belongs with—in which situation he (she) is most likely to be feeling that way. You can name any picture as many times as you want to. If the thought doesn't seem to fit any picture, just say so."

QUESTION 6 Percentage of respondents
naming each pastime as best match for various
"thoughts." For example: when the interviewer
read the "thought," *"Am I lazy!,"* 49% said it fits the
TV picture best; 12% designated the reading scene, etc.

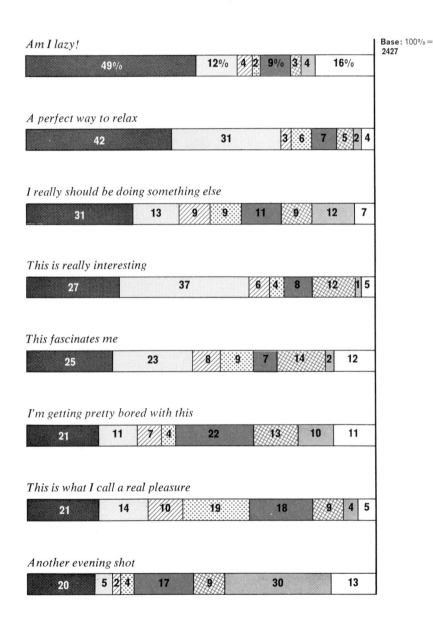

Base: 100% =
2427

Am I lazy!
49% | 12% | 4 | 2 | 9% | 3 | 4 | 16%

A perfect way to relax
42 | 31 | 3 | 6 | 7 | 5 | 2 | 4

I really should be doing something else
31 | 13 | 9 | 9 | 11 | 9 | 12 | 7

This is really interesting
27 | 37 | 6 | 4 | 8 | 12 | 1 | 5

This fascinates me
25 | 23 | 8 | 9 | 7 | 14 | 2 | 12

I'm getting pretty bored with this
21 | 11 | 7 | 4 | 22 | 13 | 10 | 11

This is what I call a real pleasure
21 | 14 | 10 | 19 | 18 | 9 | 4 | 5

Another evening shot
20 | 5 | 2 | 4 | 17 | 9 | 30 | 13

| TV | READ | CHILD | GOLF | VISIT | MOVIE | BAR | NONE |

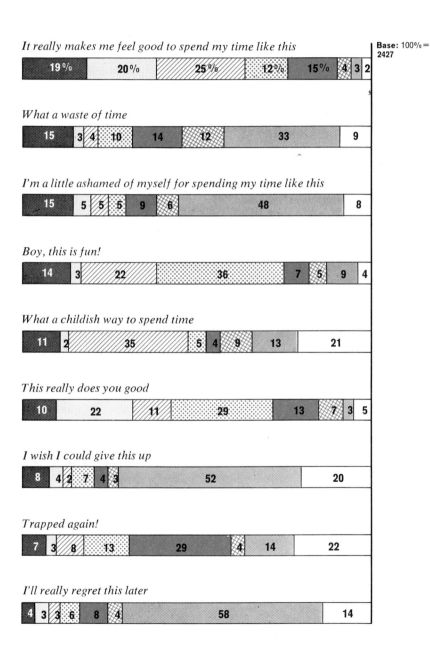

It really makes me feel good to spend my time like this

Base: 100% = 2427

19% | 20% | 25% | 12% | 15% | 4 | 3 | 2

What a waste of time

15 | 3 | 4 | 10 | 14 | 12 | 33 | 9

I'm a little ashamed of myself for spending my time like this

15 | 5 | 5 | 5 | 9 | 6 | 48 | 8

Boy, this is fun!

14 | 3 | 22 | 36 | 7 | 5 | 9 | 4

What a childish way to spend time

11 | 2 | 35 | 5 | 4 | 9 | 13 | 21

This really does you good

10 | 22 | 11 | 29 | 13 | 7 | 3 | 5

I wish I could give this up

8 | 4 | 2 | 7 | 4 | 3 | 52 | 20

Trapped again!

7 | 3 | 8 | 13 | 29 | 4 | 14 | 22

I'll really regret this later

4 | 3 | 3 | 6 | 8 | 4 | 58 | 14

The "thoughts" were designed to incorporate both the favorable feelings of interest, involvement, and relaxation, and some negative counterparts—boredom and shame or guilt about laziness. Obviously the device does not provide an exhaustive measure of the range of feelings associated with the various activities; it merely attempts to quantify the specific attitudes built into the statements. As in the case of the rating scales presented on page 45, this instrument requires quick responses so that respondents have less time to consider the "right" answer.[1]

The preceding chart shows the results, with the "thoughts" arranged in order of "TV" response. (For order of presentation in the interview, see Appendix A.)

Watching television: a perfect way to relax for lazy people who should be doing something else! The ambivalence of the total pattern of response to TV could hardly be more pronounced. Scan the chart vertically from those phrases that most frequently arouse "TV" responses down to those that almost never do: the two sides of the coin alternate continually. The depicted viewer feels, first of all, lazy but (or *and*) relaxed; interested, but he really ought to be elsewhere; fascinated and bored; it is "real pleasure" but also "another evening shot"; and so on.

And then compare this alternation to the consistent clusters of most frequent associations surrounding other activities:

Reading, for example, suggests mainly involvement and self-satisfaction, unadulterated by guilt or shame:

This is really interesting	37%
A perfect way to relax	31
This fascinates me	23
This really does you good	22
It really makes me feel good to	
spend my time like this	20

Golf also couples fun with justification:

Boy, this is fun!	36%
This really does you good	29

[1] Women saw an alternate set of pictures with a female principal in the same situations. There were also two versions of each form, varying the position of the different situations on the sheet, to control for any effect the order of pictures might have. The actual picture cards are reproduced in Appendix A.

While drinking at the bar brings the expected recriminations:

I'll really regret this later	58%
I wish I could give this up	52
I am a little ashamed of myself for spending my time like this	48
What a waste of time	33
Another evening shot (which meaning?)	30

We included the bar picture partly because of its natural appropriateness as a match for the "guilt" items. The fact is, that even against this competition, fully 15 per cent of the American public think of television as most "shameful" and 8 per cent even match TV with "I wish I could give this up."

The inconsistency in the over-all response to viewing stems partly, but only partly, from differing reactions among, rather than within, people. Some groups of viewers are less apt to consider TV most relaxing and more prone to think of it as the best match for "lazy"—and vice versa. Educational differences stand out, especially in the comparison with reading. The chart shows answers to the key phrases on both sides of the issue:

QUESTION 6 Television vs. Reading on Four Selected Comparisons

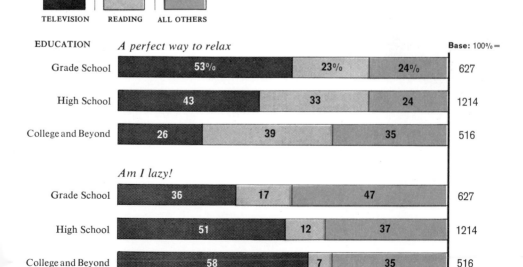

	TELEVISION	READING	ALL OTHERS	

EDUCATION   *A perfect way to relax*   Base: 100% =

	Television	Reading	All Others	Base
Grade School	53%	23%	24%	627
High School	43	33	24	1214
College and Beyond	26	39	35	516

Am I lazy!

	Television	Reading	All Others	Base
Grade School	36	17	47	627
High School	51	12	37	1214
College and Beyond	58	7	35	516

continued next page

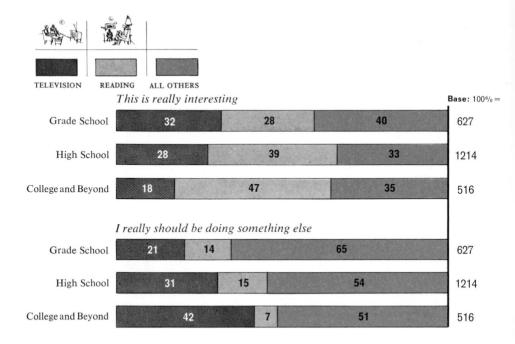

With increasing education, the vote on "interesting" shifts from TV to reading. And the same is true for "relaxing," though television remains in the lead through high school and makes a strong showing even in the college sample. Conversely, the more educated clearly express more guilt about televiewing than those with less schooling; and less reluctance about reading.

But taking these differences into account, we still find both halo and horns on television within each educational group. The high-school respondents illustrate this most clearly: 51 per cent associate "lazy" with TV, probably partly because of, not in spite of, the fact that a nearly equivalent 43 per cent find it the "perfect way to relax."

But here is a measure of ambivalence *within* given individuals: the cross-tabulation of "relax" on the one hand with "lazy" and "should be doing something else" on the other:

A perfect way to relax:		Per cent of those naming each activity as "perfect way to relax" who also match it with:	
	Base: 100% =	*Am I lazy*	*I really should be doing something else*
TV	1013	45%	25%
Read	762	10	12
Visit	176	6	10
Golf	139	1	7
Movie	113	2	4
Child	82	5	6
Bar	51	10	12

In short, of the 1013 people who select TV as "the perfect way to relax," almost half also consider viewing the most appropriate match for "am I lazy." By comparison, only 10 per cent of those who "relax" with reading attach such a conscience cost. And the same general pattern occurs with "should be doing something else."

Why these Calvinistic hesitations about televiewing, in contrast with the self-satisfaction associated with reading? The distinction is so great that guilt over indulgence in the one is sometimes directly related to neglect of the other:

"My conscience might say I spend too much time watching television because I get behind on reading. Probably won't stop though."

But nobody says the opposite, and it is hardly conceivable: "My conscience might say I spend too much time reading because I get behind on my television." Is this situation entirely attributable to differences in content between the two media?

It is unlikely that a larger share of *all* printed matter than of *all* television is "worthwhile." There is much more print to start with, and it is less visible, less subject to legal and social controls. So by weight of sheer numbers, printed trash probably outweighs the broadcast version, perhaps even on a percentage basis.

But of the books actually *read,* as against the programs *seen,* a larger share may have turned out to be worthwhile: the reader can and does exercise more selectivity. He has more to choose from in the first place; a larger range of quality, by whatever definition; little or no need to compromise with the tastes of others around him; and accidental or entirely nonselective exposure is virtually impossible. You can't wander into a room and absorb a book simply because your wife happens to be reading it.

In addition, there are structural and historical differences that may be relevant:

1. *Physical and mental demands:*   Reading is more work; and therefore it seems a less passive, "lazy" pursuit.[2] Reading Shakespeare or Mickey Spillane is harder than watching them on the screen, and both Mark Twain and modern psychologists observe that the more effort something takes, the more worthwhile the product seems.[3]

2. *The cultural halo:*   Reading is heir to worth-by-association, in the culture and in the personal history of the average American. It was the earlier means for transmission of serious ideas, and it is still best suited for the communication of much technical and other heavy material, chiefly because such learning often requires self-pacing. And reading— like spinach or music lessons—is sanctioned and required of the child in school and at home, by the child's respected and powerful elders; and it remains closely associated with formal education throughout life.

So the printed form probably dignifies a message beyond the respect it would command on the screen. Psychologically—as sometimes physically—the reader can hide Mike Hammer behind the covers of Tolstoy ("I spent the evening with a novel"). The opposite may actually occur with TV: "I watched Bernstein" could be generalized to: "I spent the afternoon in front of the idiot box."

3. *The time consumed:*   Finally, there is the absolute number of hours spent watching. Few people, even avid readers, typically spend several hours a day with books—as avid viewers do with TV. And any form of relaxation that occupies this much daily time is bound to conflict with other, productive alternatives. In the present media mix of the average viewer, television represents *the* large daily non-working expendi-

---

[2] In the construction of the questionnaire, a pro-television researcher criticized the cartoon projective because, in his words, watching television "is the only really passive activity portrayed." Even the staunchest supporters apparently feel that televiewing is somehow more "passive" than reading, talking to friends, sitting at a bar, or being at the movies.

[3] In *A Theory of Cognitive Dissonance* (Row, Peterson, 1957), Leon Festinger reports a number of demonstrations in which the same goal acquires greater value as a result of subject's having expended more energy to attain it. The point is not that people will work harder for something they want more; the point is that they will value the same thing more if it has taken more work to get it.

ture of time, and as such, is far more likely to be the villain behind neglected alternatives, real or potential, than the occasional book.

Focus on Viewing

So far the picture is comparative. Television raises more qualifications than reading, less than drinking, and so on. And questioning on the issue has been "projective"—that is, feelings were attributed to the expressionless cartoon protagonist, not reported by respondents as their own.

Now we turn to a more direct and detailed look at viewing itself. How do people say they themselves feel when they watch television—not in relation to how they feel when they do other things, but in relation to how they would like to feel? It was later in the interview, and TV alone had been the topic for several preceding questions, when we raised the issue explicity:

Q. 12 A "How does watching television usually make you feel?"
C "And how (else) would you like TV to make you feel?"

	Usually feel	Would like to feel
Relaxed, satisfied, peaceful	49%	26%
Happy, entertained, amused	27	19
Depends on show	17	0
Tired, sleepy	13	1
Good, nice, O.K.	12	7
Excited, suspenseful, thrilled	8	3
Informed, educated	7	17
Interested	6	5
Lazy, restless, guilty	6	0
Takes mind off cares	6	1
Disgusted	5	0
Bored	2	0
Sad, depressed	2	0
Active, aware	0	1
DK, NA, no other way	5	41

Base: 100% = 1218 (asked of half the sample only)

NOTE: Percentages add to more than 100% because of multiple responses.

The pattern here is much less ambivalent or conflicted, and more clearly positive. Watching television is usually relaxing and entertaining, and nearly half the respondents cannot think of any other effect they would like. Some guilt is suggested, but only infrequently.

In short, the responses here concentrate on the emotional rewards, not the costs. If hesitations often accompany the satisfactions of viewing —as strongly suggested in the cartoon comparisons—they do not "usually" predominate.

Now this is not a particularly striking finding, since, after all, viewing is largely a voluntary activity.[4] But two other small but important entries also appear in this table and both anticipate major trends.

The first is the call for more intellectual gratification. The second is the hedge: "It all depends on the program." Both of these become crucial components in the mixture of feelings about watching, especially among the intellectual critics of the medium. We pursue the matter via a detailed, quantitative description of viewing produced by a sixty-word check list that we used with three different sets of instructions:

(1) ". . . go through this list quickly and check all the words that describe how watching TV *usually* makes you feel . . ."

(2) ". . . describe how you'd like watching TV to make you feel."

(3) ". . . describe how watching (your favorite programs) makes you feel."

One half the sample answered both the first and second questions, and in that order, while the other half was asked only about their favorite programs. Favorite programs had been established for each respondent in the previous question, and were inserted by name in this probe. (For example: ". . . check all the words that describe how watching *Gunsmoke* makes you feel.")

The complete list with the score for each individual word appears in Appendix Table 6. In the following chart we group the words to simplify the comparison, and show only the average score for each cluster.[5]

---

[4] As a respondent points out: "It makes you feel pretty good or you wouldn't watch it." Also, people are now talking about themselves, not the expressionless cartoon figure, and "I" obviously do not waste as much time watching as "most people" do.

[5] For example: the words "contented," "calm," "peaceful," "satisfied," are considered together. In describing how watching television "ordinarily . . . makes me feel," 52 per cent checked "satisfied," 39 per cent checked "peaceful," 34 per cent checked "contented," and 32 per cent checked "calm." The average for the four words, 39 per cent, is used in the table. Since we take the average for all the

QUESTION 12B *"Ordinarily, watching television makes me feel . . ."* *

QUESTION 12D *"I'd like television to make me feel . . ."* *

QUESTION 14D *"Watching my favorite programs makes me feel . . ."* *

Base: 100%=1216

Base: 100%=1216

Base: 100%=1210

Average Score For The Cluster:

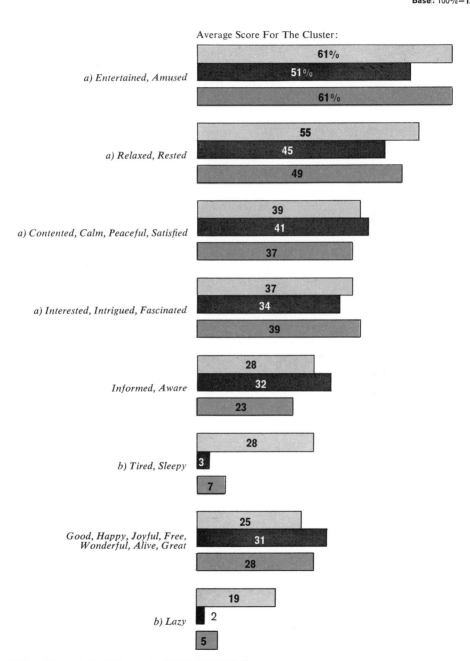

a) Entertained, Amused — 61% / 51% / 61%

a) Relaxed, Rested — 55 / 45 / 49

a) Contented, Calm, Peaceful, Satisfied — 39 / 41 / 37

a) Interested, Intrigued, Fascinated — 37 / 34 / 39

Informed, Aware — 28 / 32 / 23

b) Tired, Sleepy — 28 / 3 / 7

Good, Happy, Joyful, Free, Wonderful, Alive, Great — 25 / 31 / 28

b) Lazy — 19 / 2 / 5

*12B and D asked of half the sample; 14D of the other half

continued next page

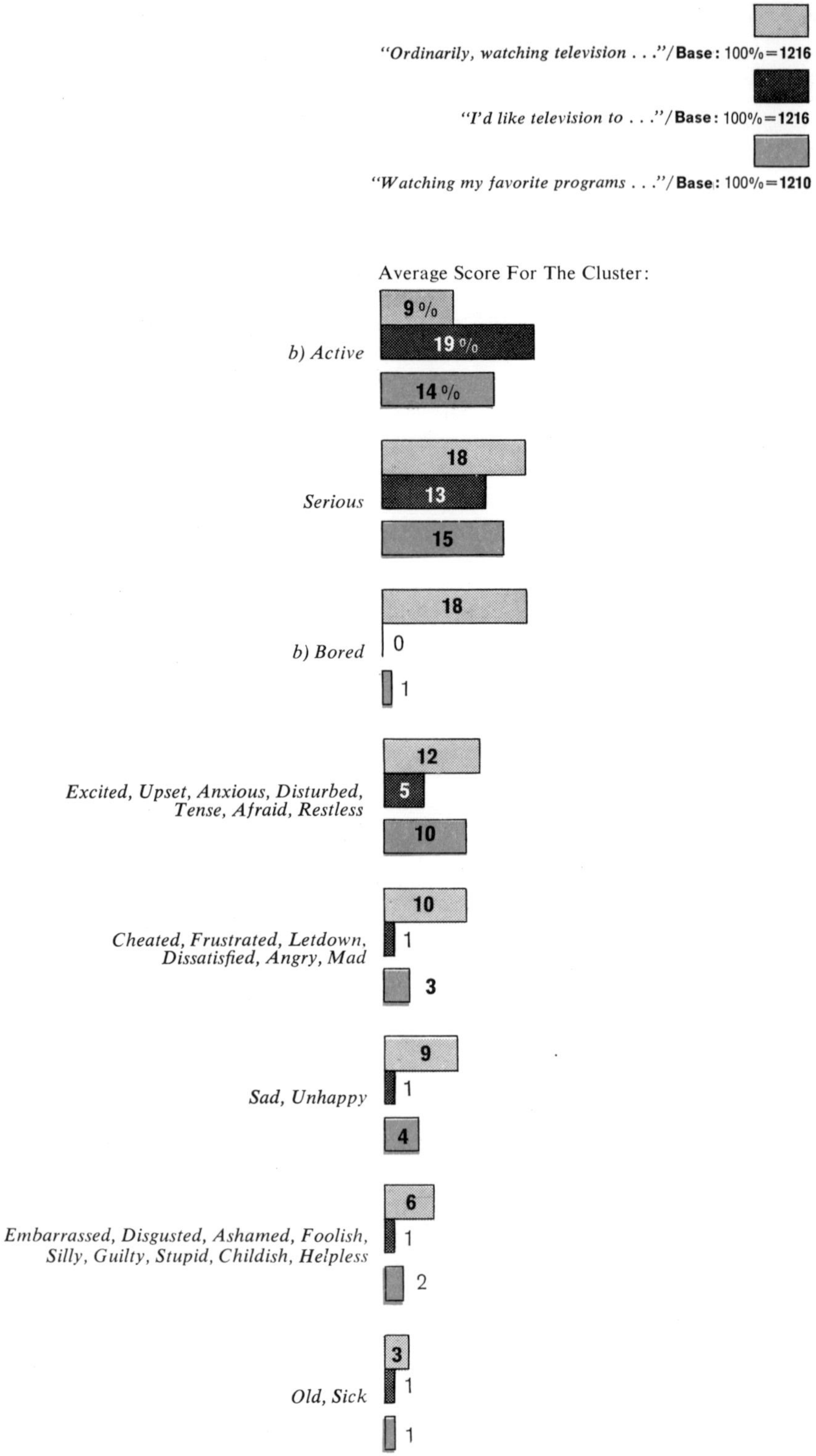

"Ordinarily, watching television . . ."/Base: 100%=1216
"I'd like television to . . ."/Base: 100%=1216
"Watching my favorite programs . . ."/Base: 100%=1210
Average Score For The Cluster:
b) Active
9%
19%
14%
Serious
18
13
15
b) Bored
18
0
1
Excited, Upset, Anxious, Disturbed, Tense, Afraid, Restless
12
5
10
Cheated, Frustrated, Letdown, Dissatisfied, Angry, Mad
10
1
3
Sad, Unhappy
9
1
4
Embarrassed, Disgusted, Ashamed, Foolish, Silly, Guilty, Stupid, Childish, Helpless
6
1
2
Old, Sick
3
1
1

a) Again, the satisfactions clearly predominate, and they are the same as in previous measures: watching television is entertaining, relaxing, satisfying, and interesting, and in that order. What is more, on all these counts, viewing "ordinarily" does as good a job as "I would like," or as "my favorite shows." In fact, "ordinarily" almost always exceeds "would like" on those clusters.

b) Again, there is the unmistakable undercurrent of ambivalence and its source, passivity: it often makes me feel "lazy," and I would like to feel "active." And "tired" and "sleepy" also probably relate psychologically to "relaxation"—as well as, physically, to *The Late Show*.

The locus of the conflict involved in the pleasures and perils of relaxation is sharpened when we divide the sample by education, as in the table on page 67.

The simplest summary is still that the more highly educated are more critical; but the effects of education differ notably among the various adjective clusters. First, let us compare what viewing *is* (12B, 14D) with what it *should be* (12D):[6]

a) The groups are in substantial agreement that TV is relaxing and entertaining; and that it should be. In all three columns, the largest entries at each educational level are in these clusters, save one which is close. And the groups all "ordinarily" note some attending laziness and sopor. But the more educated are less willing to settle for that, or at least to say they do:

b) They make far more frequent demands to feel informed and intellectually stimulated; and at the same time they more often report such benefits. Despite their generally more critical attitude, the educated are more apt to attribute informative effects to their "ordinary" viewing as well as to their favorite shows. (The selectivity this implies is given intensive scrutiny in following sections; we simply note it here.)

---

words in the cluster, the total number of words included does not affect the score. A cluster of three words is no more likely to get a high score than a single word, so cluster scores are directly comparable with each other.

[6] Because the absolute number of words checked increases with education, the most meaningful comparison is among the three check lists produced by each group, rather than across educational groups for any given list.

c) The wish to feel "active" also climbs with education, but neither "ordinary" nor "favorite" viewing satisfies that. This is the one discrepancy between what viewing is and what it should be that expands most with education. At no level do viewers ordinarily feel active watching TV, even during their favorite shows; but at high school and beyond, many say they would like to.[7]

In short, uneasiness about viewing seems once more to grow with schooling; and it appears to come largely from the laziness and passivity associated with what the educated seem to consider "contented vegetation" in front of the tube. They also admit to being relaxed and entertained, but they are less happy about it.

The role of personal values in determining reactions to pleasant, easy relaxation is further suggested when we divide the sample by religion. By and large, the pattern is similar to educational differences, with Jews, on the average, representing the college reaction. But on several crucial words, the relationship is highlighted and especially indicative of cultural differences. For example:

	12B Ordinarily, watching TV makes me feel . . .			*12D* I would like TV to make me feel . . .			*14D* Watching my favorite programs makes me feel . . .		
	Protestant	Catholic	Jew	Protestant	Catholic	Jew	Protestant	Catholic	Jew
Disturbed	10%	9%	18%	1%	1%	10%	3%	5%	5%
Dissatisfied	13	18	25	1	1	8	3	4	4
Happy	37	40	23	46	43	25	39	50	45
Base: 100% =	841	283	40	841	283	40	829	282	56

More Jews say they are ordinarily disturbed and dissatisfied by viewing (though not by their favorite programs—there are no differences there); *and* more of them say they *want* TV to disturb or dissatisfy! Similarly: fewer are ordinarily made "happy," and fewer say they *want* to be.

This apparent masochism may reflect the basic ambivalence about relaxation. (People may be saying: "I shouldn't be so complacent about wasting all this time; it would be better if I felt more disturbed about it.") But it may also represent a call for more stimulating, less Pollyanna

---

[7] This discomfort with passivity raises the possibility of programming that requires more viewer participation, in one way or another.

QUESTION 12B *"Ordinarily, watching television makes me feel . . ."*

QUESTION 12D *"I'd like television to make me feel . . ."*

QUESTION 14D *"Watching my favorite programs makes me feel . . ."*

BY EDUCATION

	Grade School			High School			College and Beyond		
	12B	12D	14D	12B	12D	14D	12B	12D	14D
Base: 100% =	313	313	314	633	633	580	241	241	275
a) *Entertained, Amused*	51%	39%	52%	65%	53%	65%	63%	61%	59%
a) *Relaxed, Rested*	53	42	50	59	45	50	46	45	44
a) *Contented, Calm, Peaceful and Satisfied*	40	37	37	41	42	40	33	41	33
b) *Interested, Intrigued, Fascinated*	31	24	34	40	35	41	38	46	39
b) *Informed, Aware*	18	18	13	29	32	22	38	48	35
a) *Tired, Sleepy*	28	4	10	29	3	7	26	2	4
Good, Happy, Joyful, Free, Wonderful, Alive, Great	30	30	33	26	32	29	18	31	21
a) *Lazy*	16	2	5	19	1	6	21	3	3
Serious	13	8	14	18	13	16	20	20	12
Bored	12	0	1	18	0	2	24	0	1
Excited, Upset, Anxious, Disturbed, Tense, Afraid, Restless	12	4	11	13	5	10	12	5	8
Cheated, Frustrated, Letdown, Dissatisfied, Angry, Mad, Impatient	7	1	3	10	1	3	14	2	3
Sad, Unhappy	8	1	6	10	1	5	7	1	2
c) *Active*	8	11	12	9	21	15	10	23	12
Embarrassed, Disgusted, Ashamed, Foolish, Silly, Guilty, Stupid, Childish, Helpless	6	0	2	6	0	2	8	1	2
Old, Sick	3	0	2	2	0	1	3	1	1
Average score for all words	**21**	**14**	**18**	**25**	**18**	**20**	**24**	**21**	**17**

programming. ("Television should wake people up to do something about the evils and dangers of today's world.") As Academicus protests, in the "great debate" cited above:

> What all of us most want to hear is how great and good and right we are; how justice triumphs, at least in the end; how good and evil are easily recognized; how rewarding it is to do one's duty; how pleasant and easy and full of fun life really is. To a major extent the mass media help us to indulge such global fantasies without recalling us sufficiently to the realities, the complexities, and the seriousness of life.[8]

But whatever the reason, general cultural factors, as reflected in educational and religious differences, seem to have a lot to do with how people feel about viewing—much more, in fact, than the effects[9] of such "basic" distinctions as age, sex, or urban-rural residence. Attitudes toward TV are not superficial; nor are they specific to the medium alone. They seem to stem as well from general and pervasive values, applied in this case to television and the reasons for watching it.

Reasons for Viewing

So far, reasons behind viewing have been implicit. Now we bring up the question directly, and in greater detail.

Because of expected differences in the "social acceptability" of various possible reasons, the question was asked in two forms. One half of the sample was asked directly: "When you watch television, how often does each of these reasons apply to you?" The others responded to a projective version, which presumably gives them the chance to be revealing without self-incrimination: "When most people watch TV, how often do you think each of these reasons apply?" Under both conditions, respondents read through the same list of fifteen possible "reasons" and checked each as "usually," "occasionally," "rarely," or "never" applicable.

Here are the results of both forms, with the reasons arranged in order of their acknowledged *self*-applicability.

---

[8] Berelson: op. cit.

[9] When we speak of the "effects" of variables such as education, we mean it only in the statistical sense: dividing the sample according to characteristic A *affects* the observed distribution of responses. It does not necessarily follow that schooling, *per se*, *produced* the difference. These cross-tabulations demonstrate only association, not causality. The latter is a matter of interpretation.

QUESTION 11A *"When you watch TV,
how often does each of these reasons apply?"*

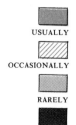

USUALLY

OCCASIONALLY

RARELY

NEVER

QUESTION 11B *"When most people watch
TV, how often do you think each
of these reasons apply?"*

a) *(I) (they)† watch to see a specific program that (I) (they) enjoy very much.* 100%*

| I watch ... | 80% | 15% | 2 | 3 |

| They watch ... | 82 | 16 | 2 |

a) *watch to see a special program that (I've) heard a lot about.*

| 54 | 35 | 7 | 4 |

| 64 | 32 | 4 |

a) *watch just because it is a pleasant way to spend an evening.*

| 55 | 26 | 11 | 8 |

| 74 | 22 | 4 |

a) *watch just because (I) feel like watching television.*

| 50 | 23 | 14 | 13 |

| 60 | 25 | 12 | 3 |

a) *watch because (I) think (I) can learn something.*

| 36 | 39 | 16 | 9 |

| 36 | 38 | 23 | 3 |

b) *start watching because (my) husband or wife is and seems to be interested.*

| 21 | 42 | 15 | 22 |

| 36 | 47 | 12 | 5 |

b) *watch mainly to be sociable when others are watching.*

| 17 | 32 | 27 | 24 |

| 24 | 39 | 30 | 7 |

c) *watch because there is nothing else to do at the time.*

| 20 | 27 | 24 | 29 |

| 36 | 37 | 19 | 8 |

† Two independent samples. All items on questions 11A were
worded "I"; on 11B, "they"

*Percentages exclude NA which varies from item to item
  Bases: "I" varies from 1060 to 1218; "they" varies from 1158 to 1183

continued next page

QUESTION 11A *"When you watch TV, how often does each of these reasons apply?"*

QUESTION 11B *"When most people watch TV, how often do you think each of these reasons apply?"*

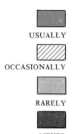

USUALLY

OCCASIONALLY

RARELY

NEVER

100%*

d) *turn on the set just "to keep me company" when (I'm) alone.*

| I watch ... | 20 | 25 | 20 | 35 |
| They watch ... | 38 | 39 | 14 | 9 |

c) *watch to get away from the ordinary cares and problems of the day.*

| 18 | 24 | 25 | 33 |
| 36 | 36 | 19 | 9 |

b) *watch because (I'm) afraid (I) might be missing something good.*

| 12 | 23 | 28 | 37 |
| 33 | 36 | 23 | 8 |

c) *start on one show and then "get stuck" for the rest of the evening.*

| 15 | 20 | 29 | 36 |
| 33 | 34 | 24 | 9 |

b) *watch because everyone (I) know is and (I) want to be able to talk about it.*

| 8 | 17 | 27 | 48 |
| 20 | 28 | 34 | 18 |

d) *watch just for "background" while (I'm) doing something else.*

| 7 | 19 | 25 | 49 |
| 15 | 37 | 30 | 18 |

c) *keep watching to put off doing something else (I) should do.*

| 2 | 12 | 27 | 59 |
| 15 | 31 | 35 | 19 |

The most striking aspect of the table is the extent to which the two sets of responses—"I" and "they"—progressively diverge from top to bottom. At the top, the self-acknowledged reasons are also attributed to others; answers on one form are like answers on the other. But down the list, those reasons that tend "never" to apply to "me" are not nearly so inapplicable when it comes to the viewing habits of "most people."

(a) "I" most often watch out of interest in specific programs, for pleasant relaxation, and for information; and so do "most people."

(b) "I" watch less frequently just to be sociable or to be in on something; but these reasons often account for other people's viewing.

(c) Similarly, "I" rarely or never watch to kill time, or for escape, or out of addiction; but others engage in these habits quite a bit.

(d) Finally, "I" seldom use TV for background, or to keep me company when I'm alone; but "most people" do so frequently, especially the latter.[1]

Bear in mind that these self-other comparisons were not explicitly made by the respondents themselves; half the sample talked only about themselves, the other half only about "most people." What do these differences in response pattern mean?

We assume that since people have little or no direct information on the reasons "most people" have for watching television, their answers to this question will draw in large measure on conscious or unconscious generalization of their own viewing habits, especially since many items, such as "for company, when alone," are by nature outside the realm of direct observation.[2]

To the extent that this interpretation is correct, the degree of discrepancy between the two sets of replies serves as a rough index to the perceived "acceptability" of each of the reasons. The greater the dis-

[1] Women, by the way, acknowledge more frequent "background" viewing than men (in the daytime?); but only slightly more watching for "company when alone" (because of the company of children?).

[2] Often, the projective interpretation of such "most people" questions is unwarranted. Someone who says: "Most people probably would object to Red China's admission to the UN," or "to Negroes moving into this area," obviously need not share these attitudes. He may simply know they exist. Not so, probably, when it comes to reasons for televiewing.

The fact that responses on the positive items do *not* differ between the two forms also gives weight to the projective interpretation of the negative ones. In view of them, it cannot readily be argued that people simply attribute all reasons more frequently to others than to themselves, or that differences in response are due to sampling differences between the two groups of respondents.

crepancy, the less willingness to admit the reason personally, so the less "legitimate" or "justified" it must appear to the respondents.

On this assumption, then, people are least proud of viewing when they watch:

—because there is nothing else to do
—for company when alone, or for "background"
—for fear of missing something good
—to put off doing something else, or for "escape"
—because everyone else is watching.

But there is no reluctance whatsoever to report watching out of interest in specific programs.

The two ends of this acceptability scale correlate strongly with the amount of deliberate selectivity exercised. All but one of the "denied" reasons involves unselective viewing—TV use in which program content is largely irrelevant. Even that one, the fear of missing something good, is dubious. The objective is content-related, but the means implied are nonselective—watching everything in sight because something might turn out to be good.

Again, selectivity or the lack of it becomes much more of an issue with increasing education. Two items at opposite ends of the continuum illustrate this dramatically: All educational groups say they and others watch out of specific program interest. But when it comes to "time-killing," the spread between "me" and "most people" increases strikingly with education. Among those with training beyond college, for example, only 14 per cent acknowledge this as one of their own "usual" reasons, as against 49 per cent who attribute it to "most"; and 46 per cent go so far as to say they *never* watch television because they have nothing else to do, while not one such respondent is willing to make this statement for "most people"!

To what extent is this an accurate perception, on the part of the intellectuals, of differences between their own viewing habits and those of the general population? And to what extent are they simply less willing to acknowledge nonselective, time-killing televiewing because it carries more of a stigma for them?

The most direct evidence comes from our later analysis of the programs they actually watch. But we have another indication at this point; namely, the sheer amount of viewing the various groups report. The information comes from this question:

USUALLY APPLIES

EDUCATION	0-6 Yrs. Grade School	7-8 Yrs. Grade School	1-3 Yrs. High School	4 Yrs. High School	1-2 Yrs. College	3-4 Yrs. College	Beyond College
"I watch to see a specific program that I enjoy very much"	76%	80%	79%	82%	76%	76%	77%
"**most people** watch to see a specific program that they enjoy very much"	81	79	81	84	82	76	69
"I watch because there is nothing else to do at the time"	30	30	22	15	15	14	14
"**most people** watch because there is nothing else to do at the time"	44	35	32	36	25	33	49

NEVER APPLIES

EDUCATION	0-6 Yrs. Grade School	7-8 Yrs. Grade School	1-3 Yrs. High School	4 Yrs. High School	1-2 Yrs. College	3-4 Yrs. College	Beyond College
"I watch to see a specific program that I enjoy very much"	2%	3%	3%	1%	1%	3%	2%
"**most people** watch to see a specific program that they enjoy very much"	0	0	0	0	0	0	0
"I watch because there is nothing else to do at the time"	24	26	24	27	26	33	46
"**most people** watch because there is nothing else to do at the time"	4	10	10	8	9	6	0

Base: 100% =

	0-6 Yrs.	7-8 Yrs.	1-3 Yrs.	4 Yrs.	1-2 Yrs.	3-4 Yrs.	Beyond
"I"	90	219	266	363	102	93	65
"most people"	113	205	265	320	106	101	49

1. 0-6 Years Grade School/**Base:** 100% = 203

2. 7-8 Years Grade School/**Base:** 100% = 424

QUESTION 17 Average Per cent Reporting
Viewing Per Hour in Various Time
Segments of an Ordinary . . .

3. 1-3 Years High School/**Base:** 100% = 531

4. 4 Years High School/**Base:** 100% = 683

5. 1-2 Years College/**Base:** 100% = 208

6. 3-4 Years College/**Base:** 100% = 194

7. Education Beyond College/**Base:** 100% = 114

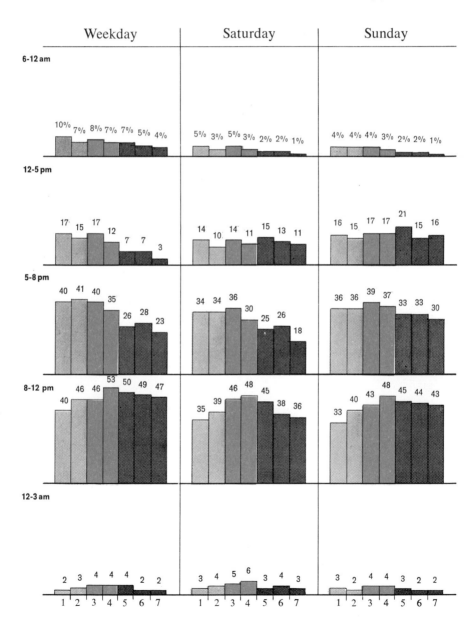

	Weekday	Saturday	Sunday

Q. 17   *"On an average day, during what hours do you yourself ordi-*
          narily watch television? . . . Please check each hour YOU
          would be likely to see at least some television."

Respondents then filled out a sheet, listing each hour from 6 a.m. to
3 a.m. and, separately, for "an ordinary weekday," "an ordinary Saturday," and "an ordinary Sunday." The self-reported ratings (average
per cent watching *per hour*) during various time periods are shown at
the left. (The objective is obviously not to compile reliable ratings;
there are more valid data on that question. The point is merely to get
a rough indication of how various groups differ in their own perception
of how much television they watch.)

The striking fact is that reported prime-time viewing is unrelated
to education! The more critical segments say they watch less during the
day, but they indicate about as much time with TV from eight to signoff. This similarity is especially impressive since response bias, if any,
should work to diminish the viewing hours reported by these more
critical groups.

More definitive data from the ARB analysis and commercial rating
services do show a decline in viewing with education, but in absolute
terms it remains high. In fact, the actual number of programs watched
during the one-week period, by the ARB panel, shows only about the
same decline with education as the average number of hours checked
by survey respondents in Question 17:

	Q. 17 Average number of hours checked per day	ARB sample Actual number of programs recorded seen, per week
0–8 yrs. G.S.	4.3	40
1–3 yrs. H.S.	4.4	37
4 yrs. H.S.	4.2	32
1–3 yrs. coll.	3.6	25
3–4 yrs. coll.	3.5	27
Beyond college	2.9	25

This result casts some doubt on the high selectivity claimed or
implied by the college-educated in several previous questions. Accordingly, their own viewing is probably less confined to specific programs
of special interest than they indicated in the foregoing discussion of
"reasons."[3] It appears, then, that they too watch a great deal but feel
worse about it:

[3] Unless, of course, there are several hours a day of programming that they
consider worthy of selection, which seems unlikely by their own stated criteria.

QUESTION 38 *"Do you think that you spend too much time watching television, or would you say that you don't have a chance to see as much as you would really like to?"*

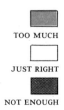

TOO MUCH

JUST RIGHT

NOT ENOUGH

EDUCATION   Base*: 100% =

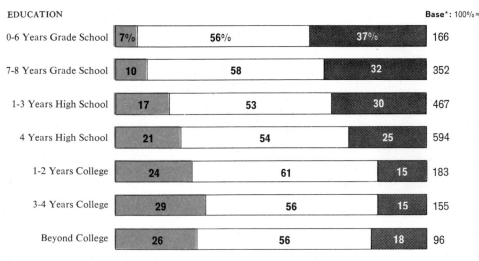

EDUCATION	TOO MUCH	JUST RIGHT	NOT ENOUGH	Base
0-6 Years Grade School	7%	56%	37%	166
7-8 Years Grade School	10	58	32	352
1-3 Years High School	17	53	30	467
4 Years High School	21	54	25	594
1-2 Years College	24	61	15	183
3-4 Years College	29	56	15	155
Beyond College	26	56	18	96

*Excludes NA

Q. 39   *"Generally, about how many hours of television would you say is 'right' for the average adult—that is, enough to keep up with the important and entertaining things but still not too much?"*

EDUCATION	Less than 1 hr. a day	1–2 hrs.	3–4 hrs.	5–6 hrs.	7–8 hrs.	8 hrs. or more	Base: 100% =	Average no. of hours
0–6 yrs. G. S.	3%	33%	51%	12%	1%	0%	183	3.1
7–8 yrs. G. S.	1	31	48	15	4	1	394	3.4
1–3 yrs. H. S.	1	29	50	15	3	2	494	3.4
4 yrs. H. S.	2	36	49	11	2	0	642	3.0
1–2 coll.	7	46	40	7	0	0	191	2.5
3–4 coll.	10	53	33	4	0	0	177	2.2
Beyond college	18	54	21	7	0	0	97	2.0

Unselective or routine viewing, then, is probably a major source of uneasiness, especially in those groups whose values are inconsistent with passive, "unproductive" use of leisure. For achievement-oriented people, relaxation needs to be justified; it is not easily accepted as an end in itself. A conscience-free vacation or game of golf must be earned ("I've got it coming after that month I put in"); or, better yet, it should be necessary to further achievement (to prolong life, store up energy for the job, develop social contacts).

Programs that provide important information, intellectual stimulation, or emotional enrichment provide such justification for viewing. When people truly restrict themselves to programs they consider worthwhile, ambivalence is probably minimal, if it exists at all. But the number of hours they watch and like to watch television makes it unlikely that even a major portion of their viewing can be that selective. And this is especially true of those who care the most, because their standards of "worth" are more stringent. Furthermore, their appetite isn't always geared to health foods. And so we hear:

> "Too often I feel that I have wasted my time. I have a country home in which I haven't installed TV because I do not want to be tempted to waste my time. I watch too much."

In its way, this is a remarkably revealing statement: in a country home presumably dedicated to pleasure, restraints are needed to keep from nonproductive enjoyment. The left hand hides the bottle from the right. And "bottle" may not be an inept analogy:

> "I don't spend too much time watching—I control myself."

> "I spend too much time. Can't help myself. A TV addict."

> "Like a drug—you shouldn't do it but you do."

> "My wife stole a tube and pretended something was wrong with the set. We went back to reading, the kids got better grades, and Mom was easier to live with. I think it was a sneaky way to do it though."

In short, television, like so many aspects of contemporary life, is considered more good than good *for* you. As is our custom with food, cigarettes, charge accounts, as well as with TV, we indulge beyond the limits we would like to set for ourselves. Whether the limits are necessary, or rational, or prudent, is beside the point. So long as they exist, and so long as they are violated, they will be a source of attendant guilt —or uneasiness, if guilt is too strong a word.

In the case of viewing, "productive" programs can potentially resolve the conflict. But in reality the resolution remains partial at best, especially for the "class" audience. By virtue of their high standards and low numbers, they will probably never find enough qualified programs to sustain the time they spend with television.

The resulting ambivalence may be historically unique to TV. The better-educated are not so ambivalent about mass magazines or popular music or run-of-the-mill movies. They care less because they themselves consume less. The dilemma appears when, for perhaps the first time in history, a truly mass medium is also, and often, attended by the elite.

Chapter 4

VIEWING AND THE FAMILY

"I used to spend most of my time at the movies and generally had to go alone. Now I find my husband and I love to stay home and watch TV. We enjoy TV together. I think it is the best thing the American people get to enjoy together."

"TV has ruined American home life. People no longer sit around and visit. Everywhere you go you have to outtalk TV. TV people have entered your home and life more than people who should be friends and companions."

Television at Home: The Natural Setting

For most people most of the time, watching television is not a solitary affair. In the prime evening hours, when television attains its maximum audience, we find an average of about two viewers per set. Nor does that figure vary much by type of program. Here, for example, are figures for the "top ten" programs (the week of May 15, 1961), according to a national rating service:[1]

| | Viewers per set | | | | | | |
	1	2	3	4	5		Average
"Emmy" Awards	37%	46%	13%	2%	2%	100%	1.85
Gunsmoke	30	48	12	5	3	100	1.99
Wagon Train	35	37	13	7	5	100	2.01
Andy Griffith	29	39	17	9	5	100	2.17
Candid Camera	24	49	16	8	3	100	2.14
Ed Sullivan	21	46	18	9	4	100	2.25
Have Gun, Will Travel	31	45	12	7	3	100	1.99
The Untouchables	31	50	12	4	2	100	1.91
Checkmate	32	44	14	6	3	100	2.01
Perry Mason	30	50	11	5	2	100	1.96

These figures most often represent members of a family, relaxing together in what, as we have seen, many consider "the most enjoyable part of the day."

Here is an indication of audience composition. There are some differences, but most programs seem to draw a family audience, at least in the over-all distribution:

| | VIEWERS PER 100 SETS | | | |
	Men 18 and over	Women 18 and over	Teen-agers 13 to 17	Children under 13
"Emmy" Awards	58	101	17	9
Gunsmoke	75	86	17	21
Wagon Train	62	84	18	37
Andy Griffith	64	94	23	36
Candid Camera	78	96	20	20
Ed Sullivan	82	95	15	33
Have Gun, Will Travel	75	76	20	28
The Untouchables	73	81	21	16
Checkmate	70	92	16	23
Perry Mason	67	98	10	21

In this section, then, we place the viewer in his most usual setting

[1] *The United States Television Audience,* May 1961, American Research Bureau, Inc. Based on a reporting sample of 1600 homes. The following table also comes from this source.

and consider its consequences: what reactions stem specifically from the use and role of television in the home? First and foremost, there is the matter of the children, and what television does to and for them and their parents. Then we take up the more general question of how viewing affects home life, and particularly how people evaluate family viewing as a form of "togetherness."

The Children

Far-reaching and profound effects on the nation's children and youth have been hypothesized and deplored in the public forum, especially on the matter of TV violence. An article in a leading women's magazine exemplifies the anxieties:

> Television is an instrument of intense pressure that convinces the immature mind that violence is an accepted way of life. It is a subtle form of American brainwashing.[2]

> It would seem that these violent shows lead children to expect, and in some cases to crave, a kind of violence that they will not encounter in real life unless they stir it up. . . . If young people watch dancing, it makes them want to dance. If they see peanut butter, or soft drinks or breakfast foods, they want to buy them. It cannot sensibly be argued that children who see violence on the screen do not acquire a liking for it, on some level of consciousness.[3]

The communications researchers are somewhat less alarmed:

> The final picture of the influence of television on children's leisure, interests, knowledge, outlook, and values proves to be far less colorful and dramatic than popular opinion is inclined to suppose. Effects occur in each one of the various fields, but not to such a degree that the children would have been fundamentally changed.[4]

But they are still concerned:

[2] Judge Frank J. Kroenberg, as quoted by Fredric Wertham in "How Movie and TV Violence Affects Children," *Ladies' Home Journal*, Vol. 77 (February 1960), pp. 58-9.

[3] Fredric Wertham: ibid.

[4] Himmelweit, Oppenheim, Vince: *Television and the Child* (London: The Nuffield Foundation; Oxford University Press; 1961), p. 40.

All in all, the values of television can make an impact if they are consistently presented in dramatic form, and if they touch on ideas or values for which the child is emotionally ready. Extrapolating from these findings, one would expect that in the crime and detective series the constant display of aggression by both the criminal and the upholder of the law would also make an impact on these children sensitized to such cues.[5]

The present study provides no direct evidence on the effects of television on children. Our information refers entirely to *parents'* beliefs, attitudes, and behavior with respect to the television set vis-à-vis the child.

We introduced the issue generally, with a question that divides the sample roughly into "pro" and "con" on the issue:

QUESTION 35A *"There has been a lot of discussion about the possible effects of television on children. Taking everything into consideration, would you say that children are better off with television or better off without television?"*

BETTER OFF WITH

BETTER OFF WITHOUT

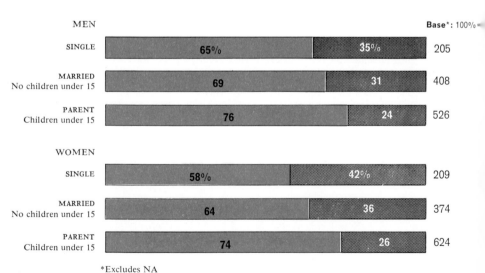

		Base*: 100% =
MEN		
SINGLE	65% / 35%	205
MARRIED No children under 15	69 / 31	408
PARENT Children under 15	76 / 24	526
WOMEN		
SINGLE	58% / 42%	209
MARRIED No children under 15	64 / 36	374
PARENT Children under 15	74 / 26	624

*Excludes NA

5 Ibid.

QUESTION 35D ASKED OF "PROS" ONLY *"Can you think of any actual example where some child you know or have heard about has benefited from television?"*

GIVE EXAMPLE

DO NOT

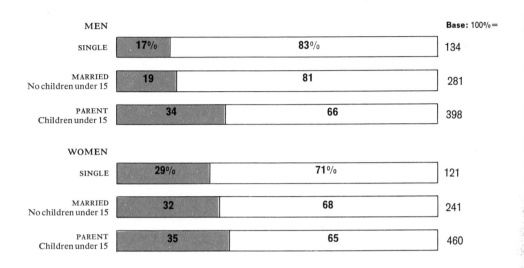

MEN

Base: 100%=

SINGLE	17%	83%	134
MARRIED No children under 15	19	81	281
PARENT Children under 15	34	66	398

WOMEN

SINGLE	29%	71%	121
MARRIED No children under 15	32	68	241
PARENT Children under 15	35	65	460

QUESTION 35G ASKED OF "CONS" ONLY *"Can you think of an actual example where some child you know or have heard of has been harmed or has done something harmful as a result of television?"*

GIVE EXAMPLE

DO NOT

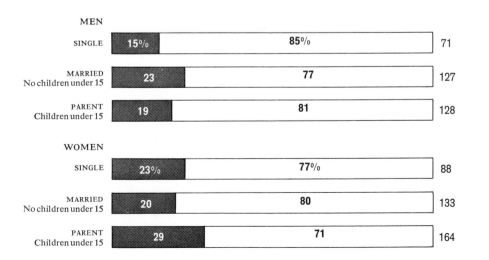

MEN

SINGLE	15%	85%	71
MARRIED No children under 15	23	77	127
PARENT Children under 15	19	81	128

WOMEN

SINGLE	23%	77%	88
MARRIED No children under 15	20	80	133
PARENT Children under 15	29	71	164

Over-all the vote is affirmative. What is more, the closer people are to having young children in the home, the more apt they are to conclude that TV's virtues outweigh its vices. Similarly, personal knowledge of benefits increases faster with parenthood than does experience with harmful effects.

We also asked everyone, regardless of their over-all vote, about the advantages *and* disadvantages of the medium "for children." Here are the perceived advantages, as categorized from free responses:

a) *Education:* The overriding advantage is mentioned by three-quarters of the parents who favor television and by half of those who don't: "Children learn by viewing." Furthermore, the educational contribution is primarily related to the serious, intellectual development of the child, not to mechanical or social skills.

> "Children have a much greater opportunity to learn than we ever had. Children today have a chance to see and learn long before they could read."

> "A more rapid acquisition of vocabulary and perhaps more stimulation of curiosity—of course, this requires selectivity. They will hear a word or phrase or see an animal and then ask about it or go to the dictionary to look it up."

> "I taught school and being around them, I could tell the ones who watched. They could add different things in class discussions just from what they had heard on TV."

Sometimes, the benefits—and responses—are more far-reaching:

> "They learn on a rabies program that bats can carry rabies. So many valuable things are given on a program, they are worthwhile for a lifetime."

The frequency with which parents cite educational benefits contrasts with the general absence of such praise in the popular press. They are not simply parroting public clichés; the attitude apparently has objective and/or subjective meaning for them.

b) *Baby-sitting:* The next advantage in order of frequency for all parents, pro or con, is the supervisory, or "baby-sitting," capacity of the

QUESTION 35B *"What do you think are some of the main advantages (of television for children)?"*

Respondents:	ALL	"PROS"			"CONS"		
		Fathers, Children under 15	Mothers, Children under 15	All Others	Fathers, Children under 15	Mothers, Children under 15	All Others
Base*: 100% = 2350		398	460	781	128	164	419
MENTION							
a) EDUCATION	65%	77%	72%	72%	45%	54%	45%
How to — social	2	2	2	2	0	2	3
How to — physical	2	2	2	3	2	2	2
Intellectual	62	74	67	70	43	50	40
Moral	2	3	3	1	2	1	1
b) BABY-SITTING	28	34	35	31	21	21	13
Keeps them occupied, quiet	9	8	13	9	5	5	5
Keeps them out of trouble	15	21	16	20	9	7	5
Kills time, something to do	7	9	12	6	9	7	4
"Company" for sick, only child	1	1	2	1	2	4	1
ENTERTAINMENT	19	19	23	23	9	20	8
Relaxing	2	2	3	3	0	4	1
Good entertainment (end in itself)	15	16	18	19	8	15	7
Good alternative to movies, etc.	7	2	3	1	2	2	0
PROGRAMS, GOOD-GENERAL	8	3	5	6	19	15	16
Children's programs	6	2	4	4	11	10	9
Other (non children)	3	0	1	2	8	5	8
STIMULATES SOCIALIZING	1	2	2	1	1	0	0
"ADULT SUPERVISION Necessary"	6	5	4	10	2	2	4
OTHER, GENERAL	2	0	1	1	8	2	6
NO ADVANTAGES (not NA)	4	1	1	1	10	6	14
DK, NA	1	0	1	1	4	5	7

*Excludes NA

Multiple responses: The detailed percentages within major categories do not necessarily add to the category totals, which show % of respondents mentioning any (one or more) of the subordinate categories

television set. There are two aspects to this. Some parents emphasize the relief that comes from having children quietly preoccupied:

> "Well, it keeps them quiet. They're not apt to go running all over the place."

> "It takes some of the burden off me teaching them games."

> "The average mother could go crazy without it."

Others stress the mischief or trouble children would get into if they were not watching:

> "It keeps them in so they're not out running around all the time."

> "It has given them a desire to stay at home and not be out where I don't know where they are at, getting into trouble."

Fathers are a little more impressed with the second of these appeals, while mothers are almost as apt to mention the first. This may reflect the differential parental responsibilities that have been alleviated. And "keeping them off the streets" is more relevant for parents of older children, while "keeping them quiet" is more likely to apply to youngsters.

What is generally striking is that over a third of the pro-television parents, and even a fifth of those who oppose it, admit to delegating some aspect of child supervision to a medium under constant authoritative attack—one whose content they themselves consider partially harmful (as we will see). And this appears, note, in response to a question regarding the advantages of television for *children,* not for parents.

Because the question was open-ended and did not itself suggest a reply; because it asked for benefits for the child, not the parent; and because baby-sitting is not a use of the medium that most parents are likely to be especially proud of—for these reasons, we take the responses as a conservative underestimate. Using TV to keep children quiet, out of trouble, and "out of my hair" is probably even more widespread than here indicated.

Nor is it confined to the less-educated group. Here, for example, are the figures for the pro-TV parents:

EDUCATION OF RESPONDENT

	Grade School		High School		College and Beyond	
	Fathers	Mothers	Fathers	Mothers	Fathers	Mothers
Mention "Baby-Sitting"	**44%**	**53%**	**38%**	**36%**	**19%**	**21%**
keeps them occupied, quiet	9	12	7	15	7	7
keeps them out of trouble	34	32	23	16	7	4
kills time, something to do	7	15	11	12	6	8
"company" for sick, only child	0	2	1	2	2	4
Don't Mention "Baby-Sitting"	**56%**	**47%**	**62%**	**64%**	**81%**	**79%**
Base: 100% =	87	66	203	298	94	83

NOTE: Subordinate entries do not necessarily add to total because of multiple responses.

Allusions to "keeping children out of trouble" drop sharply with education, but the other aspects of "baby-sitting" show smaller declines. In all, a fifth of the college-educated parents who favor television acknowledge that they use TV to occupy their children.

No other specific benefits are widely noted. There is some mention that television is entertaining, and some general praise of children's programs, although the latter comes mainly from anti-TV respondents (perhaps as an easy reply when pressed for advantages: "Some of the programs, I admit, are all right"). Note, too, that non-parents are most likely to point to the need for adult supervision!

The educational baby-sitter Could the widespread recognition of educational benefits stem, at least in part, from parents' relegation of the young to the television set in the service of their own freedom? There would naturally be less reluctance about the peaceful, quiet hours that youngsters spend in front of the set if the children are "getting something out of it." The two thoughts are frequently and revealingly linked:

> "All have some facts they can learn. It gives them something to do in the house. They can't just sit around and read a book all the time. Some people claim that all this killing gives the kids complexes but I can't see it has hurt my kids."

> "My oldest girl is pre-school age. She learns a lot on the programs in the morning. . . . Also, the children are out of your hair."

"Keeps them occupied. You take a show like *Lassie,* and they can learn a lot of things about manners. It is educational for children in a lot of respects."

"It keeps them quiet and it teaches them."

And some parents seem to reach even further:

"I don't mind what they look at, because even in those westerns with all of its shooting and killing, they show people how to protect themselves. You notice how a man will push a door open carefully before he goes in if he thinks someone may be behind it?"

Furthermore, the higher-educated are *more* likely to cite the educational benefits for children—just as they themselves more often "feel informed" when watching.

QUESTION 35B Mention of Educational Benefits,
by Parent's Education

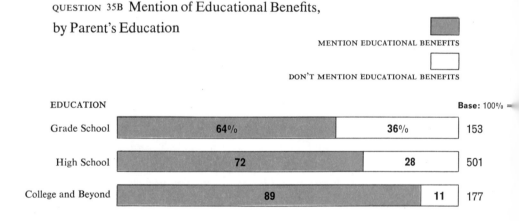

MENTION EDUCATIONAL BENEFITS

DON'T MENTION EDUCATIONAL BENEFITS

EDUCATION			Base: 100% =
Grade School	64%	36%	153
High School	72	28	501
College and Beyond	89	11	177

And this increase in the rate of acknowledged educational benefits comes entirely from those who refer to the baby-sitting advantages of television!

QUESTION 35B Per cent Who Mention Educational Benefits . . .

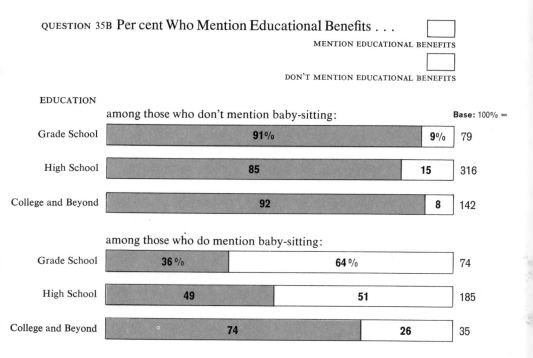

MENTION EDUCATIONAL BENEFITS

DON'T MENTION EDUCATIONAL BENEFITS

EDUCATION

among those who don't mention baby-sitting: **Base:** 100% =

Grade School   91%   9%   79

High School   85   15   316

College and Beyond   92   8   142

among those who do mention baby-sitting:

Grade School   36%   64%   74

High School   49   51   185

College and Beyond   74   26   35

In other words, among those who don't refer to baby-sitting, about 90 per cent at each educational level allude to the educational benefits of TV. But in the grade-school sample, 64 per cent are willing to cite baby-sitting without also noting educational advantages for the child; in the high-school sample, the figure shrinks to 51 per cent; and among the college-educated, only 26 per cent cite parental relief without (compensating?) intellectual gain to the child.[6]

The suggestion of some defensiveness among the well-educated TV-dependent parents is strong. Another investigator similarly concludes:

Many parents are greatly in favor of television, even to the point of being defensive about it. To some extent TV helps them to keep an eye on the children. Also, if they themselves

[6] The over-all figure for educational benefits is higher among those who don't mention baby-sitting, because many people give only one answer to the question. This produces a general negative association between any two categories of response.

enjoy television and view a lot, they have a vested interest in defending it. Perhaps for these reasons many parents do not admit to control the amount and content of children's viewing.[7]

When it comes to their children's viewing, as with their own, programming that can be considered worthwhile takes some of the stigma off an otherwise partly "unacceptable" use of the set. But in neither case is viewing confined to the programs so regarded. The number of hours people like to relax with TV, and would like their children to be preoccupied with it, almost certainly exceeds the number of programs that would survive any moderately selective test.

This situation, then, may underlie some of the demands for a higher "base" level of programming in general—more, even, than for specific outstanding shows—because viewing wants to be general. The cancer scare did not cut smoking much; it created the demand for a safer cigarette. Similarly, perhaps, we cannot or will not give up our own chain viewing or our children's; it is up to the industry to provide a filter:

"I like what I see to be clean. I don't like to have to supervise what my grandchild sees. Who am I to censor? They just shouldn't have such things on."

That brings us to the disadvantages: Parents recognize a number of ingredients that need filtering before television can, in good conscience, be cleared for general consumption by children.

a) *Bad Influence.* First and foremost, "children see things they shouldn't see." The parents who favor television acknowledge this in almost the same numbers as their more critical counterparts.

The chief irritant, clearly, is violence. And concern seems to center on the fear of imitation, rather than on moral or psychological considerations:

"You read in the paper where the kids are shooting each other or hanging by the neck, that they've seen on TV."

"I read in the paper when a boy shot another boy. They were

[7] Himmelweit *et al.:* op. cit.

QUESTION 35E *"What do you think are some of the main disadvantages (of television for children)?"*

		"PROS"			"CONS"		
Respondents:	ALL	Fathers, Children under 15	Mothers, Children under 15	All Others	Fathers, Children under 15	Mothers, Children under 15	All Others
Base*: 100% = 2350		398	460	781	128	164	419
MENTION							
a) SEE THINGS THEY SHOULDN'T – BAD INFLUENCE	**51**%	**44**%	**47**%	**48**%	**51**%	**59**%	**64**%
violence, horror	30	23	28	28	27	35	40
crime, gangsters	10	10	5	11	6	10	13
makes them anxious, nightmares	5	3	6	4	3	7	6
total violence—any of above	40	33	37	39	33	46	52
sex, suggestiveness, vulgarity	5	5	4	4	5	9	6
smoking, drinking	2	2	2	2	2	2	3
adult themes—divorce, dope, etc.	2	2	2	1	5	2	3
harmful or sinful products advertised	1	1	1	1	1	1	0
other, general	7	7	7	6	13	10	9
children will pick up above	10	7	9	9	12	15	16
teaches wrong values, morals	2	3	3	2	6	5	5
b) KEEPS THEM FROM DOING OTHER THINGS THEY SHOULD DO	**36**	**37**	**31**	**31**	**54**	**48**	**41**
homework	17	15	12	14	23	27	23
chores, bed, meals	11	15	10	11	13	9	8
active play, socializing	7	5	6	6	9	16	8
children become passive (general)	4	3	3	1	14	9	7
waste of time	6	7	6	5	13	5	6
other, general	2	3	2	2	3	4	3
OTHER PROGRAM CONTENT	**4**	**4**	**3**	**2**	**11**	**7**	**6**
unrealistic, "life isn't that way"	2	2	2	1	5	2	4
not educational enough	1	1	0	1	6	2	2
bad English	1	2	2	0	1	2	0
PROGRAMS BAD, GENERAL	**10**	**9**	**10**	**8**	**13**	**12**	**13**
children's programs	1	1	0	0	1	1	1
other (non-children)	9	9	10	8	13	11	12
PHYSICAL HARM, eye strain, posture, etc.	**5**	**4**	**3**	**4**	**5**	**8**	**8**
ADVERTISING TOO EFFECTIVE, kids drive me nuts asking for products	**1**	**1**	**2**	**1**	**2**	**3**	**0**
OTHER OR GENERAL	**2**	**1**	**3**	**1**	**2**	**3**	**3**
NO DISADVANTAGES (not NA)	**9**	**11**	**12**	**14**	**1**	**0**	**0**
DK, NA	**2**	**4**	**3**	**2**	**1**	**1**	**0**

*Excludes NA

Multiple responses: The detailed percentages within major categories do not necessarily add to the category totals, which show % of respondents mentioning any (one or more) of the subordinate categories

looking at TV and he got a gun and shot this other boy trying to imitate the TV show."

"When they see these murders the first thing they think about is to try to do what they see. If they only heard it on radio it would have a different effect. I think that's how a lot of juvenile delinquency starts."

"I don't like western shows and the like. They are learning the young generations to go astray. They do shooting and people get up after that, just like caricatures. Children are apt to get a gun and shoot their parents."

"Children learn how to kill and murder looking at TV."

"I don't believe these wild shoot-em-up westerns are too good for children. Too many youngsters play with toy guns and after a while get hold of a real one. Lots of kids get in trouble."

Much of this is undoubtedly playback of the TV violence issue in the press. But many specific and concrete remarks seem to reflect personal experience rather than the general platitude.

"Mighty Mouse is the one I'm least happy about, because they try to fly and the children try to imitate. They get rope and hang my poor daughter [to make her fly]."

Violence vis-à-vis children is also a principal negative cited without prompting by those who respond most critically to "television in general" in our introductory probes.

There is little question, then, that this is a widespread, real concern; and there is little question that it is realistically founded in program content. There may be no scientific evidence that TV violence has harmful effects, but there cannot be much of an issue regarding its presence in programs designed for children as well as in adult crime stories:

"The Three Stooges hit themselves with glass. They may imitate the crazy things the Stooges do."

This emphasis on fear of imitation probably stems largely from the fact that television is available to very young children. Parental reaction to the Three Stooges may be an example. When the Three Stooges appear in the theater, the audience is pretty well restricted to children old enough to "know better." If they are big enough to go to the Saturday matinee, they are probably big enough to know that you don't test a straight razor on your tongue, or run a saw across your brother's head, or gouge his eyes, for laughs. But does the three-year-old distinguish fact from fantasy clearly enough? The pre-school child, like modern society itself, may be in an especially vulnerable period in which physical and technological capabilities exceed discretionary controls. So violence of this type—using implements available to children in ways they can copy—may be especially dangerous.[8]

Interestingly, mothers who "oppose" TV for children mention violence more frequently than those who are "favorable," whereas the two groups of fathers refer to it with equal frequency. This suggests that violence is a more important issue with mothers; perhaps they have more opportunity to see it being imitated.

While this is by far the most frequent element associated with fear of imitation, it is not the only one. A special problem is presented by the fantastic physical abilities portrayed not only in cartoons and adventures:

> "Back East some kid put a blanket over his shoulders and jumped out of a window."

> "They shouldn't watch shows like *Superman*. It makes them want to go jump off the roof to see if they can fly."

but also in some of our most acclaimed whimsical programming:

> "My girl friend's brother saw *Peter Pan,* went out on the roof, jumped out as he saw on TV; got caught and was almost dead from strangulation. He had a dog chain around his neck. A neighborhood child saw him, ran in and told the family."

Vulgarity is also mentioned:

> "Remarks such as 'You're a dirty, double-crossing rat.' Can you believe my younger one called me that the other day? This is a sample of the language they hear on TV."

[8] As opposed to fantasied violence in cartoons (mouse steamrolls cat) or even to "realistic" adult violence, as in gangster shows, which requires tommy guns or bombs to implement.

And sex—"scantily clad girls in the dance show," "sinful things like hugging and kissing"—comes in for its expected, though in this case, small share of outrage.

But none of these latter qualifies as a genuine concern for any substantial proportion of the viewing population, certainly not as compared with violence.

With respect to generalized criticisms, note that those who simply say "Programs are bad for children" are almost always referring to adult shows. This anticipates a general dilemma discussed later: adult programming, even when good, may expose children to "things they shouldn't see."

b) *Passivity and distraction.* Violence and its "bad influence" is the major objection in terms of what is actually on the air. But an equally frequent class of objection—actually more frequent among fathers who oppose television—has little to do with the content itself. As one articulate respondent puts it:

> "I think the main disadvantage of television for children is not so much what it inspires them to do, but what they miss by sitting down and watching television. It takes time away from reading and outdoor activities, which is why we limit it. It is a form of entertainment in which they do not participate."

Some parents worry about the alternative, more "worthwhile" activities that viewing replaces, much as they worry about their own "waste of time" before the TV set and perhaps even a little more explicitly.[9]

> "We are going to grow a group of wide-bottom, one-eyed morons. They aren't going to read enough. They can't participate. They just sit and watch."

> "They become too habit-forming and you have to boot them out of the house on a sunny day."

> "Don't spend enough time playing outside with other children."

[9] Possibly children caricature some of their own tendencies; or perhaps some of the parents' unresolved feelings about their own viewing may be spilling over onto the children.

Nor does this concern with fresh air and sunshine stem entirely from pristine regard for the child's physical or social development:

> "I'd like to have them take *Sky King* off so we can get them out of the house. All of those Saturday-morning serials. I just feel they should get out of the house. We get sick of them around all the time."

So program quality is important, but clearly not the whole story. Better programs are less likely to have a "bad influence," but they may actually aggravate the conflict with other pursuits:

> "Some of the best programs come on when my girl should be practicing music."

This comment illustrates the most frequent form of parental objection to the seductiveness of the set. It isn't just that TV replaces such abstract alternatives as "active socialization"—it makes it a lot harder to get children to do the simple, concrete things they are supposed to do:

> "They don't want to eat. They don't want to help with the housework or do their homework. They're just stuck to the set."

This complaint is heard in large numbers from both parents; and, except for specific mentions of homework, with roughly equal frequency among pros and cons. Parents who oppose TV, and especially the mothers, refer to its interference with school assignments much more frequently than those who approve. Indeed, that may be a major consideration behind their over-all verdict.

So all in all, so far as adult judgments are concerned, television helps to educate the child, but watching it interferes with his education. It helps keep him busy and out of mischief, but it also keeps him too busy to do his chores. It keeps the kids in when you want them in— which is good, except for some of the bad things they see. And it keeps them in when you want them out—which is bad even if they see good things. Ideally, then, TV should provide interesting, educational programs that intrigue children when parents don't want to be bothered with them—but not when they ought to be outside or doing something else.

As in the case of adult viewing, then, there are undeniable strings attached to undeniable benefits. The resulting ambivalence is partially, but only partially, resolved by good programming.

Violence, especially of a type that children can easily imitate, certainly could be removed, and with it, a chief source of parental anxiety. And children's programs could be improved; maybe not the best of them, but certainly the average. But the most educational, least violent television imaginable will not induce children to do their homework or go outside to play (except, possibly, if it loses their interest). Viewing, *per se,* remains at issue. And parents, not programs, must cope with that.

The rules. How do they do so? The first point of interest is simply the extent to which parents report supervising or regulating their children's viewing at all. Our question was asked only of parents with children under fifteen years of age at home.

Q. 36F *"Even though they're not always enforced 100%, are there any rules or regulations in your home about when and what the children watch, or do you let them make their own decisions?"*

	Mothers	Fathers	All
We have definite rules	44%	38%	41%
We try, we make an effort	6	6	6
Kids decide with minor exceptions	4	4	4
We have no rules; kids decide	27	33	30
Don't need rules—kids too young	7	8	7
No answer, all other—rules not mentioned in response, etc.	12	11	12
Base: 100% =	632	538	1170

We tried to balance the wording of the question, but there is probably still some bias toward "rules" as the more socially acceptable response: parents who have rules will not fail to report them here but some who exercise little or no control might tend to overestimate their regulation. If anything, then, these results probably overstate the degree of parental control. Yet less than half report definite regulations and a third state the total or virtual absence of controls.

Furthermore, those who think children are "better off without television" are only slightly more likely to claim some regulation: 44 per cent of them have definite rules as against only 41 per cent of those who think children are "better off with TV."

The specific rules that are mentioned, by those who do legislate, show the degree of parental concern with the circumstances of viewing:

Q. 36F   The Rules Mentioned

Viewing Circumstances	Mothers 31%		Fathers 29% *	
Hours	24%		22%	
no later than (usually bedtime)		18		15
only certain times or days		5		6
no more than . . .		2		1
Duties	14		12	
homework first, or reward for		9		6
meals, naps, chores first, or				
reward for		3		5
withheld for punishment		2		3
play outside when nice		1		1
Programs	**28**		**20**	
Specific—prohibit or discourage	11		8	
violence, scary things		6		4
sex, adult themes		1		1
specific shows		3		3
Other		1		1
General "Supervision"	18		12	
"their shows only"		4		3
"we supervise what they see"		14		9
Other	1		1	
Base: 100% =	632		538	

* These are multiple responses. Hence, detailed percentages within major categories do not necessarily add to the total, which shows percentages of respondents mentioning any (one or more) of the subordinate categories.

Most of the specific taboos deal with when and how much children may watch. Regulations on content are less frequently mentioned, especially by fathers.

One form of program control is conspicuously small. In the same sample that has just designated "violence" the number-one irritant, only about 5 per cent specifically mention some attempt at regulation in this regard. And again, the figure is not significantly higher among those parents who actually cited the violence as a disadvantage (about 7 per cent of them, to 5 per cent of those who did not). Parents who "generally supervise what they see" may of course employ anti-violence criteria, but even then that regulation would be far less frequent than expressed concern about the harmful effects of violence.

On the whole, there is little, if any, relationship between the disadvantages the parents cite and the controls they mention. For example, those who worry about TV's interference with chores or other activities are only a shade more likely to mention appropriate limitations on the circumstances under which children can watch (14 per cent to 12 per cent).

Perhaps parents do not really mean the disadvantages they talk about; maybe the concrete restraints they impose are a better indication of their anxieties about the medium than their abstract citation of disadvantages. Or, the rules may be largely a matter of what can realistically be enforced, rather than an accurate reflection of the parents' deep concerns. Or, finally, regulations may speak more to the disadvantages of TV for parents than for children.[1]

But whatever the reason, there seems to be a general discrepancy between what parents say worries them most and what they say they do about it. The general impression left by these questions is that few parents even claim stringent controls over content; the rule in a good many homes, including those that "oppose" TV for children, is *laissez-faire*. And in the rest, regulation centers mainly on the circumstances of viewing. A noted communication researcher recently suggested to parents:

> I suggest that you do not think in terms of what television does
> to children, but rather, what do children do with television.[2]

Some may be taking his advice in the sense that they are concerned with the passivity of children, but many seem to be thinking rather, or at least also, in terms of what television does for them as parents.

---

[1] The most frequently mentioned rule, bedtime, is a case in point. Television may aggravate enforcement, but bedtime rules themselves clearly do not originate with television.

[2] Wilbur Schramm: *Children and Television—Some Advice to Parents.* Reprint of a talk delivered at the Biennial National Convention of the American Association of University Women, Kansas City, Mo., June 24, 1959.

Television and Togetherness

Adults watch television and children watch television, and frequently they watch television together. We saw that TV has become an integral part of nightly family relaxation in many homes and as such it has an important role in the social life of the family. The attraction of the set not only keeps people home together but it gives them something to do in common.

The degree of dependence on TV sealing wax in some homes is difficult to overstate:

Q. 37E "What did you do (the last time the set broke down) during the time you would ordinarily have spent watching TV?"

"The family walked around like a chicken without a head. It's like a lost friend."

"We didn't know what to do. There was so much missing, we just went to bed."

"It was terrible. We did nothing—my husband and I talked.

"Screamed constantly. Children bothered me and my nerves were on edge. Tried to interest them in games, but impossible. TV is part of them."

"I couldn't stay at home. We went over to my mother-in-law's at night. She has a TV. Even with my family there, I'm lonesome without TV."

Desperation is also reflected in the urgency with which most families cope with the emergency; as documented in the following chart.

The fact that the better-educated are slightly *slower* in repairing their sets indicates that finances are probably not the crucial factor. The fact that they are *only* slightly slower again attests to the almost equally routine usage among these groups.

"Altogether, about how long were you without a television set?"

Grade School/ **Base:** 100% = 388

High School/ **Base:** 100% = 812

College and Beyond/ **Base:** 100% = 337

FIXED OR
REPLACED
WITHIN:

HALF A DAY

28%	
28%	
22%	

ONE DAY

46	
50	
43	

THREE DAYS

66	
69	
66	

ONE WEEK

84	
85	
80	

THREE WEEKS

92	
94	
89	

But TV togetherness is not without its cost to the family. Viewers recognize at least two attending disadvantages.

1. *"Quiet! I can't hear."*   First, there is the specific family form of the general viewing ambivalence: television replaces other worthwhile activities. When family or friends are preoccupied with television, they are less occupied with other things or with each other. Some people are especially concerned with the curtailment of direct, personal communication:

> "TV has ruined American home life. People no longer sit around and visit. Everywhere you go you have to outtalk TV. TV people have entered your home and life more than people who should be friends and companions."

> "I think they should drop an atom bomb and wipe it all out. I would say that TV has smashed home life. It has not brought us closer together, it has separated us."

In fact, the seductiveness of the set to the exclusion of other family activities is among the dangers cited spontaneously by the strongest critics of the medium, while the positive counterpart, togetherness *through* viewing, is noted by the enthusiasts. Recall, for example, these data from an earlier table (page 42):

Q. 8   "How do you feel about television in general?"

OVER-ALL RESPONSE

MENTION:	Extremely positive	Positive	50/50	Negative	Extremely negative
Makes for togetherness, home life	15%	8%	1%	1%	0%
Interferes with home life, visiting	1	2	4	4	7
Good for children (or helps parents)	13	11	6	3	0
Bad for children (or makes it tough for parents)	1	6	19	23	21

Within certain limits, the better the program, the greater this particular cost. People can discuss the day's events and still keep up with a canned comedy, but it is difficult to follow meaningful programming and still make meaningful (unrelated) conversation. So TV families accommodate to a reduced level of communication, which is sometimes dramatically brought home to them by breakdown of the set:

"We got acquainted with each other all over again."

"We had a marvelous time. We read, had discussions, nobody missed TV at all."

The reduction in "normal" family interaction of all types, attending the introduction of TV, has also been noted and satirized extensively in the popular culture, as, for example, in numerous magazine cartoons.

The "opportunity cost" of an evening with TV—what it costs in *not* doing something else—obviously varies with the physical, social, and cultural alternatives that are realistically available to the family. As a rough indication:

Q. 37   *"What did you do during the time you would ordinarily have spent watching TV?"*

	0–6 yrs. G. S.	7–8 yrs. G. S.	1–3 yrs. H. S.	4 yrs. H. S.	1–2 yrs. Coll.	3–4 yrs. Coll.	Beyond College
Read	17%	19%	21%	30%	30%	38%	49%
Radio	26	16	18	13	9	13	16
Movies	1	1	2	1	1	2	1
Went out	9	3	5	4	3	2	1
Talked, visited	2	3	2	3	7	2	3
Chores, work	14	11	14	12	13	13	13
Sewed	3	4	3	3	2	3	3
Played cards, games	1	4	4	4	2	5	1
Hi-fi, records	2	2	1	5	4	4	3
Hobbies	1	1	2	1	1	2	1
Used other set	4	5	7	8	9	10	11
Fixed set	2	5	3	3	5	3	1
Missed it	9	5	4	3	1	1	4
Did not miss it	0	3	4	3	5	2	4

	0–6 yrs. G. S.	7–8 yrs. G. S.	1–3 yrs. H. S.	4 yrs. H. S.	1–2 yrs. Coll.	3–4 yrs. Coll.	Beyond College
Rested, slept	7	8	6	5	4	2	3
Nothing	5	4	4	2	5	2	3
Other	2	11	6	8	11	11	10
DK, NA	21	19	19	19	15	10	6
Base: 100% =	117	291	374	474	149	128	70

The better-educated say they read, and the others read or listen to the radio. (The slight rise in radio among the top groups may be due to FM.)

But the question has relatively little meaning, because so few families stay without a set long enough to establish alternative patterns. Many families may recognize alternatives other than fixing the set or doing nothing; and many are aware that TV exacts a price in other family pursuits:

> "[When the set broke] we went back to living normally. I'd have liked to have left it broken."

But, however grudgingly, the price is usually paid. Regardless of what they'd "like" to have done, most viewers get the set fixed, and quickly. And by their own reports, the better-educated families spend almost as many evenings with television as the more culturally deprived.

In sum, most families report that they spend many relaxing evenings watching television together, and many attribute this togetherness largely to the ability of the TV set to keep family members at home around a common center of attention. But once people are in the same room, TV noticeably restricts communication among them. When they are watching television, they are not talking much or playing bridge or chess. But they also are not at the movies, "on the streets," in a bar, or reading comic books. Does television, on balance, create more home life than it destroys? The answer involves identifying, quantifying, and evaluating the actual alternatives—an issue even harder to conceptualize than to settle.

2. Program incompatibility. Family viewing also raises problems involved in exposing children to some of the programs enjoyed by their parents. The following two questions suggest the dilemma:

Q. 36D *"Which of the programs*
your child watches do
you think are the best
programs for him?"

Q. 36E *"Which programs that he*
watches aren't you so
happy about?"

	Parents*
Children's variety, dramatic, adventure	39%
Cartoons	32
kiddie, or general	27
"sophisticated"	7
Family situation	29
more serious, "lesson"	27
strictly comedy or general	8
School, kindergarten	15
Misc. adult shows, entertainment	15
Misc, adult shows, information	11
Westerns	10
Sports	4
Teen-age dancing	4
Other	6
None	5
All of them	1
DK, NA	8

Base: 100% = 1170

	Parents
Westerns	20%
Violence, "horror," general	19
Violent children's shows	9
Violent adult shows	9
Children's shows, other	10
Adult shows with "Adult themes" (sex, divorce, etc.)	5
Other	6
None (includes "don't let them watch bad shows")	24
All of them	1
DK, NA	16

1170

Most frequently mentioned:

Captain Kangaroo	217
Lassie	178
Walt Disney	144
Romper Room	115
Father Knows Best	115
Huckleberry Hound	78
Popeye	71
Dennis the Menace	65

(Others in Appendix Table 7)

Most frequently mentioned:

Three Stooges	103
Untouchables	37
77 Sunset Strip	20
Popeye	19
Dennis the Menace	17
Have Gun, Will Travel	13
Maverick	11
Twilight Zone	11

* Multiple responses: the detailed percentages within major categories do not necessarily add to major totals, which show percentage of respondents mentioning any (one or more) of the subordinate categories. Incidentally, there are hardly any differences in these responses between mothers and fathers.

The approved programs are straightforward and create no particular issues: they are, by and large, shows designed specifically *for* children or *for* family appeal.

Among the former, *Captain Kangaroo* stands out, with by far the highest vote for a single program. The specific ingredients that make this both a child and a parent favorite bear analysis by those charged with the development of better children's programs.

In the family-show category, *Father Knows Best* leads, probably chiefly because of the "morals" children can draw:

> *"Father Knows Best.* It was when Kathy tore up a picture so some family couldn't go on a vacation and then admitted what she had done. My son took it all in and later talked to me about it."

And other "family situations" are mentioned in the same context:

> "One child I know had a little fit of telling lies, and programs like *Beaver* and *Lassie* have brought him out, maybe. Timmie in *Lassie* told lies once or twice and got into trouble and it made quite an impression on this child."

> "My children was watching *Lassie* when the little boy said thanks at mealtime. My children asked why we don't, and now we do."

So the programs parents approve of are children's programs they themselves don't watch, or those the whole family can enjoy.

But the debit side raises a conflict. First of all, criticism is less frequently linked to particular programs; and it does not center on children's shows. Violence as a general theme predominates on the black list; but only one program clearly *for* children is implicated. *The Three Stooges* worries two and a half times as many parents as it pleases. For the rest, the programs at fault are mostly unnamed. Responses tend to general categories—shooting, crime, detectives, westerns—and these, in large measure, reflect general "adult" TV fare, as do the specific mentions of "adult themes."

So family viewing can result in objectionable exposure for children whenever parents choose shows with violence or other "adult" ingredients and then let the children watch with them. And choose them they do, as the ratings document. Recall, for example, that *Gunsmoke* and *The Untouchables* (one, a western; the other, the epitome of TV violence) are both in the top ten, and each attracts close to 40 children (and about 160 adults) per 100 sets (see page 80).

Parents cannot realistically expect to send the children out of the room at the violent or passionate climax. In the first place, it is difficult to do:

> "The violence on TV is just awful. I remember one time I came into the room and he was watching a man beat someone's head in with a rock. I sent him out of the room, and he cried so loud I couldn't even see the end of the show."

But more generally, such restrictions preclude the very family satisfactions so often integral to viewing. Nor is the problem confined to deliberate family sessions with TV. So long as there is only one TV set, and the children are at home, conflicts of this type are potential whenever adults watch television.

As a result, the family watches together, and parents feel uneasy when the objectionable themes arise—whether in *The Untouchables* or *Medea, King Kong* or *King Lear*. The issue clearly surpasses quality level; it is inherent in the inevitable difference between what interests adults and what is suitable for children. There can be a few happy blends—as in family situation shows or sophisticated cartoons—but it is doubtful whether the bulk of programming can, or should, satisfy both sets of demands simultaneously. The conflict seems indigenous to a medium the whole family so frequently wants to enjoy together.

So, by and large, the discussion of television and home life reflects many of the themes that emerged in the previous, more general consideration of viewing. We see again that why, where, and how much people watch are issues of primary concern to them; and that the effects of viewing on the family as on the individual are double-edged.

There are benefits beyond those provided by the programs themselves: children are kept busy and out of mischief, the family stays together around a shared point of interest, and so on. And there are dangers or costs, again beyond those that inhere in the program content itself: children are diverted from other things, and the family and its friends may put aside normal social relationships to join a silent audience.

The intricate and intimate relationship between feelings about watching and attitudes toward program content reappears. When television appears to instill or reinforce family values or helps educate the child, people feel more justified in surrendering their family hours or their children than when it seems to subvert these purposes. So certain programs alleviate some of the problems associated with extensive family viewing while others add the burden of "bad influence." And parents' evaluations of the matter may sometimes be colored by a vested interest in viewing—their own or their children's.

But programming itself is no ultimate answer to such questions as: Does the child get enough fresh air or active play? Has the family other interests and activities? Do we visit with friends as we used to? And, in some instances, better and more involving programming may intensify such conflicts because it is less easily dismissed, more likely to be approved or even encouraged by parents.

In short, there are "good" and "bad" programs and there is "good" and "bad" viewing. While the two are related, the relationship is far from simple or complete. Feelings about the program certainly influence feeling about watching it, but the reverse may also be true. Programs inherit as well as originate important aspects of the public's response to televiewing.

With this in mind, we turn to the programs the viewers turn to.

PART III

Television
As Content

WE HAVE now arrived at the point where most discussions of television begin. The programming content of the medium—what it is and what it should be—dominates the current dialogue among the broadcasters, producers, and sponsors; their academic, intellectual, and professional critics; the FCC; and most other interested parties.

The various voices are strong and clear, but certainly not in harmony. One point of view is represented by FCC Chairman Newton Minow in his description of the "vast wasteland":

> . . . a procession of game shows, violence, audience participation shows, formula comedies about totally unbelievable families, blood and thunder, mayhem, violence, sadism, murder, Western bad men, and Western good men, private eyes, gangsters, more violence, and cartoons. And, endlessly, commercials —many screaming, cajoling and offending. And most of all, boredom.

And in his conclusion:

> We all know that people would more often prefer to be enter-
> tained than stimulated or informed. But your broadcaster's
> obligations are not satisfied if you look only to popularity as
> a test of what you broadcast. You are not only in show busi-
> ness; you are free to communicate ideas as well as relaxation.
> You must provide a wider range of choices, more diversity,
> more alternatives. It is not enough to cater to the nation's
> whims—you must also serve the nation's needs.[1]

Another is the point of view expressed by a spokesman for the
television industry:

> It is evident that today virtually every special group—educa-
> tional, civic, governmental—quite properly regards television
> as the greatest potential force for bringing information and
> cultural awareness to the total American public. The medium's
> capacity to perform this service is based on the attention paid
> it by some 87 per cent of all U.S. families who spend more than
> five hours a day looking at its programs.
>
> It is equally evident that our people made their $16 bil-
> lion investment in television sets primarily for entertainment.
> Diminish this universality and concentration of attention—
> created in the first place by entertainment programs—and you
> diminish the medium's capacity to inform the public at large
> and to enrich its cultural life.
>
> It seems to me that impractical demands for an over-
> weighing of special-interest programs can threaten this potential.
>
> Thoughtless yielding to such demands would inevitably
> reduce the overwhelming attention paid to the medium, and
> television would cease to represent the single widest avenue to
> the American public. If television's purpose is to serve the many
> instead of the few, entertainment must continue to be the single
> largest element of the television schedule.[2]

[1] From a speech delivered by Newton N. Minow before the National Association
of Broadcasters, May 9, 1961.

[2] "Television and the Pursuit of Excellence," a talk by Louis Hausman, Director, Television Information Office, at the annual luncheon of the American
Council for Better Broadcasts, held in conjunction with the Institute for Education

Our purpose here is simply to add another voice to the debate—the voice of the viewer. At present, he is conspicuously absent at the forum, except as the subject of necessary but competing assumptions:

Chairman Minow: I believe in the people's good sense and good taste, and I am not convinced that the people's taste is as low as some of you assume.[3]

NBC Board Chairman David Sarnoff: The great majority unquestionably wants diversion—Westerns, mysteries, and adventure yarns.[4]

Hallmark's (*Hall of Fame* sponsor) Joyce Hall: The trouble is, too many sponsors underrate the audience's intelligence and appreciation of culture when it is done well.[5]

Critic Harriet Van Horn: I'm convinced the audience for Westerns, situation comedies, and private eyes, checks its brains at the door and sits through the dreadful junk in a stupor.[6]

And so on.

In the following pages we let the viewer speak on these topics for himself, not through the indirect and generalized medium of ratings, which reflect only how many people watch what, but in terms of specific likes and dislikes, "great moments" and disappointments, wishes satisfied and wishes unfulfilled.

Chapter 5 deals entirely with what people say about the matter. We ask them questions and take them at their word. The inquiry proceeds from the general to the specific: first we hear what viewers think of programming in general; then what they think of different kinds of programs and of the respective proportions now available; and, finally, what specific shows have made an impression.

---

by Radio-Television at the Ohio State University, April 26, 1961, reprinted in *Vital Speeches,* Vol. 27 (July 1, 1961), p. 568.

[3] Op. cit.

[4] Quoted in Robert W. Sarnoff (as told to Stanley Frank): "What Do You Want from TV?" *The Saturday Evening Post,* July 1, 1961.

[5] Quoted in Stanley Frank: "He Refuses to Waste Your Time." *TV Guide,* July 22, 1961.

[6] Quoted in Stanley Frank: "TV Makes Her Tired," *The Saturday Evening Post,* June 3, 1961.

Then, in Chapter 6, we take a step toward answering the crucial question: How seriously are verbal responses on these matters to be taken? Do the viewers really mean it? As an indication, we compare survey replies with independent information about what the same people actually watch and don't watch when put to the choice.

Chapter 5

WHAT VIEWERS SAY

"Television could be greatly improved by getting more educational and having better type plays like Playhouse 90 *and* Circle Theatre. *I like good high-class mystery and adventure—not just kid stuff. I like* Perry Mason, *but wish it were on at a different time because it's just too early. I'd like to see more national and international events on TV. Incidentally, I want to watch the fights now, do you mind?"*

"The Programs" in General

We begin with several readings on general reactions to present TV fare, with no effort to isolate specific programs or even types of programs. The question is simply how viewers evaluate the sum total of what they are presently offered.

First, consider these two open-ended questions:

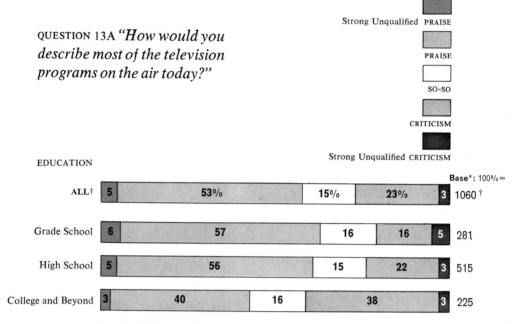

QUESTION 13A *"How would you describe most of the television programs on the air today?"*

Strong Unqualified PRAISE

PRAISE

SO-SO

CRITICISM

Strong Unqualified CRITICISM

EDUCATION

Base*: 100% =

ALL†	5	53%	15%	23%	3	1060 †
Grade School	6	57	16	16	5	281
High School	5	56	15	22	3	515
College and Beyond	3	40	16	38	3	225

*Asked of half the sample only. Excludes DK, NA, Other
† Includes 39 respondents unclassified as to education

Note: In coding these responses for general evaluation, we followed essentially the same procedure described on p. 37. Here are examples: Strong praise: great, wonderful, couldn't be better. Praise: good, entertaining, etc. *or* specific types praised. So-so: acceptable, good as they can be, *or* some praised, some criticized. Criticism: mediocre, uninteresting, *or* specific types criticized. Strong criticism: lousy, sickening, terrible

The verdict is clear, and much like the earlier response to television in general. "Most programs" are "good"; and that single word, selected by respondents themselves, captures about the amount of enthusiasm evident in the previous, more elaborate measure. For most pople, "most programs" are not great, but are clearly a cut above satisfactory.

Again, the better-educated are less satisfied when they generalize about television. The college sample is evenly divided between praise and criticism, and those among them with education beyond college become critical, on balance. (See Appendix Table 8.) But the fall-off with in-

QUESTION 13B *"What ONE word would you use to sum up most television programs?"*

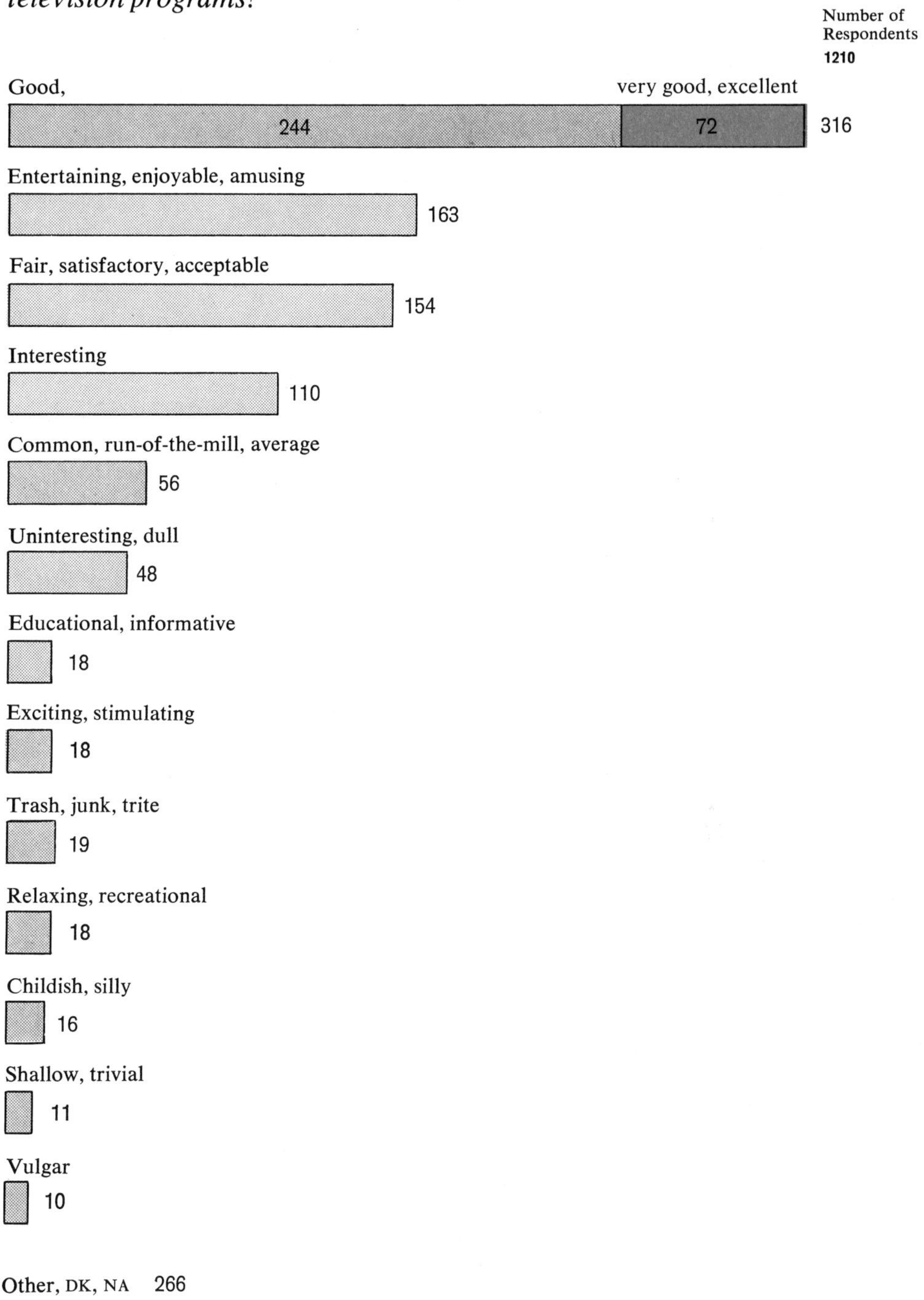

Number of Respondents
1210

Good,   very good, excellent

| 244 | 72 | 316 |

Entertaining, enjoyable, amusing

163

Fair, satisfactory, acceptable

154

Interesting

110

Common, run-of-the-mill, average

56

Uninteresting, dull

48

Educational, informative

18

Exciting, stimulating

18

Trash, junk, trite

19

Relaxing, recreational

18

Childish, silly

16

Shallow, trivial

11

Vulgar

10

Other, DK, NA   266

creasing education is not nearly so marked when we ask people to appraise only the programs they themselves generally watch:

QUESTION 28 *"Television programs, like most other things, vary in quality. Some are better than others. Considering just the programs you generally watch, what proportion would you say are: extremely enjoyable, how many are somewhat enjoyable, how many are just so-so, and how many are disappointing?"*

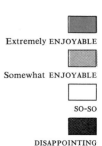

Extremely ENJOYABLE

Somewhat ENJOYABLE

SO-SO

DISAPPOINTING

EDUCATION

AVERAGE OF RESPONSES: Base[†]: 100%

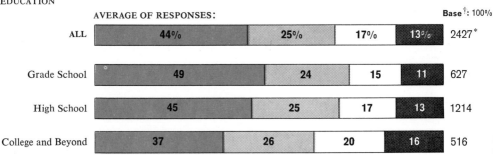

	Extremely Enjoyable	Somewhat Enjoyable	So-So	Disappointing	Base
ALL	44%	25%	17%	13%	2427[*]
Grade School	49	24	15	11	627
High School	45	25	17	13	1214
College and Beyond	37	26	20	16	516

*Includes 70 cases unclassified as to education
†Percentages exclude DK, NA which varies from response to response

Education still matters, but even the college-educated tend to find the programs they watch "extremely enjoyable."

"Most vs. *"mine"*

For a more detailed picture of reactions to "most programs" and "my programs," and how each of these compares with what programming "should be," we turn again to a word list. The comparison comes from essentially the same procedure we used in the earlier analysis of feelings associated with viewing. Half the sample read through a list of thirty-two adjectives twice, under these instructions:

Q. 13 C "Would you look at this list of words and quickly check all those that you might use to describe most *TV shows?"*

Q. 13 E "Now here's another copy of the same list. Would you look it over and check the words that describe how you'd like more *programs to be?"*

The other half, independently, used the same list only to describe programs they had previously named as favorites:

Q. 15 D "And now would you go through this list quickly and check all the words that describe (favorite program)[1] or programs of that type?"

The results appear on the next page, with the adjectives grouped as shown. Each bar shows the average score for the words in that cluster, computed as described before (footnote 5, page 62). For ready comparisons, the "positive" clusters are plotted to the right, and the corresponding "negatives" appear to the left.

"Most programs are . . ." The general pattern in the upper, light-colored bars replicates the previous free-response evaluation of "most programs." The favorable terms far outscore the critical ones; the average response to the clearly positive words on the list is 33 per cent as against 17 per cent for the negative ones.[2]

But again, praise is by no means global or undifferentiated. Most programming *is* entertaining and informative, just as most people feel entertained and informed while watching. And "honest" is also somewhat more often attributed than denied—noteworthy, in the early wake of the quiz scandals. But viewers are not willing to describe "most programs" as "creative," "tasteful," "serious," or "great." In these clusters, the negatives virtually cancel the positives, and in one case, "trivial," actually exceed them.

"More programs should be . . ." For the most part, there should be more of the same—entertaining and/or informative programming—and in general, the gray bars get shorter as the light blue ones do. So that, over-all, the comparison reveals no outstanding discrepancy between what most programs are and what more should be. (Incidentally, there is no mechanical reason for the two sets of answers to correlate so closely. In fact, there may be some response bias in the opposite direction: having just said what most programming *is,* some respondents may have felt some

[1] Respondent's first-mentioned favorite program—previously established—was inserted by name.

[2] We include "average" among the negatives, even though it applies, by definition, to "most programs," because of its connotation of mediocrity; "sinful" and "violent" are also presumed negative.

QUESTION 13C *"Most television programs are . . ."*

Base: 100% = **1210***

QUESTION 13E *"I wish most programs would be more . . ."*

Base: 100% = **1210***

QUESTION 15D *"My favorite programs are . . ."*

Base: 100% = **1217***

Average scores for the cluster:

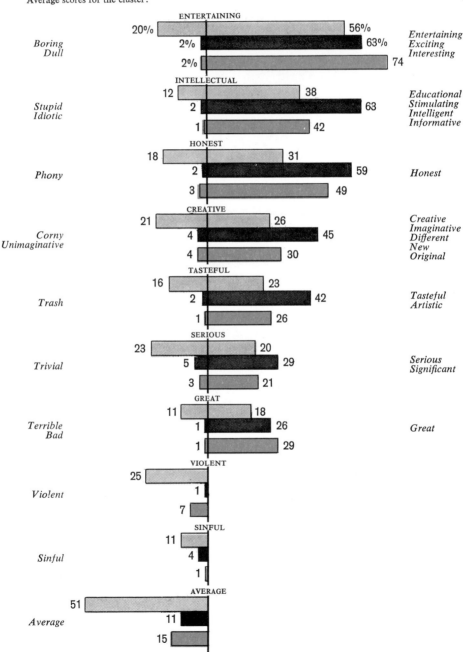

ENTERTAINING

Boring
Dull

20%   56%
2%   63%
2%   74

Entertaining
Exciting
Interesting

INTELLECTUAL

Stupid
Idiotic

12   38
2   63
1   42

Educational
Stimulating
Intelligent
Informative

HONEST

Phony

18   31
2   59
3   49

Honest

CREATIVE

Corny
Unimaginative

21   26
4   45
4   30

Creative
Imaginative
Different
New
Original

TASTEFUL

Trash

16   23
2   42
1   26

Tasteful
Artistic

SERIOUS

Trivial

23   20
5   29
3   21

Serious
Significant

GREAT

Terrible
Bad

11   18
1   26
1   29

Great

VIOLENT

Violent

25
1
7

SINFUL

Sinful

11
4
1

AVERAGE

Average

51
11
15

*13C and E asked of half the sample; 15D of the other half

pressure to produce different answers to the question of what more programs *should* be like.)

But within this overriding pattern of similarity between "is" and "should be," we find differences in the degree of agreement. First of all, note that the relative emphasis on information vs. entertainment is somewhat heavier in the "should be" profile than in the "is." This recalls the desire to feel informed, so evident in the discussion of viewing itself, and we shall see more of its origins and satisfactions in a moment.

Secondly, there are the calls for original, tasteful, serious programming—each far less frequent than the demands for entertainment and information, but each in greater contrast with the level presently attributed to the medium. If the discrepancy between "is" and "should be" is a measure of dissatisfaction, then these are the most serious criticisms expressed on this word list.

"My favorites are . . ." For the sample as a whole, favorite programs are clearly closer to "ideal" than they are to "most programs" if we take the negative entries into account. And they actually exceed the "should be" score in "entertainment." This is essentially the same relationship we saw in the analysis of viewing, where scores for "entertained" and "relaxed" surpassed even the rate of requests for these feelings.

So programs in general are good, though not as good as they could be; and *my* favorite programs are much better than most. This distinction between programs in general and those *I* watch, whether it reflects "favoritism" or "selectivity," underlies some striking educational differences—and some striking similarities as well; the data appear on the following two pages.

First, as expected, the better-educated report a much greater discrepancy between what "most programs" are, and what more programs "should be." In each cluster, the thin and heavy black lines diverge rapidly with increased schooling. But, perhaps *not* as expected, the comparison between "favorite shows" and what programming "should be" shows no such pattern at all: the discrepancy does not increase with education. The more educated viewer may be less satisfied with programming in general, but according to these responses, he is just as happy as anyone else with his *own* programs.

Actually, this finding goes even further: the educated viewer tends to speak *more* highly of his favorites than does the average man. The upper-educated are much more liberal in checking the whole range of

Word List Analysis by Education:

QUESTION 13C *"Most television programs are . . ."*

QUESTION 13E *"I wish most programs would be more . . ."*

QUESTION 15D *"My favorite programs are . . ."*

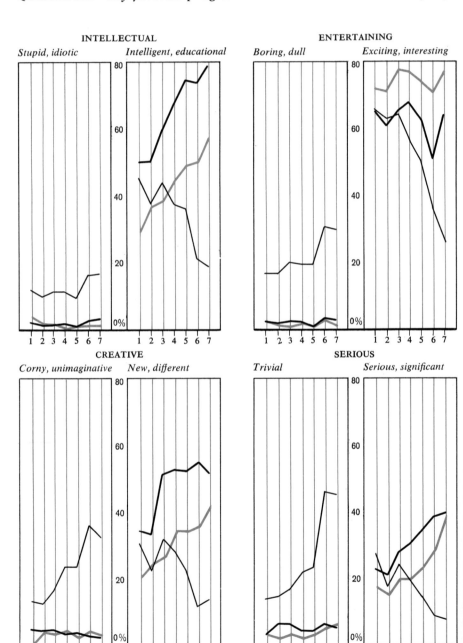

INTELLECTUAL

ENTERTAINING

Stupid, idiotic   *Intelligent, educational*

Boring, dull   *Exciting, interesting*

CREATIVE

SERIOUS

Corny, unimaginative   *New, different*

Trivial   *Serious, significant*

Viewers	Q. 13C & E*	Q. 15 D*
1. 0-6 Years Grade School	**100**	**103**
2. 7-8 Years Grade School	**214**	**210**
3. 1-3 Years High School	**262**	**269**
4. 4 Years High School	**318**	**365**
5. 1-2 Years College	**112**	**96**
6. 3-4 Years College	**98**	**96**
7. Education Beyond College	**65**	**49**

BY EDUCATION

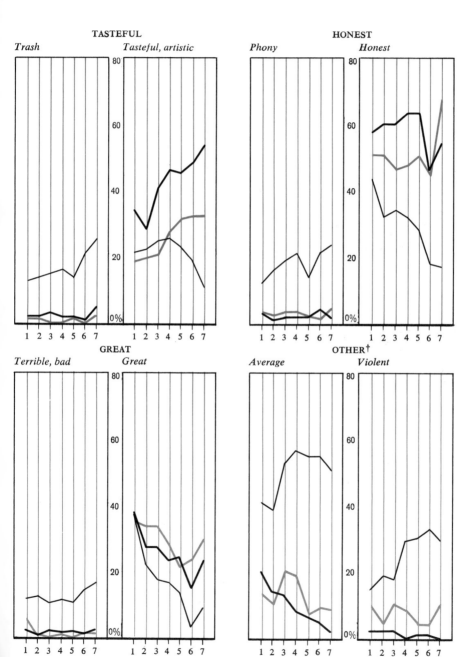

*Independent Samples
†"Sinful" not shown—see Appendix Table 29

positive adjectives. Here, for example, are the scores on individual words, for the two extreme educational groups:

Q. 15D "My Favorite Programs Are . . ." (positive words only)

	0–6 yrs. Grade School	Beyond College
Base: 100% =	103	49
interesting	76%	78%
entertaining	75	88
exciting	64	63
honest	50	67
educational	38	49
great	35	29
intelligent	32	61
different	29	47
stimulating	26	67
serious	25	39
tasteful	25	39
informative	21	53
original	19	47
new	18	27
imaginative	17	47
creative	12	43
artistic	12	27
significant	10	39
average	32%	51%

NOTE: Full data by education in Appendix Table 9.

Bear in mind that the top group is not more liberal in checking positive words when they describe "most programs"; in fact, just the opposite is true. Also, virtually no negative words are used by either group in the description of favorites. So these differences are not simply a matter of response set, or larger vocabulary on the part of the higher group.

The result is that in four of the seven clusters, the blue line actually climbs with education: the more formal schooling I have, the more intellectual, creative, serious, and tasteful I consider those programs *I* watch regularly.

These relationships are strongest, perhaps, in the key cluster, *"intellectual."* With increasing education, intellectual value is much *less* frequently attributed to most programming while much *more* frequently asked for; the thin and heavy black lines virtually explode from left to right. But favorite shows parallel the ideal, and climb steadily with education.[3]

And again, analysis by religion shows much the same pattern. Jews are considerably less favorable in their descriptions of most programs than are Protestants or Catholics—more negative, in fact, than even the highest educational groups—and they are also more demanding about what programming *should* be like. But they too have more good things to say about their own favorite shows, especially with respect to their intellectual virtues. (See Appendix Table 29.)

How is it that those most critical of television generally, are at the same time most favorably impressed by the programs they themselves watch regularly?

The discrepancy is especially significant since it does not come from a *direct* comparison of "most" vs. "mine." We would expect critics to make the claim that "my programs are better than most." But these are *independent* descriptions by *independent* samples. The only difference is that one group is generalizing about "most programs" while the other is describing specific programs watched "regularly."

One explanation is simply that they watch better shows—that the better-educated, as well as the less-educated, are realistic in appraising their own favorites. As one viewer observes:

> "[Most of the programs on the air today are designed for] other people. Part is really too high-class for me. I don't like the fancy stuff—music, dancing, etc. I'm just a hillbilly. Not much education, so I guess I can't appreciate the modern stuff."

Let us follow through by looking at the favorite programs actually named by the respondents. The programs they were describing in the "favorite" check list are tabulated on the next page.

Two points are immediately clear:

1. The viewing population, as a whole, favors light entertainment by an overwhelming majority. Now these designations need to be related to the program mix actually available—if there were *no* other programs on the air, "favorites" would have to come from this category—and we

---

[3] In fact, note that the lower groups apply the positive intellectual terms to *most* programming more frequently than to their own favorites. It is not until high school graduates and above that the perceived intellectual level of favorites climbs above that attributed to "most programs."

QUESTION 14/15A-B *"What are some of your favorite programs—those you watch regularly or whenever you get a chance?"*[§]

EDUCATION

	ALL	0-6 Yrs. Grade School	7-8 Yrs. Grade School	1-3 Yrs. High School	4 Yrs. High School	1-2 Yrs. College	3-4 Yrs. College	Education Beyond College
Base: 100% =2427*		203	424	531	683	208	194	114

FIRST MENTIONED EXAMPLE: [†]

		0-6	7-8	1-3 HS	4 HS	1-2 Col	3-4 Col	Beyond
ACTION—Westerns, Crime, Adventure	29%	27%	30%	33%	29%	26%	23%	18%
COMEDY/VARIETY	24	18	24	24	29	24	21	14
LIGHT DRAMA	12	20	12	15	11	7	8	7
LIGHT MUSIC	9	6	13	8	9	8	6	11
SPORTS	7	13	8	6	6	8	6	5
REGULAR NEWS	4	5	2	3	3	6	8	8
Other INFORMATION & PUBLIC AFFAIRS	7	2	5	5	6	11	15	21
HEAVY DRAMA includes Heavy films	3	1	0	2	3	5	9	10
RELIGION	1	2	1	1	1	0	1	2
MOVIES—excluding Heavy-films	1	1	1	1	1	1	0	1
HEAVY MUSIC	0	0	0	0	0	1	0	1
ALL OTHERS, DK, NA	3	4	4	2	2	2	4	3

SUMMARY:

		0-6	7-8	1-3 HS	4 HS	1-2 Col	3-4 Col	Beyond
LIGHT ENTERTAINMENT	82%	85%	88%	87%	85%	74%	64%	56%
HEAVY ENTERTAINMENT	3	1	0	2	3	7	9	11
NEWS	4	5	2	3	3	6	8	8
INFORMATION & PUBLIC AFFAIRS	8	4	6	6	7	11	15	23
ALL OTHERS, DK, NA	3	4	4	2	2	2	4	3

*Includes 70 cases unclassified as to education
†Only one favorite—the first mentioned—is entered for each respondent
§Here and in subsequent analyses of specific programs, responses were categorized according to a detailed code containing 47 narrow categories (see Appendix Tables 10 and 11), then collapsed into these 12 broad types, and further into the 5 major groupings shown in the summary

undertake such an analysis in later pages. For the moment, we note merely that the actual programs first thought of as "favorites" are, for the most part, those that provide pleasant relaxation rather than serious stimulation.

2. Although this remains true among all educational groups—with 56 per cent naming light-entertainment shows even at the top of the educational range—there are some marked differences. As education increases, the incidence of serious, highbrow programs (heavy drama, information) rises sharply and light drama falls off accordingly. Comedy and action also decline with education, though the differences are slight except at the very top.

Moreover, even within general categories, the named "favorites" seem to vary according to general quality distinctions built into the code on the basis of our *a priori* evaluations. Here, for example, is a more detailed analysis of programs within the "action" category.

Q. 14/15A: Favorite Programs

		EDUCATION	
	All	G. S.	H. S.	Coll. and Beyond
ACTION	28%	28%	31%	24%
Westerns, "adult"	9	9	10	7
Westerns, other, or general	10	14	10	4
Adventure, other worlds	2	1	2	2
Crime drama	4	2	5	6
Private eye, "sophisticated"	2	1	2	3
Police, detective, other, or general	2	1	2	2
Base: 100% =	2427 *	627	1214	516

* Includes 70 cases unclassified as to education.

The only form of action that declines in popularity with education is "westerns." Furthermore, while the figures are small, they suggest that this decline is largely confined to run-of-the-mill entries; those we categorized as "adult" remain favorites of roughly equal proportions of each education group.[4]

[4] If true, this clearly speaks to the issue of whether the "class" audience need be lost in the wooing of the "mass."

So the greater enthusiasm of the better-educated for their own favorite shows—far greater than their enthusiasm over most programs and greater even than the praise other groups bestow on their favorites —is due in part to the fact that they are describing different programs. These programs probably *are* more "intellectual," "creative," "serious" and "tasteful" than an unselected sample of all television fare, or even than the favorites cited by the public at large.

But at the same time, this selectivity may apply to their responses, as well as to their actual viewing habits. If a professor and a blue-collar worker watch both *The Untouchables* and *Omnibus* regularly, the professor may be relatively more apt to cite *Omnibus* as an appropriate "favorite."[5] We get some indication of the extent of this response bias in the next section.

Finally, the critics who feel worse about television and worse about watching it may find it more necessary to discover or invent saving graces in the programs they do admit to watching regularly. They may, in short, have more favorable things to say about the same programs.

Unfortunately, the numbers are too small to allow such comparisons by individual show, and the analysis by general category is confounded by the fact that highbrows probably select better shows within each category. But whatever the explanation, we do find that the better-educated find more benefits in favorites *within* the same general group of programs. Here, for example, those college-educated viewers who mention "light drama" programs as favorite find them more "intellectual," "creative," and "tasteful" than the corresponding groups with less education. The same is true in the action category, and it is not just that they use more words in total: they do not see these favorites as any more "great," "honest," or "entertaining."

Incidentally, similar differences occur in the case of comedy-variety.

In sum: most people like most programs; the more critical groups less so. Most people also like *their* programs better than programs in general; the critics even more so. This leads to the unusual yet revealing picture of a segment of viewers who are least satisfied with the medium and its products in general, but more satisfied with what they themselves consume.

---

[5] In some surveys, the "regular readers" of *Punch* or the *Saturday Review* tend to exceed their circulation, while *Confidential* apparently never sells a copy.

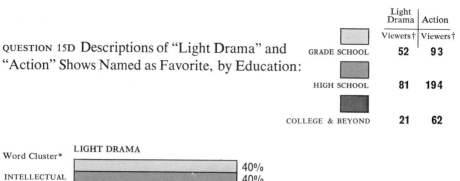

	Light Drama Viewers†	Action Viewers†
GRADE SCHOOL	52	93
HIGH SCHOOL	81	194
COLLEGE & BEYOND	21	62

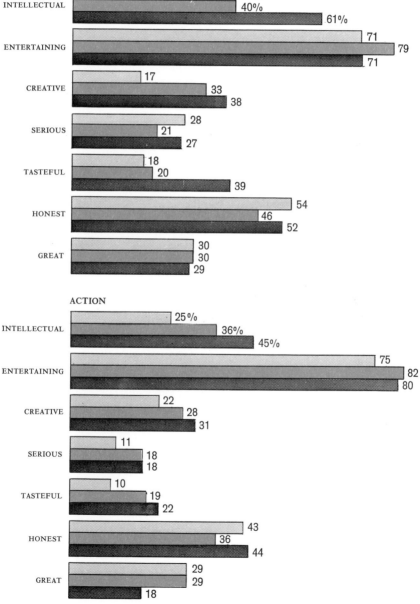

Word Cluster*

LIGHT DRAMA

INTELLECTUAL	40% / 40% / 61%
ENTERTAINING	71 / 79 / 71
CREATIVE	17 / 33 / 38
SERIOUS	28 / 21 / 27
TASTEFUL	18 / 20 / 39
HONEST	54 / 46 / 52
GREAT	30 / 30 / 29

ACTION

INTELLECTUAL	25% / 36% / 45%
ENTERTAINING	75 / 82 / 80
CREATIVE	22 / 28 / 31
SERIOUS	11 / 18 / 18
TASTEFUL	10 / 19 / 22
HONEST	43 / 36 / 44
GREAT	29 / 29 / 18

*Negatives subtracted from corresponding positives in each cluster
†15D asked of half the sample

The Present Menu—How Adequate?

"Most of the programs on the air today are designed for ignor-
amuses. Just the general public like you and me. Begging
your pardon, lady. I didn't mean to call you an ignoramus."

Differences in taste and selectivity within the audience lead naturally to a consideration of the range and mix of present offerings. To
what extent are various viewing interests adequately represented? Everyone likes his favorite shows, but does everyone get enough of the kind
of programming he likes?

Now, the criterion of "enough" is an issue in itself. There are a
variety of economic, social, and even philosophical approaches to the
matter, and each is fraught with conceptual as well as measurement
difficulties. For example: Should heavy viewers get more consideration
than light viewers because, after all, they consume more? Or would the
light viewers become "heavy" if their needs were satisfied? Do small
minorities "deserve" at least some programs in prime time, displacing
the majority interests? Or should minority interests be expected to
tolerate inconvenience or other "costs" if they are to be satisfied, just
as they expect to pay more and/or look harder for better books or foods
of limited, specialized appeal?

We confine ourselves to a simpler question. Our criterion of
"enough" is subjective, as is our information. The following pages ask
only this: Do the *viewers themselves think* their interests are adequately
represented, or do they find inequities, omissions, or other "imbalances"
in the current fare?

We begin with this general question:

Q. 20   *"What kind of people do you feel most of the programs on the*
         air today are designed for? (Would you say that the programs
         are designed pretty much with people like you in mind—or does
         it seem that most of them are aimed at people with other in-
         terests and tastes?)"

	All	G. S.	H. S.	Coll. and Beyond
People like me	31%	36%	33%	18%
General public	26	19	29	29
Something for everybody—diversity	21	26	21	15
For other interests, tastes	19	16	17	27

	All	G. S.	H. S.	Coll. and Beyond
Further information, when given: above average (intelligence, status, etc.)	2	3	1	1
below average (intelligence, status, etc.)	9	3	7	21
people who want to relax, escape	2	1	1	3
Other	7	6	6	8
NA, DK	3	7	2	2
Base: 100% =	2427 *	627	1214	516

* Includes 70 cases unclassified as to education.

A substantial minority—19 per cent of all viewers and 27 per cent of those who have been to college—say explicitly that most programs are directed at "other interests." Further, 9 per cent of the total and 21 per cent of the college-educated specify that these interests are lowbrow, childish, or otherwise beneath them:

> "People of lower intelligence. The more you teach, the more you realize that there are a lot of these. It is certain the more general programs aren't for a very high class. It is the large, more unalert class that the programs reach. That is, in general."

> "Geared for low intellects. Minimum of education. A majority of the shows never seem to be anything that makes you think, raise questions, challenge. All plots are so obvious. People with minimum education."

The nature of these observations and their locus in the upper-educated is now not surprising, but perhaps its frequency, or infrequency, is noteworthy. (Should we say that *fully* one fifth of the college-educated explicitly assert that most shows are directed at other interests and tastes —or that *only* one fifth do so?)

At the other extreme, only a very few think that the present level is over their heads:

> "Maybe people who know more than I do. Maybe people who know more English."

But the large middle-majority "identifies" with most programming:

it is adequate and appropriate for the general public and the common
man—and that's what *I* am:

> "I know a lot of people would say morons. I don't think that.
> I guess the average person. My type person, I guess."

> "Myself. I am just an average man—and I feel I'm lucky to
> be able to enjoy anything as wonderful as TV."

Or people believe that there is diversity—something for everybody:

> "It's for all people—there are programs for men, women,
> and children. The programs are designed pretty much with
> people like me in mind. I feel I have a wide range of shows to
> choose from and I love all the shows I watch. I'm a person
> who wants to learn from TV, wants to be entertained, and yet
> feel relaxed while I watch."

> "Try to please everybody. I think they do a good job with
> something for everybody, but most programs are for people
> like me. I consider myself the average."

Another indication of the relatively high regard the majority viewer
has for the majority program comes from the comparison of "regular
fare" with "specials," as shown to the right.

Only the college-educated, about a fifth of our viewing sample, vote
on balance for programs that presumably have some extra news or entertainment value.

Somewhat ironically, then, the attempts at unique, "superlative"
broadcasting often arouse antagonism among the large proportion of
viewers who prefer the familiar and the routine. NBC's David Sarnoff
reports that ". . . a barrage of protests . . . invariably comes when a
regular show is preempted for a special program."[6] And, as we shall
see, even "great moments" in television tend to come from the ranks of
the regulars.

The affinity for the familiar, as epitomized by the perpetual radio

[6] Op. cit.

QUESTION 31 *"In general, do you think that specials or spectaculars are better than the regular shows they replace, or would you generally rather see the regularly scheduled programs?"*

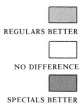

REGULARS BETTER

NO DIFFERENCE

SPECIALS BETTER

EDUCATION   **Base:** 100% =

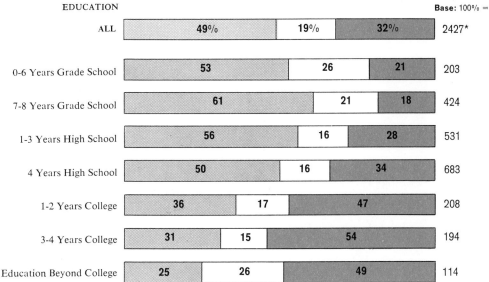

	REGULARS BETTER	NO DIFFERENCE	SPECIALS BETTER	Base: 100% =
ALL	49%	19%	32%	2427*
0-6 Years Grade School	53	26	21	203
7-8 Years Grade School	61	21	18	424
1-3 Years High School	56	16	28	531
4 Years High School	50	16	34	683
1-2 Years College	36	17	47	208
3-4 Years College	31	15	54	194
Education Beyond College	25	26	49	114

*Includes 70 cases unclassified as to education

favorites, may be involved here. But the vote may also reflect simple differences in taste: if specials *are* better by the standards of the intellectuals—as they themselves report them to be—then perhaps they are worse, or uninteresting, by the standards of the rest of the community. Why expect the masses to prefer "class" material on TV any more than they do in print or at the movies? By almost any criterion—ratings, survey, or commercial—the average viewer is not only satisfied with average programming but *most* satisfied with average programming.

The components Now we turn to some specific matters. So far, except for the revealing contrast provided by the description of "favorites," the discussion has been in general terms. Different segments of the viewing population have evaluated the TV menu *in toto,* and they have given us a rough indication of the extent to which it provides for their respective tastes. The only distinction has been between "regular" and "special" offerings. In the next few pages, we analyze programming by various types—present and potential.

First, we ask explicitly about several broad categories. How much is there of each, and how much should there be? As a check on a possible response bias toward taking an "acceptable" position on this issue, we again asked our major question in two forms—each of half the sample—as shown to the right.

The pattern is clear:

1. First, there should be more of everything except "escape." In regard to each of the other program types, substantial proportions of viewers ask for more, while the rest think the present availabilities are sufficient. In no case is there "too much" at present.

2. It is also clear that "light," entertaining programming is far more generally considered in adequate supply than is intellectually stimulating fare. Only a third ask for more "laughs," and still fewer for more "relaxation." But half of all viewers feel there should be more information, and over 60 per cent request additional "educational" programming.

Furthermore, this general pattern is maintained in both versions of the question. "Most people" are, to be sure, slightly less serious-minded in their requests than "I" am, but *only* slightly so. The rank-order of the "not enough" response is identical under the two conditions. The desire to appear discriminating and "intellectual," then, is probably *not* the major factor in the call for more educational, informative programming

"Television programs can be designed to provide different things, from your point of view, does television today have enough, not enough, or too many of each of these kinds of programs?"

NOT ENOUGH

ENOUGH

ALL OTHER

TOO MANY

PROGRAMS THAT PROVIDE:

Base: 100% = 1229

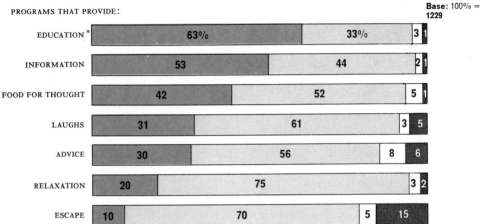

EDUCATION* 63% 33% 3 1
INFORMATION 53 44 2 1
FOOD FOR THOUGHT 42 52 5 1
LAUGHS 31 61 3 5
ADVICE 30 56 8 6
RELAXATION 20 75 3 2
ESCAPE 10 70 5 15

QUESTION 18B ASKED OF THE OTHER HALF

"Television programs can be designed to provide different things, if you had to guess, would you say that most people think that television today has enough, not enough, or too many of each of these kinds of programs?"

NOT ENOUGH

ENOUGH

ALL OTHER

TOO MANY

PROGRAMS THAT PROVIDE:

Base: 100% = 1198

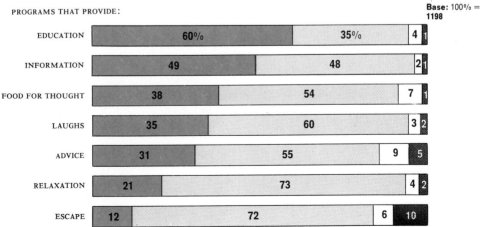

EDUCATION 60% 35% 4 1
INFORMATION 49 48 2 1
FOOD FOR THOUGHT 38 54 7 1
LAUGHS 35 60 3 2
ADVICE 31 55 9 5
RELAXATION 21 73 4 2
ESCAPE 12 72 6 10

*Program types listed in order of "not enough" response. For order of presentation, see Appendix A

—since it is attributed to "most people" with almost equal frequency[7] (except, as we will see in a moment, by those at the top of the educational ladder).

This is not to say that all those who feel there is "not enough" informative programming would actually watch more if it were available. Whether and to what extent that is true, is one of the main questions of our ARB analysis. It probably does mean, though, that they really *believe* there should be additional programming of this type—not just that interviewers would be impressed by that response.

3. It goes almost without saying that the relative emphasis on serious programming is highest among the top educational groups. "Not enough" education, information, food for thought—all climb steadily with schooling, especially in the personal responses:

Q. 18A,B

Per cent who say there is *not enough:*

		EDUCATION						
		1	2	3	4	5	6	7
"Education"	for me	46%	48%	62%	65%	84%	75%	82%
	for most	54	52	56	67	68	64	47
"Information"	for me	27	35	52	58	69	73	72
	for most	33	41	43	57	58	59	55
"Food for thought"	for me	21	25	33	46	70	63	66
	for most	24	29	31	43	48	59	65
Base: 100% =	Me	90	219	266	363	102	93	65
	Most	113	205	265	320	106	101	49

Thus, differences between "me" and "most people" do occur on this score among the top educational groups. Only 47 per cent of those with education beyond college think "most people" want more edu-

---

[7] That is, if "most people's" tastes had turned out to be much "lighter" than "mine," the possibility of such response bias would be indicated—as it was in the discussion of "reasons for watching," where marked discrepancies between the two sets of responses occurred. Technically, there are two response tendencies that may underlie discrepancies between "most" and "me" (beyond actually perceived differences). First, respondents may exaggerate "positive" attributes for themselves (but not, of course, for "most"). Secondly, they may understate or deny negatives as self-applicable (but, again, be willing to attribute them to others). In either case, the "self" description comes off more favorably, so the "most" question provides a check on the presence of either or both.

cational programs,[8] whereas 82 per cent say that they themselves do. And similar though smaller discrepancies occur in the other items. Conversely, those at the bottom of the educational ladder are actually a bit more modest in their own intellectual desires than in those they attribute to "most people."[9]

In this sense, viewers at both educational extremes—and especially those at the top—correctly indicate the direction in which the intellectual desires of "most people" depart from their own. Most people *are* in fact less likely to request additional enlightenment than are the intellectual elite; and most people *are* more likely to do so than the lowest group.

But regardless of these differences in degree, or nuances of interpretation, the stress on additional enlightenment holds at all educational levels. Here are the two extremes and a middle group; the rest fall in between.

Q. 18A

"*Not Enough*," for Me

0–6 yrs. Grade School		High School Grad.		Beyond College	
Base: 100% = 90		363		65	
Education	46%	*Education*	65%	*Education*	82%
Advice	32	*Information*	58	*Information*	72
Information	27	*Food for thought*	46	*Food for thought*	66
Laughs	24	*Laughs*	37	*Laughs*	28
Food for thought	21	*Advice*	31	*Advice*	25
Relaxation	12	*Relaxation*	20	*Relaxation*	23
Escape	8	*Escape*	11	*Escape*	8

Note that the specific form of intellectual benefit requested varies somewhat with schooling: "educational programs" lead the list for all, but for those with very little schooling, the personal and concrete "advice" category tends to replace the more abstract "food for thought" that attracts the response of the upper-educated. This is consistent with differences in their print diet: specific, personal advice is a relatively

---

[8] Note that this 47 per cent estimate is lower than the comparable projections made by those with only college training, or, indeed, any lower level of education. Is this a matter of more "insight" into the general public or more "snobbery" as a result of advanced training?

[9] This recalls the similar "realistic" relationship dealing with the intellectual level that various educational groups attribute to their favorites as against "most programs" (see page 125).

large manifest component of many mass magazines, as compared with the broader, more abstract informative content of the "class" books.[1]

In sum: all groups report that intellectual content on TV is in shortest supply—by a wide margin among the well-educated, by a smaller margin among those with less schooling. But substantial portions at all levels also ask for more entertainment; and the better-educated exceed the request rate of the mass audience even here:

Q. 18A

Per cent who say there is
"*Not Enough*," for me:

			EDUCATION			
1	2	3	4	5	6	7
Laughs 24%	28%	26%	37%	39%	31%	28%
Relaxation 12	17	17	20	26	25	23

Base:
100% = 90 · 219 · 266 · 363 · 102 · 93 · 65

Some of this can be attributed to the usually more critical response pattern of the educated. For them, TV in general is not as adequate on any score; and "not enough" is a more critical response than "enough." But so is "too much," and a critical attitude alone does not explain the rarity of the complaint that there is too much light programming. Nowhere, except "escape," is there any indication of an oversupply—and even in that case the figure for "too many" is a surprisingly small 34 per cent even at the top educational level:

Q. 18A

Per cent who say there
are "*Too Many*," for me:

			EDUCATION			
1	2	3	4	5	6	7
Laughs 8%	5%	5%	4%	5%	9%	5%
Relaxation 1	1	0	2	7	5	5
Escape 9	5	12	13	25	25	34

Base: 100% = 90 · 219 · 266 · 363 · 102 · 93 · 65

[1] In addition, the "latent" advisory function of fiction in such magazines as *True Confessions* (or in radio's soap operas) has often been discussed in the analysis of their appeal.

Cf. Herta Herzog: "Motivation and Gratifications of Daily Serial Listeners," in Paul Lazarsfeld and Frank Stanton (ed.): *Radio Research, 1942-43* (Duell, Sloan, and Pearce, 1944).

This must be attributed, at least in part, to the relaxation that the highly educated, along with the rest of the audience, want from TV.[2] Thus, on balance, even for them, there should be more, not fewer, relaxing and amusing programs on television. And that brings us to the final point in this analysis.

These have been absolute, not comparative, judgments. No choices between program types are forced, no costs assessed. By the terms of the question, viewers can request more of everything, as many of them actually do.

What happens when they are put to a choice? Here is such a question, phrased in terms of the two major program types that underlie the more specific categories of the previous analysis:

QUESTION 41A *"Generally speaking, would you say that television should do more in the way of providing informational material, or should it concentrate on providing the best entertainment possible?* IF "BOTH" TO A: *Well suppose there was a free hour on the air that could be used for any kind of television program at all, what would you like to see it used for?"*

INFORMATION

ENTERTAINMENT

BOTH, CAN'T CHOOSE, DK

	INFORMATION	ENTERTAINMENT	BOTH, CAN'T CHOOSE, DK	Base: 100% =
ALL	30%	40%	30%	2427*
EDUCATION				
0-6 Years Grade School	29	47	24	203
7-8 Years Grade School	27	47	26	424
1-3 Years High School	26	44	30	531
4 Years High School	30	41	29	683
1-2 Years College	38	25	37	208
3-4 Years College	40	27	33	194
Education Beyond College	40	20	40	114

*Includes 70 respondents unclassified as to education

[2] Realistically, the educated make far smaller distinctions between themselves and "most people" on this score, than on the "intellectual" items. Responses on the two forms are close within each educational group on all of the entertainment categories.

When it comes to selecting more information *or* better entertainment, the vote in the total population leans toward the latter. "Entertainment" loses ground mainly at the college level, and there much of the slack is taken up by those who say "both" or otherwise fail to make a choice. Even among those with education beyond college, only 40 per cent are willing to commit themselves to more information vs. better entertainment.

The increasing proportion for "both" may reflect the sophisticated position that programming should do both jobs simultaneously, that there should be entertaining shows that are informational, and vice versa:

> "Both—something musical. Guess I should specify music appreciation. Something where they tell you about it so it becomes an educational type of thing."

> "Both—I suppose the type of program that would be entertaining to the children and yet informing them on some subject."

People also mention the notion that TV fare should be varied, so as to supply the best of each:

> "Both, can't choose. . . . Should be as helpful as possible both in entertainment and education."

> "Both, can't choose, don't know—should be mixed—a happy mixture."

In any case, the difference of opinion along the educational spectrum is apparent, and in the familiar direction. But the 11 per cent rise in the requests for more informational material, from the lowest to highest educational group, is dramatically smaller here than in the previous question, where "not enough information" increased from 27 per cent to 72 per cent. When "more information" is no longer "free," but presented as an alternative to better entertainment, the educated become less clearly intellectual in their advice to the medium.

The "both" response is a perfect and perhaps realistic hedge. It recalls the role of entertainer in which even the college-educated cast the TV set in the comparison with other media, *and* their desire to feel more productive while being so entertained. Good, stimulating entertainment—that probably is the chief personal request the college-educated viewer now makes of the medium.

Complaints, suggestions, recommendations In addition to getting their reaction to the present program mix, we gave viewers several opportunities to express any unfulfilled wishes or ideas they had for program development and innovation. Although it is unrealistic to expect people to dream up ideas for program development during an interview, these responses provide a further check on the extent and nature of dissatisfaction with what is presently available.

We began with a general, open-ended question that was asked early in the interview in order to stake out the total range of possible discontent:

Q. 13D "As far as you're concerned, where is the greatest room for improvement in television programs?"

		EDUCATION		
	All	G. S.	H. S.	Coll. and Beyond
Should be more or better:				
information, news, education	23%	10%	22%	41%
drama	8	4	7	13
music	7	4	7	10
comedy, variety	6	3	6	9
religion	4	8	4	3
children's shows	4	3	3	6
westerns	4	3	4	4
other	15	13	16	16
Should be fewer				
westerns	19	16	20	18
crime	8	7	8	9
other	8	6	9	9
General				
too much violence	13	14	13	12
higher level	7	1	6	18
more variety	6	2	7	7
bad taste	4	4	6	1
more realism, honesty	4	2	5	5
too many reruns	3	3	4	1
other	6	5	6	7
Better program timing	7	6	7	8

continued next page

		EDUCATION		Coll. and
	All	G. S.	H. S.	Beyond
Criticism of commercials	13	11	15	12
fewer, shorter	8	6	9	5
content	3	2	4	4
interruptive	2	3	3	1
other	2	1	3	3
Doesn't need improving	8	17	6	3
Other, DK, NA	9	15	8	5
Base: 100% =	1210	314	580	275

NOTE: Multiple responses.

More information, fewer westerns, less violence, generally higher-level programming—these are the main and by now the familiar criticisms. "More information" and "higher level" are criticisms especially sensitive to education, while roughly equal numbers at all three levels want fewer westerns and less violence. One other specific point is noteworthy. In a question dealing explicitly with *programming,* quite a few people mention commercials—and regardless of education—suggesting the salience of this issue.

At a much later point, we asked specifically about areas of void. The question here is not whether some interests are out of balance, but whether there are recognized gaps in the broadcast spectrum—areas not *under*represented, but entirely *un*represented. Both queries are open-ended, to tap any such feelings as may exist:

Q. 22A *"Generally speaking, is there any type of program you would really like to see that isn't on at all now?"*

"No, can't think of any" (*not* NA)	49%
"Perfectly satisfied" now	8
Total: no recognized gap	57
More shows like (some present program)	20
Music	4
Religion	3
Educational, informative, general	3
Sports	2

Q. 22B *"If you could have a program tailor-made just for you, what kind of a program would it be?"*

More like (some present program)	17%
Music	16
classical, opera	3
musical comedy	3
sacred, gospel	1
ballet, dancing	2
hillbilly	1
other or general	8
Stories, plays	7
Sports	6

Q. 22A	
Travel	2%
How-to: household, hobby, social	2
Drama	2
Quiz	2
News, current events	1
Other	9
NA, DK	2
Base: 100% = 2427	

Q. 22B	
Educational, informative, general	6%
Comedy	6
Variety	6
Religion	5
Western	5
News, current events	4
Suspense, crime, action	4
How to: household, hobby, social	4
Drama—heavy, classic	4
Travel	3
Family stories	3
Classes, specific subjects	1
Other, misc. shows	10
NA, DK	13
Base: 100% = 2427	

NOTE: Multiple responses.

Looking first at the more general question: over half of the viewers can't think of any type of program they would like to see that isn't on at all now; and a number of them say explicitly that their wishes are well provided for at present:

"Good heavens. They have about everything over a week's time. I can't think of a thing."

"It has so many different kinds of programs. You can see almost anything imaginable."

In addition, 20 per cent ask specifically for other programs like some specifically named present entry. In this sense, then, such viewers also fail to demonstrate a recognized gap in the present schedule.

So over three quarters say explicitly or implicitly: "I can't think of anything *else* I'd like to see." What is more, they probably mean it. Viewing is not a rare or unimportant matter to them, and at this point in the interview they had been talking and thinking about TV for an hour or so. If specific program wishes existed, they should have crystallized to the point where they could easily be elicited. In short, the dearth of response is probably not a matter of being caught off guard on a remote or academic issue.

Those specifics that do arise center, though in very small numbers, on religion, music, and informative programming; and the "tailor-made" programs tend to substantiate these interests. For the rest, they add little in themselves save an appreciation for the idiosyncrasy of tastes, and perhaps a little comic relief:

> "Jerry Lewis, Stan Kenton, and Benny Goodman touring Switzerland and other scenic parts of the world."
>
> "I really don't care, as long as it's educational, informative, and comedy."
>
> "I'm partial to westerns—most of all one with less shooting, some comedy, a few tears, a little laugh, a little heart, a little everything."
>
> "It would be a real family. A typical American family. One that lives a typical American life. One that gets up and goes to church, that can sit and discuss as a family should—their trials."
>
> "I'd have all music. Not that stiff opera crap, but some good finger-popping music."

Possibly of greatest interest is the occasional contrast between the general categorical response to 22A and the more concrete, personal request immediately following it in 22B. Here, for example, are two respondents answering the two consecutive questions:

22A *". . . type of program you would really like to see that isn't on at all now?"*

"Maybe a lot of college or high-school courses." . . . . . .

"I'd like to hear book reviews and debates." . . . . . .

22B *"If you could have a program tailor-made just for you, what kind of a program would it be?"*

"Like Zane Grey but with more colored cowboys."

"The Lawrence Welk Show would be an over-all choice. Of course, I wouldn't watch it exclusively, but I could still listen to it for three or four hours."

These extreme examples suggest a more general tendency apparent in much of what has gone before, and in much of what is to come: viewer reaction to "programming in general" is one thing; attitudes toward generic categories (e.g., information, escape), something else again; and feelings about specific programs watched, still another matter.

We move now to our most specific queries—from the discussion of broad and somewhat abstract categories of programs to questions that demand actual names and places. Here, then, is the most concrete information on the stated program preferences and desires of our viewers:

Specifics—the present As a start, we return to the distribution of "favorites" we saw briefly before and compare it with the results of two other questions about present programs. First, how do "favorites" relate to kinds of programs viewers "would like to see more of"? And next, how do they compare with programs viewers like least of all? In both cases, the results are categorized for purposes of comparison, but the responses tabulated were names of actual programs.[3]

The differences between "favorites" and "like more of," on the next page, are striking and understandable. "Light drama" and "action" programs account for a much larger share of the "favorites" than of the programs "there should be more of," while the difference is in the opposite direction for "public affairs," "heavy drama," and "religion."

Now interestingly, the same pattern of discrepancies holds across the educational spectrum. Responses to both questions get more serious-minded with schooling, but more viewers at all levels "would like to see more" public affairs, heavy drama, and religion than name current favorites in these categories.[4] And the converse is true, everywhere, for light drama and action. (See Appendix Table 12.) So regardless of education, the requested programs are heavier than the current favorites.

In part, these differences may be due to a general response trend we have already observed: the more abstract and normative discussion of what viewers *would* like to see more of may tend to be more serious-minded than the factual recitation of their present favorites.

[3] Except in a few cases where no specific program was named. When viewers named both a "category" and an example, the example was coded according to our system, and the viewer's categoric designation ignored. For example: "Historical dramas like *Gunsmoke*" would be coded "adult western."

[4] Though the request for more religion reaches substantial proportions only in the lowest educational group.

QUESTION 14/15A-B *"What are some of your favorite programs—those you watch regularly or whenever you get a chance?"*

QUESTION 21A-B *"What kind of programs have you seen that you'd like to see more of on TV? Can you give me an example of the kind of programs you'd like to see more of?"*

"My favorite programs"

Base: 100% = **2427**

"Would like to see"

Base: 100% = **2427**

FIRST MENTIONED EXAMPLE:

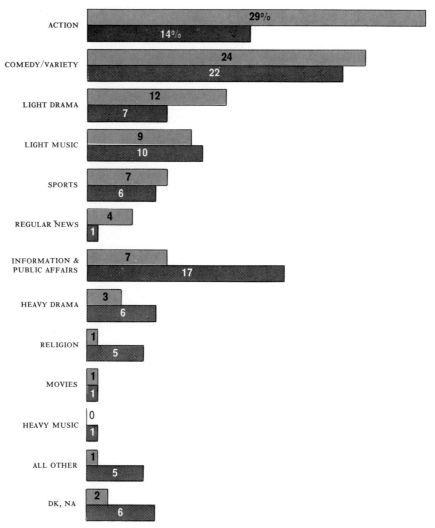

	"My favorite programs"	"Would like to see"
ACTION	29%	14%
COMEDY/VARIETY	24	22
LIGHT DRAMA	12	7
LIGHT MUSIC	9	10
SPORTS	7	6
REGULAR NEWS	4	1
INFORMATION & PUBLIC AFFAIRS	7	17
HEAVY DRAMA	3	6
RELIGION	1	5
MOVIES	1	1
HEAVY MUSIC	0	1
ALL OTHER	1	5
DK, NA	2	6

But there is another factor that may be just as important: Coca-Cola may be "my favorite drink," and yet not the one "I'd like to see more of in restaurants," because it is already available everywhere. In short: one question speaks only to preference; the other, to the relative adequacy of supply. The favorite categories of programming, for the very reasons that so often concern critics of the medium, may exist in plentiful supply, or even in excess; while second-choice programming, again for the same reasons, may be relatively difficult to find.[5]

When we look at "favorites" alongside the programs that viewers "don't care for at all" (next page), the symmetry is striking. By this measure, no *category* is far off balance; each leading type of program yields about as many fans as disowners. Action shows—and specifically westerns[6]—head both lists, with comedy-variety and light drama in second and third place, respectively. Small but noteworthy exceptions are regular news and heavy drama, which small numbers favor but virtually no one likes least; and movies and heavy music, where the opposite is true.

The mirror-image does not reflect personal inconsistency of choice, nor the same individuals discriminating within categories. As the small "overlap" percentages in the center of the chart show, few viewers designate programs within the same general category as favorite *and* least liked. The symmetry is a matter of audience differentiation: some people like some action shows best of all, while others, in about equal numbers, name their least-liked programs in this category.

These differences in taste are largely, but by no means entirely, a matter of education. The extreme groups represented show that the general preference pattern gets "heavier" with schooling, but also that there is plenty of taste difference at each level. The likes and dislikes of both segments are well spread *across* the major categories, and each has a sizable minority *within* the various major types. (See page 149.)

Incidentally, here is one of the few places where other personal characteristics come to matter. Sex and age each account for part of the remaining variance, and in the expected directions: men are relatively

[5] The bandwagon effect, in which successful program types are copied in large numbers, would produce such differential supply situations—especially in view of the one-year time lag between this season's ratings ("favorites") and the time the copies get on the air. The basic argument holds whether "second-choice" is defined as "first choice for a minority" *or* "second-choice" for everyone.

[6] Detailed breaks within each of the major categories are in Appendix Tables 13 and 13a.

QUESTION 14/15A-B *"What are some of your favorite programs—those you watch regularly or whenever you get a chance?"*

QUESTION 23A-B *"What kind of programs don't you care for at all?"*

LIGHT ENTERTAINMENT

HEAVY ENTERTAINMENT

NEWS

INFORMATION & PUBLIC AFFAIRS

ALL OTHER

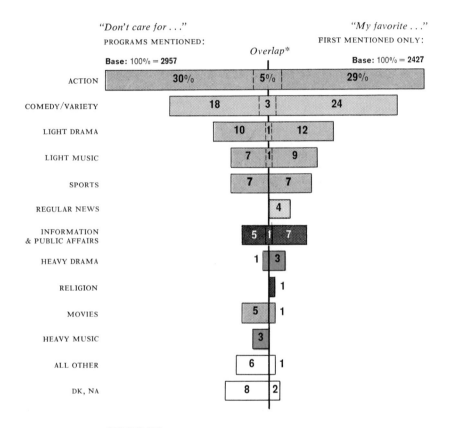

"Don't care for ..."
PROGRAMS MENTIONED:

Overlap*

"My favorite ..."
FIRST MENTIONED ONLY:

Base: 100% = 2957

Base: 100% = 2427

ACTION	30% 5%	29%
COMEDY/VARIETY	18 3	24
LIGHT DRAMA	10	12
LIGHT MUSIC	7	9
SPORTS	7	7
REGULAR NEWS		4
INFORMATION & PUBLIC AFFAIRS	5	7
HEAVY DRAMA	1	3
RELIGION		1
MOVIES	5	1
HEAVY MUSIC	3	
ALL OTHER	6	1
DK, NA	8	2

SUMMARY:

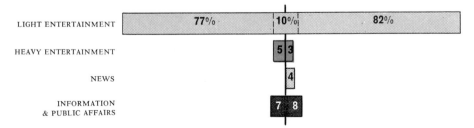

LIGHT ENTERTAINMENT	77% 10%	82%
HEAVY ENTERTAINMENT	5 3	
NEWS		4
INFORMATION & PUBLIC AFFAIRS	7	8

*Respondents who mention programs in the same category in response to both questions

QUESTION 14/15A-B *"What are some of your favorite programs—those you watch regularly or whenever you get a chance?"*

QUESTION 23A-B *"What kind of programs don't you care for at all?"*

SOME GRADE SCHOOL / **203** RESPONDENTS *

BEYOND COLLEGE / **114** RESPONDENTS †

...For Top and Bottom Educational Groups:

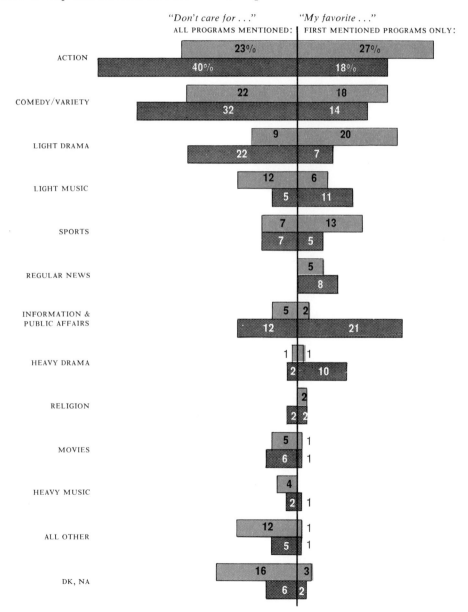

"Don't care for ..."
ALL PROGRAMS MENTIONED:

"My favorite ..."
FIRST MENTIONED PROGRAMS ONLY:

ACTION	23%	27%
	40%	18%
COMEDY/VARIETY	22	18
	32	14
LIGHT DRAMA	9	20
	22	7
LIGHT MUSIC	12	6
	5	11
SPORTS	7	13
	7	5
REGULAR NEWS		5
		8
INFORMATION & PUBLIC AFFAIRS	5	2
	12	21
HEAVY DRAMA	1	1
	2	10
RELIGION		2
	2	2
MOVIES	5	1
	6	1
HEAVY MUSIC	4	
	2	1
ALL OTHER	12	1
	5	1
DK, NA	16	3
	6	2

*211 Programs not cared for
† 130 Programs not cared for

more fond of action and sports; women lean more to comedy-variety—
especially "family situation"—and to drama of almost all kinds. Tastes
also become somewhat more gentle or "feminine" with advancing age.
(These data appear in detail in Appendix Tables 13 and 13a.)

In large measure, then, the stand-off, or "balance," in each of the
major categories is due to the combination of viewing factions with opposing opinions. And, as in elections, different candidates within the
same "party" (program type) are differentially favored. Viewers do
discriminate within these general program types when they praise or
condemn. For example, those few westerns we coded "adult"[7] are much
more frequently favored than disliked, while the opposite is true of the
rest:

QUESTION 14/15A-B *"My favorite programs . . ."*

Base: 100% = 2427†

QUESTION 23A-B *"Don't care for at all . . ."*

Base: 100% = 3246*

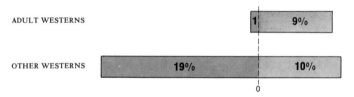

ADULT WESTERNS   1   9%

OTHER WESTERNS   19%   10%

0

*All programs mentioned. Base larger than that on page
148, which shows mentions within broader categories
†First mentioned programs only

The danger of program discussion in terms even so narrow as "westerns" is evident; when it comes to the specifics of actual viewing, responses relate to individual programs, not to broad categories.

With that, we turn to our final index of the public's reaction to
TV programming—consideration of the short but varied history of
broadcasting events.

Specifics—the past: This general probe introduces the subject:

---

[7] *Gunsmoke; Have Gun, Will Travel; Maverick; Wagon Train.*

Q. 24 *"Now I'd like to ask you about some of the things you may have seen in the past that you particularly liked. First, let's talk about programs that used to be on regularly but are no longer on the air. Are there any that you'd like to see put back on the air? I don't mean re-runs, I mean new versions. If 'yes,' which ones?"*

	All	0–6 yrs. G. S.	7–8 yrs. G. S.	1–3 yrs. H. S.	4 yrs. H. S.	1–2 yrs. Coll.	3–4 yrs. Coll.	Beyond College
Comedy-variety	47%	55%	54%	41%	50%	44%	36%	51%
Light drama	7	7	8	6	6	7	11	13
Action	20	26	22	23	17	16	19	14
Information and public affairs	20	14	14	19	20	24	32	30
Sports	2	5	1	2	3	6	3	3
Regular news	1	0	0	1	1	1	1	3
Light music	15	9	15	13	15	16	16	14
Heavy drama	4	2	1	2	5	5	7	14
Heavy music	0	0	0	0	0	2	1	2
Religion	3	2	2	4	3	2	3	3
Movies	1	0	0	2	0	2	2	0
All other—NA, DK	6	8	6	10	5	6	3	2
Base: 100% = 1377 *		98	217	312	421	121	112	63

EDUCATION

* Includes 42 cases unclassified as to education.

Most frequently mentioned:

107	I Love Lucy	55	"The quiz shows"
89	Voice of Firestone	34	Playhouse 90
88	Sid Caesar	30	Father Knows Best
84	Jackie Gleason	30	Honeymooners
66	Arthur Godfrey	30	Milton Berle
63	Omnibus	23	December Bride
60	Name That Tune	23	Studio One
60	$64,000 Question	22	Wide, Wide World
		22	Wrestling

(others in Appendix Table 14)

Again, as a group, viewers respond largely in terms of light programming. And while "action" declines in favor of "public affairs" with increasing education, "comedy-variety" remains the most frequent type of program fondly recalled, even at the top.

Further analysis of this category reveals some interesting differences within it:

Q. 24B

	All	EDUCATION							RELIGION		
		1	2	3	4	5	6	7	Prot.	Cath.	Jew.
COMEDY-VARIETY	47%	55%	54%	41%	50%	44%	36%	51%	46%	46%	62%
Family situation	2	1	0	2	3	2	4	6	2	2	6
Situation comedy	20	29	23	15	23	19	17	14	19	21	17
Stand-up, star comedian	11	9	7	6	12	18	12	22	7	14	38
Comedy-variety, regular	7	6	8	8	7	7	3	6	7	6	6
Comedy-variety, special	1	2	0	1	2	1	2	2	1	2	0
Panel, games, light quiz	8	11	13	9	8	6	2	2	8	7	11
"Adult" cartoons	0	0	0	1	0	0	0	0	0	0	0
Other cartoons	3	5	6	3	1	4	4	3	4	1	0
Comedy-variety, other	1	0	1	1	1	0	2	0	1	0	0
Base: 100% = 1377*		98	217	312	412	121	112	63	924	340	53

* Includes 42 cases unclassified as to education.

NOTE: Multiple responses.

Situation comedy declines with education, but the popularity of star comedians *increases* at roughly the same rate, and the trend is even more evident in the religious differences.[8]

Leading favorite personalities of the past are also almost entirely confined to comedians, a few popular singers, Arthur Godfrey, and Edward R. Murrow (see next page). The specific wording of the question may be partly responsible for this result: "personalities or stars" may be somewhat more appropriate labels for Sid Caesar and Imogene Coca than for Alistair Cooke or Bergen Evans, but they are not altogether inapplicable to the latter, or to dramatic or musical performers.

In addition, these objects of viewer nostalgia need to be seen against the sum total of what television has provided viewers to be nostalgic about. If TV has produced more or better comedy than anything else, it is no wonder that such programming predominates in past favorites, and hence this finding does not necessarily warrant conclusions regarding inherent or potential viewer preferences.[9]

But choosing from what they have had to choose from—and there has been a substantial range of programming within seasons and over the decade—the public seems most loyal to the comic. By almost all measures of the impact of regular programming (as against the "highlights" or "great moments" to follow), those shows that have made people laugh seem to have made the most lasting impression.

One more brief speculation regarding the exceptionally widespread loyalty surrounding Caesar-Coca and Gleason-Carney: both of these combinations, at their peak, were Saturday-night entries. In addition, such favorites as *Gunsmoke,* Palladin, Perry Mason, and the perpetual Ed Sullivan all made their mark on week-end evenings.

If Saturday and Sunday night have in fact produced more than their fair share of favorites and programs fondly recalled,[1] it may be

---

[8] Note that if "situation comedy" and "star comedian" are combined, education and religion appear to have little or no effect. This again attests to the inadequacy of the larger, general categories frequently employed in program analysis.

[9] Though specific present or past favorites are not necessarily tied to the *relative* amounts of various program types available. So long as a program is available at all, it can become a "favorite," despite, or even because of, its rarity.

[1] This is a tricky question to answer. It clearly is not enough just to show that Saturday-night ratings exceed those for other evenings, nor does it disprove the point if they do not. There may be differential tendencies to view on various nights regardless of programs, but differential ratings may also be produced by quality differences in programs on the air at different times of the week.

QUESTION 25 *"Are there any personalities or stars that you especially liked who aren't on any more?"*

Number of Respondents
2427

Sid Caesar/Imogene Coca

| Caesar 155 | Coca 49 | 204 |

Jackie Gleason/Art Carney

| Gleason 148 | AC 15 | 163 |

Arthur Godfrey

107

Milton Berle

78

Lucille Ball/Desi Arnaz

| Lucy 46 | Desi 21 | 67 |

Nat Cole

30

Bing Crosby

29

Edward R. Murrow

26

George DeWitt

22

Frank Sinatra

20

Jimmy Durante

18

Eddie Cantor

17

Red Buttons

17

Bob Hope

16

Herb Shriner

16

Jan Murray

16

Bob Cummings

15

Others in Appendix Table 15

simply because the networks tend to schedule their best then. But possibly, also, the "glamor" or relative festivity of week-end activity (party, going out, friends visiting) spills over onto programs that become part of this scene (just as the radio Jack Benny was, for so many years, an integral part of the American Sunday evening). Would the Caesar *Show of Shows* or Jackie Gleason have been quite so star-studded or sparkling on Monday night? And Ed Sullivan seems especially suited to Sunday evenings with friends and family—or is it just ten years of association?

But, as stated at the outset, this is speculation and not finding. The real point in raising the issue is to note again the possibility of an intimate connection between attitudes toward programming—in this case, toward specific shows—and the nature of the situation in which they are seen.

The great moments: These final tables represent the most limited and specific reactions of all; we turn from regular programs or program series, to single broadcast standouts, and even to single episodes *within* broadcasts. From one point of view this is minutiae; from another, it provides an important complement to preferences in "regular" fare. How do the preferences among staples relate to the most memorable viewing experiences?

QUESTION 26A *"Is there any single program or broadcast that you'd like to see again if it could be re-run? (I don't mean a whole series, I mean one particular show— either part of a series or a separate show?)"*

LIGHT ENTERTAINMENT

HEAVY ENTERTAINMENT

NO, NA, DK

INFORMATION & PUBLIC AFFAIRS

EDUCATION

Base: 100% =

ALL	20%	10%	64%	6%	2427*
Grade School	16	7	74	3	627
High School	22	9	64	5	1214
College and Beyond	20	17	54	8	516

MOST FREQUENTLY MENTIONED

Playhouse 90: 73	Science Specials: 32
Evening With Fred Astaire: 65	Green Pastures: 18
War—Documentaries, Movies: 39	I Love Lucy: 16
Peter Pan: 35	**Others in Appendix Table 16**

*Includes 70 cases unclassified as to education

The picture here is not nearly so amusement-oriented. There is still a large proportion of light entertainment, but there is also widespread agreement on particular dramatic presentations, as in the case of *Playhouse 90*—which, incidentally, included a heavy vote for "Requiem for a Heavyweight," initially broadcast more than a year before the survey. This suggests that the repertory concept may not be inherently inapplicable to television. Over time, there may develop a selected sample of "classics" that bear repetition on an annual or even a more frequent basis.[2]

Having noted that, we should also note the fact that fully two thirds of the viewers *cannot* single out any broadcast they would like to see again. The figure does decline from three fourths to one half with increasing education, reflecting the more content-centered viewing approach of the upper-educated. But even for them the response is quite limited, and it focuses strongly on entertainment, not information, and even on light entertainment.

The same lack of response occurs when, finally, we narrow the focus to one most memorable moment:

Q. 27A   *"Considering everything you've ever seen on television, is there some highlight or special moment that stands out in your mind?"*

"No, there isn't" (*not* NA, DK)	29%
Episodes or programs in regular entertainment series	24
News coverage of special events	11
Sports events	7
Documentaries, informational shows	6
Personality—interview	4
DK, NA	19

Base: 100% = 2427

"Regular entertainment" most frequently provides the most memorable single events. Even here, with the emphasis on "highlight or special moment," special programming runs a poor second to regular

[2] This may be one approach to the problem of television's ravenous appetite for talent—the demands imposed on creative abilities by the sheer number of hours in the broadcast schedule.

entertainment, for the viewing public as a whole.

Among the "entertainment" programs, Jack Paar leads with 51 mentions, including 30 for the "walk-off." The complete tabulation appears in Appendix Table 17; here are just a few of the more memorable responses about memorable moments:

> "Good Friday—the story of the Passion turned out very interesting."

> "Liberace show—fine music and high moral status."

> "Twentieth Century program. When Roosevelt said that American boys would not go overseas. I was overseas when I saw it—in the Army."

> "Boston Blackie—we used to watch Boston Blackie a lot. He got killed almost every time. That was kind of interesting, wasn't it?"

> "Ed Sullivan hugging a nigger. Because I then realized for the first time what TV is coming to. I believe it's the communists' best tool. It puts wrong ideas in people's minds and stirs up trouble."

> "What stands out in my mind is that little Kathy Fiscus down in that hole there, they done a good job on that. It was so real, and right on the spot, what was going on and the heroic deeds that went on and trying to save the little girl. I used to come home every night and turn it on to see how they were coming along. Let's see, did they save her? I can't remember."

> "The time it goes off the air."

Re-view

What picture emerges from this variety of approaches to the issue of how the viewing public regards its programs? Before we turn to the analysis of what people *see,* let us try to pull together what they have had to *say* about programming.

First, it seems clear that the General Public—the total undifferentiated audience—is well satisfied with the present fare. This is evident in their general praise of "most programs" ("good," "entertaining," "interesting," "informative"), and also in the scarcity of specific criticisms. Contrast, for example, the predominance of adults' feelings that there is too much violence on the air for children with the absence of any similar, general objections to programs for their own consumption. And nowhere, given the chance, do substantial numbers point to broad or specific oversights in the present schedule. In short, most people think most programs are good.

Dividing the general public into specific segments produces substantial variation in this picture. The response to "programming in general" is far less favorable among the higher-status groups, who are much less likely to approve television fare *in toto*. "Most programs are intended for average people, not for me"; and with this, the average man agrees.

But when the college-educated talk about programs they themselves watch, the general acceptance typical of the mass audience holds also for them, and strongly so. The intellectual viewer discusses his own programs in terms even *more* favorable than those used by his less-educated counterparts with regard to theirs. This implies a high degree of selectivity, which may be somewhat at odds with the extent of his viewing, as self-reported and as documented in the ratings. To put it another way, can and does the college-educated viewer confine himself to those programs he regards highly? The nature and extent of selectivity in various publics will be a major question under inquiry in the next chapter.

The related issue of balance in the schedule is often debated in terms of two dichotomies: *information vs. entertainment,* and *"serious" vs. "light."* These are, of course, not the same: there can be light information (how to fish) and serious entertainment (Eugene O'Neill).

Information vs. entertainment: By many measures, "more information" is the most frequent general request—using the term "information" broadly to include educational programming, advice, food for thought, and so on. Note that this is not to say that entertainment is considered any less important: it may simply be that television is already most nearly adequate on this score, and hence has less room and need for improvement there.

For example, when the question is: "What categories should there be more of?" all viewing groups, regardless of education, concentrate on informational content. But when the question is: "Should there be more information *or* better entertainment?" only the college-educated make the intellectual decision and then by a much smaller margin. More information, yes; but not at the cost of entertainment.

In addition, the higher demand for informative content among the top educational groups may be only partly attributable to their own personal desires. It may be necessary to distinguish between criticisms and requests they make on their own behalf and those that relate to some social criterion they apply to the medium ("I myself don't need more information from television, but the country does"). In short, as in so many social issues, what *"I want"* may be quite different from what *"they should have."*

Finally, when people concentrate on the informative functions of programming, they may again be expressing some ambivalence about spending so much time with TV—especially since the most "guilty" group both demand the most intellectual content *and* attribute the most to their own viewing.

Serious vs. light: As the findings reported in the preceding section move from the most general probes through the discussion of various program categories and finally into the most concrete and specific matters, people's tastes and preferences get somewhat "lighter," more amusement-oriented. The comparison is confounded by the fact that questions regarding actual programs are influenced by the present proportions of various types available, but these are also the most factual queries, those less subject to response bias of various kinds. And the fact remains that the specific present and past favorites are heavily loaded with comedy, action, and light drama—and comedy, especially, remains popular at all educational strata.

Here, for example, is the progression in response of the most highly educated and hence most critical viewing segment, as questions go from general to specific:

Viewers with Education Beyond College

Questions	Serious	Light
Q. 18A "Television today has not enough:"	Education 82% Information 72%	Laughs 28% Relaxation 23% Escape 8%
Q. 41 "Should there be more information or better entertainment?"	Information 40%	Entertainment 20% "Both" 40%

*Q. 21 "Kind of
programs you see
that you'd like to see
more of . . ."*   Information 37%   Light entertain-
                           Heavy entertain-   ment 31%
                             ment 20%

*Q. 24 "Past programs
you liked that
should be returned"*   Information 33%   Comedy-
                           Heavy entertain-   variety 51%
                             ment 16%   Action 14%
                                               Light drama 13%
                                               Light music 14%

*Q. 14-15 "Present
favorites—programs
you watch regularly
or whenever you get
the chance . . ."*   Information 31%   Light entertain-
                           Heavy entertain-   ment 56%
                             ment 11%

As a result, formal schooling, which makes such a crucial difference when people talk about what television *should* be, matters somewhat less in the discussion regarding specific programs. A substantial difference remains, but the abstract or potentially serious tastes of the upper-educated are "lightened" considerably when measured by favored program rather than by categorical response.

Is it just that their specific preferences are, of necessity, limited by the preponderance of light entertainment that has been available? Would they designate serious programs in large numbers if there had been larger numbers of them to designate? Are response biases in the more general questions responsible? Or is it simply a matter of personal versus social evaluation?

A number of interpretations seem reasonable and each involves assumptions regarding the actual viewing habits of various groups. In place of assumptions, the next chapter offers some limited data on this issue.

Chapter 6

WHAT VIEWERS SEE

EACH MONTH the American Research Bureau enlists 1600 television homes across the country to keep a detailed diary of their viewing for a one-week period. These diaries form the basis for the national monthly ratings that ARB provides to broadcasters and advertisers.

From September 1959 through March 1960, some 2700 households in the New York City metropolitan area were contacted as part of this regular national sampling procedure. About 1000 complied, to become part of the ratings for those months. Each residence maintained and returned a diary reporting not only when the set was turned on, and to what channel, but also who in the home watched each program.[1]

In May 1960, or two to eight months later, 312 of these homes were independently visited by interviewers with essentially the same

[1] Some particulars on ARB's sample and methods are in Appendix Table 18. The accuracy of national or local projections based on these sample homes is not of primary concern to our analysis; only the accuracy of the individual diaries in reporting what was seen, and by whom, in the particular homes. On that score, we should mention that the diary-reporting procedure has been checked against direct, mechanical records of hours that sets are in use, with satisfactory results.

questionnaire used in our national survey. The interviewers said nothing of the families' previous participation in the rating panel; they simply went to assigned addresses and interviewed any resident over eighteen years of age. We were then able to return to the original diary record, identify our survey respondent in the diary, and compare questionnaire answers with what he or she actually watched during one seven-day period.

Normal attrition (moving, wrong address, etc.), and cases in which it was impossible to make a positive match between the survey respondent and the various viewers listed in the diary, reduced the sample somewhat. In all, we have diary data *and* a subsequent interview for 237 individual viewers in as many households.

In the following pages, we have two main questions to ask of these viewers. First, for background, how do the program diets selected by various segments—for example, different educational groups—compare with each other and with the total proportions of various program types available during the period?

And then, of greatest interest and central importance, how do actual viewing habits compare with attitudes expressed in the survey?

The Menu vs. the Diet

To start, we need a crude base-line measure of what was available for New York viewers during the eight television-rating weeks covered in the analysis.[2] We focus on the principal viewing hours and exclude weekdays before 6 p.m. so as to maximize the *opportunity* for all members of the panel to view each program considered. (Daytime obviously excludes most of the men, and certainly all of the typical ones.[3])

To provide the fullest picture of availability, we analyzed the composition of the schedule by three different measures: number of *programs;* number of *minutes;* and number of *unduplicated minutes.*

[2] We had to span a total of seven months to get a large enough sample. There was one rating week in each month except November, which provides two. Specifically, the diaries come from the weeks beginning: September 20, October 18, November 8, November 15, December 3, January 13, February 23, March 1.

[3] Any time period rules out some people who are not usually at home then, but concentration on evenings and week-ends probably minimized the number who are ipso facto *unable* to watch. This also matches the time during which the national survey interviews were conducted with all men, and half of the women, and for the same basic reason.

The MENU —Total TV Fare:

6 pm to sign off on weekdays, and all day
Saturday and Sunday. All seven New York channels,
for weeks of September 20, October 18,
November 8, November 15, December 3, 1959;
January 13, February 23, March 1, 1960

LIGHT ENTERTAINMENT

HEAVY ENTERTAINMENT

NEWS

INFORMATION & PUBLIC AFFAIRS

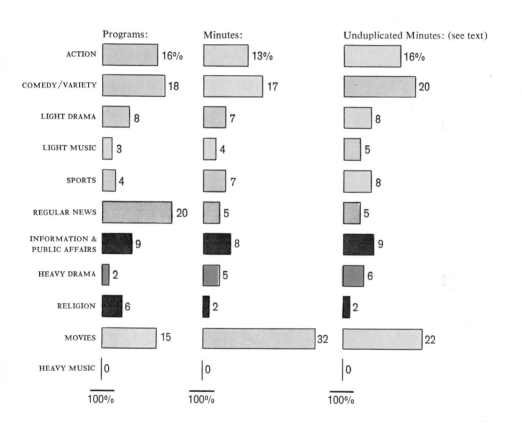

	Programs:	Minutes:	Unduplicated Minutes: (see text)
ACTION	16%	13%	16%
COMEDY/VARIETY	18	17	20
LIGHT DRAMA	8	7	8
LIGHT MUSIC	3	4	5
SPORTS	4	7	8
REGULAR NEWS	20	5	5
INFORMATION & PUBLIC AFFAIRS	9	8	9
HEAVY DRAMA	2	5	6
RELIGION	6	2	2
MOVIES	15	32	22
HEAVY MUSIC	0	0	0
	100%	100%	100%

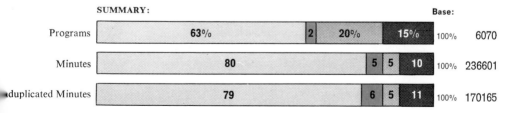

SUMMARY:						Base:
Programs	63%	2	20%	15%	100%	6070
Minutes	80	5	5	10	100%	236601
Unduplicated Minutes	79	6	5	11	100%	170165

The last is simply a measure of how many minutes a viewer could have turned to a given type of program; two one-hour westerns broadcast at the same time would produce a total of only 60 minutes of *un*duplicated availability, whereas one after another provide 120 minutes of available westerns.

This distinction turns out to be a rather elaborate way of showing that movies often tend to be on several channels at the same time. In most other categories the relative *proportions* of various program types are about the same, whether based on total or unduplicated minutes.

The comparison between programs and minutes also holds no surprises. It documents the fact that news shows are considerably shorter than the average, accounting for 20 per cent of all programs but only 5 per cent of broadcast time; and that the converse is true of movies, sports, and heavy drama.

With these technical differences in mind, and remembering that this represents all offerings by the seven channels then clearly received in the New York area, let us see what the viewers had to choose from.

First of all, it is clear that they were offered mostly "light entertainment" (comedy-variety, action, light movies, light drama, sports, and light music, in that order). Altogether, such programs account for nearly two thirds of the total number, and an even larger share of all air time (principally because of late and late-late movies). Regular newscasts and other information–public affairs shows each contribute another fifth or so, and the remaining fraction goes to "heavy entertainment" (heavy drama, including film classics; and classical music).

If we separate out Saturday and Sunday daytime broadcasts (before 6 p.m.), the "intellectual ghetto" appears, and with walls about as high as often implied:

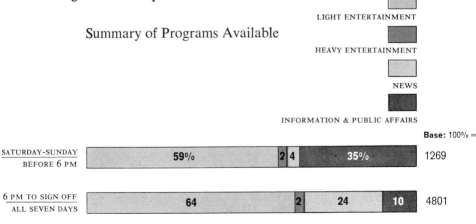

Summary of Programs Available

LIGHT ENTERTAINMENT

HEAVY ENTERTAINMENT

NEWS

INFORMATION & PUBLIC AFFAIRS

Base: 100% =

SATURDAY-SUNDAY BEFORE 6 PM	59%	2 4	35%	1269
6 PM TO SIGN OFF ALL SEVEN DAYS	64	2	24	10	4801

Over one third of all week-end "daytime" programs are information–public affairs (including religion), as against only 10 per cent during the seven evenings—though the evening hours contain more regular newscasts.

Looked at another way, the week-end concentration of public affairs appears still more striking: of all such programs broadcast during the eight weeks, fully half were on the air on Saturday or Sunday before 6 p.m. And most of these, of course, appear on Sunday. Here are the figures, separating religion from other public affairs:

Per cent of the average week's total, broadcast on:

	Saturday before 6 p.m.	Sunday before 6 p.m.	6 p.m. to signoff all seven days	Base:
Religion	14%	37%	49%	100% = 336
Information and public affairs	11	38	51	100% = 547

In general then, this program classification of eight weeks of New York television, stretching across a major part of the season, supports two observations that are often made, and often made critically:

1. Most of the schedule *is* devoted to easy entertainment—even when measured by number of programs, and overwhelmingly so when put in terms of time consumed. Heavy drama is infrequent, even by a fairly loose definition of "heavy,"[4] and classical music was so rare that rounding the percentage reduced it to zero.

2. Serious, intellectual programming *is* largely concentrated on Sundays, and then before the prime evening hours. We should point out that the early-morning educational programs, like *Continental Classroom,* are not included in this tally, which begins at 6 p.m. on weekdays; but then, neither are the daytime serials, panel shows, and re-runs.

At the same time, the more detailed program classification does reveal some exaggeration in the common critical stereotype of the program mix. For example, westerns of all types made up only 6 per cent of the schedule; and crime of all (other) kinds, only another 7 per cent. (Both these figures exclude regular movies.) This full analysis, which

---

[4] Not only *Macbeth,* or *Play of the Week,* that is, but also some items on *General Electric Theatre, Armstrong Circle Theatre,* etc.; and "substantial" movies, e.g., *The Bridge of San Luis Rey.*

Program Composition:
The DIET vs. the MENU

LIGHT ENTERTAINMENT

HEAVY ENTERTAINMENT

NEWS

INFORMATION & PUBLIC AFFAIRS

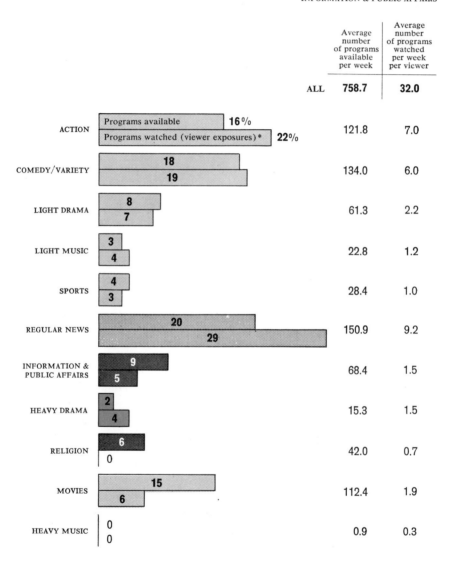

	Average number of programs available per week	Average number of programs watched per week per viewer
ALL	**758.7**	**32.0**
ACTION — Programs available 16% / Programs watched (viewer exposures)* 22%	121.8	7.0
COMEDY/VARIETY — 18 / 19	134.0	6.0
LIGHT DRAMA — 8 / 7	61.3	2.2
LIGHT MUSIC — 3 / 4	22.8	1.2
SPORTS — 4 / 3	28.4	1.0
REGULAR NEWS — 20 / 29	150.9	9.2
INFORMATION & PUBLIC AFFAIRS — 9 / 5	68.4	1.5
HEAVY DRAMA — 2 / 4	15.3	1.5
RELIGION — 6 / 0	42.0	0.7
MOVIES — 15 / 6	112.4	1.9
HEAVY MUSIC — 0 / 0	0.9	0.3

SUMMARY:

Base: 100% =

Programs Available	63%	2	20%	15	6070
Programs Watched	61	4	29	5	7406*

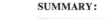

*All programs watched by all viewers

divides programs into 47 narrow groupings, appears as Appendix Table 19.

Finally, we should note that New York City did not then have an educational channel; these figures represent offerings of regular, commercial stations.

Now, how closely does the viewers' chosen diet match these availabilities? Do people take various types of programs in about the same ratios in which they are offered? We make this and all subsequent comparisons in terms of number of programs (rather than minutes).[5]

When it comes to entertainment, there is close agreement between the proportions offered and the proportions consumed. The public taste shows no concentration in rare program types; nor, more significantly, does it neglect any heavily represented category (except for movies, which are both late and duplicated). In short, the people take about as much or as little action, comedy-variety, light drama, etc., as they are given, and/or the industry gives them about as much of each major program type as they will take.

But the two classes of informational programming do diverge noticeably—menu vs. diet—and so does religion, which is sometimes offered but virtually never watched. Regular newscasts are heavily selected —they make up half again as large a share of the average diet as they do of the menu—and information-public affairs programs diverge in just the opposite direction—which must have a great deal to do with their concentration in hours that are often unattended.

The explanation for the heavy selection of news, assuming there is no bias in the diary recording,[6] may be found in the habitual, daily

---

[5] There are several reasons for this choice. First of all, the diaries do not produce detailed data on the amount of time any given viewer spent with a program —just whether or not he "watched." Thus, our basic unit of information is (any) exposure to a program; we have no information regarding how much time was spent with it. Second, and perhaps more important, our interest is chiefly in the selections made, and the more meaningful unit of selection is the program. A decision to watch a one-hour detective story is not equivalent to the selection of two independent half hours; a viewer who chooses twelve different five-minute newscasts and one ninety-minute movie for the week, is clearly more selective toward information than one who watches a one-hour news special and the same movie.

[6] Throughout this section, we will take viewers entirely at their word in the diaries. We assume that response bias in diaries, if any, would operate toward reporting an "acceptable" viewing pattern. Thus any discrepancy between what viewers say and what they see exists despite, and not because of, any tendency to "cheat" in the diaries.

viewing of one or more short newscasts, perhaps analogous to news-paper reading. Some people who "don't watch television" on a given evening may still tune to one or more news and weather reports. View-ing for information may be a more deliberate, if possibly routine, use of the set, whereas the specific type of entertainment taken is perhaps a more passive "decision," depending largely on what is there.

But by and large, all of the programs watched by all of the viewers divide roughly into the same proportions as all of the programs offered during prime hours. Except perhaps for loyalty to news, there is little indication of total-audience selectivity for or against broad or narrow[7] categories of programming. And this result matches the survey finding that the audience as a whole is satisfied with television programming in general.

But we did find marked differences between the program tastes and desires expressed by various segments of the audience, and especial-ly the amount of selectivity they report or imply. Here is our first look at the actual viewing habits of these groups.

The Diet According to "Background"

We start with the all-important analysis of programs watched by different educational groups. This chart provides an over-view of how their viewing is distributed.

With college education, people devote less of their viewing to action, and a trifle more to news, public affairs, and heavy drama. But the differences are not large, nor are they always progressive with edu-cation. The diet of the second highest group, for example, is virtually indistinguishable from that selected by the very lowest. On the whole, it is the high-school graduates who appear to have the "lightest" tastes of all.

So the program mix of different educational groups is strikingly constant especially in terms of the relative amounts of information vs. entertainment consumed. A college education, as against grade school, reduces the proportion given to all entertainment from 63 per cent to 62 per cent (for light entertainment, from 60 per cent to 56 per cent)! And even those with graduate or professional training, which makes the greatest difference, devote 53 per cent to entertainment (and 46 per cent to the light variety).

[7] See Appendix Table 20.

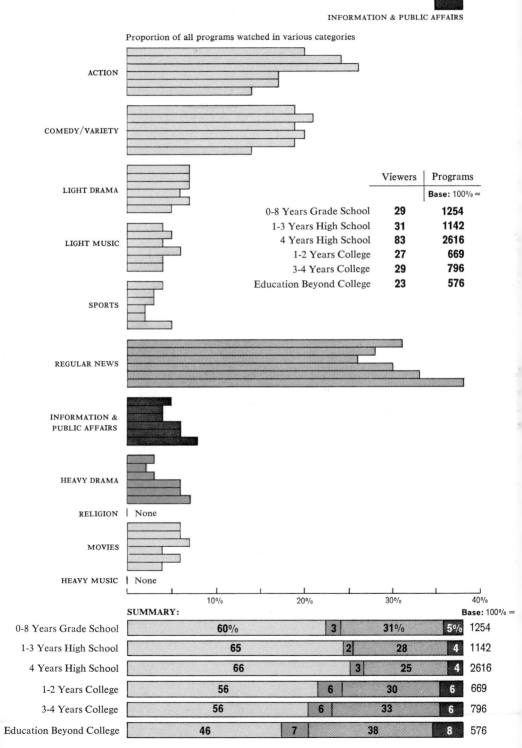

The DIET by Education:

LIGHT ENTERTAINMENT
HEAVY ENTERTAINMENT
NEWS
INFORMATION & PUBLIC AFFAIRS

Proportion of all programs watched in various categories

ACTION

COMEDY/VARIETY

LIGHT DRAMA

LIGHT MUSIC

SPORTS

REGULAR NEWS

INFORMATION &
PUBLIC AFFAIRS

HEAVY DRAMA

RELIGION | None

MOVIES

HEAVY MUSIC | None

	Viewers	Programs
		Base: 100% =
0-8 Years Grade School	29	1254
1-3 Years High School	31	1142
4 Years High School	83	2616
1-2 Years College	27	669
3-4 Years College	29	796
Education Beyond College	23	576

10%   20%   30%   40%

SUMMARY: Base: 100% =

0-8 Years Grade School	60%	3	31%	5%	1254
1-3 Years High School	65	2	28	4	1142
4 Years High School	66	3	25	4	2616
1-2 Years College	56	6	30	6	669
3-4 Years College	56	6	33	6	796
Education Beyond College	46	7	38	8	576

But *proportions* themselves do not tell the whole story, since there are clear and consistent differences in the total number of programs watched. The absolutes need to be taken into account as well as the relatives.

1. Up to the college level, people watch fewer programs per week as education increases; after that, the level remains constant.[8] This is the most consistent and overriding relationship between formal schooling and viewing. Whether these differences in total consumption are seen as surprisingly large or surprisingly small rests on one's preconceptions. The fact is that those with the most education watch (only or fully) 63 per cent as many programs, on the average, as those with the least.

2. The drop does not come equally from all program categories. Compare the two extremes: those with education beyond college watch only about a third as many movies; about half as much other light entertainment (comedy, action, light drama, and light music); three quarters as many newscasts; about the same amount of informa-tion-public affairs; and more heavy drama.

So in absolute terms, the only category of program more frequently selected by the better-educated is heavy drama. When it comes to news and public affairs, the highly educated exceed the middle groups but do not match the exposure of those with the least formal schooling.[9]

Now, whether absolute or relative comparisons are the best indica-tion of what is selected is a good question. Is someone who watches fifteen newscasts and five movies more interested in televised informa-tion than another viewer who sees thirty newscasts and twenty movies in the same period? Should a college graduate get credit for more in-terest in world affairs because he watches fewer westerns?[1]

In any case, we have both pieces of information, and the finding, if not yet the interpretation, is clear: the intellectual critics, who above all else and above all others request "more information," see no more

---

[8] In addition, there is little difference in the variability or range of exposure within each group.

[9] The U-shaped curve is interesting here. We might speculate that the lowest groups depend on television for their news, the middle groups make the classical choice of print, while those at the very top supplement their print information with newscasts.

[1] The question is similar to this one: Who "cares more" about opera—someone who never leaves the house except to attend two or three performances a year, or someone who attends the full season and also every baseball game, movie, ballet, and dog show.

Average Number of Programs Watched, Per Week, Per Viewer

 LIGHT ENTERTAINMENT

 HEAVY ENTERTAINMENT

NEWS

INFORMATION & PUBLIC AFFAIRS

 ALL

EDUCATION	0-8 Yrs. Grade School	1-3 Yrs. High School	4 Yrs. High School	1-2 Yrs. College	3-4 Yrs. College	Education Beyond College
Number of Viewers	29	31	83	27	29	23
ACTION	8.0	9.0	8.3	4.3	4.7	3.6
COMEDY/VARIETY	7.4	7.6	6.1	5.0	5.1	3.5
LIGHT DRAMA	3.0	2.5	2.3	1.4	2.0	1.3
LIGHT MUSIC	1.6	1.7	1.4	1.5	1.2	0.9
SPORTS	1.5	1.1	0.9	0.6	0.6	1.3
REGULAR NEWS	12.5	10.4	8.1	7.5	9.0	9.5
INFORMATION & PUBLIC AFFAIRS	2.0	1.6	1.2	1.6	1.7	2.0
HEAVY DRAMA	1.1	0.7	1.0	1.6	1.6	1.7
RELIGION	0.2	0	0	0.1	0	0
MOVIES	2.5	2.1	2.2	1.1	1.5	0.9
HEAVY MUSIC	0.1	0	0	0.1	0	0

SUMMARY:

	0-8 Yrs. Grade School	1-3 Yrs. High School	4 Yrs. High School	1-2 Yrs. College	3-4 Yrs. College	Education Beyond College
LIGHT ENTERTAINMENT	23.9	24.0	21.2	14.0	15.1	11.5
HEAVY ENTERTAINMENT	1.2	0.7	1.0	1.6	1.6	1.7
NEWS	12.5	10.4	8.1	7.5	9.0	9.5
INFORMATION & PUBLIC AFFAIRS	2.1	1.6	1.2	1.7	1.7	2.0
ALL	40	37	32	25	27	25

of it in total; moreover it accounts for an only slightly higher percentage of their less extensive use of the medium.

Alongside formal education, religion ranked as a most significant background variable in the survey itself. In the national sample, Jews were strikingly different from Catholics and Protestants in their attitudes toward television, its programs in general, and their own favorites. But the general mix selected by this New York sample shows only that Catholics view somewhat more and lighter programs, while Jews and Protestants turn out to be indistinguishable from one another in program diet. (Appendix Table 30.)

In part, these apparent discrepancies between survey responses and viewing may reflect the difference between measuring attitudes and behavior. But, despite these general similarities in the diets selected by various cultural groups, some differences remain. We will see these in a moment, and reserve conclusions until then.

The Diet According to Sex and Life Cycle

On page 68, after reviewing the effects of various audience characteristics on people's feelings about viewing, we concluded:

> . . . whatever the reason, general cultural factors, as reflected in educational and religious differences, seem to have a lot to do with how people feel about viewing—much more, in fact, than the effects of such "basic" distinctions as age, sex, or urban-rural differences.

Now we have some indication that actual program selections are not nearly so sensitive to these cultural variables. Does the converse hold? Do the basic factors on "life position" show relatively *more* influence on what programs people actually watch?

The most basic distinction of all has little effect: men and women report about the same amount of viewing (remember, this is for evenings and week-ends), and their diets are virtually identical. Those small differences that do appear are all in the expected direction: men take a trifle more news and public affairs, action, and sports, whereas women are somewhat more partial to comedy-variety and movies. Overall, women's diet is a little lighter than men's, but only a little: the most impressive aspect of these differences is their negligible magnitude.

A major portion of this apparent similarity in tastes no doubt comes

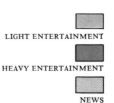

LIGHT ENTERTAINMENT

HEAVY ENTERTAINMENT

NEWS

INFORMATION & PUBLIC AFFAIRS

The DIET by Sex:

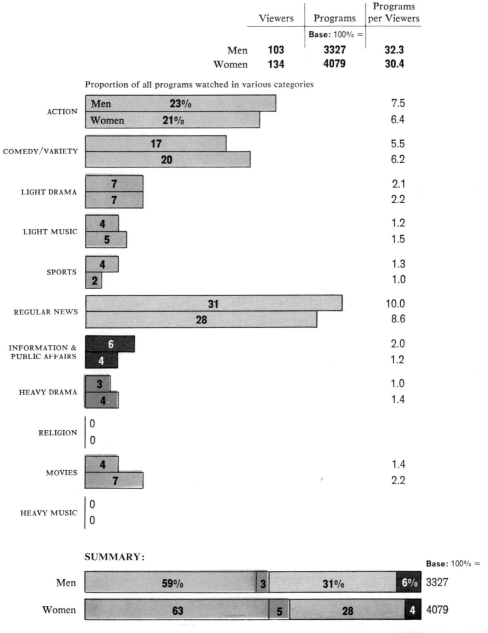

	Viewers	Programs	Programs per Viewers
		Base: 100% =	
Men	103	3327	32.3
Women	134	4079	30.4

Proportion of all programs watched in various categories

Category		Men	Women
ACTION	Men 23% / Women 21%	7.5	6.4
COMEDY/VARIETY	17 / 20	5.5	6.2
LIGHT DRAMA	7 / 7	2.1	2.2
LIGHT MUSIC	4 / 5	1.2	1.5
SPORTS	4 / 2	1.3	1.0
REGULAR NEWS	31 / 28	10.0	8.6
INFORMATION & PUBLIC AFFAIRS	6 / 4	2.0	1.2
HEAVY DRAMA	3 / 4	1.0	1.4
RELIGION	0 / 0		
MOVIES	4 / 7	1.4	2.2
HEAVY MUSIC	0 / 0		

SUMMARY:

Base: 100% =

Men	59%	3	31%	6%	3327
Women	63	5	28	4	4079

Note: Differences between summary totals and detail entries are due to rounding. For example: Heavy Entertainment shows 5% as the sum of Heavy Drama 4%, and Heavy Music 0%

from the simple fact that husband and wife cannot watch different programs on the same set at the same time. To the extent that reported
programs were viewed jointly, the diets of the two sexes necessarily
converge. This raises some interesting questions about the selection of
TV: Who chooses the "togetherness" programs? How does the decision get made? And it points again to the importance of the physical
characteristics of different media: what men read in magazines is quite
a bit different from what gets selected by women, even within the covers
of the same issue. But only single people, or unhappily married ones
with two, unshared sets, have such selective autonomy in the case of
television.

Parenthood, which tends to make a difference in so many things,
does affect the programs selected, or at least the programs *watched*—
they may often be chosen by the children, though it does not seem likely
they are picked *for* them.

First, parents of children under fifteen see fewer programs in total,
which is not to say that the set is used fewer hours—the difference probably reflects the time commandeered exclusively by the children. And
when they watch, they select substantially more action, less news and
public affairs. (These two categories can reasonably be interpreted as
the two that, respectively, interest and bore children the most.) Thus,
viewers with young children at home give no evidence of sacrificing the
kind of programming they consider most harmful for their children. If
anything, the opposite seems true: program concession to the children,
rather than compensation for their presence, is suggested.

The effects of young children vs. their absence may also have
something to do with the surprising differences between age groups. In
sheer number of programs, older viewers watch substantially more television, and most of the increment comes from newscasts and public affairs! There is also a slight over-all increase in light entertainment, but
by and large, the older segments simply switch from action to comedy-
variety for their escape.

As a result, age has more, and more consistent, effects on the information-entertainment ratio than does education. And since today's
older people, on the average, have less formal schooling, the effects of

LIGHT ENTERTAINMENT

HEAVY ENTERTAINMENT

NEWS

INFORMATION & PUBLIC AFFAIRS

The DIET:
Parents of Children Under 15 vs. All Others

	Viewers	Programs	Programs per Viewer
		Base: 100% =	
Parents	118	3196	27.1
All Others	112	4052	36.2

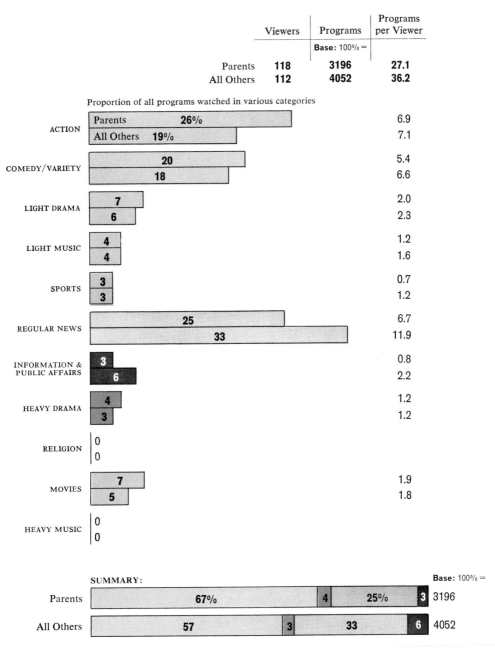

Proportion of all programs watched in various categories

Category			Programs per Viewer
ACTION	Parents	26%	6.9
	All Others	19%	7.1
COMEDY/VARIETY		20	5.4
		18	6.6
LIGHT DRAMA		7	2.0
		6	2.3
LIGHT MUSIC		4	1.2
		4	1.6
SPORTS		3	0.7
		3	1.2
REGULAR NEWS		25	6.7
		33	11.9
INFORMATION & PUBLIC AFFAIRS		3	0.8
		6	2.2
HEAVY DRAMA		4	1.2
		3	1.2
RELIGION		0	
		0	
MOVIES		7	1.9
		5	1.8
HEAVY MUSIC		0	
		0	

SUMMARY:

Base: 100% =

Parents	67% 4 25% 3	3196
All Others	57 3 33 6	4052

The DIET by Age:

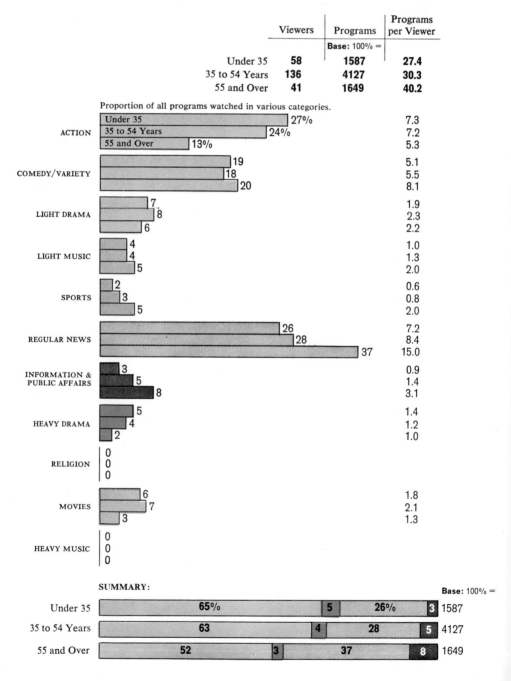

	Viewers	Programs	Programs per Viewer
		Base: 100% =	
Under 35	58	1587	27.4
35 to 54 Years	136	4127	30.3
55 and Over	41	1649	40.2

Proportion of all programs watched in various categories.

ACTION
- Under 35 — 27% — 7.3
- 35 to 54 Years — 24% — 7.2
- 55 and Over — 13% — 5.3

COMEDY/VARIETY
- 19 — 5.1
- 18 — 5.5
- 20 — 8.1

LIGHT DRAMA
- 7 — 1.9
- 8 — 2.3
- 6 — 2.2

LIGHT MUSIC
- 4 — 1.0
- 4 — 1.3
- 5 — 2.0

SPORTS
- 2 — 0.6
- 3 — 0.8
- 5 — 2.0

REGULAR NEWS
- 26 — 7.2
- 28 — 8.4
- 37 — 15.0

INFORMATION & PUBLIC AFFAIRS
- 3 — 0.9
- 5 — 1.4
- 8 — 3.1

HEAVY DRAMA
- 5 — 1.4
- 4 — 1.2
- 2 — 1.0

RELIGION
- 0
- 0
- 0

MOVIES
- 6 — 1.8
- 7 — 2.1
- 3 — 1.3

HEAVY MUSIC
- 0
- 0
- 0

SUMMARY: Base: 100% =

Under 35	65%	5	26%	3 — 1587
35 to 54 Years	63	4	28	5 — 4127
55 and Over	52	3	37	8 — 1649

age are even more pronounced than these totals indicate. Here are age differences *within* the two major educational groups:

HIGH SCHOOL OR LESS

Age	Light Entertainment	Heavy Entertainment	News	Information & Public Affairs	Viewers	Programs Base: 100%	Programs per Viewer
Under 35	73%	3%	22%	2%	30	894	30
35–54	66	3	27	4	83	2780	33
55 and over	56	3	34	7	29	1233	43

COLLEGE OR BEYOND

	Light Entertainment	Heavy Entertainment	News	Information & Public Affairs	Viewers	Programs Base: 100%	Programs per Viewer
Under 35	53%	9%	33%	5%	23	595	26
35–54	59	7	28	6	44	1027	23
55 and over	38	2	47	13	11	384	35

While the pattern is roughly progressive throughout the range, the biggest jump in the absolute and relative consumption of news occurs after fifty years of age. Perhaps increasing reading difficulties turn some of these people to TV as their principal source of news; or possibly older viewers, on a less active schedule, become more habituated to tuning to their favorite daily newscast. But whatever the reason, they average over twice as many news shows per week as those under thirty-five.

So this overview of the program mix selected by various segments provides an interesting contrast:

Cultural groups who had widely different opinions on the issues of television and its programs—especially with respect to information-entertainment—do not differ nearly so much in their viewing ratios.

On the other hand, some more prosaic and "basic" characteristics that played little if any role in expressed attitudes—parenthood and most notably age—matter a great deal in how much informational broadcasting is consumed. And that holds in absolute as well as relative amounts.

The contrast is clearly drawn in the comparison chart on the following two pages.

Responses Compared to Viewing, According to Age:

IN THE NATIONAL SURVEY: No increase in information requested with advancing age

QUESTION 41 *"Should there be more information or better entertainment?"*

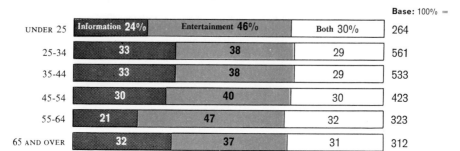

			Base: 100% =
UNDER 25	Information 24%	Entertainment 46%	Both 30%	264
25-34	33	38	29	561
35-44	33	38	29	533
45-54	30	40	30	423
55-64	21	47	32	323
65 AND OVER	32	37	31	312

QUESTION 18A *"Does television today have enough information?"*

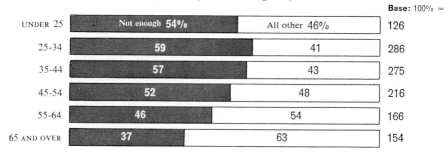

			Base: 100% =
UNDER 25	Not enough 54%	All other 46%	126
25-34	59	41	286
35-44	57	43	275
45-54	52	48	216
55-64	46	54	166
65 AND OVER	37	63	154

IN THE ARB SAMPLE: Marked increase in information consumed with advancing age

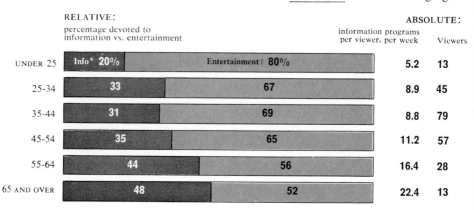

	RELATIVE: percentage devoted to information vs. entertainment		ABSOLUTE: information programs per viewer, per week	Viewers
UNDER 25	Info* 20%	Entertainment† 80%	5.2	13
25-34	33	67	8.9	45
35-44	31	69	8.8	79
45-54	35	65	11.2	57
55-64	44	56	16.4	28
65 AND OVER	48	52	22.4	13

*News, Other Information, Public Affairs
+All other

Responses Compared to Viewing, According to Education:

QUESTION 41 *"Should there be more information or better entertainment?"*

EDUCATION		Base: 100% =

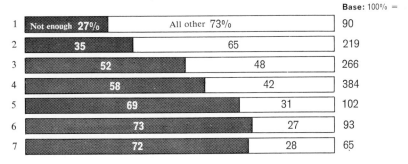

		Base: 100% =
1	Information 29% / Entertainment 47% / Both 24%	203
2	26 / 48 / 26	424
3	26 / 44 / 30	531
4	30 / 41 / 29	683
5	38 / 25 / 37	208
6	40 / 26 / 34	194
7	40 / 20 / 40	114

QUESTION 18A *"Does television today have enough information?"*

		Base: 100% =
1	Not enough 27% / All other 73%	90
2	35 / 65	219
3	52 / 48	266
4	58 / 42	384
5	69 / 31	102
6	73 / 27	93
7	72 / 28	65

IN THE ARB SAMPLE: Little if any increase in information consumed with advancing education

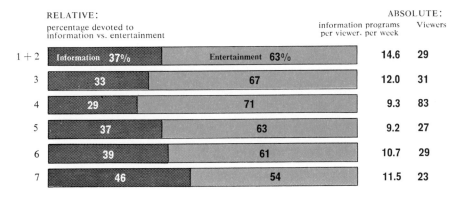

	RELATIVE: percentage devoted to information vs. entertainment	ABSOLUTE: information programs per viewer, per week	Viewers
1 + 2	Information 37% / Entertainment 63%	14.6	29
3	33 / 67	12.0	31
4	29 / 71	9.3	83
5	37 / 63	9.2	27
6	39 / 61	10.7	29
7	46 / 54	11.5	23

All of this *implies* that there is little association between attitudes on these matters, at least as expressed in an interview, and how the TV set is actually used. Is it, as critics may have said of the Kinsey report, that education and "background" does not particularly affect what people do, just what they say, how they say it, and how they feel about it—whereas the fundamental, biological facts have little influence on verbal sophistication, just on actual behavior?

But these data come from two different samples: the attitudes, from a close-to-random national sample; the behavior, from a highly selected New York Area sample. They can imply but certainly not document the relationship between survey replies and viewing. We can approach conclusions on this score only by comparing what the *same* people say and do. And that is the principal analysis to which we now put the 237 ARB viewers.

What They See by What They Say

In this section, we compare what ARB viewers told us in the survey with what they themselves saw during their previous diary-reported week. Here as before, the "programs seen" include only those watched *by the particular individual we interviewed,* not all of those reported for the entire household during the rating week.

First, the table on page 182 shows the over-all viewing of groups who take different positions on the matter of information vs. entertainment. Those who elect "more information" watch about as much television as those who vote for "better entertainment"; and they do select a slightly more informative program mix. But viewers who want "both" not only watch slightly more *in toto* but also select the *highest* rate of informational programs. These small differences are interesting, and perhaps of some theoretical significance. But in response to the primary question—How much do they mean it?—the overriding similarity implies "not much," at least not for their personal consumption. Light entertainment retains the lion's share of each group's viewing. Information, in total, ranges only from a low of 29 to a high of 39 per cent.

Furthermore, the respondents' answers to an absolute evaluation of the present supply of TV information make still less difference (page 183). People who say television has "not enough information" for themselves devote 39 per cent of their own viewing to it, whereas those who report there is already "enough" or "too much" give it only 5 per cent less. Moreover, the responses to other parts of question 18 that probed the adequacy of light entertainment were no more predictive of actual program selections: those who say there is "not enough" escape or laughs watch no more in the matching categories than does the rest of the public. (See Appendix Table 21.)

To what extent are these general similarities in diet due to the viewer's inability to be selective because TV does not offer him enough choice—at least for the amount of time he watches, or during the right hours? Perhaps people are selective whenever they get the chance; perhaps the total diets fail to differ much bcause viewers are swamped by a high percentage of programs watched under no-choice conditions. If three out of four evening hours offer *only* light entertainment, then anybody who watches during all those four hours must "choose" a minimum of 75 per cent in this category.

To be sure, he always has the option of not watching, and the

The DIET by answers to:

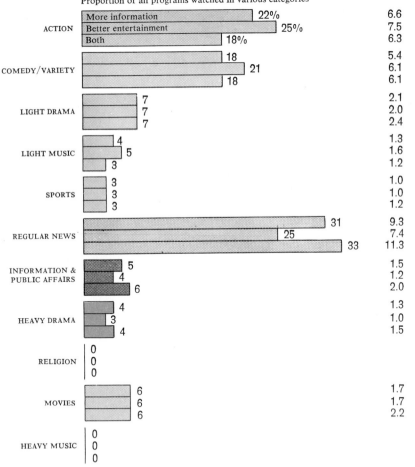

QUESTION 41 *"Generally speaking, would you say that television should do more in the way of providing informational material, or should it concentrate on providing the best entertainment possible?"*

LIGHT ENTERTAINMENT

HEAVY ENTERTAINMENT

NEWS

INFORMATION & PUBLIC AFFAIRS

	Viewers	Programs	Programs per Viewer
		Base: 100% =	
"More information"	75	2261	30.1
"Better entertainment"	89	2627	29.5
"Both"	73	2518	34.5

Proportion of all programs watched in various categories

ACTION
- More information 22% — 6.6
- Better entertainment 25% — 7.5
- Both 18% — 6.3

COMEDY/VARIETY
- 18 — 5.4
- 21 — 6.1
- 18 — 6.1

LIGHT DRAMA
- 7 — 2.1
- 7 — 2.0
- 7 — 2.4

LIGHT MUSIC
- 4 — 1.3
- 5 — 1.6
- 3 — 1.2

SPORTS
- 3 — 1.0
- 3 — 1.0
- 3 — 1.2

REGULAR NEWS
- 31 — 9.3
- 25 — 7.4
- 33 — 11.3

INFORMATION & PUBLIC AFFAIRS
- 5 — 1.5
- 4 — 1.2
- 6 — 2.0

HEAVY DRAMA
- 4 — 1.3
- 3 — 1.0
- 4 — 1.5

RELIGION
- 0 —
- 0 —
- 0 —

MOVIES
- 6 — 1.7
- 6 — 1.7
- 6 — 2.2

HEAVY MUSIC
- 0 —
- 0 —
- 0 —

SUMMARY:

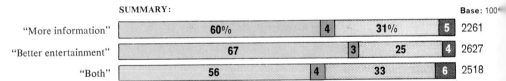

				Base: 100%
"More information"	60%	4	31%	5 — 2261
"Better entertainment"	67	3	25	4 — 2627
"Both"	56	4	33	6 — 2518

The DIET by answers to:

QUESTION 18A *"From your point of view, does television today have enough, not enough or too many . . . programs that provide information?"** *

LIGHT ENTERTAINMENT

HEAVY ENTERTAINMENT

NEWS

INFORMATION & PUBLIC AFFAIRS

	Viewers	Programs	Programs per Viewer
		Base: 100% =	
"Not enough information"	**61**	**1927**	**31.6**
"Enough," "too much," AO	**53**	**1814**	**34.2**

Proportion of **all** programs watched in various categories

ACTION	Not enough **22%**	7.1
	Enough, AO **23%**	7.9
COMEDY/VARIETY	**17**	5.3
	18	6.3
LIGHT DRAMA	**6**	2.0
	7	2.4
LIGHT MUSIC	**4**	1.3
	4	1.4
SPORTS	**2**	0.7
	4	1.2
REGULAR NEWS	**34**	10.6
	30	10.4
INFORMATION & PUBLIC AFFAIRS	**5**	1.6
	4	1.3
HEAVY DRAMA	**3**	1.0
	3	1.0
RELIGION	0	
	0	
MOVIES	**6**	1.8
	6	2.2
HEAVY MUSIC	0	
	0	

SUMMARY: Base: 100% =

ot enough information"	**58%**	**3**	**34%**	**5**	1927
ugh," "too much," AO	**62**	**3**	**30**	**4**	1814

*Recall that this question was asked in two forms, personal and projective. For purposes of this comparison, we use only those viewers who reported on their own desires, not those who were asked about "most people"

viewer who allows himself to be "forced" to consume whatever is on the air is not so selective as one who sometimes simply turns off the set. But that does not answer the essential argument: he might prefer and watch more serious programming if it were available at the time.

Similarly, it might be argued that the response "not enough information" is in no way impugned by the failure to watch a larger number or percentage of such programs: it may come in large part from precisely those who do *not* see a lot of it because it is not available when they watch.

The critical hours: To examine such arguments, we turn to our most limited but also most sensitive and most interesting data. This material provides a rough indication of viewer selectivity when given a choice between light entertainment and more serious programming.

Here is the general procedure:

First, we scanned the television listings and marked various times that provided significant alternatives—for example, hours when a documentary or news special on one channel opposed entertainment on others. We call these the "critical hours."[2]

Next, we examine each diary to see what our survey respondent was doing at the time. There are three possibilities:

a) The television set was off or the respondent himself was not watching.

b) He was watching television and saw the "critical" program.

c) He was watching, but saw something else ("missed the opportunity").

There is still the question of who in the family had the most to say about what was watched at the time. But condition (b) vs. condition (c) puts the viewer to the finest test. We know he was at home and watching TV; and we know that he had a program choice related to a basic survey question. What did he see, and how does it relate to his opinions?

[2] More accurately, they are most often "critical half hours."

What Viewers Select When Information Is Available

Analysis of the eight broadcast weeks gave us a number of opportunities to see what viewers selected when some form of information was being broadcast. As in our previous analyses, "information" divides into two classes: regular news and other information or public affairs broadcasts. For purposes of this test, we restrict the second category to "heavy" programs so that there can be little question about whether or not they qualify as informative. (That is, we exclude how-to, advice, travel, and so on. A list of examples appears in Appendix Table 22.)

Heavy information, excluding regular news Here, then, are results of the first analysis. The table on the next page reads as follows: (in the first column) the average week offered 33 different occasions for the audience to select an informational broadcast. The average viewer was watching television during nine of these hours (1.4 plus 7.5). He selected the informational programs 1.4 times.[3] The other 7.5 times, he chose competing entertainment and "missed the opportunity" to be informed. On the whole, then, viewers selected information 16 per cent of the times they were actually watching while it was available.

Now this definition of "missed opportunity" is the most liberal one, since it involves only people who actually watched something else during the hour. In any critical hour, many of those not watching at all probably could have seen the informational program if they had cared to. In this sense, they also "missed an opportunity."

There are several clear findings:

1. Most of the heavy information was broadcast during hours when our viewers were not likely to be watching at all. This fact reflects the "Sunday Ghetto," which averaged 20 of the 33 such programs for the week. (Analysis for Sunday only appears as Appendix Table 23.)

2. When the set *was* on and attended, the informational entries attracted only 16 per cent of the viewing; and the figure is the same for Sunday as for the rest of the week. So while it is true that Sunday informational broadcasts are beamed to a large number of dead sets, those who *do* watch during those hours are no more disposed than usual to select the information that *is* available then.

3. In *relative* terms, the attitudes that respondents express toward

[3] Only in the same sense that the average American has 1.4 children under eighteen. Between them, the 237 viewers watched informational broadcasts 335 times; missed 1770 opportunities, etc.

	ALL	By Survey Response: QUESTION 18A THOSE WHO SAY:				By Viewer Characteristics: EDUCATION		By Viewer Characteristics: RELIGION		
		"Not enough food for thought"	*"Enough" or "too much"*	*"Not enough information"*	*"Enough" or "too much"*	High School and Below	College and Beyond	Protestants	Catholics	Jews
Number of Viewers	**237**	117	120	136	101	143	79	63	99	65
HEAVY INFORMATION Opportunities per week, average	**33.2**	33.3	33.1	33.4	32.9	33.2	33.4	33.0	33.3	33.5
WATCHED DURING CRITICAL HOURS: HEAVY INFORMATION SELECTED										
Exposures	335	208	127	221	114	182	132	102	117	104
Per Viewer	1.4	1.8	1.1	1.6	1.1	1.3	1.7	1.6	1.2	1.6
MISSED OPPORTUNITIES saw something else										
Exposures	1770	819	951	1000	770	1190	466	457	780	466
Per Viewer	7.5	7.0	7.9	7.4	7.6	8.3	5.9	7.3	7.9	7.2
HEAVY INFORMATION Selection Rate	16%	20%	12%	18%	13%	13%	22%	18%	13%	18%
CRITICAL HOURS NOT WATCHED:										
Number	**5756**	2868	2888	3314	2442	3370	2038	1516	2392	1607
Per Viewer	**24.3**	24.5	24.1	24.4	24.2	23.6	25.8	24.1	24.2	24.7

Summary : Of All Possible
Heavy Information Exposures . . .

Watched	Missed	Not Watching
	saw something else	at all at the time

	Watched	Missed	Not Watching	Exposures†	Viewers
			Base: 100% =		
ALL	4	23%	73%	7861	237
THOSE WHO SAY:					
"Not enough food for thought"	5	21	74	3895	117
"Enough" or "too much"	3	24	73	3966	120
THOSE WHO SAY:					
"Not enough information"	5	22	73	4535	136
"Enough" or "too much"	3	24	73	3326	101
High School and Below	4	25	71	4742	143
College and Beyond	5	18	77	2636	79
Protestants	5	22	73	2075	63
Catholics	4	23	73	3289	99
Jews	5	21	74	2177	65

†Actual and possible "exposures"

serious programming is clearly related to their likelihood to select it; the proportion rises from 13 per cent to 18 per cent and from 12 per cent to 20 per cent among those who feel there is "not enough" information and "not enough" food for thought, respectively. But the *absolute* selection rate is low among all groups; the fact is that viewers who ask for more enlightenment select it only one fifth of the time that they are watching while it is actually available.

4. Dividing the sample by the relevant personal characteristics shows much the same similarity in the case of education, and even less difference in the case of religion.

With regard to the low (absolute) selection rate among the better-educated and the critics, they would probably remind us that many factors beyond program *type* enter into their choice—most importantly, perhaps, program *quality*. Possibly their criticism is directed not at the *number* of programs presently available but at their "level," to the end that better informational programs might get a bigger audience. Furthermore, we have shown only that the *average* informational program is infrequently selected—not that the outstanding or really worthwhile ones are. But the same observations hold in the other direction as well: it is *average* entertainment and entertainment at the *present* quality level that attracts these viewers away from information, four out of five times.[4]

Whatever the reason, then, those groups in the population who stress the need for more information, as well as the public in general, usually fail to select today's informative fare over today's entertainment.

Now, this is not to say that they *select* the competing entertainment programs in the sense that they actively prefer them and seek them out. After all, there are seven channels in New York, and the informational broadcasts do average 16 per cent of the audience watching at the time. Figures of this order could be produced by an entirely passive audience; one that simply tuned at random and watched whatever happened to be on.[5] What we have found here is only the absence of significant selectivity *in favor of* heavy information; and that, for the moment, may be enough.

---

[4] In fact, and in general, the critics speak more highly of the informational shows than they do of TV entertainment.

[5] Though the television ratings generally show that informational broadcasts are *underselected* by the audience at large.

An example: Eisenhower's trip   During the weeks of February 23 and March 1, 1960, the New York audience was offered special coverage of President Eisenhower's trip to Latin America. There were four such telecasts each week. The number of diaries that happen to fall into these two weeks is very small, but this analysis does provide one concrete example of the type of selective or nonselective process that produces the general pattern we have just seen.

The analysis (pages 190–1) shows that for those watching during the critical hours, the over-all selection rate was 27 per cent; so missed opportunities outscored exposures by more than 2 to 1. Among those who say television has "not enough information" the figure "rises" to 30 per cent; these viewers averaged 0.5 attendances and 1.2 missed opportunities to see this special coverage—as against 0.4 exposures and 1.3 lost chances for those who report that the present supply of TV information is adequate.[6]

Personal characteristics make more difference, and especially religion. The nine college-educated viewers selected Eisenhower 36 per cent of the time they watched during such coverage, and for the eight Jews the rate climbs to 60 per cent.[7] But these cases are far too few to "analyze," and perhaps even too few to mention other than to illustrate the fact that it is *possible* to select these critical programs.

Regular news   Each weekday between 6:30 and 7:30 p.m., six of the seven New York channels broadcast one or more newscasts. Together, they saturate the hour with news. This gives each viewer five chances during his rating week to watch some news at this time; to watch something else but *no* news; or not to watch at all. And it gives us the chance to see how the various segments differ on this score. (See data on pages 192 and 193.)

The average viewer sees at least some news in this period 1.2 times per week; but he watches telvision only a total of 1.6 times during these hours. So the news selection rate is high: given any exposure from 6:30 to 7:30, the odds are three out of four that some news will be seen.

The rate varies around this average for different groups, and usually in the expected direction, but not by much. The greatest single

[6] Here we should point out again that at least some of those not watching at all might have elected to turn the set on for these documentaries. In all, viewers "missed" 3.5 of the 4 weekly broadcasts.

[7] Only three of these, by the way, are college-educated, and their selection rate is only slightly higher.

	ALL	By Survey Response:		By Viewer Characteristics:				
		QUESTION 18A THOSE WHO SAY:		EDUCATION		RELIGION		
		"Not enough Information"	*"Enough" or "too much"*	High School and Below	College and Beyond	Protestants	Catholics	Jews
Number of Viewers	**39**	17	22	28	9	6	24	8
EISENHOWER COVERAGE Opportunities per week	**4**	4	4	4	4	4	4	4
WATCHED DURING CRITICAL HOURS:								
EISENHOWER COVERAGE SELECTED								
Exposures	**18**	9	9	13	5	3	6	9
Per Viewer	**0.5**	0.5	0.4	0.5	0.6	0.5	0.3	1.1
MISSED OPPORTUNITIES saw something else								
Exposures	**19**	21	28	39	9	9	34	6
Per Viewer	**1.3**	1.2	1.3	1.4	1.0	1.5	1.4	0.8
EISENHOWER COVERAGE Selection Rate	**27%**	**30%**	**24%**	**25%**	**36%**	**25%**	**15%**	**60%**
CRITICAL HOURS NOT WATCHED:								
Number	**88**	38	50	59	22	12	55	17
Per Viewer	**2.3**	2.2	2.3	2.1	2.4	2.0	2.3	2.1

Summary : Coverage Of Eisenhower's Trip . . .

Watched	Missed	Not Watching
	saw something else	at all at the time

				Exposures	Viewers
				Base: 100% =	
ALL	12%	32%	56%	155	39
THOSE WHO SAY:					
"Not enough information"	13	31	56	68	17
"Enough" or "too much"	10	33	57	87	22
High School and Below	12	35	53	111	28
College and Beyond	14	25	61	36	9
Protestants	13	37	50	24	6
Catholics	6	36	58	95	24
Jews	28	19	53	32	8

| | ALL | By Survey Response: | | | | By Viewer Characteristics: | | | | |
| | | QUESTION 18A THOSE WHO SAY: | | | | EDUCATION | | RELIGION | | |
		"Not enough food for thought"	*"Enough" or "too much"*	*"Not enough information"*	*"Enough" or "too much"*	High School and Below	College and Beyond	Protestants	Catholics	Jews
Number of Viewers	**237**	117	120	136	101	143	79	63	99	65
Opportunities per Week	**5.0**	5.0	5.0	5.0	5.0	5.0	5.0	5.0	5.0	5.0
WATCHED DURING CRITICAL HOURS:										
NEWS SELECTED										
Exposures	277	135	142	162	115	176	84	90	112	67
Per Viewer	1.2	1.2	1.2	1.2	1.2	1.2	1.1	1.4	1.1	1.0
MISSED OPPORTUNITIES saw something else										
Exposures	104	33	71	49	55	82	17	16	65	20
Per Viewer	0.4	0.3	0.6	0.4	0.5	0.6	0.2	0.3	0.7	0.3
NEWS Selection Rate	**73%**	**80%**	**67%**	**77%**	**68%**	**68%**	**83%**	**85%**	**63%**	**77%**
CRITICAL HOURS NOT WATCHED:										
Number	**805**	415	388	469	336	458	294	209	319	238
Per Viewer	**3.4**	3.6	3.2	3.4	3.4	3.2	3.7	3.3	3.2	3.7

Summary : Daily Newscast(s)
Between 6:30 and 7:30 pm . . .

Watched	Missed	Not Watching
	saw something else	at all at the time

				Exposures	Viewers
				Base: 100% =	
ALL	23%	9%	68%	**1186**	**237**
THOSE WHO SAY: *"Not enough food for thought"*	23	6	71	585	117
"Enough" or "too much"	24	12	64	601	120
THOSE WHO SAY: *"Not enough information"*	24	7	69	680	136
"Enough" or "too much"	23	11	66	506	101
High School and Below	25	11	64	716	143
College and Beyond	21	4	75	395	79
Protestants	29	5	66	315	63
Catholics	23	13	64	496	99
Jews	21	6	73	325	65

difference is between Catholics (63 per cent) and Protestants (85 per cent); and in no group do average exposures exceed 1.4 per week, nor fall below 1.0. Further, survey responses make no difference at all in the number of news exposures, just in the missed opportunities. Viewers who request more information average exactly the same number of news-days (1.2), but they are somewhat less likely to turn on the set just for other programs.

This consumption of regular news stands in marked contrast to the comparative apathy surrounding other information–public affairs broadcasting. In part, this no doubt reflects the multiple-channel availability of newscasts during the hour. It takes a little doing in New York to watch from 6:30 to 7:30 and miss the news entirely. But again, people do not have to watch at all then (and most of them usually do not), so that the intrinsic interest of the day's news must be largely responsible for the exposures that do occur.

This one hour, of course, is just a specific demonstration of the general pattern we saw in the over-all diets selected by the New York viewers. Regular news is the only substantial category heavily "over-selected," whereas other information–public affairs earns the opposite distinction.

On television, as in print, the newspaper outsells the serious magazine. But unlike the situation in print, the highly educated audiences and/or the proponents of more informational content are not much more likely to select the "think" piece when it *is* at their fingertips.

Now, let us turn to the other class of serious programming. Perhaps audience segments exercise more selectivity when it comes to heavy entertainment.

What Viewers Select When Heavy Entertainment Is Available

Serious drama (live, taped, or movie[8]) and classical music constitute "heavy entertainment." Excluding *Play of the Week* (a special case that we take up in a moment), the eight weeks produced an average of six occasions per week when viewers could tune to such fare.[9] What

---

[8] Including television originals and "regular" (theater) movies.

[9] Again, as in the case of "heavy information," we use stringent criteria to make sure these programs qualify. Examples, during the week of March 1: *Bitter Rice, The Mikado, Playhouse 90* ("Tomorrow"), Bernstein's *Young People's Concerts, Sunday Showcase* ("Turn the Key Deftly"), *Show of the Month* ("Treasure Island").

did the viewers do with such opportunities? The answer appears on pages 196 and 197.

On the average, they were not watching at all during three of them; during two more, they chose the competing light entertainment; and they watched the remaining program. So the over-all attraction of heavy entertainment, for those watching at the time, is twice that of heavy information (32 per cent as against 16 per cent in the latter case).[1]

In addition, we see much more substantial differences in the choices made by various parts of the population. College education boosts the selection rate to 50 per cent, and religion shows a similar spread: Jews are twice as likely to select heavy entertainment as Catholics, while Protestants fall in the middle. Although survey responses on "food for thought" are still not as predictive of viewing behavior as these personal characteristics, they clearly get more behavioral backing here than in the case of information.

A special case: Play of the Week began in the New York area in October 1959, the start of our viewing season. It presented a serious, adult drama that was broadcast each day throughout the week and during prime time (e.g. 8 p.m. on weekdays; 10:30 p.m. on Saturday; and Sunday afternoon).

Because of technical difficulties introduced by a program rebroadcast several times during the week, this unique yet perhaps prototypic "heavy entertainment" entry was excluded from the above summary analysis. Instad, we took a special look at how the New York audience behaved with respect to this pioneering venture. The chart on page 199 shows what happened during five of the eight rating weeks.[2]

---

[1] This also speaks to the question of whether the 16 per cent figure for information is a necessary "mechanical" result of the fact that only one out of the seven channels is carrying the critical program. Here, just as in the case of information, the heavy-entertainment entry is usually confined to one of the stations. Yet the selection rate is double; and the missed opportunities are only half of what they were before.

[2] Diary weeks do not necessarily begin on Monday, as does the week's Play, so that in some cases the rating week "straddles" three telecasts of one week's entry and four of the next. In the five weeks we use, each viewer had six chances to see *The Power and the Glory, A Month in the Country, The Waltz of the Toreadors, A Very Special Baby,* or *The Climate of Eden.*

	ALL	By Survey Response:		By Viewer Characteristics:				
		QUESTION 18A THOSE WHO SAY:		EDUCATION		RELIGION		
		"Not enough food for thought"	*"Enough" or "too much"*	High School and Below	College and Beyond	Protestants	Catholics	Jews
Number of Viewers	**237**	117	120	143	79	63	99	65
HEAVY ENTERTAINMENT Opportunities per week, average	**5.8**	6.0	5.8	5.8	6.0	5.6	6.0	5.9
WATCHED DURING CRITICAL HOURS: HEAVY ENTERTAINMENT SELECTED								
Exposures	**210**	124	86	101	93	54	66	81
Per Viewer	**0.9**	1.1	0.7	0.7	1.2	0.9	0.7	1.2
MISSED OPPORTUNITIES saw something else								
Exposures	**437**	190	247	319	93	103	226	93
Per Viewer	**1.8**	1.6	2.1	2.2	1.2	1.6	2.3	1.4
HEAVY ENTERTAINMENT Selection Rate	**32%**	**39%**	**26%**	**24%**	**50%**	**34%**	**23%**	**47%**
CRITICAL HOURS NOT WATCHED:								
Number	**743**	387	356	416	286	198	295	215
Per Viewer	**3.1**	3.3	3.0	2.9	3.6	3.1	3.0	3.3

Summary : Of All Possible
Heavy Entertainment Exposures . . .

Watched	Missed	Not Watching
	saw something else	at all at the time

		Exposures	Viewers
		Base: 100% =	
ALL	**15%** **31%** **53%**	**1390**	**237**
THOSE WHO SAY:			
"Not enough food for thought"	18 27 55	701	117
"Enough" or *"too much"*	12 36 52	689	120
High School and Below	12 38 50	836	143
College and Beyond	20 20 60	472	79
Protestants	15 29 56	355	63
Catholics	11 39 50	587	99
Jews	21 24 55	389	65

First of all, note that although this highly acclaimed and then novel offering was available daily, only one fifth of the viewers saw it during the average week. The rest averaged four missed opportunities apiece; that is, they selected and watched something else on four separate, competing occasions during the week. Only two viewers in the entire analysis failed to be present at the TV set at least once during their week when they could have tuned to the Play. So program availability, in and of itself, certainly does not guarantee viewer exposure, at least over this period of time.

Again, as with heavy entertainment in general, both personal characteristics and survey responses are of considerable help in predicting *who* will watch. College-educated viewers were three times as likely to see the Play as those who had not attained that educational level; in the average week, 36 per cent of them saw the week's Play at one time or another. Similarly, those who want more "food for thought" outscore viewers who do not, by almost the same rate. Finally, Jews show a substantially higher allegiance to the program than others.

On the whole, then, differences in taste are far more evident when it comes to serious entertainment than they are in the case of information–public affairs broadcasts. Not only is heavy entertainment a generally more popular (i.e., more highly selected) category, but here, unlike the former case, the differential selectivity reaches dimensions of practical significance: those who assert the need for a more serious, higher-level television also watch substantially more of such entertainment when it is available. In contrast with "more information," they not only say they want more, but their program choices suggest that they want at least some of it for themselves.

In Sum: Information vs. Entertainment

For a final, direct comparison of the value placed on serious entertainment vs. serious information by various groups, we examine some occasions when they could choose *between* them. These critical hours provide the chance to see either type of heavy fare, or miss both opportunities in favor of light entertainment—in effect, a viewing decision equivalent to the verbal choice forced by our Question 41: ". . . should TV provide more information *or* concentrate on providing the best entertainment possible?"

Critical Hours : Play Of The Week, Five Weeks Only

	ALL	By Survey Response:		By Viewer Characteristics:				
		QUESTION 18A THOSE WHO SAY:		EDUCATION		RELIGION		
		"Not enough food for thought"	"Enough" or "too much"	High School and Below	College and Beyond	Protestants	Catholics	Jews
Number of Viewers	**141**	70	71	86	45	· 39	63	34
WATCHED DURING CRITICAL HOURS:								
Saw play anytime during the week								
Viewers	29	21	8	10	16	7	10	10
Percentage	**21%**	**30%**	**11%**	**12%**	**36%**	**18%**	**16%**	**29%**
Watched during telecast(s) but never saw play								
Viewers	110	47	63	75	28	31	52	24
Percentage	**78%**	**67%**	**89%**	**87%**	**62%**	**79%**	**83%**	**71%**
Total Missed Opportunities	442	190	252	308	101	122	220	88
Per Viewer	3.9	3.9	4.0	4.1	3.7	3.8	4.2	3.7
CRITICAL HOURS NOT WATCHED:								
Never watched during any play telecast								
Viewers	2	2	0	1	1	1	1	0

	ALL	By Survey Response:							By Viewer Characteristics:				
		QUESTION 18A				QUESTION 41A			EDUCATION		RELIGION		
		"Not enough food for thought"	*"Enough" or "too much"*	*"Not enough information"*	*"Enough" or "too much"*	*"More Information"*	*"Better Entertainment"*	*"Both"*	High School and Below	College and Beyond	Protestants	Catholics	Jews
Number of Viewers	**152**	75	77	86	66	44	61	47	95	49	42	64	39
HEAVY ENTERTAINMENT VS. HEAVY INFORMATION Opportunities per week, average	**3.8**	4.0	3.6	4.0	3.5	4.0	3.7	3.9	3.7	4.0	3.7	3.7	4.0
WATCHED DURING CRITICAL HOURS:													
HEAVY ENTERTAINMENT													
Exposures	80	47	33	53	27	23	23	34	38	34	25	25	27
Per Viewer	0.5	0.6	0.4	0.6	0.4	0.5	0.4	0.7	0.4	0.7	0.6	0.4	0.7
Selection Rate	31%	36%	26%	35%	26%	30%	24%	41%	22%	53%	35%	24%	40%
HEAVY INFORMATION													
Exposures	13	9	4	7	6	2	4	7	7	6	6	2	5
Per Viewer	0.09	.12	.05	.08	.09	.05	.07	.15	.07	.12	.14	.03	.13
Selection Rate	5%	7%	3%	5%	6%	3%	4%	8%	4%	9%	8%	2%	7%
MISSED OPPORTUNITIES saw something else	162	74	88	93	69	51	69	42	125	27	45	76	36
Per Viewer	1.1	1.0	1.1	1.1	1.0	1.2	1.1	0.9	1.3	0.6	1.0	1.2	0.9
CRITICAL HOURS NOT WATCHED:													
Number	322	166	156	187	135	96	127	99	183	126	84	132	88
Per Viewer	2.1	2.2	2.0	2.2	2.0	2.2	2.1	2.1	1.9	2.6	2.0	2.1	2.3

Summary : when Heavy Entertainment and Heavy Information are available at the same time, here is what is selected by those watching at the time:

HEAVY ENTERTAINMENT

HEAVY INFORMATION

MISSED OPPORTUNITIES
watched light entertainment

	Heavy Ent.	Heavy Inf.	Missed Opp.	Exposures Base: 100% =	Viewers
ALL	31%	5	64%	**255**	**152**
THOSE WHO SAY: "Not enough food for thought"	36	7	57	130	75
"Enough" or "too much"	26	3	70	125	77
THOSE WHO SAY: "Not enough information"	35	5	61	153	86
"Enough" or "too much"	26	6	68	102	66
THOSE WHO SAY: "More information" vs.	30	3	67	76	44
"Better entertainment"	24	4	72	96	61
"Both"	41	8	51	83	47
High School and Below	22	4	74	170	95
College and Beyond	53	9	40	67	49
Protestants	32	8	59	76	42
Catholics	24	2	74	103	64
Jews	40	7	53	68	39

The results could hardly be more clear-cut. The audience at large takes two shares of light entertainment to one share of the heavy variety, and virtually no information. Even the well-educated, when faced with this choice, turn in large numbers from light to heavy entertainment— but rarely to information. College viewers select the informative program only 9 per cent of the time under these competitive conditions, and that is the highest selection rate it attains in any group in this comparison.

Those who ask for "more information" in Question 18 choose it five times in one hundred; and even the viewers who put "more information" *ahead* of "better entertainment" in Question 41, back up this response with only a 3 per cent selection rate in that direction.[3] By this measure as by the previous ones, "food for thought" seems to mean emotional or aesthetic, rather than strictly intellectual, nourishment.

Now, these over-all preferences are no surprise to anyone who follows the ratings. Heavy information is rarely represented in the top ten. In general, a rating that would alarm the backers of an action show is remarkably successful in a public affairs presentation. Substantial entertainment, on the other hand, sometimes holds its own with the public at large; and there have been several notable successes in this category, by commercial as well as by critical standards.

What is of particular interest is that the number-one suggestion for TV improvement—"more information"—that comes mostly and almost unanimously from the educated critics of the medium, is not backed up *by them* in *their own* program selections. Perhaps they mean something else by "information"; perhaps they feel the present programs are not good enough; perhaps they feel there should be more of the same but not for their own consumption. But whatever the reason, they do not select present informational programs, as they *do* select heavy entertainment, when they have the chance to do so.

So the more critical, or less enthusiastic, segments of the audience are not nearly so selective as their survey responses suggest. They certainly do not confine themselves to the programming they sanction, at least verbally; nor do they devote even the major portion of their own viewing to such material. In this ARB analysis, they do not watch 40 programs a week, but they do watch 25. Sixty per cent of their viewing

---

[3] Again, it is those who say "both" who select the "highest level" fare of all. But even among them, information doesn't compete with heavy entertainment (8 per cent to 41 per cent, respectively).

is not devoted to light entertainment, but about 50 per cent is. News accounts for a slightly higher *percentage* of their diet than it does in the case of the "less discriminating," but they do not watch as *many* newscasts per week as the common man. And when it comes to other information–public affairs, that accounts not for a mere 4 per cent of their television week, but for a mere 8 per cent.

Serious drama and music does attract them in larger numbers; it is the only program category that the highly educated see more of, in absolute terms—and they are far more apt than others to select it if it happens to be on the air while they are watching. But it still accounts for a negligible share of their television week; and it still fails to capture as much as half their viewing even while such programs are on the air.

So the argument that viewers consume so much trivia because trivia fill the schedule is confronted with the hard fact that even the most discriminating viewers choose the trivia more often than not when something else *is* available—especially when that something else is a serious, informative show. That is to say, they *watch* the light diversion, whether or not they *"prefer"* it. This may often reflect nonselective dial twisting or dial leaving alone, rather than active selection. But in either case, the effort to find and watch the "best," by their own verbal criterion of best, is not often made.

These findings are all the more impressive since they come from diary-reported viewing that might be subject to some response bias in the direction of turning in an acceptable report for the family. There may be subtle changes in what people actually watch during the observed week and/or more direct influences on what gets written down. To the extent that such effects occur, the differences in viewing patterns are probably even smaller than the diary reports indicate, and the critics even less selective in real life than in their diaries.

Before we leave this section, we should take explicit account of the limitations in this ARB check on viewing behavior vs. survey response. To repeat, these are all New York viewers. The "average" American, regardless of where he lives, lives in a smaller city and one with fewer television alternatives.

Next, these are all people who have chosen to comply with the request that they participate in an ARB panel; furthermore, they have agreed to our interview. People who co-operate in such matters are probably different on some counts from the rest of the population.

These sampling effects may well have some influence on our results

—but only if they relate to the basic comparison. ARB New Yorkers may have more favorable or less favorable attitudes toward television; they may watch more or watch less; they may be friendlier or more hostile to TV than the general population. But so long as the *relationship* between what they do and what they say is not systematically affected, neither would our general conclusions be. Our essential comparisons are all *within* the ARB sample, not between these people and others. In short, while we should not make too much of this limited look at a very few viewers, neither should we make too little of it.

Chapter 7

THE COMMERCIALS

FINALLY, we return to our national survey for a word about the sponsors.

On the average, between one and two of every ten minutes of air time is devoted to advertising. The exact figure varies by type of program, by type of station, and by time of day, but it rarely exceeds 20 per cent and almost never falls below 10. In terms of time, then, commercials are the number-three content category: behind movies (32 per cent) and comedy-variety (17 per cent), but ahead of action (13 per cent) and the other eight categories.[1]

In the great debate over television, as well as for the viewers, "the commercials" represent a twofold issue. First, there is the matter of the commercial messages themselves, including what they say, how they say it, and, especially, how often. And secondly, there is concern with the nature of the commercial sponsorship *system,* what it does and fails to do for American television.

The Commercials Themselves

Again, before raising any specific issues, we gave viewers a chance to discuss commercials in terms they themselves chose. The issue was introduced by this general probe:

[1] Based on the content analysis of New York programming, as reported in the ARB section.

QUESTION 42A *"Now about commercials on television...What, if anything do you like most about commercials?"*

Respondents:	ALL	SEX		EDUCATION		
		Men	Women	Grade School	High School	College & Beyond
Base: 100% = 2427		1177	1246	627	1214	516

ASPECT OF COMMERCIALS MENTIONED

	ALL	Men	Women	Grade School	High School	College & Beyond
ENTERTAINMENT	**38%***	**35%**	**42%**	**27%**	**42%**	**44%**
animated cartoons	9	8	11	7	9	12
tunes, jingles, songs	8	5	10	5	9	7
imagination, ingenuity, variety	3	3	3	1	2	5
other or general	22	22	22	16	24	23
INFORMATION	**22**	**19**	**24**	**23**	**22**	**19**
learn about products, general	8	7	8	9	7	7
learn about *new* products	9	7	12	8	11	7
comparative prices, deals	1	1	1	1	0	1
other or general	4	5	4	4	4	4
THEY PAY FOR TELEVISION	**18**	**20**	**16**	**19**	**19**	**15**
PROVIDE BREAK FOR FOOD, CHORES	**3**	**2**	**3**	**4**	**2**	**3**
PARTICULAR COMMERCIAL LIKED	**13**	**14**	**13**	**8**	**14**	**17**
NEGATIVE RESPONSE	**28**	**31**	**25**	**32**	**26**	**29**
nothing, absence of, etc.	23	26	20	26	22	23
short commercials	3	4	3	3	3	5
pay no attention, don't watch, other negative	2	2	2	3	2	2
GENERAL OR OTHER	**3**	**5**	**2**	**6**	**3**	**2**
NA, DK	**6**	**6**	**6**	**9**	**5**	**4**

* Multiple responses: The detailed percentages within major categories do not necessarily add to the category totals, which show % of respondents mentioning any (one or more) of the subordinate categories

So commercials (at least some of them), like programs (at least some of them), *entertain* and/or *inform*. As in the case of programming, entertainment seems to be the primary or overriding appeal. However, unlike the former case, the relative emphasis on entertainment *increases* with education. Perhaps there is less "bias" here, toward information as the acceptable response; or possibly the better-educated are more responsive to satire in commercials, as they are to satire in general.

In any event, the entertainment value of some television advertising is most often mentioned as "most liked"—by men as well as women, by viewers at all educational levels, and frequently in quite enthusiastic terms:

> "Some are better than the shows. I like the cartoons, especially those musicals."

> "Some are clever, like the Piel's Beer commercial. They are amusing and I look forward to seeing them."

The discussion of the *information* in commercials reflects some of the economists' formulations about the functions of advertising, though with the greatest emphasis on *new* products and product *uses* (rather than comparative price, which is a negligible aspect of all but some local television advertising):

> "Learning about new products and what they can do for you."

> "Keep up with the kinds of products on the market and their uses. Help to make up your mind on some subjects."

> "It tells you how to use lots of new stuff."

> "Acquaint you with the product volume, and content, and locales of products. Suppose it was wine—was it in Italy or California?"

In addition to such appeals in the message itself, its presence "pays for the program," and that is mentioned spontaneously by a sizable portion of the audience—often with an air of tolerance or "fair play" toward the advertiser:

> "They are entitled to the time because they are paying for it."

"They pay for the shows, so the least we can do is watch."

"It isn't fair to criticize them when they make the shows possible."

But despite all this, perhaps the most significant entry in the table is the last one. In response to a question directed explicitly at what is "most *liked*," over one quarter say directly or in effect, "nothing." This points clearly to audience annoyances with present commercials, and these are elaborated in specific, often heated, detail in our next question, tabulated to the right:

First, note that over-all, objections divide evenly between the *content* of commercials on the one hand and their *timing* and *frequency* on the other. (There is no mention at all of disadvantages of the sponsorship *system*, but that may be largely because of the frame of reference established in these two questions.) Men and women respond in about the same way, but differences in education produce substantial effects. All objections to *content* rise with schooling, so that the college-educated produce almost twice as much criticism of what commercials contain than do the viewers with only a grade-school education. On the other hand, annoyance with *timing* is equally frequent at each educational extreme, and still higher in the largest, middle group. In this sense, *timing* is clearly the most general complaint.

Let us spell out each of these major objections in a little more detail, with an eye to their implications for broadcasters and advertisers.

Timing: This issue divides into three distinct but closely related objections, voiced in almost equal proportions: commercials *interrupt* programming; there are too *many* of them; and they are too *long*.[2] Interruption seems to be the major annoyance; it is mentioned most frequently, and the discussion of frustration surrounding commercial intrusion into an interesting program is often impassioned:

"There are three or four sponsors not related in product or presentation and most of the shows are this way. There is no

[2] At present, these may often refer to basically the same annoyance, but their implications are clearly not identical, and it is possible to take one notion into account and still neglect the others: e.g., short commercials that interrupt; or long ones that don't; or few but long commercials; etc. Since there is probably more latitude among such alternative allocations of commercial time than in the question of whether or not to have them, it would probably be helpful to isolate these criticisms even further.

QUESTION 42B *"And what, if anything, do you dislike most about commercials?"*

Respondents:	ALL	SEX		EDUCATION		
		Men	Women	Grade School	High School	College & Beyond
Base: 100% = 2427		1177	1246	627	1214	516
ASPECT OF COMMERCIALS MENTIONED						
CONTENT	48%*	51%	46%	34%	49%	62%
boring, dull, repetitive	17	18	17	13	18	20
misleading, dishonest	16	18	14	11	15	20
stupid, insulting to intelligence	11	11	10	5	10	18
bad taste, "private" products	8	7	10	6	8	13
hard sell, aggressive, overdone	5	6	4	3	4	7
other, or general	1	1	1	1	1	1
TIMING	48	46	50	42	53	41
interruptions in program	21	19	22	19	23	16
too many, too frequent	19	19	20	15	22	18
too long	18	18	18	16	19	17
TOO LOUD	4	4	5	2	4	7
TOO EFFECTIVE ON CHILDREN	2	1	2	2	1	2
DISLIKE EVERYTHING	1	1	1	1	1	1
DISLIKE NOTHING	11	11	11	19	9	5
PAY NO ATTENTION —DON'T WATCH	2	2	2	3	1	2
PARTICULAR COMMERCIAL DISLIKED	3	3	3	4	4	3
GENERAL OR OTHER	2	2	1	2	1	2
DK, NA	5	4	5	7	4	3

*Multiple responses: The detailed percentages within major categories do not necessarily add to the category totals, which show % of respondents mentioning any (one or more) of the subordinate categories

thought or connection between the play and commercial—as if one were produced in New York and one in Hollywood. These people don't realize the author is trying to get your interest in his play, and all of a sudden they break in with a filter cigarette or hair tonic. This is like a dash of cold water. Completely destroys the mood the author is trying to build up."

"They break the mood of the show. There should be one at the beginning and at the middle and at the end."

"Interruptions—when there's a play or movie on. That is really aggravating when they do that."

"What these programs need are psychologists to realize that when they have a program and then continually interrupt it as they usually do, they are destroying the whole effect that the program tries to build up."[3]

This problem is especially far-reaching, in that it is largely unrelated to the "quality" of the commercial; perhaps even positively associated with program quality. An entertaining or informative commercial still disturbs at a critical program moment, and good programs are more likely to be engrossing than bad. Under the present placing of commercials, then, better commercials would not diminish this annoyance, and better programs might make it worse.

The references to length and frequency of commercials also relate implicitly to their interruption:

"The automobile commercials are too long. They put me in a bad mood. I lose the good feeling I had while watching the first show."

[3] Probably more relevant to the interests of the advertisers is the general psychological principle that an individual in a state of "interruption" or "unresolved tension" is especially unreceptive to unrelated intervening material. The tendency to resume or complete unfinished business often overrides or precludes irrelevant "stimuli." If this is applicable to commercials within the context of a program, it suggests that a commercial placed at the point of maximum program interest (e.g., just before we find out "whodunit," or whether Sally survives) pays for its minimized loss in physical audience with maximized audience apathy, possibly even resentment.

But by and large, "too many" and, especially, "too long" are annoyances that stem in large part from content. Boring or repetitious messages are more likely to become "too long" or "too frequent" than interesting ones, and that brings us to the other major set of irritations.

Content: 1. The single most frequent objection here is not to what commercials *do* contain, but rather to what they do *not*. Commercials are often "dull," "boring," "repetitious." Moral indignation, disgust, sales resistance—all of these follow the simple yawn as the predominant negative reaction to commercial content:

"They are just constant, repetitious, always the same."

"I dislike commercials that tell over and over and over and over."

"The ones that keep repeating the same story, over and over again. The same song or the same rhyme. They never change. They interrupt . . . with the same things day in and day out. Sometimes it's soap or coffee or beer or cigarettes. It's always the same."

Thus entertainment and information, when present, are what is most liked about commercial content; the lack of interest, accordingly, is least liked.

2. Misleading or exaggerated claims do not go unmentioned. They qualify as a close second, which is not surprising in the wake of the quiz scandals and the succeeding rash of exposés of the various props, photographic tricks, and other "fraudulent" advertising practices. Still, the reaction seems quite mild, and not very moralistic. Here are some typical statements:

"You have a feeling that some of the big statements they put on are not exactly that way. They stretch it just a little."

"One time they were shaving some sandpaper, and I don't think it can be done. It was so silly and it isn't true."

"I did not like the hair dyer that claimed to work such miracles with the hair. It stated that the hair would be beautified and made new and young-looking. I did not like for it to fool people into spending their money."

"They overdo things so. You know as well as I that when they rub grease into a piece of cloth no soap will take it out just presto! They must think we're terribly simple to swallow their line."

The last quote puts explicitly what the others may imply—and that, rather than "dishonesty," might be the major source of annoyance with misleading claims: exaggeration implies gullibility in the audience.

3. A commercial that appears incredible, exaggerated, or simply stupid carries insulting connotations that are resented by large numbers, especially among the college-educated:

"I dislike the tendency they have to regard me as an idiot. That's what I dislike most."

"Most of them put on as though we were dummies. True advertising I can go for, but not those that knock the other one down."

"They are degrading—make the public feel stupid."

This recalls the feeling among many college viewers that "most" television programs are aimed at people of lesser intellectual achievement. But whereas viewers *can* be selective in programming, commercials are unselected, intrusive riders.[4]

The degree to which commercials intrude on an audience self-selected, if at all, only for program, aggravates the offense or at least increases the likelihood of its occurrence.[5]

---

[4] To some extent, commercials less offensive to the intelligence are no doubt associated with better programming, but probably only at the extremes. "Highbrow" specials frequently incorporate high-toned advertising, and the worst commercial offenders are probably associated with programming of questionable cultural worth. But within standard network entertainment fare, there is probably little connection between the aesthetic and intellectual levels of the commercial and the program.

[5] This also speaks to the proposed "magazine" concept of TV advertising, in which advertisers would buy commercial time, not programs. One of the potential disadvantages of such a plan would be the inability of the advertiser to gear the commercials to the specific level of the program. In such a system, all commercials would perforce aim at the broadest possible base, and thus grate considerably on the nerves of the more selective segments of the audience.

4. Finally, there is the matter of vulgarity, invasion of privacy, "bringing the bathroom into the living room." Our field work followed a *Reader's Digest* article on the subject,[6] so this complaint may be swelled beyond its "normal" level. But, whether in response to the commercials or in response to the article, the objection is made in several forms.

First, there is the exposure of private products:

> "The bras and girdles. They talked about the lift and separation. That's embarrassing when there's teen-age boys around. An ad like that is unnecessary—it starts the imagination."

> "There's one about deodorants. You know, with the armpits. That's sickening."

> "Clorets for bad breath should be a personal problem, not to be discussed in public."

And, for some, of "sinful" or harmful ones:

> "The advertising of different kinds of beer. Most of the sports advertise beer, and that isn't good for children. . . . I don't think such evil things should be put before young people so convincingly."

> "Most of the deodorants and cigarettes and beer commercials. Most of these things are put in front of the children to be almost virtues."

And, finally, there are various symbolic assaults on the viewer's body:

> "I think all those headache pills where they show a hammer pounding your head are bad. Boy, if you didn't have a headache before, you'd sure have one after seeing that hammer pound you."

> "They use demonstrations like stomach acid burning a hole in a napkin, and then they tell you how their product pre-

[6] B. Clark: "Must TV Bring the Bathroom into Our Living Rooms?" *Reader's Digest,* Vol. 76 (April 1960), pp. 61-3.

vents this. It's a disagreeable subject anyway and I don't like
to sit and look at it."

Such themes, incidentally, suggest a new line of inquiry for advertising research. The consumer's brand image—*his* total picture *of*
the product—has long been a key concept in marketing and advertising
strategy. Perhaps an important area for investigation is the brand's
consumer image as perceived by the consumer himself. What does the
message communicate to the viewer about how *he* is seen and regarded
by the advertiser?[7] And how does that relate to his own picture of
himself—as he is, and as he would like to be?

"Flattering the prospect," or at least treating him with some respect,
is a cardinal rule in all but the most high-pressured personal selling. Yet
selling via the mass media often departs in several directions:

a) unflattering or insulting depiction of the consumer in the
commercial itself
b) direct or symbolic assaults on his person
c) threats and ultimatums regarding what happens if he fails
to comply
d) a level of communication that "talks down" to large portions of the audience, or otherwise implies that the advertiser has little respect for the viewer's aesthetic or critical
capacities

Some commercials embodying one or all of these are no doubt on the
lists of the most successful. But when, why, and how such appeals work
—and at what long-term cost—are issues worthy of investigation.

Favorites and offenders: Some hints as to the locus of satisfactions and grievances with commercials appear in Questions 43 and 44.

The most striking finding is the *a*symmetry of the graph. With only
two exceptions,[8] all of the major product categories are primarily praised
or primarily criticized. Thus viewers are in general agreement on the
types of commercials they like best and least; unlike the general program categories (page 148), these commercial groupings generally run
two or three to one on one side or the other.

[7] The advertiser's *actual* conception of the consumer might be a study of interest
in its own right.

[8] Laundry soaps-detergents and cosmetics—the latter, probably, because deodorants were unfortunately coded in the same category as lipstick, nail polish, etc.

QUESTION 43 *"Can you give me an example of the best advertising you've seen on TV? (I mean the advertising you personally like best.)…"*

Respondents: **1221**

QUESTION 44 *"Can you give me an example of the worst advertising you've seen on TV?…"*

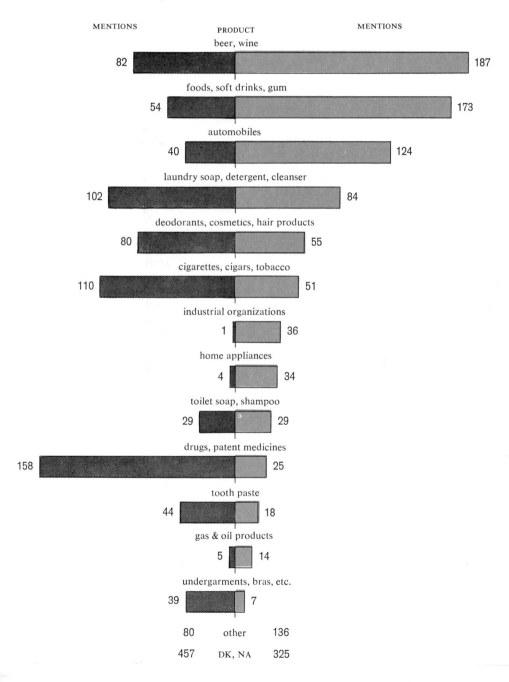

MENTIONS   PRODUCT   MENTIONS

beer, wine
82 — 187

foods, soft drinks, gum
54 — 173

automobiles
40 — 124

laundry soap, detergent, cleanser
102 — 84

deodorants, cosmetics, hair products
80 — 55

cigarettes, cigars, tobacco
110 — 51

industrial organizations
1 — 36

home appliances
4 — 34

toilet soap, shampoo
29 — 29

drugs, patent medicines
158 — 25

tooth paste
44 — 18

gas & oil products
5 — 14

undergarments, bras, etc.
39 — 7

80   other   136

457   DK, NA   325

QUESTION 43 "Can you give me an example of the best advertising you've seen on TV?"

"What did you like about it?"

PRODUCT	New Products, Ideas	Factual, Believable	Good Product	Price, Sales, Institutional, Informative, General	Cartoon	Music	Variety	Specific Characters, Elements	Unobtrusive	Entertaining, General Children, Other Content	Short, to The Point	Base*: 100% =
ALL†	8%	7%	3%	7%	17%	13%	6%	8%	4%	19%	7%	976
Beer, Wine	1	1	1	1	43	17	9	10	5	26	15	153
Food, Gum, Soft Drinks, Baby Food	16	5	3	3	18	19	9	11	5	18	11	150
Autos, Farm Equipment Accessories	14	16	3	13	9	11	10	10	5	16	4	115
Laundry Soap, Household Cleaners	12	3	14	9	9	24	8	5	3	20	6	66
Deodorants, Cosmetics, etc.	12	7	0	7	19	12	5	0	0	31	9	42
Cigarettes, Cigars, Tobacco	0	15	0	0	5	25	15	8	3	20	12	40
Industrial Goods, Institutional	22	12	0	56	3	0	0	0	0	6	6	32
Home Appliances, Aluminum Foil	20	10	0	17	23	0	0	7	7	17	10	30
Personal Soaps, Shampoos	4	4	4	4	0	17	8	17	4	42	0	24
Drugs, Patent Medicine	0	11	28	11	6	7	0	6	6	22	0	18
Tooth Pastes	7	7	7	0	13	7	0	20	0	40	0	15
Gas, Oil Products	0	14	0	50	7	0	0	0	0	43	7	14
Other Personal Products	8	9	2	8	21	10	4	13	5	17	13	121

*Includes those mentioning commercials in *one* category only
†Includes product categories not shown because of infrequent mention
Note: More than one reason can be mentioned

QUESTION 44 *"Can you give me an example of the worst advertising you've seen on TV?"* *"What didn't you like about it?"*

	Misleading, Exaggerated Claims	Products Too Personal to be Advertised	Presentation in Bad Taste	Silly, Insult to Intelligence	Boring, Repetitive	Poor Timing	Too Hard a Sell, Too Loud	Particular Personality, Element Disliked	Pointless, Confusing	Base*: 100% =
ALL†	18%	12%	11%	14%	12%	7%	5%	4%	6%	890
PRODUCT										
Beer, Wine	3	53	3	16	3	6	2	2	26	62
Food, Gum, Soft Drinks, Baby Food	13	6	4	28	13	6	6	11	15	47
Autos, Farm Equipment Accessories	29	0	3	11	20	31	17	11	0	35
Laundry Soap, Household Cleaners	48	1	3	16	13	5	8	8	1	92
Deodorants, Cosmetics, etc.	13	25	29	21	6	3	0	3	6	72
Cigarettes, Cigars, Tobacco	33	13	4	25	10	6	4	5	7	84
Personal Soaps, Shampoos	13	0	17	22	17	13	0	17	4	23
Drugs, Patent Medicine	24	11	30	11	22	4	7	1	1	142
Tooth Pastes	31	3	10	5	33	13	5	3	3	39
Women's Undergarments	0	76	12	0	3	0	0	0	15	33
Other Personal Products	12	3	8	23	18	11	7	5	11	73

*Includes those mentioning commercials in *one* category only
†Includes product categories not shown because of infrequent mention
Note: More than one reason can be mentioned

The favorites tend to come from beer (amusing), food (entertaining and informative), and automobile (news) commercials. Certain drugs and patent medicines are far and away the most objectionable (exaggerated, in bad taste, repetitive), followed by cigarettes (exaggerated, silly), undergarments (in bad taste), and toothpaste (exaggerated, repetitive). Laundry soaps, cleaners, and cosmetics each produce sizable reactions in both directions; these categories are undoubtedly too broad and hide differences within them.

The specificity of praise and criticism regarding the content of commercials indicates the difference in acceptability among the various approaches presently being used. In one sense, this should encourage and challenge those who wonder whether commercials *can* be improved. Clearly, commercial content *per se* is not objectionable. Some are good and some are bad; and viewers pretty well agree on which is which, and why. None of this, of course, speaks to effectiveness; "good" and "bad" here means only "liked" and "disliked," and perhaps that distinction is at the root of the problem. The point, however, is that advertising agencies—unlike program producers—would face relatively few dilemmas if their object were only to please their audience.

"The System"

Commercial sponsorship, as an economic system of financing television, is probably not a matter the average viewer has given a great deal of thought to. He certainly has not to its alternatives. In this study, we included only a few quick measures of viewers' feelings on this issue, principally as "insurance" to turn up any surprising views for further study. We have already seen that substantial numbers raise the matter of sponsorship spontaneously as "most liked" about commercials: "they pay for the programs" (and so they are entitled to their say).

To quantify this attitude and some others, we introduced the following self-administered check sheet:

QUESTION 42C *"Here are some statements about commercials. I'd like you to read each statement and mark whether you generally agree or disagree with each statement?"*

		SEX		EDUCATION		
Respondents:	ALL	Men	Women	Grade School	High School	College & Beyond
Base: 100% = 2427		1177	1246	627	1214	516

PER CENT WHO "AGREE" THAT *

I. Commercials are a fair price to pay for the entertainment you get	75%	74%	77%	76%	78%	70%
A. Most commercials are too long	63	62	64	56	66	65
E. I find some commercials are very helpful in keeping me informed	58	54	61	64	62	41
D. Some commercials are so good that they are more entertaining than the program	43	44	43	42	45	42
F. I would prefer TV without commercials	43	45	42	38	44	49
G. Commercials are ordinarily in poor taste and very annoying	40	43	38	37	40	46
B. I frequently find myself welcoming a commercial break	36	33	38	39	38	26
H. I dislike long movies without the movies that commercials provide	27	25	28	31	28	21
C. I'd rather pay a small amount yearly if I could have television without commercials	24	28	20	18	24	30

*Phrases arranged in order of "agree"

The two statements accepted most and least often tell the story quite clearly. Men and women; grade school, high school and college—all agree that commercials are a fair price to pay for the entertainment you get (I). At the opposite extreme (C), the suggestion that small individual fees be substituted arouses the least enthusiasm; such expressed willingness to pay even "a small amount" rises above 25 per cent only among the very highest income and educational groups (see Appendix Table 24), and then only to the order of 35 to 40 per cent. And those who do agree to pay a small amount are further reduced in number by the follow-up question: "How much?"

Q. 42 G "What would be the most you might be willing to pay per year to have television without commercials (that is, the same programs that are on now)?"

$ 0	6%
1–5	11
6–15	17
16–30	10
31–100	13
over 100	1
DK, NA	42

Base: 100% = 580

Six per cent in effect renege, and over 40 per cent really don't know. Perhaps this large residual response suggests how little meaning the question has for most people; they simply do not think in terms of annual charges for TV. And those remaining do not consider that commercial-free TV, at least with present programming, is worth a great deal in cash.

Similarly, most people would *not* prefer TV without commercials (F)—even when no costs are stipulated. Possibly alternative costs are inferred by some; but possibly, too, this response refers to the entertainment and information the commercials sometimes provide (E, D).[9]

The price that commercials often exact, however fair, is a real one. Here again, dissatisfaction with the commercials themselves appears, with the single "timing" item (A) far outscoring the single

[9] The second interpretation is supported by the fact that those most likely to recognize alternative costs—the well-educated—are also most likely to "prefer" TV without commercials and to state their willingness to pay.

content criticism (G). (It is noteworthy that 60 per cent *fail* to agree that commercials are ordinarily in poor taste and very annoying; and that the majority, though just barely, refrains from this indictment even among the college-educated.)[1]

But as critics of the commercial system often point out, the viewers' boredom or irritation with the ad message is not the only, and perhaps not the most important "cost" of the system. Beyond that, there is the "commercial control of TV content," with the debilitating, common-denominator influence so often postulated. How do the viewers feel about that?

Our information comes from a question in another context. During the discussion of programming, we asked:

Q. 19   "Who do you think has the most to say about what kinds of programs are on the air—who really decides?"

Advertisers	45%	
Sponsors		43
Ad agencies, Madison Ave.		3
Television industry	27%	
Networks, stations, executives		20
Producers		8
Writers, actors		2
The Public	26%	
Viewing public, general		23
Specific segment—men, children, etc.		1
Polls, ratings		5
Government	1%	
Censors	1%	
Critics	0% *	
Other	3%	
DK, NA	6%	

Base: 100% = 2427

*Less than 0.5.

NOTE: Multiple responses.

[1] As shown, sex makes little difference in general response to commercials; neither does age, region, race, national origin, or any other variable we examined save the education-occupation-income cluster and religion.

Why do men and women not differ *more* in their attitudes toward commercials when so many more of them are directed at the housewife? Perhaps because the relevant attitudes are associated with non-product considerations—e.g., length, interruption, entertainment value. A few more women do in fact agree that "commercials are very helpful in keeping me informed."

So the plurality clearly thinks that "sponsors" control program content, and some people view this with alarm:

> "The sponsors. You talk about your crookedness. Some of the sponsors were proven to be the ones on the quiz shows."

But far more frequently, sponsors are granted control in much the same "fair play" spirit we encountered before:

> "It has to be paid for, so whoever is paying for it decides what to show."

> "Whoever sponsors the program would have something to say about it, I would think—it's their nickel that's paying for the show."

> "If I were the sponsor, I'd decide what programs should be on."

Furthermore, many people identify the *public* interest with the sponsor's control, through his desire to attain maximum audience appeal:

> "I believe the sponsors—the ones who pay for the advertising. They are trying to come up with something new all the time to catch the viewer's eye."

> "The advertising agencies through their polls and things. . . . Layout of the program must suit the advertiser. He pays the bills and he knows what he wants for his money. Mainly, audience. Number of people. The producer merely tries to please the sponsor. That is his responsibility."

Possibly because commercial sponsorship and program control are not seen by most viewers as much of a detriment to programming, people seem cool toward "pay TV" as an alternative *or* an adjunct to the present system, at least as rudimentarily described in our question. We made no attempt, here, to spell out what "pay TV" might actually mean, under various systems. But here is a first reading on two variables:

Q. 45A,B *"You may have heard something about 'Pay TV' — this would be a system where, in addition to the regular stations, there would be some stations without advertising which would charge (fifty cents) (one dollar) or so per program for special programs. Do you think this should be tried out, or not?"*

Q. 52C,D *"You may have heard something about 'Pay TV' — this would be a system where some of the present TV stations would not have advertising but would charge (fifty cents) (one dollar) or so per program for special programs. Do you think this should be tried out, or not?"*

Per Cent "Should Be Tried"

	All *	Education			Income			Religion		
		Grade School	High School	College and Beyond	Low	Med.	High	P	C	J
Additional stations 50¢ per program	31%	22%	28%	52%	22%	33%	42%	28%	34%	47%
Additional stations $1.00 per program	22	18	17	38	17	16	39	22	19	29
Present stations 50¢ per program	20	15	16	34	14	18	28	13	24	37
Present stations $1.00 per program	22	10	22	37	15	20	37	21	20	38

* Each per cent based on a different number of respondents. See Appendix Table 25.

1. Audience enthusiasm is not impressive; especially in view of the fact that the question is not whether it should be *done,* but just whether it should be *tried.* Over-all, about three fourths say "don't try it," and the price does not make much difference.

2. The college-educated, high-income viewers are more receptive, but the idea, even there, fails to capture a majority (except under the 50 cents, additional-stations condition).

3. The "additional stations" substantially outscore "present stations" under the 50-cents conditions; but when the price goes up to $1.00, it makes no difference—both present and additional seem equally acceptable, or unacceptable.

The possible advantages of the system, cited by those who favor as well as those who oppose the trial, center mainly on its freedom from commercials. Only among the better-educated does higher-level programming become a major issue. (See Appendix Table 26.) Again, this provides some evidence of the level of annoyance with commercials.

On the other side, the projected disadvantages simply have to do with the outlay of funds, though some viewers raise interesting psychological consequences: for example, you wouldn't be as prone to turn off a program you had paid for if it turned out to be no good; or, you couldn't really relax watching something that was costing money. (See Appendix Table 27.)

At the moment, then, the public ("highbrow" included) shows no signs of clamoring for an alternative "system," though the public ("highbrow" included) probably has a very hazy idea of what it would entail.

But the public ("lowbrow" included) finds plenty of room for improvement in the way the present system is operated, with regard to commercials. So this review of the matter—pedestrian as some aspects of the issue may be—has produced three unique results:

1. For the first time in the study, we have found a source of rather general annoyance with what appears on the TV screen. Programming yielded a variety of specific suggestions and complaints, but nothing approaching a widespread dissatisfaction. Commercials undeniably qualify on this score. All of them don't annoy everybody all of the time, but there are probably very few viewers who are not often unhappy on one count or another.

2. By the same token, we find the different viewing elements in somewhat closer agreement than they have been on most issues. To be sure, the "highbrow" is still *more* critical of commercials, and on somewhat different grounds, but he and his less-educated counterparts are in substantial agreement in the direction, if not the intensity and frequency, of their criticisms and their implicit requests.

3. Thus we have the now surprising situation of the audience in substantial agreement on what *should* be changed, and on matters that *could* be changed, and rather easily (in principle, if not in practice). In short, viewer response gives clear direction to those who would increase viewer satisfaction. Here, unlike the case of programming, we can at least say what would please more of the people more of the time: shorter, fewer, and especially less interruptive messages; less aggres-

sive and distasteful messages (by common, middle-class standards). And if, with regard to timing, commercials cannot be all three—shorter, fewer, *and* non-interruptive—the priority is probably in the reverse order.

Conclusions
and Commentary

As THE heading suggests, we attempt two tasks in these final pages.

First, we assemble and condense the major findings, interpret them, and reach some tentative conclusions. What does it all seem to come to? What have we learned from and about the American television audience, and what does it all mean—to the people at both ends of the television broadcast as well as to the student of mass communication?

Second, we allow ourselves some personal observations, speculations, and questions—not always tied directly to the research findings, but suggested by the study or simply by the experience of conducting such an inquiry.

The Findings

To begin, we should restate the limits and say once again exactly what this investigation has and has not been. Our subject was the adult television *audience*—not the television industry or its programs or the economic foundations of the present system (though we have asked how the audience regards each of these).

Furthermore, we have had no direct concern with the *effects* of the medium upon that audience—only with how some of these effects are perceived by its members. Our data, like our interests, have dealt mainly with the attitudes and feelings generated by the television set. Except for the special ARB check, designed to compare some interview statements with actual viewing, there has been no direct evidence on how the audience actually behaves in regard to television, or as a result of watching it.

So a host of crucial questions are untouched in these pages: for example, what does TV really do to children—not in the opinion of their parents, but as independently and objectively assessed? Or, the same question with respect to the parents themselves.

What does "viewing" mean in behavioral terms—how much real attention is ordinarily devoted to the programs? When, and for whom, is viewing a primary or exclusive pursuit like reading, and when is it only of secondary or "background" significance? What alternatives does television replace, in what types of homes; and what alternatives does it perhaps develop? And so on.

At the same time, we have generated a broad and fairly consistent picture of the public image of the medium; what people think of the industry; how viewers feel about viewing; what part television plays in daily life, and vis-à-vis the other media; what parents consider its most important effects on their children and on the family; how people evaluate most of the programs they are offered and those they watch most often; what changes they would like to see *made* (as against what they would like to *see*); and how they regard commercials and their implications. And we have observed some clear differentiation within the audience on many of these issues.

As promised, and hedged, in the introduction, the entire book has been a brief overview of the main results. Many interesting and productive analyses have not been pursued in depth in these pages. But leaving aside the more detailed analyses that may follow, we can now make the following points, and with some confidence:

1. *The "average American viewer"*   The average American viewer spends hours a day in front of his TV set and finds it a relaxing and pleasant—now an integral—part of his daily life: certainly not without important costs, but by and large, in his judgment, well worth them. TV's contributions to home life, on balance, are somewhat more apparent than the other forms of family interaction it may replace; and its advantages for the children and for him (especially *her*), as parent, outweigh the dangers and problems it poses in this regard.

Though he has come to depend a great deal on routine, daily viewing—or perhaps *because* he has—television is not often terribly exciting. In the beginning, it was "really something to talk about"; today, the viewer gives little evidence of extreme response in either direction. He is not often overwhelmed by what he sees; nor is he often bored or disgusted. When he does tend to use superlatives in his discussion of television, it is less likely to be about the programs than about the good or evil that stems from viewing *per se*.

The programs, on the whole, he considers good—somewhat better than satisfactory; and among them he finds many favorites that are extremely enjoyable. There is no reservoir of specific unfulfilled desires; nor does he find an oversupply or an imbalance in what the industry offers him. Accordingly, he watches pretty much what happens to be on the air, as he must do to sustain the number of hours he spends at it: how selective can one be when total consumption approaches a substantial proportion of what is available?

There have been some memorable serious moments in his viewing history, especially some original television dramas, but by and large he recalls the comedy stars that TV has made: Caesar, Gleason, Desi and Lucy, Berle, *et al.* And this, of course, is consistent with the principal use to which he now puts the medium—easy, relaxing entertainment. Accordingly, his favorites in the current season are most likely to fall into "action" and "comedy-variety" categories; he finds these shows entertaining, interesting, and relaxing—but by no means especially original or creative.

He would like TV to be more informative and educational but certainly not at the expense of entertainment. Aside from the day's news and weather—which he watches regularly—he rarely uses the set as a deliberate source of information, and he is extremely unlikely to turn on serious and informative public affairs presentations, even if he is watching while they are on the air.

All of this reflects the present division of labor between the various media. Television, among the home sources of mass communication, has its greatest comparative advantage in the field of entertainment. According to the average viewer, and no doubt in reality, newspapers presently provide more thorough reports of the important happenings on the local and larger scene; radio is quicker with frequent, capsule summaries; and magazines best provide for limited, specialized interests. It is television, and by a wide margin, that is turned to for relaxation and diversion.

This division is certainly not complete, but rather one of relative emphasis. Nor is it the necessary, *a priori* allocation of function: newspapers *could* carry more entertainment and television *could* devote more time to news and editorials. And if that occurred, there would probably be some shifts in what the public expects from these media and seeks in them. But this is where we stand at the moment.

TV brought moving sight-and-sound—the nation's number-one pastime for twenty years—from the theater into the living room, from fee to "free." It seems unlikely that a medium more restricted in its sensory dimensions will displace television as the principal source of mass amusement. Conversely, and by complement, print has clear advantages in the transmission of serious material that requires concentration or self-pacing.

The problems and frustrations that surround television in the average home are several. They deal principally with how the viewer regards himself and his use of the set. But there are two notable exceptions that deal directly with content:

a) The average viewer thinks that programs depict too much imitable violence that children see both in "their shows" and in those designed for adults. This problem he places squarely on those in charge of programming. True, parental acquiescence is a necessary ingredient, he feels, but why should broadcasters put parents on that spot? There should be less need for vigilance to keep the children from potentially dangerous material, particularly since the parents usually enjoy and often benefit from the children's hours in front of the set.

b) He also thinks that there are too many commercials, and especially too many that are boring, repetitious, and/or irritating. Here, again, the responsibility is not that of the viewer; and he wishes that those in charge would do something to improve the situation.

But his most serious and pervasive hesitations are not so easily disposed of. They rest at home—precisely, in part, because *he* rests, so often and so long, at home.

Television wastes so much time! Which means, of course, that he often wastes time watching it. To watch TV is to be not "doing" anything, except relaxing; and to be doing nothing for so many leisure hours (and perhaps, for women, many "working hours") arouses some ambivalence.

There may be an inherent conflict between extensive and time-consuming "passive" amusement and the stress on achievement among mobile Americans. Television, unlike many other pastimes, does not come with a ready-made set of justifications. Golf is healthful; reading, admirable; sleep, restorative. Even liquor helps to combat those dangerous daily tensions. Keeping informed and learning something may be potential counterparts—but this particular ambivalence and its resolution reach greater significance in the case of the non-average, better-educated viewer, and we turn to him in a moment.

Some underlying "laziness" is not the only disquieting concomitant of daily viewing in the average American home. Many families have a sometimes vague, sometimes well-articulated feeling that television replaces other past or potential family activities. It does tend to keep them at home and together, but by the same token it curtails conversation, visiting, going out.

In addition, family viewing often creates conflict between what adults enjoy (and, in most cases, the children also) and what the parents think is good or appropriate for the youngsters. The issue is usually resolved in the predictable way; at the cost of some qualms about the "effects" on the children, and perhaps an accompanying annoyance at the broadcasters who provided the seductive but dangerous alternative.

But real as these and other hesitations are, they certainly do not overshadow the basic satisfaction that the television set provides. That was apparent from the beginning, in the ubiquitous and extensive consumption the medium enjoys. All things considered, television is among the most significant contributions to everyday pleasure that modern technology has produced. The average viewer would not give it up if he could—as, of course, he *could* if he wanted to. When the house is temporarily without television, as it sometimes is for mechanical reasons beyond his control, he sees to it that it is temporary indeed.

This average American viewer in the average American home is a concept of convenience, which enables us to summarize the most common patterns in personal terms. But he is not a statistical artifact, "average" only in the arithmetic sense: that is, he is not the result of adding an enthusiast to an indifferent viewer and dividing by two. He exists, and in the largest numbers.[1]

He has no more than a high-school education, an annual income of less than $8000, and he accounts for over three quarters of all television homes and a still higher percentage of the effective audience at any given time because he watches somewhat more often than those with higher social-economic standing. Thus, the thoughts and reactions we have attributed to him are broadly characteristic of the major segment of the American television audience.

2. *The average non-average viewer* The higher-educated, higher-income, big-city viewer shares many of the above responses, but departs notably in others. In general, his verbal focus shifts visibly to the negative: he finds the same basic satisfactions in television but he takes its costs more seriously.

He too turns to television principally for relaxation and entertainment. More than the rest, he has other sources of serious information available to him—especially magazines—and only slightly more often than the common man does he select information from what is available when he watches. He too has been most impressed by the comic greats of past seasons and would like to see them return. He too watches a great deal of television—quite a bit less than the average, but that is still quite a bit. And he too generally finds the programs he watches "extremely enjoyable"; indeed, his own favorites get even more glowing praise then the mass audience lavishes on its own.

On the other hand, he is far less impressed with "television in general" and its "programs in general." Accordingly, he is especially likely to put great emphasis on the related issues of "productive" programming and selective viewing.

Selectivity is a matter of some importance in his personal approach to the subject of TV: he may claim a bit more than he exercises but

[1] In this sense, technically, he is modal, not mean.

probably no more than he would like to. He does tend to be attracted to specific, outstanding dramatic programs, but they account for an infinitesimal share of his television week. That, as with the average viewer, is devoted mostly to light entertainment.

Thus, his consistent call for more informative television is possibly the clearest finding with the least clear interpretation. To summarize the survey results is simple: the more educated and informed the viewer, the more education and information he says television should provide—to the point where this becomes the number-one criticism or suggestion of the number-one educational group.

But why does he say it, and what does he mean? Apparently not that he, personally, would like to see more programs like the present informational ones on the air. He has a long way to go before he comes close to exhausting those—even on the commercial channels, let alone the educational outlets. He takes little of the first and still less of the second, when he *has* the opportunity to do so.

Perhaps he means something else by information and education; something different, or better, than what now goes by that name. But if so, he fails to tell us about it when he has the chance. On the contrary, he often lists current informational shows as his favorites, and he has little else to suggest when we get to specifics.

Is it just a matter of response bias—of saying what is appropriate, approved, expected of a well-educated, sophisticated respondent? Probably in large part; certainly not entirely. There are at least two other possibilities.

First, he may be sincerely convinced that television should be more informative *beyond* the extent to which he himself needs or wants more enlightment from it. Social, not personal criteria may be involved. Listen again to Academicus, for a clear exposition of the extreme position:

> . . . precisely my complaint about the mass media arises from the fact that they do occupy the center of attention in America . . . television itself gets more hours of attention each week than anything but home and work, and perhaps it rivals them. You can't get people to think about the great values because they're watching TV. So the media *are* reaching vulnerable people who, from our standpoint, do not give attention to other things. With that huge slice of attention,

then, goes responsibility for our values. And what values are they serving?"[2]

Academicus obviously watches little if any television himself, and certainly does not depend on it for serious information. His chief concern is with the social and cultural implications of so much television "escape" among the masses. To him, the country *needs* a more informative and educational schedule, as it needs speed limits, better public schools, and racial integration—not necessarily for his personal benefit or use, but for the common good when adopted by others.

This argument is not reduced to "hypocrisy" by the intellectuals' own neglect of TV information; in fact, it is entirely untouched by whatever they do or fail to do. If it is to be met, it must be met on its own ground; and we will give both sides a platform in the next section.

Or, his call may be for information *with,* not *instead of,* entertainment, so as to make his own relaxation more rewarding or at least more psychologically comfortable. Recall that, in large numbers, he refused to choose between the two and asked, instead, for "both"—for programs at once enjoyable and intellectually satisfying.

As a middle-class, striving American, he more acutely feels the need to spend time usefully than his less ambitious counterparts; and his formal schooling has placed a high value on reading and serious study. This combination attaches more than a little uneasiness to the hours he spends being entertained without effort by materials he regards of little intrinsic worth. "Waste," which probably tends to be an issue with him in many areas, seems especially evident here in the case of time, his most valuable resource.

If he could only learn something—historical, political, scientific, cultural—that would justify this otherwise unproductive use of time. Maybe he asks for "more information" partly out of the desire for such a justification.

There is at least some evidence in that direction: first, in the widespread agreement that TV is educational for children—which increases with parental schooling only among those who admit to using the set as a baby-sitter; secondly, in the far greater intellectual benefits the educated viewer already attributes to his favorites, even when these come from the "action" or "light drama" categories.

[2] In Berelson: op. cit.

(The best rationalizations, of course, are the true ones. The psychological functions of a belief say nothing of its validity, just about the reasons for clinging to it. Television may *be* highly educational for children; and a more informative adult schedule *would* reward the mind as well as salve the conscience—but only if it were watched.)

Finally, our "class" viewer has financial and cultural resources which make "more meaningful" alternatives psychologically available, if not always actually so. He "could have" gone to the opera or read something provocative instead. Whether he actually would have, except for television, is another matter. The mere presence of these more highly sanctioned and probably more satisfying alternatives raises the issue; and its expression may often take the form of dissatisfaction with the seductive "influence" of the easier time-killer.

Who or what is really to "blame," if evenings at home with television are sometimes or even generally preferred to more worthwhile ways of spending time? This is not an empirical question—but investigation does point out that there are at least two components in the decision: the presence of the television alternative, and its actual selection by those who prefer it. As we have said, watching television is not, like outdoor advertising, imposed or interposed between the viewer and better things by an industry; it is, after all, an activity initiated by those who have the final option in the matter. If the TV set "intrudes," it is by invitation.

In sum, then, the great mass of the American television audience divides roughly into two major segments according to the social-economic standing of the household, with formal schooling the single factor that makes the most difference. The number of slices on this continuum if of course arbitrary; but on most matters we do little violence to the data by dividing the public into those with and those without college training.

These two groups differ markedly in what they have to say about television, but not so markedly in how they use it and what they choose to see. There are significant differences in taste, but most tastes are already represented in the present range of television programming, though not in equal proportions. The behavioral distinction (not the verbal one) is between *Gunsmoke* and nondescript westerns; between Sid Caesar and the canned comedy; between *Play of the Week* and anthology light drama. It is *not* between occasional selective viewing of a few outstanding presentations and daily hours of escape. To see that contrast, we must sample not the college-educated but the teachers of their teachers.[3]

The big and real difference seems to lie not in what they do but how they feel about it. What the majority accepts as a legitimate use of television, the minority may think of as abuse of it (or *its* abuse of *them*). The mass audience is more likely to thank TV for keeping the family together, physically; the class viewer is more apt to blame it for keeping them apart, socially. The large segment concentrates on the help it gives them in keeping their children out of mischief; the small, on the fact that it (also) keeps them out of books or bed.

But while they focus on different sides, all examine the same coin. In the average and non-average home alike, we have seen at least as much concern with *how* people watch as with *what* they watch. Thus, the audience itself is aware of what sociologists might call the "structure" (as against the content) of television, and in this awareness, isolates the unique effects of TV. For the content is not unique: westerns did not originate with television and do not end with it, and neither, of course, does Shakespeare.

So it is that one commentator can say today of the video tube:

> We have triumphantly invented, perfected, and distributed to the humblest cottage throughout the land one of the greatest technical marvels in history, television, and have used it for what? To bring Coney Island into every home. It is as though movable type had been devoted exclusively since Gutenberg's time to the publication of comic books.[4]

[3] The extremes, at either end, account for relatively few people; but on matters of policy their voices are perhaps the most and least important, respectively.

The true upper-crust intellectual—the thought leader at the national level—certainly accounts for a negligible portion of the audience, but hardly a negligible portion of the effective critical voice. He writes the articles, teaches the classes, and runs the government agencies that direct attention to the shortcomings of television—as well as those of the other media, and indeed American society in general. And he has by far the least rosy picture of the state and effects of today's TV.

At the opposite extreme, we have a larger number of unqualified enthusiasts (some argue, in both senses of unqualified), with neither the articulation, the platform, or the power—not even the consumer dollar—to make themselves heard.

[4] From an address delivered by Robert M. Hutchins, Center for the Study of Democratic Institutions, Washington, D.C., June 1, 1961.

precisely what another said one hundred years ago about that movable type:

> Communications has just about reached the lowest point, with respect to its importance; and contemporaneously the means of communications have pretty nearly attained the highest point, with respect to quick and overwhelming distribution. For what is in such haste to get out, and on the other hand, what has such widespread distribution as . . . twaddle? Oh, procure silence![5]

But, watching at the dinner table, pre-school children engrossed quietly for hours, the family at the movies in the living room—these things did originate less than fifteen years ago. They are the effects of the medium itself, as against the more general implications of the type of content found before and at present in other channels of mass communication.[6]

Interestingly, too, the popular critics and observers (as against the professional ones) seem to have trained their sights mainly on such issues. As both class and mass cartoons illustrate, satirists have treated television largely in terms of its demands on us, and ours on it. Programming, as such, has been far less important.[7]

None of this is to deny the significance of programming, its level and its diversity. In the last analysis, that is in large measure responsible for the way television *is* used. The point is that the relationship is clearly two-way: the actual uses of the medium influence programming (by determining what fare will be most appropriate and thus most popular) and they certainly affect how the public regards its shows and what it says about them. But to understand popular praise and popular criticism and to know how much stock to put in each, they must be read against the criteria the public actually applies—the criteria not readily admitted as well as those held with pride.

[5] Kierkegaard as quoted in Berelson: op. cit.

[6] And here, also, we know precisely which is chicken and which egg, unlike content considerations, which are always subject to such argument: do the values portrayed in programming reflect, produce, or just reinforce the general cultural norms and trends? For example, to what extent does TV violence or immorality foster such behavior; to what extent does it simply express our national acceptance of these patterns?

[7] A short content analysis of all TV cartoons in four publications documents this point. (See Appendix Table 28.)

In the case of television, as in the case of most issues that people are personally involved in, their attitudes, stereotypes, and reactions stem only in part from the actual nature of the "object." They also reflect the nature of the holder, and exist in the service of his needs. The lesson has been learned in almost every important realm of social policy—from political affiliation, to religious and racial discrimination, to birth control, to fallout shelters.

Television is no exception. Hence, it provides scholars with fertile territory for social and psychological exploration; and it provides practical men with enigmas in deciding what it is they are and should be doing with the medium.

Commentary

Q. 65   *"If you personally were in charge of a leading television network, what changes would you like to make?"*

> "I wouldn't want to make any radical changes until I'd taken a poll and saw what the people wanted to see."
>
> *   *   *
>
> > "Well, I think I'd like a lot of comedy and something that takes our mind off everyday troubles."
> >
> > "To secure better material for all programs. Material that has meaning and teaches us the meaning of life."
> >
> > *   *   *
> >
> > "I would make everything factual whether the churches and hypocrites approved or not."
> >
> > "I'd have church services and some good singing and praying."
> >
> > *   *   *
> >
> > "I would have nothing but westerns."
> >
> > "Have less cowboy shows."
> >
> > *   *   *
> >
> > "I'd put more Negroes on the shows."
> >
> > "I'd set dynamite under it. Then I'd build two new ones—one for the whites, one for the Negroes."
> >
> > *   *   *
> >
> > "Put on more interesting but informative programs. Would like to feel entertained but have my mind stimulated at the same time."

"I'd fix it so all of the news shows wouldn't all come on at the same time, so if you didn't want to watch it, you could watch a program."

*   *   *

"I am very well satisfied with the programs the way they are."

"I would cut it off—that's what I'd do."

*   *   *

"I'd put *I Love Lucy* on for four hours a day for my family; and I'd put *Restless Gun* on every day for two hours; and *Air Power* for nine hours every day, and that's it."

*   *   *

"The first thing I would do is change places with somebody else."

"I can't answer that. That's just like being President of the United States."

"I wouldn't like that. You can't please everybody."

"You might as well ask, 'What would you do if you were God?' "

"Lady, I'm a welder—a union welder. I don't even want to *think* about being manager of a TV network. They are doing a fine job, and I don't know how to make it better."

Now for a long step back from the data. The following comments are mostly personal conjecture and opinion, and to make that perfectly clear and keep it in view, I put them in the first person.

During two years of preoccupation with television and its implications, I encountered many recurring questions and arguments. I learned early and often that the operational translation of some of the most appealing clichés is either impossible or quite surprising in its results. My main purpose here is to put some of these questions—and most of them still unanswered—in terms explicit enough to make their consequences evident, or at least open to investigation.

The question(s) of "cultural democracy"   The most general issue divides into two basic questions: Do we want "cultural democracy" in the case of television? And if so, what is it and how do we know when we have it?

Do we want it? Many critics and critical positions rest on the assumption that we do not, or at least that we cannot afford to have it, or to have it entirely. The argument, complicated or simple, embeds the basic premise that what the public *wants* is irrelevant, at least to some extent. Here are two of the key spokesmen.

For the Government:

You will get no argument from me if you say that, given a choice between a Western and a symphony, more people will watch the Western. I like Westerns and private eyes too—but a steady diet for the whole country is obviously not in the public interest. We all know that people would more often prefer to be entertained than stimulated or informed. But your broadcaster's obligations are not satisfied if you look only to popularity as a test of what to broadcast. You are not only in show business; you are free to communicate ideas as well as relaxation. You must provide a wider range of choice, more diversity, more alternatives. It is not enough to cater to the nation's whims—you must also serve the nation's needs."[8]

For the critics:

. . . recognition of the importance of escapism must be accompanied by an awareness that a mass audience also can be childlike; it generally will choose candy over spinach. To surrender to this tendency on the ground that doing so epitomizes "cultural democracy" or "giving the public what it wants" is hogwash.[9]

In short: "We don't ask children whether or not they want to go to school. We make them do it for their own sake and for that of the country."[1]

---

[8] Newton N. Minow, in an address delivered to the National Association of Broadcasters, Washington, D.C., May 9, 1961.

[9] Jack Gould: *The New York Times Magazine,* January 14, 1962.

[1] On the other hand, of course, we do ask the voters who should run the country and assume that they can make that decision. The question is whether the adult American is more properly regarded as a dependent child when it comes to matters of his own entertainment and enlightenment than he is in his role as voter. One answer is that we *need* to enlighten him—despite himself if necessary—precisely in order to qualify him as a dependable citizen: "Today, as never before, we need an enlightened public to make judgments on matters crucial to the nation and the world . . ."

To what extent, then, should television be pre-empted in the public service, like land for highways or the school system? To what extent should it be left entirely free to try to please its audience, like the movies or magazines? That is a policy matter based on value judgments not open to empirical discussion. Sir Robert Fraser has clearly stated the logical alternatives:

> If, like Plato, we believe in Golden Men who know best and if we get our way, we will not be troubled by problems of quantity and quality in television, not if we have the luck, that is, to be Golden Men ourselves, for we will provide ordinary people with the amount and kind of television we think is good for them. But if we agree not with Plato but with Mill about the great social problem of human happiness, then we must face the logic of our preference. The television that is produced will reflect what people do like, not what we think they ought to like, and it is not of great relevance to criticize television.[2]

It is often pointed out that TV is not comparable to films or magazines because of the limited number of channels available. This, the argument runs, makes it necessary to regulate and license TV broadcasters in the public interest. But that coin has two sides. The Mill democrats might counter that the government has even less business pre-empting a limited resource. If one or two newspapers are regulated "in the public interest," the public can reject the regulator's decision by turning to others. But if *all* available television is geared to an authority's conception of what the public needs, the latter is left no choice but to take it that way or not at all. Why, counter the Platonists, should the network bosses' control of content be more acceptable? Because, return the Millites, they are under pressure to maximize the audience (and therefore to please it); and the government agency is not.

What television *should* do is not, then, an empirical matter. But what television *could* do, is—and that is the main reason for raising the issue. It seems to me that the weak, or at least the questionable, link in the Platonic position is the absence of a truant officer. We can and do force children into the classroom, but can we force adults to attend the necessary or beneficial programs?

[2] Sir Robert Fraser, in an address given at Scarborough, England.

In principle, we can certainly prevent them from seeing those we consider harmful, by censorship—but no one is really in favor of that. The real question is to what extent, or how often, people would choose to watch the *better,* more enlightening, less escape-filled schedule. Both the ratings and our limited data suggest that the answer is "not often," at least under conditions where a choice exists.

If all channels were simultaneously elevated, at least during some hours, some attendance would undoubtedly be forced—but how much, or for how long, no one really knows. That, as has already been proposed, can only be answered by a great natural experiment in that direction.[3]

The program distinctions implicit in these considerations usually take the form of two general dichotomies: information or public service vs. entertainment; and within the second, "class culture" vs. "mass culture." Let me pursue each of these in a little more detail.

"Public service" vs. "entertainment"   To date, our national answer to this value issue has been a compromise. The Government in effect tithes the industry: for 10 per cent devoted to Caesar, it allows 90 per cent to be devoted to Circus. The industry *may* entertain most of the time so long as it also provides a share of "public service."

Now, I think it worthwhile to question the consequences of this dichotomy, especially the rather narrow and specific definition of "public service" or "public affairs" programming invoked by the FCC and thus by the industry. In effect, the consideration of "public service" is restricted to news coverage, informational programming, and religious or secular editorializing. Each station is charged with fulfilling a limited quota—as much as it has "promised" in its license application. In turn, it is apt to consider its "service" obligations fulfilled if and when it can point to x hours, regardless of quality or intrinsic interest.

It seems to me that the FCC and other evaluators of broadcaster performance must recognize entertainment as a legitimate and perhaps most significant "public service." Even *within* the civic objectives presently implicit in the "public service" category, there can be serious question as to which program form really does the most good—especially if the size of the audience is included in the comparison. If the objective is spiritual "uplift," are five unwatched minutes of incantation

<hr/>

[3] Bernard Berelson: "The Great Experiment in Cultural Democracy," forthcoming.

by a local preacher really worth more than *Martin Luther* or some equivalent on *The Late Show?* Is the serious consideration of civic issues more often aroused by three aldermen or professors around a table, or by dramatic presentation in an entertainment context—e.g., "message" films *(Snake Pit, Blackboard Jungle, Pinky, Gentlemen's Agreement,* etc.), or social drama (Ibsen, Williams, O'Neill, Chayevsky), and so on?

And beyond the present civic objectives of "public service," there is the matter of enriching, provoking, stimulating, even soothing the emotional or aesthetic sensitivities. In short, entertainment and recreation *per se,* when really good, certainly contribute a valuable public service. That under the present system a station might well feel more pressure to present sectarian religion or the water commissioner than an opera or serious drama,[4] strikes me as a curious misapplication of a communications resource, and certainly raises questions about the underlying value judgment.

In short, *if* broadcasters are to be evaluated on how well they serve the public, the consideration might be expanded—at least conceptually —to the total schedule. Entertainment shows do many of the things the present "public service" shows are supposed to do: often better, certainly for more people. Secondly, good, enriching entertainment should be recognized *as* public service, perhaps the most important public service performed by TV.

Now, clearly this cuts two ways, and perhaps that is why the industry has not made this obvious point long ago and defended it vigorously. If there is to be a public service credit for the moral lessons contained in a serious drama, there will be debits for programs that appear to subvert American values; if broadcasters can claim civic benefits in a dramatic presentation, or personal tragic-catharsis in a good western, they will be held responsible for the juvenile delinquency or emotional disturbance that someone else sees as an obvious consequence of other (or even the same) programs.

So this line of reasoning tends to open a Pandora's box of questions to which there are no real answers—some, because there is not enough

---

[4] And this is perhaps the most realistic alternative. Broadcasters are far less likely to displace a highly rated western or comedy show with such classic presentations than they are to consider substituting them for the required "public service," which gets still lower ratings.

evidence (do crime shows really induce crime?); others, because they are normative and entirely outside the realm of scientific inquiry (*should the public be stimulated or provoked by television programming that may disturb some immature or susceptible minds? What values should drama reinforce? Nihilism? Middle-class? Integration or segregation? Pacifism? Patriotism? Etc.*). Once entertainment is examined in the light of service or disservice, we have to face such issues and their related consequences, censorship or control of content, which nobody wants and nobody can implement.

But, if not formally, then at least informally, there should be a mutual awareness that great good and harm to the community probably rest in the type of entertainment a station presents. Station operators should not sleep soundly just because they have exceeded their quota of "public service"; neither should the critics continue to talk almost entirely in such easy dichotomies of program classification.[5]

Entertainment level—vast wasteland or mass tasteland? It is clear that most of today's entertainment programs are designed to please most of the people—and our study indicates that they usually succeed. It is equally clear that most of the programs do not please all of the people—at least not equally; that significant differences in taste exist, especially between audience segments with different levels of cultural attainment.

By definition, the better-educated, more sophisticated viewers will have tastes different from (and in their opinion, better than) those with less exposure to the finer things. So long as differential education and cultural levels exist in the population, so will different capacities to appreciate and enjoy various forms of diversion and recreation. That is inevitable. So it is probably inevitable that programs catering to the "mass taste" are, for the intellectual, synonymous with "vast waste"— though he may not always take explicit account of that fact and its consequences:

> If you decide to have a system of people's television, then people's television you must expect it to be . . . and it will

---

[5] All discussants, of course, should give up clichés in favor of specific evaluations. *The Untouchables* can't touch Shakespeare or the Greeks when it comes to real (audience-experienced) "violence"; *Alice in Wonderland* and Gulliver "escape from reality" as few canned comedies do; and religion, as I am not the first to point out, may be an even more effective soporific or opiate than *The Late Show.*

reflect their likes and dislikes, what they can comprehend and what is beyond them. Every person of common sense knows that people of superior mental constitutions are bound to find much of television intellectually beneath them. If such innately fortunate people cannot realize this gently and with good manners, if in their hearts they despise popular pleasures and interests, then, of course, they will be angrily dissatisfied with television. But it is not really television with which they are dissatisfied. It is with people.[6]

"Balance"—the answer, or the question?   These and other taste distinctions within the total audience raise questions about what the general level and nature of TV entertainment *should* be, and most important, about the range of its coverage and the relative proportions at various points. Should television "cater to" or should it "elevate"? *Whom* should television serve, and how often?

From the democratic point of view,[7] an appealing answer is "balance." These are not issues to be decided one way or the other; the obvious resolution is to spread the medium across the diversity of tastes and interests represented in the audience. The air waves belong to the people—everyone should have his fair share:

> Let me make clear that what I am talking about is balance. I believe that the public interest is made up of many interests. There are many people in this great country and you must serve all of us.[8]

But that, of course, simply states the problem. The issue lies not in the principle of "balance," but in its practical translation. What does "fair share" mean? Who is, and who is not, getting his at present?

This is the locus of the debate, and the question is not just one of information. Suppose we *really* knew what every viewer *really* wanted to see, how much of it, and during what hours. How would that information, complete and final as it would be, translate into a balanced schedule

---

[6] Sir Robert Fraser, at the Manchester Lunch Club, May 17, 1960.

[7] The Platonic alternative, of course, removes all issues other than who will decide, and who will decide *that*.

[8] Minow: op. cit.

that takes these conflicting interests into account, each in its fair measure?

Here are some of the issues in vastly oversimplified form. Suppose there are only *two* audience segments, A and B; and only two types of programs, "a" and "b." Assume, further, that tastes are obligingly differentiated in the simplest possible manner—A will watch only "a," and B, only "b." Finally, let us say that A's outnumber B's by three to one, and that A's, on the average, presently watch twice as much TV.

Now, what would a perfectly balanced schedule look like? Should there be equal amounts of "a" and "b," so that every individual audience member has an equal chance of having his interests served? Should there be three times as much "a" material because it has three times the potential audience? Or twice as much, on the grounds that each "a" consumer has twice the appetite? Or should it be sixfold over "b," to take both of these differences into account?

In real life, of course, the picture is not nearly so "simple," and the conceptual problems (unsolved in the simple case) multiply unbelievably. In the first place, we need at least all the letters in the alphabet, and some of their combinations, to describe the possible taste and program categories. Next, the audience groupings are not really mutually exclusive, and what is worse, they have differential taste flexibility. A's will watch some "b," and vice versa; but the chances are not the same: for example, the college-educated watch comedy or adventure far more frequently than the barely literate will tune to heavy information. In some cases, then, the first choice for one segment is a close second choice for another; while the preferred fare of the second may be entirely uninteresting or incomprehensible to the first. That, too, should get into the equation.

In real life, also, the different segments make differential use of the total medium. Some depend almost entirely upon TV for entertainment and information, while others have many other sources that cater to their special tastes. Should that be a factor; if so, how much weight should it get?

In the economic sphere, we ordinarily leave such problems to the "invisible hand," or free market. That giant computer assumes that willingness to pay is a good indicator of need or want, puts all the facts together, adds the appropriate weights, and decides what shall be produced, and in what quantities. It makes both Chevrolets and Cadillacs, rock-and-roll records and stereophonic tapes of organ recitals. And it makes each in about the quantities that people want (and, incidentally, at appropriate differential costs).

But some argue that that model is largely unworkable or inapplicable here, where a limited resource is allocated to a limited number of licensed "producers" or distributors, under certain constraints, who sell not directly to the public but to advertisers.[9]

According to them, "balance" cannot be defined as what happens of itself when you simply leave the present system alone. And so it seems to me to rest with those employing the concept—whether to argue that television is or is not balanced—to state precisely what they mean, and how they know. If "balance" is to be a real and not just a rhetorical goal, we have to know how far away we are, and especially how we know when we get there.

A Final Look

This book, like most other books about "issues," should probably end with a list of clear and workable recommendations. But to make recommendations on the basis of personal opinion would be presumptuous, and to base them solely on this study, largely irrelevant. For television, like politics, is an art of the possible. Recommendations worthy of the name must center on means as well as ends. Hence they must come from a careful study of the practical alternatives as well as the needs and desires of the audience.

I would like to substitute another set of presumptions; namely, to say, as faithfully as possible, what the composite viewer would request of the broadcaster: not just his manifest requests—the general ones are few, the specific ones conflicting—but the latent requests that seem to emerge from his general pattern of television attitudes and reactions. On this basis, here is what large numbers[1] of the audience would like to see happen.

The reader should bear in mind that these requests are made in complete ignorance of their technical feasibility or of any economic or

---

[9] Most free-market economists consider the licensing procedure the *only* relevant constraint.

[1] There is no effort to restrict the list to requests that "all" viewers would share nor to distinguish those made by various audience segments. The criterion is simply that each of these applies to audience components of practical significance, and in most cases to a large majority.

artistic constraints. I report them not necessarily in the belief that they should be implemented, but primarily as a final summary of what viewer feelings come to, in action terms:

1. First, give me more programs that are fun *and* worthwhile. Along these lines, there are at least three basic benefits that you might *add* or *incorporate* in my entertainment. (Please remember, I'm not talking about special "good-for-me" programs; there are plenty of those on educational television and sometimes on the regular channels, and usually they bore me.)

    a) Any time I can *learn* something—say, of the history of the country, or about arts and crafts, or the present political system or world situation, or about the latest national fad or craze—I feel I haven't wasted my time.

    b) Programs that introduce me to higher-level culture—in a way I can understand and enjoy now—also make me feel good about having watched. But please move realistically.

    c) Often I wish I could *participate* more. Maybe that's why I liked some of the quiz shows and panel games. Is there some way that television could give me something to *do*? Maybe some other ways to "test myself," or compare my feelings and reactions with others, or even talk back to the programs.

2. Give us more programs that are safe for the children *and* also attract them. You really should be able to figure out how to do that. If you must have some "violence" or slapstick in their shows, please make it unrealistic, as it is in westerns or fairy stories, *not* the way it is in some children's shows where children can copy ridiculous and dangerous things. Bear in mind that the physical harm one such program can do outweighs the good that all the rest might do. And that brings me to another point:

3. I like to watch television every day, and so do the children —so the most important thing to me is the *usual* level of television programming, not how it is at its *best*. I think I would rather have you improve all programs by 10 per cent, than add two or three simply marvellous programs during the sea-

son. It would be more useful to raise the level of the worst shows than make the best still better. The improvement would go farther, spread to more people, more often. And this is especially true in the case of children's shows, where I can't be sure they won't see the worst. By the same token, of course, if you give me five evenings of bad movies on *The Late Show,* you can't really make up for it by putting two good ones on on Saturday night. (I know some of my neighbors on the hill who only watch once or twice a week wouldn't agree.) In short, I feel about it as I would feel about a restaurant where the kids and I ate lunch every day: I'd much rather be sure they never have any spoiled food than have them serve gourmet dishes once in a while.

4. If you're interested in my specific program tastes, I might say that by now I am getting a little tired of all the westerns. Not that I don't like westerns in general—and especially the good ones—but I've had something of an overdose and I would like to see you replace some of them with fun, family-type entertainment. It seems to me that in past years there were some really great funny programs, and we didn't have to worry about the children watching them with us. How about some more *I Love Lucy, Sid Caesar, Jackie Gleason,* and so on? [Bear in mind that this is May, 1960.]

5. Now about those commercials. I know they pay for the shows, and I appreciate that, but please don't allow the advertisers to interrupt at crucial points in the movies or in regular shows. In the first place, it makes me angry and probably backfires much of the time—I'm so interested in the show I don't give a hoot about the product at that moment. But even if it works, you shouldn't allow it. After all, magazines don't print slogans in the middle of their stories.

You fellows have such a valuable advertising medium, and a virtual monopoly, that you should be able to put some limits on the sponsors and still sell just as much. Maybe if one of the networks did it, while the others continued to interrupt, that network's audience and revenues would even go up.

Also, so many commercials are silly or insulting, especially the ones for drugs and other bathroom products. But you're not really responsible for that—as you are for commercial placement.

6. I'm sorry I really can't think of much else; I'd like to be of more help. It's not that I don't have plenty of other problems with television, but many of them don't have much to do with the programs. By and large, you're doing a good job. I'm sure television could be improved, and it could certainly be more creative and surprising at times, but I don't know exactly how.

And so, in the final look, or at least in *my* final look, at the survey, the results appear quite fruitful and interesting to the social psychologist but perhaps of less direct bearing on how broadcasters should change the way they conduct their business. In the main, the people have had a great deal more to say about themselves than they have about TV, and in so doing, they may have provided the communicators with a clearer picture of the audience(s) they are serving, and how they are serving them. At the same time, they may have provided the critics with a better look at the audience(s) they are arguing for and against. That can not fail to be of some help, when it is taken seriously into account.

This book will have served its purpose if interested parties have found, in these pages, some clarification of how, when, and especially *why* the people look at television.

Appendices

APPENDIX A

COMPOSITE QUESTIONNAIRE

THE FOLLOWING composite questionnaire contains all of the questions used in the survey, including alternate forms as well as alternate questions. No single respondent answered all of these, and the actual order of questioning is often interrupted in the composite in order to show the alternate forms in the appropriate place.

There were sixteen questionnaire versions employed, eight by each field service, and these were "rotated" from interview to interview.

The questionnaire versions are specified by question number in the following chart:

NATIONAL OPINION RESEARCH CENTER VERSIONS

Questions	1	2	3	4	5	6	7	8
1 A	x	x	x	x	x	x	x	x
B	x	x	x	x	x	x	x	x
2	x	x	x	x	x	x	x	x
3 A	x	x	x	x	x	x	x	x
B	x	x	x	x	x	x	x	x
C	x	x	x	x	x	x	x	x
4 A	x	x	x	x	x	x	x	x
B	x	x	x	x	x	x	x	x
5 A	x	x			x	x		
B		x	x				x	x
6	x	x	x	x	x	x	x	x
7 (a)	x	x					x	x
7 (b)			x	x	x	x		
8	x	x	x	x	x	x	x	x
9	x	x	x	x	x	x	x	x
10 A	x	x	x	x	x	x	x	x
B	x	x	x	x	x	x	x	x
C	x	x	x	x	x	x	x	x
D	x	x	x	x	x	x	x	x
E (11 B) (a)*	x	x	x	x	x	x	x	x
11 A (a)	x	x	x	x	x	x	x	x
12 A	x		x		x		x	
B (a)	x		x		x		x	
C	x		x		x		x	
D (a)	x		x		x		x	
13 A		x		x		x		x
B		x		x		x		x
C (a)		x		x		x		x
D		x		x		x		x
E (a)		x		x		x		x
14 A		x		x		x		x
B		x		x		x		x
C		x		x		x		x
D (a)		x		x		x		x

* The lower-case letters (a) or (b), following question numbers, designate variations in item-orders within the question, to control for position effects.

NATIONAL OPINION RESEARCH CENTER VERSIONS (*Cont.*)

Questions	1	2	3	4	5	6	7	8
15 A	x		x		x		x	
B	x		x		x		x	
C	x		x		x		x	
D (a)	x		x		x		x	
16 A	x	x	x	x	x	x	x	x
B	x	x	x	x	x	x	x	x
C	x	x	x	x	x	x	x	x
17	x	x	x	x	x	x	x	x
18 A	x	x	x	x				
B					x	x	x	x
19 through 42	x	x	x	x	x	x	x	x
43 A	x	x	x	x	x	x	x	x
B	x	x	x	x	x	x	x	x
C	x	x	x	x	x	x	x	x
D	x	x	x	x	x	x	x	x
44 A	x	x	x	x	x	x	x	x
B	x	x	x	x	x	x	x	x
C	x	x	x	x	x	x	x	x
D	x	x	x	x	x	x	x	x
45 (52) A	x	x	x	x				
B					x	x	x	x
C (52)								
D								
E	x	x	x	x	x	x	x	x
F	x	x	x	x	x	x	x	x
46 (53) A	x	x	x	x				
B					x	x	x	x
C								
D								
E	x	x	x	x	x	x	x	x
47	x	x	x	x	x	x	x	x
48 A	x	x	x	x	x	x	x	x
B	x	x	x	x	x	x	x	x
C	x	x	x	x	x	x	x	x
D	x	x	x	x	x	x	x	x
49	x	x	x	x	x	x	x	x
50 A	x	x	x	x	x	x	x	x

NATIONAL OPINION RESEARCH CENTER VERSIONS (*Cont.*)

Questions	1	2	3	4	5	6	7	8
B	x	x	x	x	x	x	x	x
51 A	x	x	x	x	x	x	x	x
B	x	x	x	x	x	x	x	x
C	x	x	x	x	x	x	x	x
52 A								
B								
C								
D								
E								
F								
53 A								
B								
C								
D								
E								
54								
55 A								
B								
C								
D								
56 A								
B								
C								
57 A								
B								
C								
D								
58								
59 A								
B								
C								
D								
60								
61								
62								
63 through 101	x	x	x	x	x	x	x	x

ROPER QUESTIONNAIRE VERSIONS

Questions	9	10	11	12	13	14	15	16
1 A	x	x	x	x	x	x	x	x
B	x	x	x	x	x	x	x	x
2	x	x	x	x	x	x	x	x
3 A	x	x	x	x	x	x	x	x
B	x	x	x	x	x	x	x	x
C	x	x	x	x	x	x	x	x
4 A	x	x	x	x	x	x	x	x
B	x	x	x	x	x	x	x	x
5 A	x	x			x	x		
B			x	x			x	x
6	x	x	x	x	x	x	x	x
7 (a)	x	x					x	x
7 (b)			x	x	x	x		
8	x	x	x	x	x	x	x	x
9	x	x	x	x	x	x	x	x
10 A	x	x	x	x	x	x	x	x
B	x	x	x	x	x	x	x	x
C	x	x	x	x	x	x	x	x
D	x	x	x	x	x	x	x	x
E (11 B) (b)	x	x	x	x	x	x	x	x
11 A (b)	x	x	x	x				
12 A	x		x		x		x	
B (b)	x		x		x		x	
C	x		x		x		x	
D (b)	x		x		x		x	
13 A		x		x		x		x
B		x		x		x		x
C (b)		x		x		x		x
D		x		x		x		x
E (b)		x		x		x		x
14 A		x		x		x		x
B		x		x		x		x
C		x		x		x		x
D (b)		x		x		x		x
15 A	x		x		x		x	
B	x		x		x		x	
C	x		x		x		x	

ROPER VERSIONS—*Continued*

Questions	9	10	11	12	13	14	15	16
15 D (b)	x		x		x		x	
16 A	x	x	x	x	x	x	x	x
B	x	x	x	x	x	x	x	x
C	x	x	x	x	x	x	x	x
17	x	x	x	x	x	x	x	x
18 A	x	x	x	x				
B					x	x	x	x
19 through 42	x	x	x	x	x	x	x	x
43 A								
B								
C								
D								
44 A								
B								
C								
D								
45 A								
B								
C								
D								
E								
F								
46 A								
B								
C								
D								
E								
47								
48 A								
B								
C								
D								
49								
50 A								
B								
51 A								
B								

ROPER VERSIONS—*Continued*

Questions	9	10	11	12	13	14	15	16
C								
52 (45) A								
B								
C	x	x	x	x				
D					x	x	x	x
E	x	x	x	x	x	x	x	x
F	x	x	x	x	x	x	x	x
53 (46) A								
B								
C	x	x	x	x				
D					x	x	x	x
E	x	x	x	x	x	x	x	x
54	x	x	x	x	x	x	x	x
55 A	x	x	x	x	x	x	x	x
B	x	x	x	x	x	x	x	x
C	x	x	x	x	x	x	x	x
D	x	x	x	x	x	x	x	x
56 A	x	x	x	x	x	x	x	x
B	x	x	x	x	x	x	x	x
C	x	x	x	x	x	x	x	x
57 A	x	x	x	x	x	x	x	x
B	x	x	x	x	x	x	x	x
C	x	x	x	x	x	x	x	x
D	x	x	x	x	x	x	x	x
58	x	x	x	x	x	x	x	x
59 A	x	x	x	x	x	x	x	x
B	x	x	x	x	x	x	x	x
C	x	x	x	x	x	x	x	x
D	x	x	x	x	x	x	x	x
60	x	x	x	x	x	x	x	x
61 A, B	x	x	x	x	x	x	x	x
62 A, B	x	x	x	x	x	x	x	x
63 through 101	x	x	x	x	x	x	x	x

COMPOSITE QUESTIONNAIRE
WITH MARGINAL FREQUENCIES FOR ALL VIEWERS,
FOR PRE-CODED QUESTIONS, BY FIELD SERVICE

BUREAU OF APPLIED SOCIAL RESEARCH
Columbia University

in conjunction with

National Opinion Research Center   Elmo Roper and Associates
University of Chicago   *New York City*

1. A.   First, think of the way you spend an ordinary day—just a typical
        weekday when nothing special is happening. What part of the
        day do you enjoy most?
   B.   What makes that part of the day particularly enjoyable? (PROBE
        FULLY FOR SPECIFICS)
2. Considering all the new inventions, new products and new developments of the past 25 years or so, which—if any—have done the
   most to make *your* life more enjoyable, pleasant, or interesting?
   (What else?)
3. Here is a list of five different products and services designed to
   please the general public. (HAND RESPONDENT WHITE CARD)
   A.   Generally speaking, which of these do you think people are
        most satisfied with today?
   B.   Which does the next best job of satisfying most people?
   C.   And which, if any, don't seem to be designed with people's
        real interests and tastes in mind?

NORC Base: 1221	A (Best)		B (Next)		C (Worst)	
ROPER Base: 1206	NORC	ROPER	NORC	ROPER	NORC	ROPER
Today's:						
Fashions for women	6%	6%	13%	11%	23%	19%
Automobiles	57	57	25	25	3	3
Television programs	29	27	42	41	7	7
Movies	2	1	7	7	19	17
Popular music	5	6	10	10	30	24
None of them	0	0	0	1	7	8
DK, can't decide	1	3	2	4	10	19

4. A. And which of these five things are you *personally* most satisfied with?
   B. And which is next best, in your opinion?

NORC Base: 1221 ROPER Base: 1206	A (Best)		B (Next Best)	
	NORC	ROPER	NORC	ROPER
Today's:				
Fashions for women	10%	12%	14%	13%
Automobiles	47	48	24	23
Television programs	32	27	36	35
Movies	2	2	9	8
Popular music	7	8	11	12
DK	1	3	5	7

5. A. Here are some things that many people take for granted today. (HAND RESPONDENT GREEN CARD) But imagine, if you can, that for two or three months you could have only *one* of these and you'd have to do without the rest.
   (1) If you could only have one of those things, which one would you choose?
   (2) Suppose you could have two of them, what would be the second item you'd want?
   (3) And which would be the third?

NORC Base: 608 ROPER Base: 595	(1) 1st choice		(2) 2nd choice		(3) 3rd choice	
	NORC	ROPER	NORC	ROPER	NORC	ROPER
Telephone	9%	11%	23%	19%	26%	27%
Refrigerator	45	41	23	25	14	16
Automobile	32	29	28	28	17	16
Television	5	5	13	15	26	22
Newspaper	9	12	13	10	16	15

   B. Here are some things that many people take for granted today. (HAND RESPONDENT GREEN CARD) But suppose the clock were suddenly turned back and all of these things were gone.
   (1) Which do you think you *personally* would miss the most?
   (2) Which would you miss next most?
   (3) And next?

	(1)		(2)		(3)	
NORC Base: 613	Miss Most		Next		Next	
ROPER Base: 611	NORC	ROPER	NORC	ROPER	NORC	ROPER
Home freezers	21%	21%	11%	16%	9%	10%
Air conditioning	4	6	7	6	8	12
Hi-fidelity	3	2	3	4	2	4
Power brakes and						
steering	4	5	3	5	7	5
Television	34	34	23	23	17	15
Miracle fabrics—						
nylon, orlon, etc.	9	8	14	16	18	15
Frozen foods	9	9	17	13	15	15
Vacuum cleaner	16	13	19	14	16	17

6. Now would you take a look at these pictures. (HAND RESPONDENT PICTURE CARD)* I'm going to read some thoughts this (man) (woman) might be having, and I'd like you to tell me which picture each thought belongs with—in which situation (he) (she) is most likely to be feeling that way. You can name any picture as many times as you want to. If a thought doesn't seem to fit *any* picture, just say so.

I'll read the thought, and you just tell me the letter of the picture it fits best.

A. Here's the first one: Boy, this is fun!
B. Next: I'm a little ashamed of myself for spending my time like this.
C. I'll really regret this later.
D. It really makes me feel good to spend my time like this.
E. This fascinates me.
F. I really should be doing something else.
G. This is what I call real pleasure.
H. What a waste of time.
I. This really does you good.
J. Another evening shot.
K. I'm getting pretty bored with this.
L. I wish I could give this up.
M. What a childish way to spend time.
N. Trapped again!
O. A perfect way to relax.
P. This is really interesting.
Q. Am I lazy!

* Reproduced on the following pages.

NORC Base: 1221
ROPER Base: 1206

	None		C (TV)		L (READ)		M (CHILD)		P (GOLF)		T (VISIT)		R (MOVIE)		S (BAR)	
	NORC	ROPER	NORC	ROPER	NORC	ROPER	NORC	ROPER	NORC	ROPER	NORC	ROPER	NORC	ROPER	NORC	ROPER
	3%	3%	15%	13%	2%	4%	23%	22%	36%	35%	7%	7%	4%	6%	10%	8%
A.	6	6	14	15	6	4	5	5	5	5	9	9	5	6	48	49
B.	12	11	4	5	4	4	3	2	7	5	8	8	3	4	57	59
C.	1	2	19	18	22	19	23	26	13	10	14	16	4	4	3	3
D.	9	10	24	27	24	23	7	9	10	8	7	7	16	11	2	2
E.	4	5	30	31	13	13	9	8	9	9	11	11	10	9	12	12
F.	3	4	22	21	13	14	10	10	19	18	18	17	9	8	4	4
G.	5	8	13	17	4	2	4	4	9	11	15	13	13	10	35	32
H.	4	3	10	10	23	22	11	11	30	28	13	13	6	7	3	3
I.	9	10	18	22	5	5	2	3	4	3	19	15	10	8	29	31
J.	7	10	21	21	10	11	7	7	4	5	23	22	14	12	10	9
K.	16	17	8	9	3	4	2	3	7	7	5	4	3	3	53	50
L.	18	17	9	12	2	2	36	34	5	4	5	4	10	8	13	13
M.	18	17	7	8	3	3	6	9	14	12	30	29	4	4	14	15
N.	1	2	42	41	31	32	4	3	6	5	7	7	5	5	2	2
O.	3	3	28	26	36	39	6	6	5	4	8	8	12	11	1	1
P.	12	13	48	50	11	14	5	4	2	3	12	6	3	3	5	4

SPECIMEN PICTURE CARD
(*male respondents*)

NOTE: There were alternate for ~~m~~ with scenes arranged in different po~~si~~ tions to control for position effect.

SPECIMEN PICTURE CARD
(female respondents)

7. Now I would like to get your opinions about how radio, newspapers, television, and magazines compare. (HAND RESPONDENT GRAY CARD) Generally speaking, which of these would you say . . .
   A. Is the most entertaining?
   B. Which gives the most complete news coverage?
   C. Presents things most intelligently?
   D. Is the most educational?
   E. Brings you the latest news most quickly?
   F. Does the most for the public?
   G. Seems to be getting worse all the time?
   H. Presents the fairest, most unbiased news?
   I. Is doing its job best?
   J. Is the most important to you?
   K. Is the least important to you?
   L. Creates the most interest in new things going on?
   M. Does the least for the public?
   N. Seems to be getting better all the time?
   O. Which of these gives you the clearest understanding of the candidates and issues in national elections?
   P. And which has the hardest job to do?

NORC Base: 1221
ROPER Base: 1206

	Television		Magazines		Newspapers		Radio		None or Don't Know	
	NORC	ROPER	NORC	ROPER	NORC	ROPER	NORC	ROPER	NORC	ROPER
A.	69%	67%	8%	9%	14%	12%	9%	10%	1%	2%
B.	21	18	4	3	60	58	15	20	1	1
C.	26	27	30	24	34	33	6	10	4	7
D.	32	32	32	29	30	31	2	3	3	5
E.	36	36	0	0	6	4	57	58	1	2
F.	35	34	3	2	46	43	11	12	6	10
G.	23	26	18	15	9	10	16	11	34	37
H.	29	29	9	10	31	27	22	22	9	12
I.	31	27	9	8	35	31	14	15	11	19
J.	38	36	5	7	40	37	14	16	2	4
K.	14	16	50	48	7	7	24	21	5	8
L.	56	56	17	18	19	17	4	4	4	5
M.	14	12	49	44	5	5	13	12	19	26
N.	52	45	9	12	12	10	10	11	17	22
O.	43	41	10	10	36	36	5	6	7	8
P.	46	43	5	5	30	30	8	6	11	17

8. Now let's just consider television. How do you feel about television in general?

9. Here are some "opposites." (HAND PINK PAGE TO RESPONDENT) Please read each pair quickly and put a check mark some place between them, wherever you think it belongs to describe television. Just your off-hand impression. (IF NECESSARY, EXPLAIN: For example, take that first pair—exciting or dull. If you think television is *very* exciting, you'd put a check all the way over here in the FIRST space, or if you think it's pretty exciting, you'd put a check in the next space, or if you think it's very dull you'd put your check all the way over in the right-hand space. Now where would you put it to indicate how *you* feel about television?) I just want your quick, off-hand reaction. Don't spend a lot of time worrying about it. (IF "SOME TV ONE WAY AND SOME THE OTHER," PROBE: "How would you generally describe it?")

9. Put a check ($\sqrt{}$) between each pair—wherever you think it belongs —to describe television.

NORC Base: 1221

ROPER Base: 1206

TELEVISION IS GENERALLY:

Exciting	N	30%	20%	27%	13%	6%	4%	Dull
	R	29%	18%	29%	13%	4%	5%	
In good taste	N	23%	21%	31%	14%	6%	4%	In bad taste
	R	25%	20%	29%	14%	6%	4%	
Important	N	36%	17%	21%	11%	7%	7%	Unimportant
	R	40%	16%	19%	10%	7%	6%	
Generally bad	N	4%	6%	15%	33%	18%	21%	Generally excellent
	R	4%	5%	19%	28%	18%	22%	
Lots of variety	N	33%	17%	19%	12%	10%	7%	All the same
	R	34%	15%	18%	13%	11%	8%	
Upsetting	N	3%	3%	9%	20%	22%	41%	Relaxing
	R	4%	3%	9%	18%	21%	42%	
Interesting	N	41%	23%	19%	9%	4%	3%	Uninteresting
	R	42%	19%	19%	10%	4%	3%	
Wonderful	N	26%	17%	33%	15%	4%	2%	Terrible
	R	28%	15%	32%	16%	3%	3%	
Nobody cares much	N	3%	4%	15%	26%	21%	29%	On everyone's mind
	R	3%	4%	14%	21%	20%	35%	
For me	N	40%	18%	18%	10%	5%	8%	Not for me
	R	40%	15%	18%	10%	7%	8%	
Too "simple-minded"	N	9%	11%	39%	28%	3%	3%	Too "highbrow"
	R	9%	11%	39%	28%	3%	4%	
Getting worse	N	8%	7%	16%	22%	20%	24%	Getting better
	R	9%	8%	14%	24%	16%	25%	
Stays the same	N	7%	9%	19%	21%	18%	23%	Keeps changing
	R	10%	9%	17%	22%	15%	23%	
Informative	N	36%	26%	20%	8%	4%	3%	Not informative
	R	40%	23%	18%	8%	5%	4%	
Lots of fun	N	31%	21%	25%	11%	5%	5%	Not much fun
	R	32%	18%	23%	13%	6%	6%	
Serious	N	8%	8%	27%	28%	12%	13%	Playful
	R	8%	8%	32%	28%	11%	9%	
Imaginative	N	25%	21%	27%	13%	6%	4%	No imagination
	R	25%	21%	27%	13%	6%	5%	

10. A. Do you have a television set?

> NORC Base: 1221
> ROPER Base: 1206

	NORC	ROPER
Yes	94%	95%
No	6	5

IF "NO," ASK B–E (IF APPROPRIATE):

B. Where do you get a chance to watch television?

C. IF "NO PLACE" OR "NEVER" IN B: Did you ever watch?

D. IF "YES" TO C: About how often *do* you see TV?

E. (Respondents who "never" or "very rarely" watch were asked Q. 11 B next in all cases. All others, 11 A *or* 11 B, on a random basis.)

IMPORTANT: If respondent has NEVER watched television, skip Q. 11 and all subsequent questions in which the question number is circled.

⑪ A. Now let's talk for a moment about *reasons* for watching television. Here is a list of possible reasons. When you watch TV, how often does each of these reasons apply to you? (HAND RESPONDENT SECOND YELLOW PAGE AND HAVE HIM CHECK ONE CATEGORY FOR EACH REASON) For example, take (READ FIRST ITEM FROM LIST HANDED TO RESPONDENT) When you watch TV, is that usually one of your reasons, occasionally a reason, rarely, or never?

[YELLOW PAGE]

When you watch TV, how often does each of these reasons apply?

NORC Base: 614
ROPER Base: 615

		Usually	Occa-sionally	Rarely	Never	All Other
I watch to see a special program that I've heard a lot about.	N	56%	33%	9%	2%	1%
	R	53	37	5	4	1
I watch because there is nothing else to do at the time.	N	21	29	26	23	1
	R	19	23	23	33	2

		Usually	Occa-sionally	Rarely	Never	All Other
I watch to get away from the ordinary cares and problems of the day.	N	19	25	27	27	2
	R	17	23	21	37	2
I turn on the set just "to keep me company" when I'm alone.	N	22	23	20	34	1
	R	19	26	20	34	2
I watch because I think I can learn something.	N	35	35	20	8	1
	R	37	43	11	8	1
I watch because I'm afraid I might be missing something good.	N	16	23	29	31	2
	R	13	17	28	39	2
I keep watching to put off doing something else I should do.	N	4	12	27	56	1
	R	4	12	26	56	2
I start watching because my husband or wife is watching and seems to be interested.	N	18	37	13	17	15
	R	17	34	15	21	12
I start on one show and then "get stuck" for the rest of the evening.	N	12	25	30	31	2
	R	13	21	26	39	1
I watch because everyone I know is watching and I want to be able to talk about it afterwards.	N	9	19	24	47	2
	R	8	16	28	47	1
I watch just for "background" while I am doing something else.	N	6	19	25	49	1
	R	7	19	23	49	2
I watch just because I feel like watching television.	N	52	24	11	11	1
	R	47	20	16	15	3
I watch mainly to be sociable when others are watching.	N	18	35	24	21	3
	R	15	27	29	27	3

		Usually	Occa- sionally	Rarely	Never	All Other
I watch to see a specific pro- gram that I enjoy very much.	N	82	12	3	2	1
	R	77	19	2	2	1
I watch just because it is a pleasant way to spend an eve- ning.	N	50	28	12	9	2
	R	58	25	11	5	1

10. E. Now let's talk for a moment about *reasons* for watching tele-
11. B. vision. Here is a list of possible reasons. When most people
watch TV, how often does each one of these reasons apply?
(HAND RESPONDENT YELLOW PAGE AND HAVE HIM CHECK ONE
CATEGORY FOR EACH REASON) For example, take (READ FIRST
ITEM FROM LIST HANDED TO RESPONDENT) When people
watch TV, do you think that is usually one of their reasons,
occasionally a reason, rarely, or never? (Asked of all non-
viewers and sub-sample of viewers. Figures below show viewer
responses only.)

[YELLOW PAGE]

When most people watch TV, how often do you think each of these reasons
apply?

NORC Base: 607
ROPER Base: 591

		Usually	Occa- sionally	Rarely	Never	All Other
They watch to see a special program that they've heard a lot about.	N	64%	31%	4%	0%	1%
	R	62	32	3	1	2
They watch because there is nothing else to do at the time.	N	38	39	16	5	2
	R	33	34	20	11	3
They watch to get away from the ordinary cares and prob- lems of the day.	N	37	35	18	6	3
	R	31	34	19	12	3
They turn on the set just "to keep them company" when they're alone.	N	41	37	15	7	1
	R	34	40	13	9	4

		Usually	Occa-sionally	Rarely	Never	All Other
They watch because they think they can learn something.	N	34	35	24	4	3
	R	35	37	21	4	3
They watch because they're afraid they might be missing something good.	N	35	32	23	8	2
	R	29	34	23	11	3
They keep watching to put off something else they should do.	N	13	31	35	18	3
	R	14	29	31	23	3
They start watching because their husband or wife is watching and seems to be interested.	N	37	45	10	6	2
	R	33	45	13	5	4
They start on one show and then "get stuck" for the rest of the evening.	N	33	32	22	10	2
	R	29	37	22	10	3
They watch because everyone they know is watching and they want to be able to talk about it afterwards.	N	22	27	33	16	2
	R	19	28	33	18	3
They watch for "background" while they are doing something else.	N	13	38	27	19	2
	R	14	35	32	15	4
They watch just because they feel like watching television.	N	58	24	11	5	2
	R	55	24	12	4	4
They watch mainly to be sociable when others are watching.	N	26	39	24	9	3
	R	21	36	34	6	4
They watch to see a specific program that they enjoy very much.	N	84	13	2	0	1
	R	78	18	2	0	2
They watch because it is a pleasant way to spend an evening.	N	73	21	5	0	1
	R	73	24	2	0	1

⑫ A. How does watching television *usually* make you feel? (IF
        NEVER OR RARELY WATCH: When you have watched, how did
        it make you feel?)

    B. Would you go through this list quickly and check all the words
        that describe how watching TV usually makes you feel?
        (HAND WHITE PAGE TO RESPONDENT)
        IF RESPONDENT SPENDS MUCH TIME ON LIST, EXPLAIN: Don't
        worry too much about it. Just go through the list as fast as
        you can. I don't want to take up too much of your time on it.
        IF RESPONDENT OBVIOUSLY CANNOT READ, READ LIST QUICKLY,
        BUT FIRST OFFER THIS EXPLANATION: I'll read the list off and
        you stop me whenever I mention a word that describes how
        watching TV makes you feel.

[WHITE PAGE]

⑫　　B.　Ordinarily, watching television makes me feel . . .
　　　　　(CHECK √ ALL THAT APPLY)

Per Cent		Per Cent		Per Cent	
18	Bored	6	Unhappy	51	Good
23	Wonderful	11	Let down	15	Dissatisfied
63	Interested	14	Tense	4	Helpless
45	Rested	64	Relaxed	15	Aware
3	Childish	54	Amused	12	Anxious
9	Angry	6	Embarrassed	9	Upset
68	Entertained	10	Restless	9	Active
18	Hungry	17	Disgusted	41	Sleepy
15	Tired	3	Old	11	Mad
5	Silly	34	Contented	37	Happy
4	Foolish	11	Thirsty	32	Calm
26	Excited	10	Disturbed	5	Ashamed
19	Lazy	12	Great	6	Cheated
41	Informed	2	Sick	6	Afraid
2	Jealous	12	Sad	18	Serious
11	Impatient	26	Joyful	5	Guilty
20	Disappointed	8	Frustrated	11	Eager
18	Intrigued	5	Stupid	39	Peaceful
2	Sexy	12	Free	52	Satisfied
17	Alive	31	Fascinated		

Base: All 1217

NOTE: NORC and ROPER are not comparable on this and subsequent check
　　　 lists because order of adjectives was varied to control position effect.
　　　 Entries are for all respondents.

12. C. And how (else) would you *like* TV to make you feel?

D. ASK UNLESS ANSWERS TO A AND C IDENTICAL: Now would you go through this list again and check all the words that describe how you'd like watching TV to make you feel? (HAND WHITE PAGE TO RESPONDENT AND PROCEED AS IN 12B, ABOVE)

[WHITE PAGE]

⑫ D. I'd like television to make me feel . . .
(CHECK √ ALL THAT APPLY)

Per Cent		Per Cent		Per Cent	
0	Bored	1	Unhappy	50	Good
33	Wonderful	0	Let down	2	Dissatisfied
55	Interested	3	Tense	1	Helpless
38	Rested	51	Relaxed	20	Aware
1	Childish	43	Amused	7	Anxious
2	Angry	2	Embarrassed	1	Upset
59	Entertained	1	Restless	19	Active
2	Hungry	1	Disgusted	5	Sleepy
1	Tired	1	Old	1	Mad
1	Silly	38	Contented	45	Happy
0	Foolish	2	Thirsty	30	Calm
23	Excited	2	Disturbed	1	Ashamed
2	Lazy	20	Great	1	Cheated
43	Informed	0	Sick	1	Afraid
0	Jealous	1	Sad	13	Serious
1	Impatient	33	Joyful	1	Guilty
1	Disappointed	1	Frustrated	14	Eager
18	Intrigued	1	Stupid	39	Peaceful
2	Sexy	15	Free	56	Satisfied
26	Alive	31	Fascinated		

Base: All 1217

⑬ A. How would you describe *most* of the television programs on
        the air today? (Just however they strike you. Even though you
        haven't seen much TV, just go by what you have seen.)

    B. ASK UNLESS RESPONSE TO 13A WAS ONE WORD: What ONE
        word would you use to sum up most television programs?

    C. Would you look at this list of words and quickly check all
        those that you might use to describe *most* TV shows? (HAND
        BUFF PAGE TO RESPONDENT)

                        [BUFF PAGE]

⑬ C. Most television programs are . . .
        (QUICKLY CHECK √ ALL THAT APPLY)

Per Cent		Per Cent	
35	Exciting	18	Great
24	New	27	Creative
21	Boring	20	Artistic
28	Different	26	Tasteful
19	Dull	18	Phony
33	Intelligent	11	Bad
61	Interesting	44	Educational
23	Trivial	22	Corny
71	Entertaining	24	Violent
11	Sinful	24	Serious
43	Informative	16	Trash
14	Stupid	30	Stimulating
15	Significant	20	Original
29	Imaginative	51	Average
12	Terrible	19	Unimaginative
9	Idiotic	31	Honest

Base: All 1217

⑬ D. As far as you're concerned, where is the greatest room for improvement in television programs? (What kinds of things need to be improved?) (What kinds of improvements are needed?) (What kinds of programs do you have in mind?)

E. Now here's another copy of the same list. Would you look it over and check the words that describe how you'd *like* more programs to be? (HAND BUFF PAGE TO RESPONDENT)

[BUFF PAGE]

⑬ E. I wish most programs would be more . . .
(QUICKLY CHECK √ ALL THAT APPLY)

Per Cent		Per Cent	
48	Exciting	26	Great
46	New	53	Creative
2	Boring	36	Artistic
44	Different	47	Tasteful
2	Dull	2	Phony
65	Intelligent	1	Bad
70	Interesting	75	Educational
5	Trivial	3	Corny
72	Entertaining	2	Violent
4	Sinful	34	Serious
61	Informative	2	Trash
2	Stupid	50	Stimulating
24	Significant	46	Original
38	Imaginative	11	Average
2	Terrible	4	Unimaginative
1	Idiotic	59	Honest

Base: All 1217

⑭   A. What are some of your favorite programs—those you watch
        regularly or whenever you get a chance?

    B. IF NO SPECIAL PROGRAMS MENTIONED, ASK: Can you give me
        an example of the kind of (WESTERN) (MUSICAL) (KIND OF
        PROGRAM MENTIONED) you have in mind?

    C. How does watching (FIRST SPECIFIC SHOW MENTIONED) or
        programs of that type make you feel?

    D. And now would you go through this list quickly and check all
        the words that describe how watching (SAME PROGRAMS DIS-
        CUSSED IN C ABOVE) makes you feel? (HAND WHITE PAGE TO
        RESPONDENT)

[WHITE PAGE]

⑭   D.   Watching my favorite programs makes me feel . . .
          (CHECK √ ALL THAT APPLY)

Per Cent		Per Cent		Per Cent	
1	Bored	3	Unhappy	53	Good
27	Wonderful	3	Let down	3	Dissatisfied
69	Interested	9	Tense	2	Helpless
36	Rested	61	Relaxed	14	Aware
2	Childish	46	Amused	16	Anxious
4	Angry	2	Embarrassed	3	Upset
75	Entertained	2	Restless	14	Active
8	Hungry	4	Disgusted	10	Sleepy
4	Tired	1	Old	4	Mad
2	Silly	35	Contented	41	Happy
2	Foolish	5	Thirsty	23	Calm
31	Excited	4	Disturbed	2	Ashamed
5	Lazy	15	Great	2	Cheated
32	Informed	1	Sick	3	Afraid
1	Jealous	5	Sad	15	Serious
5	Impatient	28	Joyful	2	Guilty
5	Disappointed	3	Frustrated	13	Eager
16	Intrigued	1	Stupid	32	Peaceful
1	Sexy	10	Free	59	Satisfied
21	Alive	33	Fascinated		

Base: All 1210

⑮ A. What are some of your favorite programs—those you watch
       regularly or whenever you get a chance?

    B. IF NO SPECIFIC PROGRAMS MENTIONED IN A, ASK: Can you give
        me an example of the kind of (WESTERN) (MUSICAL) (KIND
        OF PROGRAM MENTIONED) you have in mind?

    C. How would you describe (FIRST SPECIFIC PROGRAM MEN-
        TIONED) or programs of that type?

    D. And now would you go through this list quickly and check all
        the words that describe (FIRST SPECIFIC PROGRAM MEN-
        TIONED) or programs of that type? (HAND BUFF LIST TO

        RESPONDENT)

                              [BUFF PAGE]
⑮ D. My favorite programs are . . .
        (QUICKLY CHECK √ ALL THAT APPLY)

Per Cent		Per Cent	
62	Exciting	29	Great
21	New	28	Creative
1	Boring	17	Artistic
36	Different	34	Tasteful
2	Dull	2	Phony
44	Intelligent	1	Bad
79	Interesting	41	Educational
3	Trivial	3	Corny
82	Entertaining	7	Violent
2	Sinful	27	Serious
37	Informative	1	Trash
1	Stupid	45	Stimulating
14	Significant	32	Original
34	Imaginative	15	Average
1	Terrible	4	Unimaginative
1	Idiotic	49	Honest

Base: All 1217

⑯ NOTE TIME AND WHETHER TV SET WAS ON WHEN YOU ENTERED?
   DO NOT ASK:
   Was TV set on when you entered?   ☐ Yes   ☐ No
   Is it on now?   ☐ Yes   ☐ No
   What time did interview begin?

   _____AM.
   _____P.M.*

   ⎧IF BEFORE 5:00 P.M., ASK ABOUT "TONIGHT."
   ⎪IF BETWEEN 5:00 and 7:30 P.M., ASK ABOUT "LATER TO-
 * ⎨NIGHT."
   ⎩IF AFTER 7:30 P.M., ASK ABOUT "TOMORROW."

A. Do you think you will probably watch some television (to-
    night) (later tonight) (tomorrow)?

       NORC Base: 1221
       ROPER Base: 1206

	NORC	ROPER
Yes, probably will watch	68%	65%
May watch, but may not	6	8
No, probably won't watch	22	24
Television set out of order	3	2
All other	1	1

    IF "YES" OR "MAYBE," ASK B AND C:

B. Are there any particular programs you plan to watch?

       NORC Base: 903
       ROPER Base: 877

	NORC	ROPER
Yes	69%	70%
No	26	26
All other	5	5

    IF "YES": Which ones?

C. Do you happen to know any (other) shows that are on tonight?

       NORC Base: 903
       ROPER Base: 877

	NORC	ROPER
Yes	45%	41%
No	46	48
All other	9	11

    IF "YES": Which ones?

D.   IF "PROBABLY WON'T WATCH" OR "TV OUT OF ORDER," ASK:
     Do you happen to know some programs that will be on to-
     night?

NORC Base: 300
ROPER Base: 314

	NORC	ROPER
Yes	37%	33%
No	56	57
All other	7	10

IF "YES": Which ones?

⑰ On an average day, during what hours do you yourself ordinarily
   watch television? (HAND GRAY PAGE TO RESPONDENT) Would you
   fill this out—just put check marks in each appropriate column—
   for a weekday, for Saturday, and for Sunday.
   Please check each hour YOU would be likely to see at least some
   television. (DON'T COUNT TIMES WHEN SET IS ON BUT RESPONDENT
   IS NOT WATCHING AT ALL)

[GRAY PAGE]

⑰   Please check each hour *you* would be likely to see at least some
     television.
NORC Base: 1221
ROPER Base: 1206

	An ordinary weekday		An ordinary Saturday		An ordinary Sunday	
	N	R	N	R	N	R
6–7 A.M........	3%	1%	1%	0%	1%	0%
7–8 A.M........	5%	5%	1%	1%	1%	1%
8–9 A.M........	7%	5%	3%	2%	2%	2%
9–10 A.M........	8%	7%	5%	4%	4%	3%
10–11 A.M........	10%	9%	6%	5%	5%	4%
11 A.M.–12 Noon..	12%	11%	7%	6%	6%	7%
12–1 P.M.........	15%	13%	8%	9%	9%	9%
1–2 P.M.........	11%	13%	12%	14%	13%	15%
2–3 P.M.........	13%	13%	14%	17%	19%	20%
3–4 P.M.........	11%	12%	13%	14%	20%	19%
4–5 P.M.........	11%	11%	12%	11%	22%	19%
5–6 P.M.........	16%	15%	15%	12%	23%	21%
6–7 P.M.........	35%	36%	29%	29%	37%	33%
7–8 P.M.........	57%	56%	50%	50%	53%	51%
8–9 P.M.........	69%	70%	56%	58%	62%	60%
9–10 P.M.........	65%	67%	55%	57%	57%	59%
10–11 P.M.........	42%	42%	40%	40%	38%	37%
11–12 P.M.........	14%	17%	18%	22%	13%	16%
12–1 A.M........	6%	8%	9%	10%	5%	7%
1–2 A.M........	2%	2%	3%	4%	1%	3%
2–3 A.M........	1%	1%	1%	1%	1%	1%
N.A.............	6%	5%	15%	17%	12%	13%

18. A. Television programs can be designed to provide different things. From your point of view, does television today have enough, not enough, or too many of each of these kinds of programs?

(1) First, how about programs that provide information—does television today have enough, not enough, or too many programs of that type?

	NORC Base: 614	ROPER Base: 615
Not enough	51%	54%
Enough	46	42
Too many	1	1
NA	2	2

If "not enough" or "too many": Can you give me (an idea) (an example) of the kind of program you have in mind?

(2) How about programs that provide escape from every-day life—does television today have enough, not enough, or too many programs of that type?

	NORC	ROPER
Not enough	10%	11%
Enough	71	69
Too many	15	14
NA	3	6

If "not enough" or "too many": Can you give me (an idea) (an example) of the kind of program you have in mind?

(3) Educational programs? Would you say there are enough, not enough, or too many educational programs?

	NORC	ROPER
Not enough	61%	65%
Enough	35	31
Too many	0	1
NA	3	3

If "not enough" or "too many": Can you give me (an idea) (an example) of the kind of program you have in mind?

(4) And what about programs that help you relax?

	NORC	ROPER
Not enough	19%	20%
Enough	76	73
Too many	2	3
NA	3	4

If "not enough" or "too many": Can you give me (an idea) (an example) of the kind of program you have in mind?

(5) Programs that provide food for thought?

	NORC	ROPER
Not enough	40%	44%
Enough	54	50
Too many	1	1
NA	5	5

If "not enough" or "too many": Can you give me (an idea) (an example) of the kind of program you have in mind?

(6) How about programs that offer advice or help solve problems?

	NORC	ROPER
Not enough	29%	30%
Enough	58	55
Too many	6	5
NA	7	10

If "not enough" or "too many": Can you give me (an idea) (an example) of the kind of program you have in mind?

(7) And the last kind of program I want to ask about is programs that provide just plain laughs. Are there enough, not enough or too many?

	NORC	ROPER
Not enough	29%	33%
Enough	63	59
Too many	5	4
NA	3	4

If "not enough" or "too many": Can you give me (an idea) (an example) of the kind of program you have in mind?

18. B. Television programs can be designed to provide different things. If you had to guess, would you say that most people think that television today has enough, not enough, or too many of each of these kinds of programs?

(1) First, how about programs that provide information? Do you think most people would say there are enough, not enough, or too many programs of that type?

	NORC	ROPER
	Base: 607	Base: 591
Not enough	47%	50%
Enough	49	48
Too many	2	1
NA	2	2

If "not enough" or "too many": Can you give me (an idea) (an example) of the kind of program you have in mind?

(2) What about programs that provide "escape" from everyday life? Do you think most people would say there are enough, not enough, or too many programs of that type?

	NORC	ROPER
Not enough	10%	14%
Enough	76	69
Too many	8	11
NA	6	6

If "not enough" or "too many": Can you give me (an idea) (an example) of the kind of program you have in mind?

(3) Educational programs? Do you think most people would say there are enough, not enough, or too many educational programs?

	NORC	ROPER
Not enough	59%	59%
Enough	35	37
Too many	1	1
NA	5	3

If "not enough" or "too many": Can you give me (an idea) (an example) of the kind of program you have in mind?

(4) How about programs that help you relax—does television today have enough, not enough, or too many programs of that type?

	NORC	ROPER
Not enough	20%	22%
Enough	74	73
Too many	2	1
NA	4	4

If "not enough" or "too many": Can you give me (an idea) (an example) of the kind of program you have in mind?

(5) Programs that provide food for thought?

	NORC	ROPER
Not enough	37%	39%
Enough	55	53
Too many	1	2
NA	7	6

If "not enough" or "too many": Can you give me (an idea) (an example) of the kind of program you have in mind?

(6) How about programs that offer advice or help solve problems?

	NORC	ROPER
Not enough	31%	32%
Enough	55	55
Too many	6	4
NA	8	9

If "not enough" or "too many": Can you give me (an idea) (an example) of the kind of program you have in mind?

(7) And the last kind of program I want to ask about is programs that provide just plain laughs. Would most people say there are enough, not enough, or too many?

	NORC	ROPER
Not enough	32%	37%
Enough	63	58
Too many	2	3
NA	3	2

If "not enough" or "too many": Can you give me (an idea) (an example) of the kind of program you have in mind?

19. Who do you think has the most to say about what kind of programs are put on the air—who *really* decides? (USE FOLLOWING OR COMPARABLE NEUTRAL PROBES TO GET AS DETAILED AND SPECIFIC ANSWERS AS POSSIBLE BUT DO NOT SUGGEST SUCH CATEGORIES: Who on the networks? What do you have in mind when you say "Madison Avenue"? What TV people? In what positions? Who do you have in mind when you say "they"? What do you have in mind when you say "the people who produce the programs"?)

20. What kind of people do you feel most of the programs on the air today are designed for? (Would you say that the programs are designed pretty much with people like you in mind—or does it seem that most of them are aimed at people with other interests and tastes?)

㉑ A. What kind of programs have you seen that you'd like to see more of on TV?

   B. Can you give me an example of the kind of programs you'd like to see more of?

㉒ A. Generally speaking, is there any type of program you would really like to see *that isn't on at all now?*

   B. If you could have a program tailor-made just for you, what kind of program would it be?

㉓ What kind of programs don't you care for at all? (Can you describe them for me?) (Can you give me an example?)

㉔ A. Now I'd like to ask you about some of the things you may have seen in the past that you particularly liked.
First, let's talk about programs that *used* to be on *regularly* but

are no longer on the air. Are there any that you'd like to see put back on the air? I don't mean re-runs, I mean new versions.

NORC Base: 1221
ROPER Base: 1206

	NORC	ROPER
Yes	58%	56%
No	40	41
All other	3	3

IF "YES": Which ones?

㉕ And are there any personalities or stars that you especially liked who aren't on any more? (Which ones?)

㉖ A. Is there any single program or broadcast that you'd like to see again if it could be re-run? (I don't mean a whole series, I mean one particular show—either part of a series or a separate show.) (Which one?)

    B. Any others?

㉗ A. Considering everything you've ever seen on television, is there some highlight or special moment that stands out in your mind? (It can be either a whole program, an event, or something that happened during a program—just anything that impressed you.) (What was it?)

    B. IF NOT OBVIOUS: What made it special (What happened?)

㉘ Television programs, like most other things, vary in quality. Some are better than others. Considering just the programs you generally watch, what proportion would you say are extremely enjoyable, how many are somewhat enjoyable, how many are just so-so, and how many are disappointing? First, roughly, what percentage of the TV programs you watch would you call "extremely enjoyable"? (WHEREVER POSSIBLE, GET PERCENTAGE FOR EACH CATEGORY— IT'S OK IF THEY DON'T ADD UP TO 100%)

NORC Base: 1221
ROPER Base: 1206

Response:	0–5%	6–15%	16–25%	26–35%	36–45%	46–55%	56–65%	66–75%	76–85%	86–95%	96–100%	NA
Extremely enjoyable												
NORC	8%	11	13	7	8	19	4	11	4	5	5	5
ROPER	5%	12	11	8	8	17	7	10	4	3	5	10
Somewhat enjoyable												
NORC	11%	19	28	14	8	10	2	2	0	0	1	4
ROPER	10%	17	27	17	7	5	2	2	0	0	0	11
So-so												
NORC	27%	27	22	7	5	5	1	1	0	0	0	4
ROPER	21%	28	21	8	5	4	1	1	0	0	0	11
Disappointing												
NORC	44%	26	13	5	3	2	1	1	0	0	0	4
ROPER	31%	30	13	5	3	3	1	0	0	0	0	12

(29) Have you ever seen a program that you thought wouldn't interest you much but that turned out to be fascinating? (Tell me about it— what was it?) (What was it like?)

(30) A. When you watch, how often, if ever, are you disappointed by shows that don't live up to your expectations—does this happen frequently, occasionally, only rarely, or never? (I mean how often you find that a show isn't as good as you expected it to be.)

NORC Base: 1221
ROPER Base: 1206

	NORC	ROPER
Frequently disappointed	12%	15%
Occasionally disappointed	43	43
Rarely disappointed	28	27
Never disappointed	16	14
All other	1	1

B. IF EVER DISAPPOINTED: Can you give me an example of a recent program you found disappointing?

(31) A. In general, do you think that specials or spectaculars are better than the regular shows they replace, or would you generally rather see the regularly scheduled programs?

NORC Base: 1221
ROPER Base: 1206

	NORC	ROPER
Specials better	33%	32%
Regular shows better	50	49
No difference	14	16
All other	3	3

㉜ Now a couple of questions about people outside your own family. First, would you think of one of your closest friends (outside of the home). (I don't want the name, but I would like you to have a specific person in mind.)

A. Do you happen to know any of his or her favorite programs? (Which programs are they?)

B. And do you know any he or she dislikes? (Which programs?)

33. A. Did you talk to anybody (excluding your immediate family and others who live within this house/apartment) today (IF MORNING INTERVIEW: yesterday) about television—either in person or on the phone? Just think a minute.

NORC Base: 1221
ROPER Base: 1206

	NORC	ROPER
Yes, talked about television	10%	12%
No discussion about television	89	88
All other	1	0

IF "YES," ASK B–D:

B. Who did you talk with? (I don't need the *name,* but can you tell me who the person was?)

C. What were you and the other person talking about?

D. And can you tell me briefly what was said?

34. DO NOT ASK, BUT CIRCLE ONE CODE TO SHOW DAY OF WEEK AND ONE CODE TO SHOW TIME INTERVIEW BEGAN:

NORC Base: 1221
ROPER Base: 1206

INTERVIEW CONDUCTED ON:			INTERVIEW BEGAN AT:		
	NORC	ROPER		NORC	ROPER
Sunday	9%	5%	Before noon	15%	12%
Monday	11	14	12:00–12:59	5	4
Tuesday	13	14	1:00– 1:59	10	7
Wednesday	15	18	2:00– 2:59	8	8
Thursday	16	16	3:00 –3:59	7	7
Friday	11	14	4:00– 4:59	7	5
Saturday	24	19	5:00– 5:59	12	18
			6:00– 6:59	12	12
			7:00– 7:59	15	15
			8:00 or later	8	10
			No answer	1	2

35. A. There has been a lot of discussion about the possible effects of television on children. Taking everything into consideration, would you say that children are better off with television or better off without television?

NORC Base: 1221
ROPER Base: 1206

	NORC	ROPER
With	69%	66%
Without	29	30
All other	2	4

IF "WITH," ASK B–D:

B. What do you think are some of the main advantages?

C. And what are some of the disadvantages, if any?

D. Can you think of any actual example where some child you know or have heard about has benefited from television? (What program was it that helped?) (Just what happened? In what way did the child benefit?)

IF "WITHOUT," ASK E–G:

E. What do you think are some of the main disadvantages?

F. And what might be some of the advantages, if any?

G. Can you think of an actual example where some child you know or have heard of has been harmed or has done something harmful as a result of television? (Just what happened? What harm resulted?)

36. A. Do you have any children under 15 years old who live here now?

NORC Base: 1221
ROPER Base: 1206

	NORC	ROPER
Yes	50%	52%
No	49	47
Other	1	1

IF "YES," ASK B–F:

B. First, I'd like to know how *many* children you have under 15?

C. PROBE FOR AND RECORD AGE AND SEX OF EACH CHILD

D. IF ANY CHILDREN BETWEEN 1 AND 15 YEARS OLD: Which of the programs your (child watches) (children watch) do you think are the best programs for (him) (her) (them)?

E. And which programs (that they watch) aren't you too happy about?

F. Even though they're not always enforced 100%, are there any rules or regulations in your home about when and what the (child) (children) watch or do you let (him) (her) (them) make their own decisions?

㊲ A. Do you recall the last time your television set broke down?

NORC Base: 1221
ROPER Base: 1206

	NORC	ROPER
Yes, can remember	72%	64%
No, can't remember	10	14
Never broke down	10	11
All other	8	11

IF "YES," ASK B–E:

B.   Who fixed it—did you or someone in the family fix it, did a repairman come to the house, or did you take the set to a repair shop?

NORC Base: 885
ROPER Base: 777

	NORC	ROPER
Family member fixed it	14%	13%
Repairman came to house	55	59
Took set to a repair shop	21	20
Bought a new set	5	4
Still broken and unreplaced	4	4
All other	1	1

C.   How soon after the set broke down did you (call in the repairman) (take it to the shop) (start fixing it) (buy a new one)? (About how long?)

D.   Altogether, about how long (were you) (have you been) without a TV set?

NORC Base: 885
ROPER Base: 777

	NORC	ROPER
½ day or less	25%	26%
1 day	19	21
2 days	12	11
3 days	8	8
4–6 days	5	5
1 week	10	10
2–3 weeks	8	9
1–2 months	5	5
3–6 months	2	1
7 or more months	1	1
NA	4	4

E.   IF SET WAS DOWN FOR MORE THAN AN HOUR OR TWO: What did you do during the time you would ordinarily have spent watching TV?

⊛   Do you think that you spend too much time watching television, or would you say that you don't have a chance to see as much as you would really like to? (RECORD VERBATIM AND DON'T TRY TO FORCE CHOICE IF RESPONSE IS "RIGHT AMOUNT")

39. A. About how much television would you say is "right" for the average adult—that is, enough to keep up with the important and entertaining things but still not too much.

B. IF ANSWER TO A DOES NOT GIVE ACTUAL NUMBER OF HOURS: Generally, about how many hours would it be?
NORC Base: 1221
ROPER Base: 1206

	NORC	ROPER
Less than one hour a day	0%	0%
One or two hours a day	3	3
Three or four hours	34	33
Five or six	43	43
Seven or eight	11	10
Eight or more	2	2
All other	7	10

40. A. (Aside from TV) what are some of the (other) things you like to do in your spare time nowadays?

B. Is there anything you would like to study or take up if you had the time and opportunity?

C. What are some of the opportunities for adult education in (IF NON-URBAN AREAS) this community? (IF URBAN AREAS) this community and this city?

D. Is there any subject that interests you that you would like to see presented or taught on television? (What subject would that be?)

41. A. Generally speaking, would you say that television should do more in the way of providing informational material, or should it concentrate on providing the best entertainment possible?

NORC Base: 1221
ROPER Base: 1206

	NORC	ROPER
Provide more informational material	32%	29%
Provide best entertainment	43	36
Both, can't choose, don't know	25	33
All other	0	1

B.   IF "BOTH" TO A: Well, suppose there was a free hour on the air that could be used for any kind of television program at all, what would you like to see it used for?

㊷   Now about commercials on television? (PAUSE BRIEFLY AND RECORD ANY SPONTANEOUS COMMENTS MADE AT THIS POINT)

A.   What, if anything, do you like most about commercials?

B.   And what, if anything, do you dislike most about commercials?

C.   Here are some statements about commercials. I'd like you to read each statement and mark whether you generally agree or disagree with each statement. (HAND GREEN PAGE TO RESPONDENT)

㊷   C.   (QUICKLY CHECK √ ONE COLUMN FOR EACH OF THE FOL-
            LOWING TO SHOW WHETHER YOU GENERALLY AGREE OR DIS-
            AGREE WITH THE STATEMENT)

			Agree	Disagree	N.A.
A.	Most commercials are too long.	N	63%	34%	3%
		R	63%	32%	5%
B.	I frequently find myself welcoming	N	34%	61%	5%
	a commercial break	R	37%	57%	6%
C.	I'd rather pay a small amount yearly if I could, to have tele-	N	23%	73%	4%
	vision without commercials . .	R	24%	70%	6%
D.	Some commercials are so good that they are more entertaining	N	42%	55%	3%
	than the program	R	45%	50%	5%
E.	I find some commercials very	N	57%	40%	3%
	helpful in keeping me informed	R	59%	35%	6%
F.	I would prefer TV without com-	N	45%	50%	5%
	mercials	R	42%	51%	7%
G.	Commercials are ordinarily in	N	40%	56%	4%
	poor taste and very annoying.	R	40%	53%	7%
H.	I dislike long movies without the breaks that commercials pro-	N	26%	68%	6%
	vide	R	28%	64%	9%
I.	Commercials are a fair "price" to pay for the entertainment	N	75%	22%	3%
	you get	R	76%	19%	5%

NORC Base: 1221
ROPER Base: 1206

㊷ D. Before skipping to next question, glance at completed green list and note whether respondent agreed with statement A, C, or G. Ask all of following, if appropriate:

If agree with statement A:

    A. I see that you agree with the statement that commercials are too long. Can you give me an example of programs where the commercials are too long?

If agree with statement C:

    C. You (also) indicate that you find commercials ordinarily in poor taste and annoying. May I have an example of the kind of commercial you have in mind on that?

If agree with statement G:

    G. What would be the most you might be willing to pay per year to have television without commercials? (IF RESPONDENT ASKS ABOUT KIND OF PROGRAMS ON PAY TV, EXPLAIN THAT YOU MEAN FOR SAME PROGRAMS AS PRESENT ONES)

㊸ A. Can you give me an example of the best advertising you've seen on TV? (I mean the advertising you personally like best.)

    IF NOT COVERED IN A ABOVE, ASK B–D, AS NECESSARY:

    B. What were they advertising?

    C. Can you describe the commercial itself? (What was it like?) (What did they show or say?)

    D. What did you like about it?

㊹ A. And can you give me an example of the worst advertising you've seen on TV?

    IF NOT COVERED IN A, ASK B–D, AS NECESSARY:

    B. What were they advertising?

    C. And would you describe the commercial itself?

    D. What didn't you like about it?

45. A. You may have heard something about "Pay TV"—this would be a system where, in addition to the regular stations, there would be some stations without advertising which would charge fifty cents or so per program for special programs. Do you think this should be tried out or not?

NORC only, Base: 614

	NORC
Should be tried out	31%
Should not be tried out	54
Don't know	14
NA	1

B. You may have heard something about "Pay TV"—this would be a system where, in addition to the regular stations, there would be some stations without advertising which would charge $1.00 or so per program for special programs. Do you think this should be tried out or not?

ROPER only, Base: 607

	ROPER
Should be tried out	22%
Should not be tried out	62
Don't know	15
NA	1

C. (Same as Q. 52C)
You may have heard something about "Pay TV"—this would be a system where some of the present TV stations would not have advertising, but would charge fifty cents or so per program for special programs. Do you think this should be tried out or not?

NORC only, Base: 615

	NORC
Should be tried out	20%
Should not be tried out	64
Don't know	15
NA	1

D. (Same as Q. 52D)
You may have heard something about "Pay TV"—this would be a system where some of the present TV stations would not have advertising, but would charge $1.00 or so per pro-

gram for special programs. Do you think this should be tried
out or not?

ROPER only, Base: 591

	ROPER
Should be tried out	22%
Should not be tried out	63
Don't know	13
NA	2

E. (And) what, if anything, do you think might be some of the
advantages of such a system?

F. (And) what do you think might be some of the disadvantages
it (would) (might) lead to?

(46) Now I'd like to get your estimates or guesses about a few things.
You may not have any information at all on some of these, but
I'd like your off-hand guesses anyway.

A. Considering only the *regular* evening programs for adults—
those scheduled between seven-thirty and ten or so—this season, what percentage of the time would you say is devoted
to humorous or comedy programs (including both the [situa-
tion] [story] type comedies like *I Love Lucy* or *The Danny
Thomas Show* and variety shows with star comedians like Red
Skelton or Bob Hope)? (IF "DEPENDS ON CHANNEL," SPECIFY
FOR EACH)

NORC Base: 614

0–5%	6–15%	16–25%	26–35%	36–45%	46–55%	56–65%	66–75%	76–85%	86–95%	96–100%	NA
2%	9%	19%	18%	5%	23%	5%	5%	2%	1%	0%	0%

E. Would you say that's enough, not enough, or too much?

Enough	60%
Not enough	26
Too much	8
NA	6

B. Considering only the *regular* evening programs for adults—
those scheduled between seven-thirty and ten or so—this
season, what percentage of the time would you say is devoted
to mystery, detective, or police programs? (IF "DEPENDS ON
CHANNEL," SPECIFY FOR EACH)

ROPER Base: 607

0–5%	6–15%	16–25%	26–35%	36–45%	46–55%	56–65%	66–75%	76–85%	86–95%	96–100%	NA
1%	3%	16%	14%	7%	27%	4%	9%	3%	1%	1%	12%

    E.   Would you say that's enough, not enough, or too much?

Enough	55%
Not enough	8
Too much	30
NA	6

    C.   (Same as Q. 53C)

Considering only the *regular* evening programs for adults—those scheduled between seven-thirty and ten or so—this season, what percentage of the time would you say is devoted to westerns? (IF "DEPENDS ON CHANNEL," SPECIFY FOR EACH)

NORC Base: 615

0–5%	6–15%	16–25%	26–35%	36–45%	46–55%	56–65%	66–75%	76–85%	86–95%	96–100%	NA
3%	8%	9%	6%	31%	5%	13%	3%	2%	1%	18%	0%

    E.   Would you say that's enough, not enough, or too much?

Enough	42%
Not enough	6
Too much	46
NA	7

46. D.   (Same as Q. 53D)

Considering only the *regular* evening programs for adults—those scheduled between seven-thirty and ten or so—this season, what percentage of the time would you say is devoted to news, public affairs, and documentaries—programs that deal with current events or important issues of the day? (IF "DE-PENDS ON CHANNEL," SPECIFY FOR EACH)

ROPER Base: 591

0–5%	6–15%	16–25%	26–35%	36–45%	46–55%	56–65%	66–75%	76–85%	86–95%	96–100%	NA
21%	31%	18%	5%	2%	2%	1%	1%	1%	0%	0%	10%

E.   Would you say that's enough, not enough, or too much?

Enough	55%
Not enough	8
Too much	30
NA	6

47. In a regular fifteen-minute news broadcast, about how many minutes do you think should be devoted to news about people and events (around NAME OF CITY) (around here) and about how many to national and international affairs?

48. Do you recall the publicity about quiz shows a few months ago? (Do you remember anything about it at all?)

NORC Base: 1221	
Yes, some recollection	83%
No, no recollection	17

IF ANY RECOLLECTION AT ALL, ASK B–D:

B.   Do you happen to recall any of the shows that were under investigation? (Which ones can you remember?)

C.   As far as you know, which of these actually was found to be fixed in some way? (Try to remember the name of the show.)

D.   How do you feel about the whole affair?

IF NO RECOLLECTION (TO A IN Q. 48), SKIP TO QUESTION 63

49. Which of these statements come closest to expressing your opinion about what these investigations into television have shown about the industry?

NORC Base: 1221

These shocking disclosures show just how bad television is.	4%
These practices are very wrong and should be stopped immediately, but you can't condemn all of television because of them.	60
No one can really be in favor of this kind of thing, but there's nothing very wrong about it either.	12
What happened is a normal part of show business and is perfectly all right	6
DK	3
NA	16

50. A. Who do you think is responsible for the rigged quiz shows—the contestants, the television broadcasting companies, the independent show-producing companies, the companies sponsoring these shows, the sponsors' advertising agencies, or who? (Anyone else?)

NORC Base: 1221

Contestants	11%
The broadcasters	12
Independent producers	29
Sponsors	34
Agencies	16
The public	3
Other (SPECIFY)	3
None or DK	10
NA	16

B. When you say the (broadcasters) (independent show-producing companies) (the companies sponsoring the shows) the sponsors' advertising agencies) are responsible, do you mean the companies as a whole or just a few individuals in these companies?

NORC Base: 836

Companies as a whole	20%
Just a few people	71
DK	4
NA	5

51. A. Do you think that misleading or deceptive practices were pretty much confined to quiz shows or are there some other misleading or deceptive practices on television?

   IF "OTHER MISLEADING OR DECEPTIVE PRACTICES ON TELE-VISION," ASK B AND C

   B. What sort of (misleading) (deceptive) practices do you have in mind? (Can you describe the sort of thing you mean?)

   C. How are they deceptive? (In what way are they misleading?) (Questions 52 and 53 same as 45 and 46)

54. What channel(s) or station(s) do you get on your set? (ENTER EACH CHANNEL MENTIONED, IN ORDER NAMED, AT TOP OF A SEPA-RATE COLUMN)

	Channel Number DK	All the same
A. In general, which channel do you think has the best reception (CHECK ONE ONLY)		
B. Which one has the best news coverage?	[Data vary	
C. Which has the most sports?	by location.]	
D. Which one most frequently presents local personalities or events?		
E. Which has the best all-around entertainment?		
F. Which has the most annoying commercials?		
G. The most serious programs?		
H. The most believable advertising?		
I. The most westerns?		
J. The most movies?		
K. And which needs the most improvement (in programming)?		
L. Which channel will probably have the best coverage of the political conventions?		
M. Which gives you the most information and news about things going on around (NAME OF CITY)?		

55. A.   Taking everything into consideration, if you could watch only *one* channel on your set, which would you choose?

    B.   Why?

    C.   IF THREE OR MORE CHANNELS MENTIONED IN Q. 54: What would be your second choice?

    D.   Why?

56. A.   Are there any channels that you almost never watch?

         ROPER Base: 1206
         Yes   51%
         No   41
         NA   8

    IF "YES," ASK B AND C:

    B.   Which ones?

    C.   Why is it that you don't watch (it) (them)?

57. A.   As you understand it, are any of these channels (READ BACK THOSE MENTIONED IN Q. 54) associated with a network?

         ROPER Base: 1206
         Yes   65%
         No   3
         DK   22
         NA   10

    IF "YES," ASK B–D:

    B.   Which ones are associated with which network?

    C.   As you understand it, what is the nature of the association between (this) (these) channel(s) and the network(s)?

    D.   IF NO APPARENT UNDERSTANDING OR DON'T KNOW IN C, CONTINUE: For example, does (FIRST MENTIONED NETWORK) own Channel (NUMBER), does Channel (NUMBER) simply agree to show (NETWORK) programs or what? (SPECIFY FOR EACH CHANNEL IF RESPONDENT SAYS ARRANGEMENTS VARY)

58. A. IF CBS, NBC, OR ABC NOT MENTIONED IN Q. 57, ASK: Do you know of any other television networks?

> ROPER Base: 1206
> Yes   10%
> No   44
> NA   46

59. A. IF TWO OR MORE NETWORKS MENTIONED IN Q. 57 AND/OR Q. 58:

Which of these would you think of as the leading network in the country? (IF RESPONDENT SAYS ONE LEADS IN SOME RESPECTS AND ONE IN OTHERS, SPECIFY HOW EACH LEADS)

B. Why do you think that's the best?

C. IF THREE OR MORE NETWORKS MENTIONED IN Q. 57 AND/OR Q. 58:
Which would you put in second place?

D. And why do you consider (NETWORK) second best?

60. Do you think about any particular network in connection with the broadcasting of news, public affairs, and documentaries—programs that deal with current events or important issues of the day? (Which?)

61. A. Do you happen to recognize this symbol? (HAND CARD WITH CBS EYE)

B. Do you happen to know who uses it and what it stands for?

62. A. How about this one? (HAND ABC CARD TO RESPONDENT)

B. And do you know who uses it and what it stands for?

63. A. Is there an educational channel in this area?

IF "YES," ASK B–F:

B. Which channel is that?

C. During what hours do you think (it) (Channel __) is on the air? (I'd like your best guess on when it goes on and when it goes off.)

D. What type of programs do you think it broadcasts? (How do you mean, educational?)

E. Have you ever seen a program on (the educational channel) (Channel ___)?

> NORC Base: 1221
> ROPER Base: 1206

	NORC	ROPER
Yes	18%	17%
NA, DK	16	13
All other	66	70

IF "YES" TO E, ASK (1) AND (2):

(1) About how frequently do you watch (Channel ___)?

(2) IF ACTUAL NUMBER OF HOURS NOT MENTIONED: About how many hours a month would you say you watch it?

F. Do other members of your family ever watch (the educational channel (Channel ___)?

> NORC Base: 1221
> ROPER Base: 1206

	NORC	ROPER
Yes	10%	8%
No	18	18
All other	72	74

IF "YES" TO F, ASK (1)–(3):

(1) Who in the family watches?
(2) Which programs do they watch?
(3) How frequently do they watch?

64. A. Have you ever written (or called) a newspaper, television station, columnist, congressman, or anyone like that to express your opinions about television?

> NORC Base: 1221
> ROPER Base: 1206

	NORC	ROPER
Yes	4%	5%
No	95	95
Other	1	0

IF "YES," ASK B–D:

B. Whom did you write?

C. What did you write about? (What did you say about it?)

D. What, if anything, happened? (Did you get an answer?) (Were there any changes made that might have resulted from your letter?)

65. If you personally were in charge of a leading television network, what changes would you like to make? (If it were completely up to you, what changes would you try to make?)

BACKGROUND INFORMATION

Base for all classifying questions:
NORC: 1221
ROPER: 1206

66. Composition of household:

ASCERTAIN AND DESCRIBE ALL THE MEMBERS OF HOUSEHOLD AND THEIR RELATIONSHIP TO EACH OTHER—E.G., "HUSBAND, WIFE, AND THREE CHILDREN," "TWO SINGLE GIRLS SHARING AN APARTMENT," "A YOUNG COUPLE, STILL IN COLLEGE, LIVING WITH HIS PARENTS," ETC.

67. WHICH ONE DID YOU INTERVIEW?

Respondent is head (or wife of head) of household and lives with:

	NORC	ROPER
(1) Spouse and dependent children	54%	59%
(2) Spouse only	28	25
(3) Children only	2	2
(4) Neither—shares with relative	3	2
(5) Neither—shares with non-relative	2	1
(6) Lives alone	7	5

Respondent is not head of household, and lives with:

	NORC	ROPER
(7) Parents, in-laws	2	4
(8) Adult children	1	1
(9) With relatives	1	1
(10) NA	0	0

68. SEX OF RESPONDENT

	NORC	ROPER
Male	48%	50%
Female	52	50

69. Are you now married, single, widowed, divorced, or separated?

	NORC	ROPER
Married	80%	81%
Single	9	10
Widowed	8	7
Divorced	2	2
Separated	1	1

70. What is your (approximate) age?

	NORC	ROPER
Under 20	4%	3%
20–24	6	9
25–29	12	12
30–34	11	11
35–39	12	11
40–44	10	10
45–49	9	8
50–54	9	8
55–59	6	10
60–64	5	6
65–69	7	5
Over 70	8	6
NA	0	1

71. ASK UNLESS OBVIOUS, BUT CODE IN EVERY CASE:

A. What do you usually do—work full time, work part time (keep house, go to school), or something else?

	NORC	ROPER
Work full time	45%	46%
Work part time only	3	5
Work part time and keep house	4	4
Work part time and go to school	1	1
Keep house only	36	36
Go to school only	2	1
Retired	7	6
Other	0	0
NA	2	1

B.   IF "WORKS": Exactly what sort of work do you do?

	NORC	ROPER
Top professional	1%	1%
Lesser professional	10	9
Proprietor	5	5
White collar	23	28
Skilled labor	21	19
Unskilled–semi-skilled labor	26	22
Farmer	5	6
NA	10	10

C.   IF "KEEP HOUSE," "GO TO SCHOOL," "RETIRED," OR "OTHER":
Have you ever worked for pay?

	NORC	ROPER
Yes	71%	69%
No	19	18
NA	10	13

(1) IF "YES": Exactly what sort of work did you do when
you worked? (Last job held?)

72.   IF RESPONDENT IS A MARRIED WOMAN LIVING WITH HER HUSBAND,
ASK THE FOLLOWING ABOUT HIM. IF RESPONDENT IS A MARRIED
MAN LIVING WITH HIS WIFE, ASK THE FOLLOWING ABOUT HER.
IF RESPONDENT IS A DEPENDENT OR SEMI-DEPENDENT (E.G., YOUNG
ADULT OR COUPLE LIVING WITH PARENT(S) OR ELDERLY PARENT
LIVING WITH CHILDREN, ETC.), ASK ABOUT THE MAIN EARNER IN
THE FAMILY, WHATEVER THE SEX.

A.   What does your (husband, wife, father, etc.) usually do—
work full time, work part time (keep house, go to school), or
something else?

	NORC	ROPER
Works full time	46%	50%
Works part time only	3	4
Works part time and keeps house	3	2
Works part time and goes to school	0	0
Keeps house only	28	28
Goes to school only	0	0
Retired	5	3
NA, other	15	14

B. IF "WORKS": Exactly what sort of work does (he, she) do?

	NORC	ROPER
Top professional	1%	1%
Lesser professional	8	9
Proprietor	5	5
White collar	19	22
Skilled labor	21	21
Unskilled–semi-skilled labor	20	20
Farmer	5	6
NA, other	21	15

C. IF "KEEPS HOUSE," "GOES TO SCHOOL," "RETIRED," OR "OTHER": Has (he, she) ever worked for pay?

	NORC	ROPER
Yes	39%	43%
No	23	16
NA, other	38	41

IF "YES": What sort of work did (he, she) do when (he, she) worked? (Last job held?)

73. A. Do you rent this (house, apartment), or do you own it?

	NORC	ROPER
Own house	63%	62%
Rent house	23	23
Own apartment	1	1
Rent apartment	11	10
Other	0	0
All other	2	4

B. How many rooms are there (not counting bathrooms)?

74. A. What was the name of the last school you attended?

B. What was the last grade you completed in this school?

	NORC	ROPER
0– 4 years	4%	2%
5– 6 years	5	5
7– 8 years	18	17
9–11 years	23	21
12 years	25	31
1–2 years college	9	9
3–4 years college	8	8

	NORC	ROPER
Some graduate work (specify		
degree, if any)	5	4
Trade or technical school in		
addition to above (specify)	8	9
NA	1	1

75. A. What newspapers do you usually read?

    B. Any others that your (husband, wife) reads?

76. How many TV sets do you now have in your home?

NUMBER OF SETS	NORC	ROPER
1	78%	79%
2	14	13
3	2	1
4	0	0
5 +	0	0
NA	6	6

LOCATION OF SETS	NORC	ROPER
Living room	80%	77%
Dining room	2	3
Bedroom	10	12
Play room, basement	11	11
Kitchen	1	2
Porch	1	1
Portable	0	0
Other	1	0
NA	7	9

77. How about other sound equipment? Do you have at home . . .

		NORC	ROPER
Regular AM radio	Yes	92%	91%
	No	8	6
	NA	0	3
FM radio	Yes	26	28
	No	70	56
	NA	4	15
Phonograph	Yes	55	51
	No	43	38
	NA	2	11
Tape recorder	Yes	6	5
	No	89	78
	NA	4	17

		NORC	ROPER
Custom high-fidelity or	Yes	17	17
stereophonic equipment	No	79	68
	NA	4	15
Piano	Yes	18	19
	No	79	68
	NA	3	13
Other musical instruments	Yes	18	15
	No	76	66
	NA	6	19

78. Do you ever go to the movies?

	NORC	ROPER
Yes	61%	60%
No	38	39
NA	1	1

IF "YES": What was the name of the last movie you saw?

79. Have you had a chance to read any books in the last year?

	NORC	ROPER
Yes	44%	44%
No	55	55
NA	1	1

IF "YES": Do you happen to recall the title of the last book you read?

80. A. During what hours were you not at home yesterday?

    B. And the day before?

    C. How about your (husband, wife)—during what hours was (he, she) not at home yesterday?

    D. And the day before?

81. Did you take a vacation last year?

	NORC	ROPER
Yes	51%	48%
No	48	51
NA	1	1

IF "YES": Where did you spend it?

82. A. Do you have any vacation plans for this year? (How and where will you probably spend it?)

B. Is there any particular place you would like to see or visit if you had unlimited time and money? (Where would you go and what would you do?)

83. A. Do you smoke?

	NORC	ROPER
Yes	50%	50%
No	49	50
NA	1	0

IF "YES," ASK B AND C:

B. About how many cigarettes (cigars, pipes) a day?

C. Have you ever tried to give up smoking?

NORC Base: 616
ROPER Base: 603

	NORC	ROPER
Yes	50%	46%
No	46	43
NA	4	11

D. IF "NO" TO A: Have you ever smoked regularly?

NORC Base: 604
ROPER Base: 603

	NORC	ROPER
Yes	19%	17%
No	54	51
NA	27	32

84. Do you belong to any clubs or organizations at present? Which ones?

Now just four more questions for classification purposes.

85. Which of these general groups did your total (family) income fall in last year—before taxes, that is?

		NORC	ROPER
A.	Under $1000	5%	4%
B.	$1000 to $1999	7	5
C.	$2000 to $2999	9	7
D.	$3000 to $3999	11	11
E.	$4000 to $4999	13	12
F.	$5000 to $5999	14	11
G.	$6000 to $6999	10	8

		NORC	ROPER
H.	$7000 to $7999	7	7
I.	$8000 to $8999	5	6
J.	$9000 to $9999	3	3
K.	$10,000 or over	10	8
L.	DK	3	14
	NA	2	3

86. A. Where were you born? (What state or foreign country?)

	NORC	ROPER
Foreign-born	10%	6%

  B. IF IN THIS COUNTRY: Where were your parents born?

	NORC	ROPER
U.S.-born, foreign parents	19%	16%
U.S.-born, U.S. parents	71	76
NA	0	2

87. A. Generally speaking, what is your political preference?

	NORC	ROPER
Democratic	52%	47%
Republican	28	30
Independent	14	15
Other	4	2
NA	2	5

  B. What is your religious preference? (What do you consider yourself?)

	NORC	ROPER
Protestant	66%	71%
Catholic	24	22
Jewish	5	3
Other	4	1
NA	1	2

88. May I have your name and phone number (in case I have to check back for any reason)?

89. Closed book.

THANK RESPONDENT AND PREPARE TO LEAVE. ASK THE FOLLOWING QUESTIONS AS IF FOR YOUR OWN INTEREST, AND RECORD THE RESPONSES AS CLOSE TO VERBATIM AS POSSIBLE IMMEDIATELY AFTER YOU LEAVE THE RESPONDENT'S HOME AND BEFORE YOU GO ON TO ANOTHER INTERVIEW.

A. You know, TV has changed quite a bit since it began. What do you think it'll be like ten years from now?

B. How would you personally like to see it change—if anything at all were possible?

90. A. RECORD THE NAMES OF ANY MAGAZINES YOU HAVE OBSERVED IN THE HOME.

B. ARE THERE ENOUGH SHELVES OF BOOKS VISIBLE IN THE HOME TO SAY THERE IS A "HOME LIBRARY"?

	NORC	ROPER
Yes	19%	21%
No	53	48
Didn't observe enough rooms to know	26	28
NA	2	3

91. WHAT WAS RESPONDENT'S ATTITUDE DURING MOST OF THE INTERVIEW?

	NORC	ROPER
Friendly	81%	85%
So-So	17	12
Hostile	1	1
NA	1	2

92. A. WERE THERE ANY OTHERS PRESENT FOR MORE THAN A MINUTE OR TWO DURING THE INTERVIEW?

	NORC	ROPER
Yes	48%	64%
No	50	34
NA	1	2

B. IF "YES": Who? (GIVE NUMBER OF PERSONS AND RELATIONSHIP OF EACH TO RESPONDENT)

93. RESPONDENT'S RACE:

	NORC	ROPER
Negro	10%	12%
White	89	86
Oriental	0	0
NA	1	2

94. PLEASE USE THIS SPACE (AND THE BACK OF THIS PAGE) TO TELL
    US ANYTHING ABOUT THE RESPONDENT THAT MIGHT HELP US IN
    ANALYZING THE DATA

95. A. CIRCLE ONE OF THE FOLLOWING CODES TO SHOW TYPE OF
        DWELLING UNIT:

	NORC	ROPER
Located on a farm	13%	17%
Non-farm, single-family house	60	56
Non-farm, duplex or two-family structure	11	13
Non-farm; multi-unit structure (e.g., apt. house)	13	11
Other	1	1
NA	2	2

96. A. CIRCLE ONE OF THE FOLLOWING CODES TO SHOW LOCATION OF
        DWELLING UNIT:

	NORC	ROPER
Inside the largest city in the area	53%	43%
In a suburb of the largest city in the area	14	13
In the outskirts (including nearby small towns) of the largest city in area	19	17
In open country	15	27
NA	0	0

B. PLEASE TELL US WHATEVER ELSE WE NEED TO KNOW TO HAVE
    A CLEAR PICTURE OF HOW AND WHERE RESPONDENT LIVES:

CITY SIZE	NORC	ROPER
1 million and over	22%	12%
250 thousand to 1 million	21	13
100 thousand to 250 thousand	11	8
25 thousand to 100 thousand	10	11
25 hundred to 25 thousand	18	18
Under 2500	3	6
Open country	15	27
Urban fringe	0	6

Geographic Region (Census Definitions)		
Northeast	4%	9%
Middle Atlantic	23	17
E. N. Central	19	21
W. N. Central	10	9

	NORC	ROPER
S. Atlantic	13	13
E. S. Central	6	8
W. S. Central	10	9
Mountain	4	3
Pacific	11	10

97. NAME OF PRIMARY SAMPLING UNIT:
County _____
Met. Area _____

98. SAMPLING UNIT NO. _____

99. LINE NO. FROM LISTING SHEET

100. DATE OF INTERVIEW

101. INTERVIEWER'S SIGNATURE

Questionnaires used in ARB New York sub-sample were NORC Versions 1 and 8, with Questions 42D(a,c,g); 43A,B,C,D; 44A,B,C,D; 45A,E,F; and 46A,E deleted in Version 1, and Questions 42D(a,c,g); 43A,B,C,D; 44A,B,C,D; 45B,E,F; and 46B,E deleted in Version 8, replaced by the following Questions 42X and 42Y,Z in both versions. Questions 42C and 47 were also deleted in ARB questionnaires.

42x. Now I'd like to ask you about any TV you or anyone else in the (family, household) saw last night. I don't care if last night was typical or not. Here is a copy of the TV Guide for last night—would you start at 7 o'clock in the evening and pick out all the programs that *anyone* watched. IF NO VIEWING LAST NIGHT, SKIP TO QUESTION 48; IF ANY VIEWING BY ANYONE, FILL IN BELOW, PROGRAM BY PROGRAM.

A. Name of Program
WHEN R DIDN'T WATCH BUT OTHERS DID, GET GUESS AS TO PROGRAM SEEN. IF R HAS NO IDEA, RECORD "?" IN THIS COLUMN AND ASK C ONLY.

B. Channel

C. Viewers (Any who saw some or all)
R / Spouse / Children / Other (specify)

D. ASK FOR EACH PROGRAM VIEWED BY MORE THAN ONE PERSON. Who especially enjoys that program?
R / Spouse / Children / "All equally" / Other (specify)

E. ASK FOR EACH, UNLESS SPECIAL TELECAST—ACADEMY AWARD, SPECTACULAR, ETC. Was this something you (they) watch nearly every time it's on, or once in a while, or was it just the first or second time you've (they've) watched it?
Regularly / Once in a while / 1st or second time / Other (specify)

F. (IF "ONCE IN A WHILE," "1st OR 2nd TIME," or "SPECIAL TELECAST") How did you happen to run across it last night? (IF NECESSARY PROBE . . . because it came on the station you happened to be watching, or turned up when you twisted the dial, or was the best thing you could find in the guide . . . or what?) Verbatim

Time
7:00– 7:30
7:30– 8:00
8:00– 8:30
8:30– 9:00
9:00– 9:30
9:30–10:00
10:00–10:30
10:30–11:00
11:00–11:30
11:30–12:00
12:00–12:30
12:30– 1:00
1:00– 1:30
1:30– 2:00

42y. A. IF FIRST PROGRAM WATCHED WAS AFTER 7:00–7:30 P.M.:
          You (your wife, etc.) started watching at _____. How
          did you (she, they) happen to start watching at that par-
          ticular time? (IF NECESSARY, PROBE . . . because that is your
          regular time, or because a favorite program was on, or what?)

      B. ASK OF ALL:
          How did you (they) happen to stop watching at _____?
          (IF NECESSARY, PROBE . . . because it was a good time to do
          something else, or because you (they) were tired of watching,
          or there wasn't anything good on, or because you were going
          to bed, or what?)

      C. IF R WATCHED MORE THAN TWO PROGRAMS: Of all the
          things you saw last night, which did you personally enjoy
          most? VERBATIM (What did you like about it?)

42z.   Now, thinking not just about last night, but about most of the
          times you watch television at home . . . are there other things
          you like to do while you watch television? (PROBE, IF NECES-
          SARY . . . things you like to combine or do along with watch-
          ing.)

SKIP TO Q. 48

BROADCAST SCHEDULES OF THE THREE NATIONAL TELEVISION NETWORKS

The following pages summarize the network programming broadcast during the months of interviewing in the national survey.

SCHEDULES OF THE THREE NATIONAL TELEVISION NETWORKS
MARCH AND APRIL, 1960

(Places where no entries are given represent time periods in which no network programs were scheduled.)

ABC-TV DAYTIME

Day/Time	Regular Programs	Special Programs
SUNDAY		
12:00–12:30 p.m.	JOHNS HOPKINS FILE 7	
12:30– 1:00	BISHOP PIKE	
1:00– 1:30	COLLEGE NEWS CONFERENCE	
3:00– 3:30	OPEN HEARING	3 / 6 Presidential Mission—Latin America
		4/10 The Everlasting Road
		4/17 To Win a Crown
3:30– 4:00	CHAMPIONSHIP BRIDGE WITH CHARLES GOREN (thru 4/10)	
	CAMPAIGN ROUNDUP (eff. 4/17)	
4:00– 4:30	PAUL WINCHELL SHOW (thru 4/3) (no network service thereafter)	
4:30– 5:00	BROKEN ARROW (thru 3/27)	
	CAMPAIGN ROUNDUP (4/3–4/10) (no network service thereafter)	
5:00– 5:30	MATTY'S FUNDAY FUNNIES	
5:30– 6:00	THE LONE RANGER	

4/15 The Shroud of Turin

MONDAY–FRIDAY
12:00–12:30 p.m.	THE RESTLESS GUN
12:30– 1:00	LOVE THAT BOB
1:00– 1:30	ABOUT FACES
1:30– 2:00	DAY IN COURT
2:00– 2:30	THE GALE STORM SHOW
2:30– 3:00	BEAT THE CLOCK
3:00– 3:30	WHO DO YOU TRUST?
3:30– 4:00	AMERICAN BANDSTAND
4:00– 5:30	THE ADVENTURES OF RIN TIN TIN (Mon. & Fri.) (also Tues. thru 3/1)
5:30– 6:00	MY FRIEND FLICKA (Wed.) ROCKY AND HIS FRIENDS (Thurs.) (also Tues. eff. 3/8)

SATURDAY
12:00–12:30 p.m.	LUNCH WITH SOUPY SALES
12:30– 1:00	THE RESTLESS GUN (thru 3/5) (no network service thereafter)
4:00–con.	BIG LEAGUE BASEBALL (eff. 4/16)
5:00– 6:00	ALL-STAR GOLF (thru 4/2)

ABC-TV EVENING

Day/Time	Regular Programs	Special Programs
SUNDAY		
7:00– 7:30 p.m.	COLT .45 (thru 3/27)	
	BROKEN ARROW (eff. 4/3)	
7:30– 8:30	MAVERICK	
8:30– 9:00	LAWMAN	
9:00– 9:30	THE REBEL	
9:30–10:30	THE ALASKANS	
10:30–11:00	21 BEACON STREET (thru 3/20)	
	JOHNNY STACCATO (eff. 3/27)	
MONDAY		
6:45– 7:00 p.m.	JOHN DALY AND THE NEWS	
7:30– 8:30	CHEYENNE	
8:30– 9:30	BOURBON STREET BEAT	
9:30–10:30	ADVENTURES IN PARADISE	
10:30–11:00	TED MACK AND THE ORIGINAL AMATEUR HOUR	
TUESDAY		
6:45– 7:00 p.m.	JOHN DALY AND THE NEWS	
7:00– 7:15		3/ 8 Presidential Mission—South American Trip
7:30– 8:30	SUGARFOOT (3/1) alternating with	
	BRONCO (3/8)	
8:30– 9:00	WYATT EARP	

9:00– 9:30	THE RIFLEMAN	
9:30–10:00	PHILIP MARLOWE (thru 3/29)	
	COLT .45 (eff. 4/5)	
10:00–10:30	ALCOA PRESENTS	3/29 Korea—No Parallel (60 min.)
10:30–11:00	KEEP TALKING	3/ 2 Governor Rockefeller (N. Y. State only)
WEDNESDAY		
6:30– 6:45 p.m.		
6:45– 7:00	JOHN DALY AND THE NEWS	
7:30– 8:00	MUSIC FOR A SPRING NIGHT	4/27 The Dark and the Light (a report on Africa) (60 min.)
8:00– 8:30	THE CHARLEY WEAVER SHOW (thru 3/23)	
	MUSIC FOR A SPRING NIGHT, cont. (eff. 3/30)	
8:30– 9:00	THE ADVENTURES OF OZZIE AND HARRIET	4/20 Special Tonight—Ninotchka (90 min.)
9:00–10:00	HAWAIIAN EYE	
10:00–11:00	WEDNESDAY NIGHT FIGHTS	4/27 Invitation to Paris
THURSDAY		
6:45– 7:00 p.m.	JOHN DALY AND THE NEWS	
7:30– 8:00	THE GALE STORM SHOW (thru 3/24)	3/31 All-Star Circus (60 min.)
	STEVE CANYON (eff. 4/7)	
8:00– 8:30	THE DONNA REED SHOW	
8:30– 9:00	THE REAL McCOYS	
9:00– 9:30	PAT BOONE CHEVY SHOWROOM	
9:30–10:30	THE UNTOUCHABLES	
10:30–11:00	TAKE A GOOD LOOK	

FRIDAY
6:45– 7:00 p.m.   JOHN DALY AND THE NEWS
7:30– 8:30   WALT DISNEY PRESENTS
8:30– 9:00   MAN FROM BLACKHAWK
9:00–10:00   77 SUNSET STRIP
10:00–10:30   THE DETECTIVES
10:30–11:00   BLACK SADDLE

SATURDAY
7:30– 8:00 p.m.   THE DICK CLARK SHOW
8:00– 8:30   JOHN GUNTHER'S HIGH ROAD
8:30– 9:00   LEAVE IT TO BEAVER
9:00–10:00   LAWRENCE WELK'S DODGE DANCING PARTY
10:00–11:00   JUBILEE USA

SCHEDULES OF THE THREE NATIONAL TELEVISION NETWORKS
MARCH AND APRIL, 1960

CBS-TV DAYTIME

Day/Time	Regular Programs	Special Programs
SUNDAY		
10:00–10:30 a.m.	LAMP UNTO MY FEET	4/17 Easter Sunday Service (Catholic) (60 min.)
10:30–11:00	LOOK UP AND LIVE	4/17 Easter Sunday Service (Protestant) (60 min.)
11:00–11:30	FYI	
11:30–12:00 n.	CAMERA THREE	
12:00–12:55 p.m.	THE CBS TELEVISION WORKSHOP	
12:55– 1:00	HARRY REASONER WITH THE NEWS	
1:00– 2:00		3/ 6 The New York Philharmonic Young People's Concerts (also 3/27 and 4/24)
1:30– 2:30	BASEBALL GAME OF THE WEEK (eff. 4/17)	4/10 The Great Challenge
1:45–con.		
2:00– 3:00		3/27 The Great Challenge (also 4/3)
3:00– 4:30	SUNDAY SPORTS SPECTACULAR (4/10 only 2:30–4:00 p.m.)	
4:00– 5:30		4/10 Masters' Golf Tournament
4:30– 5:00	FACE THE NATION	3/13 Leonard Bernstein and the New York Philharmonic (60 min.)

5:00– 5:30	CONQUEST	
5:30– 6:00	G-E COLLEGE BOWL	
MONDAY–FRIDAY		
8:00– 8:15 a.m.	RICHARD C. HOTTELET WITH THE NEWS	
8:15– 9:00	CAPTAIN KANGAROO	
10:00–10:30	THE RED ROWE SHOW	3/29 Woman! You Can't Raise Children by the Book (60 min.)
10:30–11:00	ON THE GO	
11:00–11:30	I LOVE LUCY	
11:30–12:00 n.	DECEMBER BRIDE	
12:00–12:30 p.m.	LOVE OF LIFE	
12:30–12:45	SEARCH FOR TOMORROW	
12:45– 1:00	THE GUIDING LIGHT	
1:00– 1:05	CHARLES KURALT WITH THE NEWS	
1:30– 2:00	AS THE WORLD TURNS	
2:00– 2:30	FOR BETTER OR WORSE	
2:30– 3:00	ART LINKLETTER'S HOUSE PARTY	
3:00– 3:30	THE MILLIONAIRE	3/ 1 Woman! The Lonely Years (60 min.)
3:30– 4:00	THE VERDICT IS YOURS	
4:00– 4:15	THE BRIGHTER DAY	
4:15– 4:30	THE SECRET STORM	
4:30– 5:00	THE EDGE OF NIGHT	

SATURDAY

8:00– 9 00 a.m.	CAPTAIN KANGAROO
10:00–10:30	THE HECKLE & JECKLE CARTOON SHOW
10:30–11:00	MIGHTY MOUSE PLAYHOUSE
11:00–11:30	THE LONE RANGER
11:30–12:00 n.	I LOVE LUCY
12:00–12:30 p.m.	SKY KING
1:00– 1:30	THE SATURDAY NEWS WITH ROBERT TROUT
1:45–con.	BASEBALL GAME OF THE WEEK (eff. 4/16)
2:00–con.	PROFESSIONAL HOCKEY (thru 3/19)
4:30– 5:30	
5:00– 6:00	

Special Programs

4/23 De Gaulle at the National Press Club (60 min.)

3/ 5 Olympic Medal Winners
4/ 9 Masters' Golf Tournament

CBS-TV EVENING

Day/Time   *Regular Programs*

SUNDAY

6:00– 6:30 p.m.	SMALL WORLD
6:30– 7:00	THE TWENTIETH CENTURY
7:00– 7:30	LASSIE
7:30– 8:00	DENNIS THE MENACE
8:00– 9:00	THE ED SULLIVAN SHOW
9:00– 9:30	GENERAL ELECTRIC THEATER
9:30–10:00	ALFRED HITCHCOCK PRESENTS

Special Programs

4/ 3 PLAYHOUSE 90: Alas, Babylon (90 min.)

3/20 Special Tonight: The Valley of Decision (90 min.)

10:00–10:30	THE JACK BENNY PROGRAM (3/6) alternating with THE GEORGE GOBEL SHOW (3/13)	
10:30–11:00	WHAT'S MY LINE?	3/ 7 PLAYHOUSE 90: Tomorrow (90 min.)
11:00–11:15	SUNDAY NEWS SPECIAL	
MONDAY		3/22 PLAYHOUSE 90: The Hiding Place (90 min.)
6:45– 7:00 p.m.	DOUGLAS EDWARDS WITH THE NEWS	
7:30– 8:00	THE KATE SMITH SHOW	
8:00– 8:30	THE TEXAN	4/ 5 What Happened in Wisconsin
8:30– 9:00	FATHER KNOWS BEST	
9:00– 9:30	THE DANNY THOMAS SHOW	
9:30–10:00	THE ANN SOTHERN SHOW	
10:00–10:30	HENNESEY	
10:30–11:00	THE DUPONT SHOW WITH JUNE ALLYSON	
TUESDAY		
6:45– 7:00 p.m.	DOUGLAS EDWARDS WITH THE NEWS	
8:00– 8:30	THE DENNIS O'KEEFE SHOW	
8:30– 9:00	THE MANY LOVES OF DOBIE GILLIS	
9:00– 9:30	TIGHTROPE!	
9:30–10:00	THE RED SKELTON SHOW	
10:00–11:00	THE GARRY MOORE SHOW	
11:15–12:00 mid.	MEN INTO SPACE	
WEDNESDAY		
6:45– 7:00 p.m.	DOUGLAS EDWARDS WITH THE NEWS	
7:30– 8:30	BE OUR GUEST	
8:30– 9:00	MEN INTO SPACE	

WEDNESDAY
9:00– 9:30 THE MILLIONAIRE
9:30–10:00 I'VE GOT A SECRET
10:00–11:00 ARMSTRONG CIRCLE THEATRE (3/2) alternating with
THE UNITED STATES STEEL HOUR (3/9)

4/21 DUPONT SHOW OF THE MONTH: Years Ago (90 min.)

THURSDAY
6:45– 7:00 p.m. DOUGLAS EDWARDS WITH THE NEWS
7:30– 8:00 TO TELL THE TRUTH
8:00– 8:30 THE BETTY HUTTON SHOW
8:30– 9:00 JOHNNY RINGO
9:00– 9:30 DICK POWELL'S ZANE GREY THEATRE
9:30–10:00 MARKHAM
10:00–11:00 REVLON REVUE

CBS REPORTS:
3/17 Trujillo: Portrait of a Dictator
4/21 Biography of a Cancer

FRIDAY
6:45– 7:00 p.m. DOUGLAS EDWARDS WITH THE NEWS
7:30– 8:30 RAWHIDE
8:30– 9:00 HOTEL DE PAREE
9:00–10:00 WESTINGHOUSE . . . .

3/25 THE BUICK ELECTRA PLAYHOUSE: The Snows of Kilimanjaro (90 min.)

3/11 MANHATTAN: If I Should Die (60 min.)

LUCILLE BALL–DESI ARNAZ SHOW (3/4, 4/1, 4/29)

4/ 8 A Salute to the American Theatre (60 min.)

DESILU PLAYHOUSE (3/18, 4/15)

4/22 PLAYHOUSE 90: Journey to the Day (90 min.)

10:00–10:30 THE TWILIGHT ZONE
10:30–11:00 PERSON TO PERSON

EYEWITNESS TO HISTORY:

3/25 Khrushchev in France
4/29 De Gaulle in America

SATURDAY

6:00– 6:15 p.m.

4/ 9 Conclusion of Masters' Golf

7:30– 8:30 PERRY MASON

3/ 5 DUPONT SHOW OF THE MONTH: Treasure Island (90 min.)

8:30– 9:00 WANTED: DEAD OR ALIVE
9:00– 9:30 MR. LUCKY
9:30–10:00 HAVE GUN, WILL TRAVEL
10:00–10:30 GUNSMOKE

3/19 Jack Benny Hour with Polly Bergen and Phil Silvers (60 min.)

10:30–11:00

3/ 5 EYEWITNESS TO HISTORY: The President in Argentina

SCHEDULES OF THE THREE NATIONAL TELEVISION NETWORKS
MARCH AND APRIL, 1960

NBC-TV DAYTIME

Day/Time	Regular Programs	Special Programs
SUNDAY		
11:00–12:00 n.		4/10 Palm Sunday Service 4/17 Roman Catholic Easter Mass
12:30– 1:00 p.m.		3/20 New York Times Youth Forum
1:00– 1:30		3/20 A Priest Forever 4/10 Eternal Light 4/24 The Key
1:30– 2:00	FRONTIERS OF FAITH (thru 4/24) (no network service thereafter)	
2:00– 2:15	NBA SPOTLIGHT (thru 4/3)	4/10 NBC Opera Company: Don Giovanni (150 min.)
2:00– con.	MAJOR LEAGUE BASEBALL AND PRE-GAME SHOW (eff. 4/17)	4/24 Korea in Turmoil (15 min.)
2:15– con.	NBC-NBA PRO BASKETBALL (thru 4/3)	
4:00– 4:30	ASK WASHINGTON (thru 4/3)	3/20 MEET THE PRESS
4:30– 5:30	WORLD CHAMPIONSHIP GOLF	
5:30– 6:00	TIME: PRESENT—CHET HUNTLEY REPORTING	4/24 Conventions 1960

MONDAY–FRIDAY

6:00– 7:00 a.m.	CONTINENTAL CLASSROOM
7:00– 9:00	TODAY
10:00–10:30	DOUGH RE MI
10:30–11:00	PLAY YOUR HUNCH
11:00–11:30	THE PRICE IS RIGHT
11:30–12:00 n.	CONCENTRATION
12:00–12:30 p.m.	TRUTH OR CONSEQUENCES
12:30– 1:00	IT COULD BE YOU
2:00– 2:30	QUEEN FOR A DAY
2:30– 3:00	THE LORETTA YOUNG THEATRE
3:00– 3:30	YOUNG DOCTOR MALONE
3:30– 4:00	FROM THESE ROOTS
4:00– 4:30	COMEDY PLAYHOUSE
4:30– 5:00	ADVENTURE TIME

SATURDAY

10:00–10:30 a.m.	HOWDY DOODY
10:30–11:00	THE RUFF AND REDDY SHOW
11:00–11:30	FURY
11:30–12:00 n.	CIRCUS BOY
12:00–12:30 p.m.	TRUE STORY
12:30– 1:00	DETECTIVE'S DIARY
1:00– 1:30	WATCH MR WIZARD
1:30–con.	MAJOR LEAGUE BASEBALL AND PRE-GAME SHOW (eff. 4/16)

4/ 4 Address by Secretary of State
Herter (NAB)

2:00–con.
4:00– 6:00   NBC-NBA PRO BASKETBALL
  3/12 National Invitational Tournament Basketball Game and Sports fill (also 3/19)
4:30– 5:00   4/ 2 Florida Derby

NBC-TV EVENING

Day/Time	Regular Programs
SUNDAY	
6:00– 6:30 p.m.	MEET THE PRESS
6:30– 7:00	SABER OF LONDON
7:00– 8:00	OVERLAND TRAIL
8:00– 9:00	SUNDAY SHOWCASE
9:00–10:00	THE CHEVY SHOW
	3/ 6 Houston Championship Rodeo
	3/13 The Dinah Shore Show (also 3/20, 4/3, 4/24)
	3/27 Janet Blair—Mexican Fiesta
	4/17 Children Are People
10:00–10:30	THE LORETTA YOUNG SHOW
	4/10 The Road (60 min.)

Special Programs

3/20 BELL SYSTEM SCIENCE SERIES: Alphabet (60 min.)

4/10 HALLMARK HALL OF FAME: The Cradle Song (90 min.)

4/24 THE DOW HOUR OF GREAT MYSTERIES: The Burning Court (60 min.)

MONDAY
6:45– 7:00 p.m.   THE HUNTLEY-BRINKLEY REPORT
7:30– 8:30   RIVERBOAT
8:30– 9:00   TALES OF WELLS FARGO
9:00– 9:30   PETER GUNN
9:30–10:00   ALCOA THEATRE (3/7) alternating with
                  GOODYEAR THEATRE (3/14)
10:00–11:00   THE STEVE ALLEN SHOW   4/ 4 Oscar Night in Hollywood
                                                                and the 32nd Annual Oscar
                                                                Awards Show (142 min.)
11:15– 1:00 a.m. THE JACK PAAR SHOW   4/ 4 THE BEST OF PAAR
                                                                (12:22–1:00 a.m.)

TUESDAY
6:45– 7:00 p.m.   THE HUNTLEY-BRINKLEY REPORT
7:00– 7:15   3/ 8 President Eisenhower's Re-
                                                                port on His South Ameri-
                                                                can Trip
7:30– 8:30   LARAMIE
8:30– 9:30   FORD STARTIME PRESENTS
9:30–10:00   THE ARTHUR MURRAY PARTY
10:00–10:30   M SQUAD   4/26 Jack Paar Presents (60 min.)
11:15– 1:00 a.m. THE JACK PAAR SHOW   4/ 5 Wisconsin Primary—Elec-
                                                                tion Returns (15 min.)

WEDNESDAY
6:15– 6:30 p.m.   3/16 Governor Rockefeller—
                                                                Your Future in New York
                                                                State (N. Y. State only)

6:45– 7:00	THE HUNTLEY-BRINKLEY REPORT	
7:30– 8:30	WAGON TRAIN	
8:30– 9:00	THE PRICE IS RIGHT	
9:00–10:00	PERRY COMO'S KRAFT MUSIC HALL	4/20 Bob Hope Buick Show
10:00–10:30	THIS IS YOUR LIFE	
10:30–11:00	WICHITA TOWN (thru 4/6)	
	PEOPLE ARE FUNNY (eff. 4/13)	
11:15– 1:00 a.m.	THE JACK PAAR SHOW	

THURSDAY

6:45– 7:00 p.m.	THE HUNTLEY-BRINKLEY REPORT	JOURNEY TO UNDER-STANDING:
7:30– 8:00	THE LAW OF THE PLAINSMAN	
		3/ 3 Eisenhower in South America and Puerto Rico
		4/28 De Gaulle Tours the Nation
8:00– 8:30	BAT MASTERSON	
8:30– 9:00	JOHNNY STACCATO (thru 3/24)	
	PRODUCER'S CHOICE (eff. 3/31)	3/31 THE DOW HOUR OF GREAT MYSTERIES: The Bat (60 min.)
9:00– 9:30	BACHELOR FATHER	
9:30–10:00	THE FORD SHOW STARRING TENNESSEE ERNIE FORD	
10:00–10:30	YOU BET YOUR LIFE	

THURSDAY

| 10:30–11:00 | THE LAWLESS YEARS (thru 3/24) (no network service thereafter) |
| 11:15– 1:00 a.m. | THE JACK PAAR SHOW |

FRIDAY

6:45– 7:00 p.m.	THE HUNTLEY-BRINKLEY REPORT
7:30– 8:00	PEOPLE ARE FUNNY (thru 4/8) PLAY YOUR HUNCH (eff. 4/15)
8:00– 8:30	THE TROUBLESHOOTERS
8:30– 9:30	4/22 JOURNEY TO UNDER-STANDING: De Gaulle in Washington 3/ 4 THE ART CARNEY SHOW 3/11 THE BELL TELEPHONE HOUR (also 4/1, 4/29) 3/18 PONTIAC STAR PARADE: Victor Borge 3/25 TV Guide Award Show 4/ 8 THE ART CARNEY SHOW: Joseph Conrad's "Victory" (90 min.) 4/15 The Jerry Lewis Show 4/22 PROJECT 20: Mark Twain's America
9:30–10:00	MASQUERADE PARTY
10:00–10:45	CAVALCADE OF SPORTS—BOXING
10:45–11:00	JACKPOT BOWLING
11:15– 1:00 a.m.	THE BEST OF PAAR

SATURDAY

Time	Program	
7:00– 7:30 p.m.		4/23 De Gaulle Press Conference
		4/16 PONTIAC STAR PARADE: Andy Williams (60 min.)
7:30– 8:30	BONANZA	
8:30– 9:00	THE MAN AND THE CHALLENGE	JOURNEY TO UNDERSTANDING:
		3 / 5 Summary of President Eisenhower's Complete South American Trip
9:00– 9:30	THE DEPUTY	4 / 2 Mr. K. in Paris
9:30–10:30	WORLD WIDE 60	
10:30–11:00	MAN FROM INTERPOL	

APPENDIX C

REFERENCE TABLES
AND DETAILS ON
ARB DIARY PROCEDURE

TABLE 1

Q. 1A, 1B Time Most enjoyed, by reasons

Q. 1A First, think of the way you spend an ordinary day—just a typical weekday when nothing special is happening.
     What part of the day do you enjoy most?

Q. 1B What makes that part of the day particularly enjoyable?

		Work done	Relax	Leisure (total)	Watch TV	Listen to radio	Kids out of way	Read	Listen to music	Hobbies	Gardening, outdoors	Outside organizations, activities	Friends, socialize	Be with family	Enjoy work	Feel fresh	Eating	Housework, cooking	Other	NA	Base: 100%
		%	%	%	%	%	%	%	%	%	%	%	%	%	%	%	%	%	%	%	
Morning	Men	1	8	9	4	1	1	3	0	3	29	3	1	2	12	50	4	2	9	3	147
	Women	10	17	25	9	1	1	8	0	2	21	1	3	5	8	31	2	6	20	0	216
Noon	Men	6	24	26	6	3	0	6	0	9	9	4	8	12	35	1	22	5	1	1	80
	Women	13	28	35	20	1	13	9	1	9	6	6	6	14	24	2	5	7	5	1	85
Afternoon	Men	28	39	58	12	4	0	5	1	17	11	7	7	5	6	6	1	3	6	3	100
	Women	40	49	70	30	2	19	10	0	7	5	6	7	10	1	3	1	3	2	0	308
Evening	Men	33	50	68	29	1	3	11	2	7	6	5	6	25	1	1	5	2	3	1	719
	Women	33	53	68	37	2	18	10	2	7	3	4	8	30	0	1	1	1	4	0	539
NA	Men	3	4	5	12	1	1	2	1	5	7	2	3	9	13	0	3	0	3	58	111
	Women	4	9	10	10	1	4	9	1	5	3	4	9	12	6	0	4	5	6	56	78

TABLE 2

Sample Characteristics and Census Data, Where Directly Comparable

	CENSUS—U.S. POPULATION*	SAMPLE CHARACTERISTICS FROM INTERVIEW DATA	
		Viewers	Non-viewers
Sex			
Men	49%	48%	46%
Women	51	52	54
Income			
under $2000	14	11	45
$2000–$2999	10	8	18
3000– 3999	11	11	4
4000– 4999	11	12	7
5000– 5999	11	13	0
6000– 9999	27	24	3
over 10,000	15	9	3
DK, NA	0	11	19
Religion			
Protestants	66	69	86
Catholics	26	23	8
Jews	3	4	0
Others	5	3	4
NA	0	1	1
Race			
Caucasians	89	87	66
Negroes	11	11	32
Orientals	1	0	1
NA	0	1	0
Age			
20–30	20	19	13
31–40	21	23	8
41–50	20	19	14
51–60	18	17	17
61–70	13	11	17
over 70	10	7	27

NOTE: See classifying data in questionnaire for further characteristics.
* From *Statistical Abstract of the United States, 1960.*

TABLE 3

Q. 7. *Now I would like to get your opinions about how Radio, Newspapers, Television and Magazines compare. Generally speaking, which of these would you say . . .*

AGE

	Under 20	20–24	25–29	30–34	35–39	40–44	45–49	50–54	55–59	60–64	65–69	Over 70
Base: 100% =	84	180	294	267	280	253	212	211	193	130	138	174
A. Is the most entertaining												
NEWSPAPERS	6%	6%	10%	10%	14%	12%	15%	12%	15%	14%	18%	25%
MAGAZINES	4	6	9	12	11	9	9	12	3	12	4	9
NONE OR DK	0	2	1	1	2	1	1	1	3	2	1	1
RADIO	17	10	6	9	7	9	7	11	8	14	14	10
TELEVISION	74	76	74	68	67	70	68	63	72	58	63	56
B. Gives the most complete news coverage												
NEWSPAPERS	64	60	64	60	58	57	60	56	56	64	46	61
MAGAZINES	6	5	4	4	4	4	3	2	4	1	3	1
NONE OR DK	0	2	0	0	3	1	1	1	2	0	1	1
RADIO	14	13	14	16	18	16	19	18	20	20	25	21
TELEVISION	15	20	18	19	17	22	18	23	19	15	25	16

C. Presents things most intelligently

NEWSPAPERS	26	37	40	31	30	35	37	29	34	30	33	29
MAGAZINES	33	26	26	25	34	29	26	30	24	22	22	24
NONE OR DK	10	3	3	3	5	2	4	5	9	9	8	9
RADIO	7	6	8	9	8	6	7	10	7	6	10	10
TELEVISION	24	29	22	31	24	28	26	26	25	33	28	29

D. Is the most educational

NEWSPAPERS	38	32	35	35	28	25	33	24	28	34	29	33
MAGAZINES	29	27	35	34	36	30	28	36	29	18	25	28
NONE OR DK	4	5	3	3	4	4	5	3	6	5	6	6
RADIO	1	2	1	1	2	5	1	3	3	5	4	5
TELEVISION	29	34	26	27	31	35	33	34	35	38	37	29

E. Brings you the latest news most quickly

NEWSPAPERS	6	4	7	4	5	2	5	4	4	8	7	8
MAGAZINES	0	1	0	0	1	0	0	0	0	0	0	0
NONE OR DK	0	1	2	0	2	2	0	1	2	2	1	2
RADIO	64	61	59	55	58	62	58	55	57	55	55	50
TELEVISION	31	33	32	40	35	34	37	39	37	35	38	40

F. Does the most for the public

NEWSPAPERS	55	48	49	39	44	43	41	43	43	43	40	47
MAGAZINES	4	3	4	4	3	2	1	2	2	1	1	3
NONE OR DK	2	5	5	8	8	9	11	8	11	11	8	10
RADIO	10	9	9	13	9	17	11	13	8	13	13	9
TELEVISION	30	36	34	35	38	31	36	35	36	32	38	30

AGE

	Under 20	20–24	25–29	30–34	35–39	40–44	45–49	50–54	55–59	60–64	65–69	Over 70
Base: 100% =	84	180	294	267	280	253	212	211	193	130	138	174
G. Seems to be getting worse all the time												
NEWSPAPERS	14	8	7	10	13	12	11	10	9	5	13	5
MAGAZINES	17	26	19	16	15	15	21	17	17	15	9	10
NONE OR DK	30	27	32	36	29	36	35	38	37	42	49	47
RADIO	23	13	18	15	16	13	11	12	11	8	10	10
TELEVISION	17	27	24	23	27	25	23	22	25	29	19	29
H. Presents the fairest, most unbiased news												
NEWSPAPERS	25	32	31	28	24	28	25	25	31	38	30	35
MAGAZINES	12	9	13	8	12	10	7	9	7	5	8	10
NONE OR DK	11	7	9	9	13	10	9	10	20	9	7	11
RADIO	26	25	19	27	25	20	23	21	18	18	22	20
TELEVISION	26	27	28	28	26	32	36	35	25	29	33	24
I. Is doing its job best												
NEWSPAPERS	43	34	37	31	31	28	32	29	34	35	33	37
MAGAZINES	11	7	10	9	13	13	7	6	7	5	6	6
NONE OR DK	7	10	15	13	15	16	14	15	20	23	12	18
RADIO	13	17	12	17	16	17	15	14	12	12	12	16
TELEVISION	26	33	28	29	25	26	33	37	26	25	37	24

J. Is the most important to you

NEWSPAPERS	32	29	38	31	35	37	49	38	41	45	45	44
MAGAZINES	7	8	5	10	9	8	7	3	5	4	2	6
NONE OR DK	0	3	4	2	4	3	2	4	5	4	4	2
RADIO	24	18	15	16	16	16	10	16	11	14	11	15
TELEVISION	37	42	38	40	36	37	33	39	39	33	38	33

K. Is the least important to you

NEWSPAPERS	10	8	10	9	7	7	4	7	7	5	7	5
MAGAZINES	55	54	52	44	42	42	57	49	48	49	52	51
NONE OR DK	6	6	4	8	5	10	4	7	7	8	7	10
RADIO	19	15	20	23	28	24	20	23	24	25	22	22
TELEVISION	11	16	14	15	18	18	15	14	14	13	13	13

L. Creates the most interest in new things going on

NEWSPAPERS	21	15	18	15	20	15	20	19	21	25	14	20
MAGAZINES	18	18	23	21	22	18	11	16	19	11	14	13
NONE OR DK	5	3	1	1	5	3	5	5	7	4	7	11
RADIO	2	1	5	4	4	4	3	5	4	2	5	6
TELEVISION	54	63	53	58	50	60	61	55	49	58	61	49

M. Does the least for the public

NEWSPAPERS	10	4	5	6	6	6	3	6	5	3	7	3
MAGAZINES	45	52	48	43	44	52	53	45	41	52	43	43
NONE OR DK	17	13	20	21	23	21	21	25	28	26	30	29
RADIO	14	14	11	18	14	11	9	12	12	8	11	13
TELEVISION	14	17	16	13	14	9	13	12	14	10	9	13

		Under 20	20–24	25–29	30–34	35–39	40–44	45–49	50–54	55–59	60–64	65–69	Over 70
	Base: 100% =	84	180	294	267	280	253	212	211	193	130	138	174
N.	Seems to be getting better all the time												
	NEWSPAPERS	11	11	10	12	9	11	11	8	12	15	12	13
	MAGAZINES	11	10	9	11	14	13	9	13	12	5	8	8
	NONE OR DK	12	14	12	15	21	17	23	23	24	28	25	26
	RADIO	13	12	11	9	9	11	10	11	10	10	8	14
	TELEVISION	54	53	58	54	47	48	48	45	42	42	47	39
O.	Gives you the clearest understanding of the candidates and issues, in national elections												
	NEWSPAPERS	30	32	39	35	35	32	38	33	42	36	44	35
	MAGAZINES	10	13	13	12	15	11	8	9	6	6	3	5
	NONE OR DK	6	4	7	4	5	6	5	7	11	9	12	13
	RADIO	5	4	6	5	5	4	4	9	4	9	2	7
	TELEVISION	50	46	35	44	40	46	45	43	38	40	41	40
P.	Has the hardest job to do												
	NEWSPAPERS	26	32	30	26	24	23	34	32	31	34	36	40
	MAGAZINES	7	6	4	6	6	4	5	6	5	4	3	5
	NONE OR DK	10	12	10	10	12	14	13	14	16	24	20	18
	RADIO	5	7	6	7	8	7	8	8	5	6	4	6
	TELEVISION	52	43	49	51	50	52	40	41	44	32	38	32

AGE

COMPOSITION OF THE HOUSEHOLD

	RESPONDENT IS HEAD OF HOUSEHOLD						RESPONDENT NOT HEAD		
	With spouse & children	Spouse Only	Child Only	With Relatives	With Non-Relatives	Alone	With Parents	With Child	With Relative
Base: 100% =	1374	633	46	69	30	147	74	30	24
A. Is the most entertaining									
NEWSPAPERS	11	15	33	13	10	14	8	40	17
MAGAZINES	9	8	9	16	10	12	8	3	4
NONE OR DK	1	1	0	3	3	1	0	0	0
RADIO	8	10	7	10	17	16	11	17	13
TELEVISION	71	66	52	58	60	57	73	40	67
B. Gives the most complete news coverage									
NEWSPAPERS	61	56	61	57	57	56	58	43	50
MAGAZINES	4	2	2	4	7	5	5	0	4
NONE OR DK	1	1	0	3	0	1	0	0	0
RADIO	16	20	17	16	23	25	15	30	29
TELEVISION	18	22	20	20	13	15	22	27	17
C. Presents things most intelligently									
NEWSPAPERS	34	33	41	26	40	31	30	30	29
MAGAZINES	28	26	15	29	27	18	30	13	38
NONE OR DK	5	6	0	3	0	10	8	3	0
RADIO	7	8	11	10	0	10	8	23	13
TELEVISION	26	27	33	32	33	30	24	30	21

COMPOSITION OF THE HOUSEHOLD

| | With spouse & children | RESPONDENT IS HEAD OF HOUSEHOLD | | | | | RESPONDENT NOT HEAD | | |
		Spouse Only	Child Only	With Relatives	With Non-Relatives	Alone	With Parents	With Child	With Relative
Base: 100% =	1374	633	46	69	30	147	74	30	24
D. Is the most educational									
NEWSPAPERS	31	29	26	38	33	31	39	33	21
MAGAZINES	33	28	35	29	20	25	30	17	29
NONE OR DK	4	4	4	4	3	5	3	10	4
RADIO	2	4	2	1	3	4	1	3	0
TELEVISION	30	35	33	28	40	36	27	37	46
E. Brings you the latest news most quickly									
NEWSPAPERS	4	7	2	4	3	5	1	10	4
MAGAZINES	0	0	2	0	0	0	0	0	0
NONE OR DK	2	1	2	1	0	2	0	0	0
RADIO	59	53	59	54	67	62	58	67	75
TELEVISION	36	38	37	41	30	31	41	23	21
F. Does the most for the public									
NEWSPAPERS	44	42	54	45	50	46	51	53	38
MAGAZINES	3	2	7	3	0	3	1	0	4
NONE OR DK	8	9	2	9	0	10	5	13	8
RADIO	11	13	9	10	7	8	12	13	21
TELEVISION	35	35	30	33	43	33	30	20	29

G. Seems to be getting worse all the time

NEWSPAPERS	10	10	7	3	13	10	14	3	13
MAGAZINES	17	16	15	17	10	12	22	10	13
NONE OR DK	34	40	26	32	37	44	27	57	25
RADIO	15	11	13	20	10	8	22	3	8
TELEVISION	24	24	39	28	30	26	16	27	42

H. Presents the fairest, most unbiased news

NEWSPAPERS	29	29	33	32	20	28	35	33	13
MAGAZINES	11	8	7	7	10	8	5	3	13
NONE OR DK	10	11	11	7	10	11	11	10	17
RADIO	21	19	28	20	30	29	24	33	42
TELEVISION	29	32	22	33	30	24	24	20	17

I. Is doing its job best

NEWSPAPERS	33	30	50	35	37	35	39	37	25
MAGAZINES	10	8	7	9	10	5	8	3	8
NONE OR DK	14	19	7	14	10	18	7	13	13
RADIO	15	13	13	9	17	16	16	17	29
TELEVISION	28	31	24	33	27	27	30	30	25

COMPOSITION OF THE HOUSEHOLD

	RESPONDENT IS HEAD OF HOUSEHOLD						RESPONDENT NOT HEAD		
	With spouse & children	Spouse Only	Child Only	With Relatives	With Non-Relatives	Alone	With Parents	With Child	With Relative
Base: 100% =	1374	633	46	69	30	147	74	30	24
J. Is the most important to you									
NEWSPAPERS	38	40	43	43	53	35	34	40	17
MAGAZINES	7	6	2	3	10	7	9	0	0
NONE OR DK	3	4	0	4	3	3	0	0	4
RADIO	15	13	11	12	13	21	22	17	33
TELEVISION	37	38	43	38	20	35	35	43	46
K. Is the least important to you									
NEWSPAPERS	7	6	9	10	13	8	7	7	4
MAGAZINES	49	51	33	35	50	48	53	53	63
NONE OR DK	7	6	9	7	13	7	7	10	8
RADIO	23	24	20	30	7	14	24	13	0
TELEVISION	14	13	30	17	17	22	9	17	25
L. Creates the most interest in new things going on									
NEWSPAPERS	18	19	15	17	13	23	18	23	8
MAGAZINES	19	16	17	19	30	12	14	7	17
NONE OR DK	4	5	2	4	0	10	4	17	8
RADIO	3	4	4	3	3	9	5	3	13
TELEVISION	56	56	61	57	53	46	59	50	54

M. Does the least for the public

NEWSPAPERS	5	5	2	4	13	5	7	10	4
MAGAZINES	48	45	46	43	30	45	46	37	46
NONE OR DK	21	25	20	23	30	28	19	33	17
RADIO	13	12	17	13	10	7	14	7	17
TELEVISION	13	11	17	16	17	15	15	13	17

N. Seems to be getting better all the time

NEWSPAPERS	11	10	17	12	10	10	8	13	17
MAGAZINES	11	10	11	7	20	9	11	10	8
NONE OR DK	17	23	11	30	17	25	9	27	29
RADIO	10	11	15	9	3	13	18	7	13
TELEVISION	51	45	48	42	50	44	54	43	33

O. Gives you the clearest understanding of the candidates and issues, in national elections

NEWSPAPERS	36	37	46	45	30	33	34	30	33
MAGAZINES	11	7	13	9	17	7	18	3	13
NONE OR DK	6	8	0	7	13	11	7	23	0
RADIO	5	5	9	4	0	10	8	3	13
TELEVISION	42	44	33	36	40	39	34	40	42

P. Has the hardest job to do

NEWSPAPERS	27	34	37	33	27	34	34	33	29
MAGAZINES	6	3	7	9	3	5	7	0	0
NONE OR DK	12	16	11	12	17	18	8	27	21
RADIO	8	5	7	4	0	9	4	7	8
TELEVISION	47	42	39	42	53	33	47	33	42

INCOME

	Under $1000	$1000–$1999	$2000–$2999	$3000–$3999	$4000–$4999	$5000–$5999	$6000–$6999	$7000–$7999	$8000–$8999	$9000–$9999	$10,000 and Over
Base: 100% =	110	155	192	265	301	310	225	180	130	82	214
A. Is the most entertaining											
NEWSPAPERS	10	19	14	10	11	13	12	12	17	20	14
MAGAZINES	10	2	7	7	7	9	8	11	12	15	15
NONE OR DK	3	1	2	1	0	1	2	2	3	0	1
RADIO	16	16	11	11	7	8	4	11	2	10	8
TELEVISION	61	63	67	71	73	69	73	64	66	56	61
B. Gives the most complete news coverage											
NEWSPAPERS	50	54	48	57	57	58	66	60	75	57	71
MAGAZINES	3	2	2	3	4	1	4	5	3	6	7
NONE OR DK	3	0	2	2	1	2	0	1	1	0	1
RADIO	24	22	17	16	17	18	12	18	12	24	14
TELEVISION	21	23	31	23	21	21	18	16	8	12	7
C. Presents things most intelligently											
NEWSPAPERS	25	25	27	30	36	32	39	45	45	34	31
MAGAZINES	25	18	23	21	28	25	27	27	32	38	43
NONE OR DK	11	5	4	3	3	5	3	6	8	9	3
RADIO	9	13	6	8	6	7	10	7	3	9	8
TELEVISION	30	39	39	37	28	30	21	15	13	11	15

D.	Is the most educational											
	NEWSPAPERS	35	30	26	29	31	33	28	33	42	28	28
	MAGAZINES	17	25	21	32	30	29	36	34	36	34	44
	NONE OR DK	5	5	7	3	3	2	4	3	6	7	4
	RADIO	6	6	3	2	2	3	0	2	1	1	2
	TELEVISION	36	33	43	34	35	33	31	27	15	29	22
E.	Brings you the latest news most quickly											
	NEWSPAPERS	6	2	6	6	4	4	4	5	5	5	9
	MAGAZINES	0	0	0	0	0	0	0	0	1	0	0
	NONE OR DK	3	1	2	2	2	1	1	1	1	0	0
	RADIO	61	56	53	55	59	51	63	57	62	65	66
	TELEVISION	30	41	39	37	36	44	32	37	33	30	24
F.	Does the most for the public											
	NEWSPAPERS	44	48	37	40	44	46	42	49	58	49	48
	MAGAZINES	5	2	1	2	3	1	3	4	2	5	5
	NONE OR DK	12	8	6	8	6	7	8	4	9	5	9
	RADIO	16	9	11	9	10	10	13	13	8	7	14
	TELEVISION	24	33	45	41	38	35	34	30	22	34	24
G.	Seems to be getting worse all the time											
	NEWSPAPERS	6	13	11	10	10	12	7	13	6	6	12
	MAGAZINES	13	21	19	19	18	16	20	19	12	10	10
	NONE OR DK	45	41	35	39	37	37	30	32	35	28	27
	RADIO	13	7	13	13	14	12	18	13	14	18	17
	TELEVISION	24	18	21	19	22	23	26	23	34	39	34

INCOME

	Under $1000	$1000–$1999	$2000–$2999	$3000–$3999	$4000–$4999	$5000–$5999	$6000–$6999	$7000–$7999	$8000–$8999	$9000–$9999	Over $10,000
Base: 100% =	110	155	192	265	301	310	225	180	130	82	214
H. Presents the fairest, most unbiased news											
NEWSPAPERS	34	26	33	24	34	29	29	32	27	28	30
MAGAZINES	6	9	7	10	7	8	9	11	12	11	14
NONE OR DK	11	8	12	10	7	10	10	7	8	10	11
RADIO	25	28	19	23	18	20	24	21	28	22	25
TELEVISION	24	29	30	32	34	33	28	29	25	29	19
I. Is doing its job best											
NEWSPAPERS	27	30	34	35	31	33	33	37	41	32	36
MAGAZINES	6	5	4	7	7	8	8	9	9	18	21
NONE OR DK	17	17	13	11	12	16	13	11	18	10	15
RADIO	15	20	10	14	15	13	16	17	14	16	14
TELEVISION	34	28	39	35	35	30	30	27	18	24	14
J. Is the most important to you											
NEWSPAPERS	30	30	35	31	34	39	40	47	53	45	52
MAGAZINES	5	3	3	6	6	4	6	8	7	21	11
NONE OR DK	5	3	4	3	3	4	4	2	2	0	3
RADIO	25	16	15	15	14	16	12	16	11	12	14
TELEVISION	36	48	44	45	44	37	38	27	28	22	21

K. Is the least important to you

NEWSPAPERS	12	11	4	11	10	5	6	3	3	11	6
MAGAZINES	55	51	58	51	51	48	48	49	48	30	29
NONE OR DK	7	9	6	8	5	7	6	4	6	11	6
RADIO	12	16	19	16	22	27	25	28	23	22	33
TELEVISION	15	13	13	14	11	12	15	16	20	26	26

L. Creates the most interest in new things going on

NEWSPAPERS	13	14	14	17	21	18	21	18	22	16	22
MAGAZINES	10	8	13	16	15	21	19	21	25	33	27
NONE OR DK	11	6	5	4	4	4	3	2	5	2	3
RADIO	10	10	5	4	3	2	2	3	2	6	5
TELEVISION	56	61	64	60	58	55	56	56	47	43	43

M. Does the least for the public

NEWSPAPERS	5	7	6	4	5	6	5	3	3	6	6
MAGAZINES	47	53	44	47	48	48	52	51	45	43	36
NONE OR DK	27	20	29	25	21	23	19	13	19	23	20
RADIO	9	10	13	11	13	13	12	13	14	17	15
TELEVISION	11	10	9	13	13	10	12	19	19	11	22

N. Seems to be getting better all the time

NEWSPAPERS	10	18	8	11	10	9	14	12	12	15	8
MAGAZINES	8	5	8	12	7	10	7	11	16	26	17
NONE OR DK	27	17	20	17	17	21	15	14	25	15	24
RADIO	15	8	9	6	13	8	9	15	14	12	13
TELEVISION	40	52	55	55	53	53	56	48	33	33	38

INCOME

	Under $1000	$1000–$1999	$2000–$2999	$3000–$3999	$4000–$4999	$5000–$5999	$6000–$6999	$7000–$7999	$8000–$8999	$9000–$9999	Over $10,000
Base: 100% =	110	155	192	265	301	310	225	180	130	82	214
O. Gives the clearest understanding of candidates and issues, in national elections											
NEWSPAPERS	24	30	28	38	34	38	40	44	44	40	38
MAGAZINES	6	2	6	7	5	9	12	12	13	13	27
NONE OR DK	17	7	11	9	5	6	5	7	6	6	3
RADIO	7	12	5	5	5	3	5	3	4	7	4
TELEVISION	45	48	51	42	52	44	38	33	33	34	29
P. Has the hardest job to do											
NEWSPAPERS	33	37	28	27	32	29	32	28	30	28	27
MAGAZINES	4	4	6	3	4	5	6	7	5	7	7
NONE OR DK	17	19	17	14	11	14	8	11	15	11	9
RADIO	11	6	4	7	7	6	7	7	8	7	10
TELEVISION	35	33	46	45	46	46	47	47	42	46	47

| | CITY SIZE | | | | | | | | SEX | |
	Over 1 Million	250,000–1 Million	100,000–250,000	25,000–100,000	2500–25,000	Towns to 2500	Open Country	Urban Fringe	Men	Women
Base: 100% =	420	404	228	255	432	111	503	74	1177	1246
A. Is the most entertaining										
NEWSPAPERS	15	12	14	14	13	14	11	15	14	12
MAGAZINES	10	7	7	11	9	7	8	14	7	10
NONE OR DK	1	2	2	2	1	0	2	1	1	1
RADIO	10	12	10	5	6	7	12	7	8	10
TELEVISION	65	67	68	69	72	72	67	64	69	67
B. Gives the most complete news coverage										
NEWSPAPERS	62	65	62	56	59	66	50	61	60	58
MAGAZINES	5	1	6	5	4	0	2	4	4	2
NONE OR DK	0	0	1	1	0	1	2	3	1	1
RADIO	15	14	17	18	17	21	24	14	16	19
TELEVISION	19	19	14	21	20	13	21	19	18	20
C. Presents things most intelligently										
NEWSPAPERS	35	37	32	31	36	41	26	39	33	33
MAGAZINES	25	30	38	27	28	23	22	16	29	25
NONE OR DK	5	3	3	4	5	6	8	11	5	6
RADIO	8	6	8	10	7	8	8	8	8	8
TELEVISION	27	24	18	28	25	22	35	26	25	29

| | CITY SIZE | | | | | | | | SEX | |
	Over 1 Million	250,000– 1 Million	100,000– 250,000	25,000– 100,000	2500– 25,000	Towns to 2500	Open Country	Urban Fringe	Men	Women
Base: 100% =	420	404	228	255	432	111	503	74	1177	1246
D. Is the most educational										
NEWSPAPERS	33	31	39	31	32	30	24	38	31	31
MAGAZINES	33	32	30	27	33	30	30	16	34	28
NONE OR DK	4	3	2	4	5	2	6	5	4	5
RADIO	2	4	3	2	2	4	3	1	2	3
TELEVISION	29	31	26	35	28	35	38	39	30	33
E. Brings you the latest news most quickly										
NEWSPAPERS	9	4	8	4	5	4	3	4	5	5
MAGAZINES	0	0	1	0	0	0	0	0	0	0
NONE OR DK	1	1	0	1	1	1	3	3	1	1
RADIO	56	60	59	66	48	55	58	65	58	57
TELEVISION	34	35	32	29	46	41	36	28	35	37
F. Does the most for the public										
NEWSPAPERS	45	50	49	43	44	39	39	39	46	43
MAGAZINES	3	2	4	2	4	5	1	3	3	2
NONE OR DK	6	6	7	9	9	8	10	14	8	8
RADIO	11	11	9	12	8	11	14	11	11	11
TELEVISION	35	31	32	35	35	38	36	38	32	36

G. Seems to be getting worse all the time

NEWSPAPERS	10	12	11	7	10	8	10	7	10	10
MAGAZINES	15	17	18	15	14	18	19	18	17	16
NONE OR DK	37	29	25	44	36	37	38	49	34	37
RADIO	12	16	16	13	17	12	11	9	16	12
TELEVISION	26	27	30	22	23	25	22	18	24	25

H. Presents the fairest, most unbiased news

NEWSPAPERS	31	28	34	26	30	32	26	23	31	27
MAGAZINES	9	13	13	7	9	5	8	12	11	8
NONE OR DK	8	10	9	10	12	9	13	12	10	11
RADIO	22	22	23	25	19	22	24	16	20	24
TELEVISION	30	28	21	32	31	32	29	36	28	30

I. Is doing its job best

NEWSPAPERS	36	37	35	29	34	33	28	32	35	31
MAGAZINES	8	10	10	9	9	8	6	7	9	8
NONE OR DK	12	12	14	15	14	21	18	27	14	16
RADIO	14	14	17	17	12	9	17	12	14	15
TELEVISION	31	26	24	31	31	29	31	22	28	30

	CITY SIZE								SEX	
	Over 1 Million	250,000–1 Million	100,000–250,000	25,000–100,000	2500–25,000	Towns to 2500	Open Country	Urban Fringe	Men	Women
Base: 100% =	420	404	228	255	432	111	503	74	1177	1246
J. Is the most important to you										
NEWSPAPERS	45	42	50	37	37	38	28	39	43	34
MAGAZINES	6	5	6	6	8	6	5	11	6	6
NONE OR DK	3	2	3	3	3	5	3	7	3	3
RADIO	12	14	16	13	12	15	21	14	3	3
TELEVISION	34	37	26	41	40	36	42	30	13	17
K. Is the least important to you										
NEWSPAPERS	6	7	5	5	8	8	9	5	6	8
MAGAZINES	48	50	48	52	42	46	54	43	51	47
NONE OR DK	8	5	4	8	6	13	7	4	7	7
RADIO	22	22	27	19	30	23	16	27	21	24
TELEVISION	15	17	16	15	14	11	14	20	15	15
L. Creates the most interest in new things going on										
NEWSPAPERS	25	20	23	20	17	13	12	14	20	17
MAGAZINES	21	18	18	16	21	16	13	15	16	19
NONE OR DK	4	3	4	4	5	9	5	5	4	5
RADIO	4	4	3	5	4	1	6	1	4	4
TELEVISION	47	55	52	56	53	61	64	65	56	55

M. Does the least for the public

NEWSPAPERS	4	7	4	4	5	7	6	4	6	4
MAGAZINES	45	42	50	48	44	51	50	51	46	47
NONE OR DK	23	18	16	27	28	22	24	14	20	25
RADIO	13	16	15	9	13	10	10	18	13	12
TELEVISION	16	17	15	12	10	10	10	15	15	11

N. Seems to be getting better all the time

NEWSPAPERS	13	11	13	10	10	9	10	9	9	12
MAGAZINES	11	13	10	12	10	9	8	9	9	12
NONE OR DK	17	15	23	20	22	18	21	31	19	20
RADIO	10	12	10	12	9	14	10	7	12	9
TELEVISION	49	50	44	46	49	51	51	43	51	47

O. Gives you the clearest understanding of the candidates and issues, in national elections

NEWSPAPERS	41	36	41	35	37	25	30	47	37	35
MAGAZINES	11	12	11	13	8	9	7	5	11	8
NONE OR DK	5	6	5	9	6	6	10	5	6	8
RADIO	6	4	2	4	5	9	9	4	6	5
TELEVISION	37	42	40	39	44	50	45	38	40	44

P. Has the hardest job to do

NEWSPAPERS	35	30	29	32	30	26	28	24	31	29
MAGAZINES	2	7	7	4	4	8	6	4	6	4
NONE OR DK	10	10	12	14	15	18	18	23	12	15
RADIO	7	7	8	6	6	9	6	8	8	5
TELEVISION	46	47	45	44	46	39	42	41	43	46

TABLE 4

Q. 8 General Evaluation by Religion, Within City Size and Within Educational Groups

How do you feel about television in general?	City Size									Education*					
	Over One Million Population			250,000 to One Million			Under 250,000			High School			College and Beyond		
	P	C	J	P	C	J	P	C	J	P	C	J	P	C	J
Extreme, unqualified positive	12%	14%	9%	16%	13%	8%	14%	16%	6%	12%	16%	8%	9%	7%	4%
Qualified positive	49	53	41	45	51	33	49	46	39	52	49	51	38	44	26
So-so	19	15	9	14	14	25	15	16	11	17	15	13	18	15	13
Qualified negative	16	16	38	21	19	25	18	20	39	16	18	26	30	30	50
Extreme, unqualified negative	4	1	3	4	3	8	4	3	6	3	1	3	5	3	7
Base 100%=	178	150	66	267	115	12	736	229	18	832	299	39	357	126	46

Legend: P=Protestants
　　　　 C=Catholics
　　　　 J=Jews

* Grade-school analysis omitted—too few Jews in sample.

TABLE 5

QUESTION 9 Put a (√) between each pair—wherever you think it belongs—to describe television.

Grade School/**Base:*** 100% = **571-613**

High School/**Base:*** 100% = **1130-1205**

College and Beyond/**Base:*** 100% = **497-512**

BY EDUCATION

TELEVISION IS GENERALLY:

	46%	19%	21%	7%	2%	5%	
EXCITING	29	21	30	14	3	3	DULL
	13	15	32	19	14	7	
IN GOOD TASTE	36	20	26	8	4	6	IN BAD TASTE
	24	23	32	13	5	3	
	11	17	34	22	11	5	
IMPORTANT	50	17	17	7	3	6	UNIMPORTANT
	40	18	21	9	6	6	
	23	15	24	18	13	7	
GENERALLY BAD	5	4	13	25	17	36	GENERALLY EXCELLENT
	4	5	17	34	19	21	
	6	11	24	33	18	8	
LOTS OF VARIETY	46	16	15	9	6	8	ALL THE SAME
	36	16	19	11	10	8	
	18	15	22	19	18	8	
UPSETTING	5	4	7	15	17	52	RELAXING
	3	3	9	18	22	45	
	4	5	11	27	26	27	
INTERESTING	55	20	13	6	2	4	UNINTERESTING
	44	22	19	9	3	3	
	21	20	28	15	11	5	
WONDERFUL	44	17	24	10	2	3	TERRIBLE
	26	18	36	15	3	2	
	12	11	39	26	9	3	
NOBODY CARES MUCH	4	3	12	21	19	41	ON EVERYONE'S MIND
	3	4	15	26	19	33	
	3	6	17	25	28	21	
FOR ME	54	13	14	7	3	9	NOT FOR ME
	42	19	19	9	4	7	
	20	15	24	17	13	11	
TOO "SIMPLE-MINDED"	11	6	39	34	4	6	TOO "HIGH-BROW"
	7	11	44	32	2	3	
	14	19	40	21	4	2	
GETTING WORSE	8	6	13	20	17	36	GETTING BETTER
	9	7	16	24	19	25	
	9	13	19	28	18	13	
STAYS THE SAME	12	7	13	18	18	32	KEEPS CHANGING
	8	10	18	22	17	25	
	8	13	25	27	16	11	
INFORMATIVE	47	22	18	6	3	4	NOT INFORMATIVE
	41	26	19	7	4	3	
	27	26	23	12	8	4	
LOTS OF FUN	47	17	19	7	3	7	NOT MUCH FUN
	31	21	26	12	5	5	
	15	19	30	19	11	6	
SERIOUS	13	10	27	24	9	17	PLAYFUL
	8	8	33	30	11	10	
	4	6	30	35	18	7	
IMAGINATIVE	32	18	28	12	3	7	NO IMAGINATION
	27	24	28	12	5	4	
	16	20	27	18	13	6	

*Excludes NA, which varies from item to item

TABLE 6

Check List Analysis

	12B TV ordinarily makes me feel...				12D I'd like TV to make me feel...				14D My favorite programs make me feel...			
Base: 100% =	All 1217	G.S. 313	H.S. 654	C.&B. 241	All 1217	G.S. 313	H.S. 654	C.&B. 241	All 1210	G.S. 314	H.S. 604	C.&B. 275
Contented	34%	32%	36%	32%	38%	31%	40%	37%	35%	33%	37%	35%
Satisfied	52	56	54	32	56	49	57	61	59	60	59	58
Calm	32	29	34	30	30	26	31	33	23	22	29	17
Peaceful	39	42	41	29	39	40	41	33	32	34	36	23
Interested	63	58	66	59	55	46	55	66	69	63	70	69
Intrigued	18	9	21	24	18	7	17	32	16	8	19	20
Fascinated	31	26	33	31	31	20	31	41	33	32	35	28
Rested	45	44	48	37	38	36	37	39	36	38	39	30
Relaxed	64	62	70	55	51	47	53	51	61	61	63	59
Entertained	68	61	71	70	59	45	62	70	75	65	79	78
Amused	54	41	59	57	43	32	44	52	46	39	51	41
Good	51	55	54	35	50	48	51	48	53	54	55	46
Happy	37	45	37	28	45	43	46	42	41	42	45	33
Joyful	26	29	28	18	33	32	34	30	28	36	28	20
Free	12	15	11	11	15	14	15	12	10	13	10	8
Wonderful	23	30	23	15	33	35	33	30	27	38	27	16
Alive	17	20	17	12	26	19	28	31	21	26	22	15
Great	12	13	12	8	20	16	20	21	15	19	16	9

Cheated	6	4	6	11	1	1	0	2	2	1	2	3
Frustrated	8	5	7	11	1	1	1	2	3	3	2	4
Let down	11	8	12	14	0	0	0	0	3	2	4	3
Dissatisfied	15	9	15	24	2	3	1	2	3	4	3	4
Angry	9	9	9	8	2	1	0	2	4	4	4	3
Mad	11	9	12	11	1	0	1	2	4	4	4	2
Impatient	11	6	11	16	1	1	1	2	5	4	5	4
Tired	15	12	15	18	1	1	1	2	4	4	4	1
Sleepy	41	43	43	34	5	6	5	3	10	16	9	7
Lazy	19	16	19	21	2	2	1	3	5	5	6	3
Old	3	3	2	2	1	1	0	1	1	2	1	0
Sick	2	3	1	3	0	0	0	1	1	2	0	1
Embarrassed	6	7	6	5	2	1	1	2	2	2	2	2
Disgusted	17	12	19	0	1	1	0	2	4	3	6	2
Ashamed	5	5	4	6	1	0	1	2	2	2	2	1
Foolish	4	5	4	6	0	0	0	0	2	3	2	2
Guilty	5	4	5	7	1	0	1	1	2	2	1	2
Silly	5	5	5	6	1	1	0	0	2	2	2	0
Stupid	5	5	4	5	1	1	1	1	1	2	1	1
Childish	3	3	4	4	1	1	0	0	2	3	2	3
Helpless	5	4	5	4	1	1	0	0	2	2	2	2
Informed	41	31	41	51	43	28	44	61	32	21	30	48
Aware	15	5	17	26	20	7	20	34	14	4	15	22
Excited	26	29	28	20	23	17	25	23	31	34	34	23
Upset	9	11	8	10	1	1	0	2	3	4	3	2
Anxious	12	12	14	7	7	6	8	5	16	18	16	12

TABLE 6—continued

Check List Analysis

Base: 100% =	12B TV ordinarily makes me feel...				12D I'd like TV to make me feel...				14D My favorite programs make me feel...			
	All 1217	G.S. 313	H.S. 654	C. & B. 241	All 1217	G.S. 313	H.S. 659	C. & B. 241	All 1210	G.S. 314	H.S. 604	C. & B. 275
Disturbed	10	7	10	13	2	1	1	3	4	3	4	5
Tense	14	12	14	18	3	1	3	4	9	8	11	6
Afraid	6	6	8	5	1	1	0	1	3	2	2	2
Restless	10	6	11	12	1	1	1	2	2	4	2	1
Bored	18	12	18	24	0	0	0	0	1	1	2	1
Sad	12	10	14	10	1	1	1	2	3	6	6	2
Unhappy	6	5	6	4	1	1	0	0	3	5	2	1
Active	9	8	9	10	19	11	21	23	14	12	14	12
Serious	18	13	18	20	13	8	13	20	15	14	16	12

TABLE 7

Q. 36D *Which of the programs your child watches (children watch)*
do you think are the best programs for (him) (her) (them)?

	Times Mentioned
Captain Kangaroo	217
Lassie	178
Disney	144
Father Knows Best	115
Romper Room	115
Huckleberry Hound	78
Popeye	71
Dennis the Menace	65
Leave It to Beaver	64
Danny Thomas	53
Fury	50
Three Stooges	43
Ding Dong School	36
Circus Boy	31
Donna Reed	31
Red Skelton	29
Real McCoys	27
Shirley Temple	26
Howdy Doody	25
Dick Clark	24
High Road	22
Wagon Train	22
Bozo the Clown	21
Rin-Tin-Tin	20
American Bandstand (*or* Bandstand)	17
Baseball	17
Commercials	17
Mr. Wizard	15
Twentieth Century	15
I Love Lucy	14
News	14
Flicka	13
Sea Hunt	13
Dobie Gillis	12
Ozzie and Harriet	12
Ruff and Ready	12
Little Rascals	11
Roy Rogers	10
Quick Draw McGraw	10

NOTE: Programs with fewer than 10 mentions not shown.

TABLE 8

Q. 13A   How would you describe most of the television programs on the air today?

Education	Strong Praise	Qualified Praise	50-50	Qualified Criticism	Strong Criticism	Other	NA-DK
Base: 100%							
0–6 G.S. (100)	7%	49%	19%	8%	6%	3%	2%
7–8 G.S. (213)	5	53	12	16	6	3	1
1–3 H.S. (262)	3	52	13	17	6	3	0
4 H.S. (318)	5	48	13	22	5	1	1
1–2 coll. (112)	4	42	13	27	12	1	0
3–4 coll. (98)	3	28	12	35	12	4	3
Beyond coll. (65)	0	25	14	32	18	2	2

TABLE 9

Check List Analysis

	Q. 13C Most television programs are . . .							Q. 13E I wish most programs would be more . . .							Q. 15D My favorite programs are . . .						
	0-6 G.S.	7-8 G.S.	1-3 H.S.	4 H.S.	1-2 Coll.	3-4 Coll.	Be-yond Coll.	0-6 G.S.	7-8 G.S.	1-3 H.S.	4 H.S.	1-2 Coll.	3-4 Coll.	Be-yond Coll.	0-6 G.S.	7-8 G.S.	1-3 H.S.	4 H.S.	1-2 Coll.	3-4 Coll.	Be-yond Coll.
	%	%	%	%	%	%	%	%	%	%	%	%	%	%	%	%	%	%	%	%	%
Intelligent	50	33	40	30	29	17	20	55	49	63	67	77	76	86	32	40	45	46	49	46	61
Informative	38	41	50	45	48	29	20	44	49	55	68	76	72	75	21	30	32	42	48	48	53
Educational	58	52	51	43	37	20	23	72	68	73	77	86	79	74	38	41	39	40	40	47	49
Stimulating	34	29	34	32	30	18	12	30	34	45	57	59	67	80	26	36	38	51	59	58	67
Exciting	49	45	43	33	24	19	3	57	47	52	49	43	33	42	64	59	67	63	57	50	63
Interesting	70	70	70	61	57	36	32	69	66	69	76	72	59	75	76	75	81	81	80	81	78
Entertaining	78	73	78	74	68	51	46	70	69	73	77	71	60	75	75	79	84	85	84	80	88
New	34	26	28	22	21	9	9	43	36	52	51	50	43	38	18	16	18	24	19	24	27
Different	45	23	36	28	25	14	11	46	39	46	50	44	43	35	29	35	39	38	36	27	47
Imaginative	20	22	36	35	28	18	22	20	19	32	45	51	61	51	17	21	27	41	46	52	47
Creative	27	23	32	32	22	11	14	34	39	45	59	65	68	75	12	24	21	33	30	40	43
Original	22	18	27	23	14	5	15	28	32	43	57	48	60	57	19	25	29	36	40	35	47
Serious	37	23	29	24	19	9	9	31	30	38	34	36	38	29	25	24	31	25	28	29	39
Significant	18	12	19	17	11	9	6	15	12	18	27	33	40	51	10	6	9	15	19	27	39
Tasteful	25	26	27	28	31	23	11	44	35	50	51	51	48	49	25	26	28	38	39	45	39
Artistic	17	18	22	25	14	15	11	23	21	31	41	39	48	58	12	13	13	17	22	28	27
Honest	43	32	34	32	28	18	17	57	60	60	63	63	46	54	50	50	46	47	50	44	67
Great	37	22	18	17	14	3	9	38	18	27	23	24	15	25	35	33	33	27	21	23	29
Stupid	16	13	12	14	13	19	22	4	2	2	2	1	4	3	4	2	2	1	0	1	2
Idiotic	8	7	11	9	6	14	14	0	0	2	1	0	1	3	3	0	1	1	1	1	0
Boring	14	17	22	20	21	28	31	2	2	2	1	0	3	2	1	0	1	1	0	2	0

TABLE 9—continued

Check List Analysis

	Q. 13C Most television programs are ...							Q. 13E I wish most programs would be more ...							Q. 15D My favorite programs are ...						
	0-6 G.S.	7-8 G.S.	1-3 H.S.	4 H.S.	1-2 Coll.	3-4 Coll.	Be-yond Coll.	0-6 G.S.	7-8 G.S.	1-3 H.S.	4 H.S.	1-2 Coll.	3-4 Coll.	Be-yond Coll.	0-6 G.S.	7-8 G.S.	1-3 H.S.	4 H.S.	1-2 Coll.	3-4 Coll.	Be-yond Coll.
Dull	17	16	18	19	18	33	27	2	1	2	3	1	3	5	3	1	1	2	1	3	2
Unimaginative	10	11	15	20	23	41	34	6	4	6	3	5	1	2	0	5	4	4	2	4	4
Corny	17	14	18	27	24	31	31	3	4	3	3	2	4	2	1	3	3	4	3	4	2
Trivial	14	15	17	22	23	46	45	3	6	6	4	4	6	5	3	2	3	2	3	5	6
Trash	13	14	15	16	14	21	25	2	2	3	2	2	1	5	1	1	1	1	1	0	2
Phony	12	16	19	21	14	21	23	3	1	2	2	2	4	2	3	2	3	3	2	1	4
Bad	11	10	9	12	13	18	18	1	0	2	1	2	0	3	4	0	1	1	0	1	2
Terrible	12	15	12	11	8	11	15	3	1	2	2	0	2	2	6	1	1	1	0	1	2
Violent	15	19	18	30	28	31	29	2	2	2	3	1	1	0	10	4	10	8	4	4	10
Sinful	13	13	12	9	8	9	11	4	3	4	4	1	6	8	5	2	1	1	0	3	2
Average	41	39	54	57	55	55	51	20	14	13	8	6	5	2	13	10	20	19	7	9	8
Base: 100%	100	214	262	318	112	98	65	100	214	262	318	112	98	65	103	210	269	305	96	96	49

TABLE 10

Detailed Master Program Code

5/1 *Family* situation comedy
2 Situation *comedy*
3 Standup or *star comedian*
4 Comedy—*variety regular*
5 Comedy—*variety specials*
6 Light musical *specials*
7 Panel, games, light quiz
8 *Adult* cartoons
9 Comedy—variety
0 Child cartoon

6/1 *Light and medium* drama
2 *Heavy* drama
3 Daytime serials
4 Personal, "real life" drama
5 Courtroom enactments— crime or general
6 Courtroom enactments— family relations
7 Western, *adult*
8 Westerns, other or general
9 Adventure—"other worlds"
0 Child—non-cartoon
X Drama, stories—other or general

7/1 Crime *drama*
2 Private-eye—sophisticated
3 Police, detective, private- eye

8/1 Star, *light* music
2 *Medium* music
3 *Heavy* music
4 *Teen* music or dance
9 Music, other or general

9/1 American sports, *regular*
2 Sports coverage, *special* or *unusual*
3 Boxing
4 Wrestling
0 Other sports

10/1 *Regular* news coverage
2 *Special* coverage of *current* events, *heavy*
3 Special coverage of *current* events, *light*
4 *Documentaries* on issues
5 Documentary, interview, emphasis on *people*
6 More *academic* issues or approach
7 Variety—information
8 Quiz shows—serious or general
9 Other information or "information general"

11/1 Religion

12/1 Movies, *heavy*
2 Movies, *medium*
3 Movies, *other*
4 Movies, other or general

TABLE 11

Master Program Code Summaries

Summary I

1.	Comedy—variety	5/1, 2, 3, 4, 5, 6, 7, 8, 9, 0, and 6/0
2.	Light drama	6/1, 3, 4, 5, 6
3.	Action (westerns, crime, adventure)	7/1, 2, 3, and 6/7, 8, 9
4.	Light music	8/1, 2, 4, 9
5.	Sports	9/1, 2, 3, 4, 0
6.	Regular news	10/1
7.	Information—public affairs	10/2, 3, 4, 5, 6, 7, 8, 9, and 11/2, 3
8.	Heavy drama (including film "classics")	6/2 and 12/1
9.	Heavy music	8/3
10.	Religion	11/1
11.	Movies (excludes "classics")	12/2, 3, 4
12.	All others	

Summary II

A.	Light entertainment	1. 2. 3. 4. 5. 11.
B.	Heavy entertainment	8. 9.
C.	News	6.
D.	Information—public affairs	7. 10.
E.	All others	12.

TABLE 12

Q. 14, 15A   *Favorite programs (first-mentioned example)*

Q. 21   . . . *Kind of programs I'd like to see more of on TV*

	All		0–6 G.S.		7–8 G.S.		1–3 H.S.		4 H.S.		1–2 Coll.		3–4 Coll.		Beyond Coll.	
	Q. 14, 15A	Q. 21	Q. 14, 15A	Q. 21	Q. 14, 15A	Q. 21	Q. 14, 15A	Q. 21	Q. 14, 15A	Q. 21	Q. 14, 15A	Q. 21	Q. 14, 15A	Q. 21	Q. 14, 15A	Q. 21
Comedy-variety	24%	22%	18%	15%	24%	23%	24%	23%	29%	26%	24%	20%	21%	14%	14%	9%
Light drama	12	1	20	3	12	1	15	2	11	1	7	0	8	1	7	0
Action	29	14	27	18	30	16	33	17	29	12	26	11	23	7	18	5
Light music	9	10	6	6	13	14	8	9	9	9	8	8	6	10	11	12
Sports	7	6	13	11	8	6	6	4	6	6	8	5	6	3	5	5
Regular news	4	1	5	3	2	1	3	1	3	0	6	3	8	4	8	1
Information— public affairs	7	17	2	8	5	12	5	13	6	18	11	25	15	27	21	34
Heavy drama	3	6	1	1	0	2	2	4	3	9	5	7	9	13	10	14
Heavy music	0	1	0	0	0	0	0	1	0	1	1	3	0	4	1	6
Religion	1	5	2	13	1	6	1	5	1	3	0	4	1	3	2	3
Movies	1	1	1	1	1	1	1	1	1	0	1	1	0	1	1	0
AO, DK, NA	3	16	4	21	4	18	2	20	2	15	2	12	4	13	3	11
Base: 100% =	2427		203		424		531		683		208		194		114	

TABLE 13

Q. 14/15A What are some of your favorite programs? (first-mentioned) Base: 100% =	All	EDUCATION				RELIGION			AGE			SEX	
	All 2427	G.S. 627	H.S. 1214	1-4 Coll. Coll. 402	Beyond Coll. 114	P 1670	C 566	J 96	34— 825	35-55 956	55+ 635	M 1177	F 1246
5/1 Family situation comedy	6%	4%	7%	6%	3%	6%	6%	8%	6%	6%	5%	3%	8%
2 Situation comedy	3	3	3	3	0	2	4	1	3	3	2	2	3
3 Standup or star comedian	3	1	3	3	3	2	3	4	2	3	2	3	2
4 Comedy—variety regular	5	4	5	6	5	5	6	7	4	5	5	4	6
5 Comedy—variety specials	0	0	0	1	0	0	0	0	0	0	0	0	0
6 Light musical specials	0	0	0	0	1	0	0	0	0	0	0	0	0
7 Panel, games, light quiz	6	8	7	4	2	7	6	5	4	7	9	4	9
8 Adult cartoons	0	0	0	0	0	0	0	0	0	0	0	0	0
9 Comedy—variety	1	1	1	0	0	1	0	0	1	0	1	0	1
0 Child cartoon	0	0	0	0	0	0	0	0	0	0	0	0	0
6/1 Light and medium drama	3	2	3	3	4	3	3	3	5	2	1	2	4
2 Heavy drama	3	0	3	7	10	2	4	22	5	3	1	3	4
3 Daytime serials	6	8	7	4	2	8	5	2	8	6	5	1	12
4 Personal, "real life" drama	1	2	2	0	1	2	0	1	1	1	2	1	2
5 Courtroom enactments—crime or general	1	2	1	0	1	1	1	0	1	1	2	0	2
6 Courtroom enactments—family relations	0	0	0	0	0	0	0	0	0	0	0	0	0
7 Westerns, adult	9	9	10	8	6	9	10	2	9	10	7	13	5
8 Westerns, other or general	10	14	10	4	3	11	7	5	12	10	8	14	6
9 Adventure—"other worlds"	2	1	2	2	1	1	3	2	2	2	0	3	1
0 Child—non-cartoon	0	1	0	0	0	0	0	0	0	0	0	0	0
X Drama, stories—other or general	0	0	0	0	0	0	0	0	0	0	0	0	0
7/1 Crime drama	4	2	5	6	4	4	5	4	4	4	4	5	3
2 Private-eye—sophisticated	2	1	2	2	4	2	3	1	4	2	0	2	2
3 Police, detective, private-eye	2	1	2	2	0	1	3	0	3	1	1	2	1

Category	1	2	3	4	5	6	7	8	9	10	11	12	13
8/1 Star, *light* music	9	6	12	7	5	4	9	8	11	5	8	9	8
2 *Medium* music	1	1	1	1	0	0	1	0	0	2	0	0	1
3 *Heavy* music	0	0	0	0	0	1	0	0	1	1	0	0	0
4 *Teen* music or dance	1	0	0	0	2	0	0	1	0	1	1	0	0
9 Music, other or general	0	0	0	0	0	0	0	0	0	0	0	0	0
9/1 American sports, *regular*	1	8	5	5	2	4	5	4	5	5	4	4	4
2 Sports coverage, *special or unusual*	0	0	0	0	0	0	0	0	0	1	0	0	0
3 Boxing	0	3	2	2	0	1	2	2	0	1	1	3	2
4 Wrestling	1	2	2	0	1	0	1	1	0	0	0	2	1
0 Other sports	0	0	0	0	0	0	0	0	0	0	0	0	0
10/1 *Regular* news coverage	3	5	6	4	2	4	3	4	8	7	3	3	4
2 *Special* coverage of *current* events, *heavy*	0	0	0	0	0	0	0	0	0	0	0	0	0
3 *Special* coverage of *current* events, *light*	0	0	0	0	0	0	0	0	0	0	0	0	0
4 *Documentaries* on issues	1	2	1	2	2	2	1	2	4	4	1	0	2
5 Documentary, interview, emphasis on *people*	1	2	2	1	8	1	1	11	2	1	2	1	1
6 More *academic* issues or approach	1	1	0	0	0	1	1	0	1	1	0	1	0
7 Variety—information	4	2	5	3	2	2	2	3	4	5	3	2	3
8 Quiz shows—serious or general	0	0	1	0	0	0	0	0	0	0	0	0	0
9 Other information or "information general"	0	0	0	0	0	0	0	0	0	0	0	0	0
11/1 Religion	1	1	2	1	1	0	1	1	2	0	1	2	1
12/1 Movies, *heavy*	0	0	0	0	0	0	0	0	0	0	0	0	0
2 Movies, *medium*	1	0	0	0	0	1	0	0	0	0	0	0	0
3 Movies, *other*	0	0	0	0	1	0	0	0	0	0	0	0	0
4 Movies, other or general	0	0	0	0	0	0	0	0	1	0	0	0	0

TABLE 13A

Q. 23 What kind of programs don't you care for at all?

	All	EDUCATION				RELIGION			AGE			SEX	
		G.S.	H.S.	1–4 Coll.	Beyond Coll.	P	C	J	34–	35–55	55+	M	F
Base: 100% =	2427	627	1214	402	114	1670	566	96	825	956	635	1177	1246
	1%	0%	0%	2%	2%	0%	1%	0%	0%	1%	0%	1%	0%
5/1 *Family situation comedy*	4	4	3	4	12	3	4	10	4	5	3	5	4
2 Situation *comedy*	3	3	4	3	4	3	3	2	3	4	3	3	4
3 Standup or *star comedian*	5	4	5	5	7	5	5	2	5	5	3	6	4
4 Comedy—*variety regular*	0	0	1	1	1	0	0	2	0	0	0	1	1
5 Comedy—*variety specials*	1	2	1	2	2	1	1	2	2	1	1	2	1
6 Light musical specials	2	2	1	3	2	2	1	6	2	1	1	2	1
7 Panel, games, light quiz	5	4	5	6	7	4	6	6	7	5	2	5	4
8 *Adult* cartoons	0	0	0	0	0	0	0	0	0	0	0	0	0
9 Comedy—variety	2	2	1	3	2	1	1	0	2	2	1	2	1
0 Child cartoon	3	3	3	2	3	3	2	3	3	3	3	3	3
6/1 *Light and medium drama*	1	1	1	1	0	1	1	0	1	1	2	1	1
2 *Heavy* drama	1	1	2	1	2	2	0	0	1	1	2	2	1
3 Daytime serials	10	6	10	13	18	9	11	12	13	11	5	13	6
4 Personal, "real life" drama	1	1	1	1	3	1	1	0	2	1	1	1	1
5 Courtroom enactments—crime or general	0	0	0	0	0	0	0	0	0	0	0	0	0
6 Courtroom enactments—family relations	0	0	0	0	0	0	0	0	0	0	0	0	0
7 Westerns, *adult*	2	2	2	2	4	2	2	4	2	2	3	1	3
8 Westerns, other or general	25	20	25	33	33	25	24	46	24	25	27	16	34
9 Adventure—"other worlds"	3	2	4	3	0	3	3	3	4	2	2	3	4
0 Child—non-cartoon	1	1	1	3	0	1	1	1	1	1	1	2	1
X Drama, stories—other or general	0	1	1	0	2	0	1	1	1	0	0	1	0
7/1 Crime *drama*	2	1	2	2	1	2	2	0	2	1	2	1	2
2 Private-eye—*sophisticated*	1	1	1	1	2	1	1	3	1	1	1	1	2
3 Police, detective, private-eye	9	7	8	14	12	9	8	13	7	11	9	7	10

	1	2	3	4	5	6	7	8	9	10	11	12	13
8/1 Star, *light* music	5	7	4	6	4	6	4	1	6	4	5	7	3
2 *Medium* music	0	0	0	0	0	0	2	0	0	0	0	1	0
3 *Heavy* music	3	4	4	2	2	4	2	0	3	4	3	5	2
4 *Teen* music or dance	3	4	2	4	2	3	2	4	2	3	4	4	2
9 Music, other or general	0	0	0	1	0	0	0	2	0	0	1	1	0
9/1 American sports, *regular*	3	4	4	2	4	4	2	5	4	3	3	2	4
2 Sports coverage, *special* or *unusual*	0	0	0	0	1	0	0	0	0	0	0	0	0
3 Boxing	3	4	4	2	3	4	3	5	3	4	3	1	5
4 Wrestling	4	5	5	3	3	4	4	4	3	5	5	2	6
0 Other sports	0	0	0	0	0	0	0	0	0	0	0	0	0
10/1 *Regular* news coverage	0	0	0	0	0	0	0	0	0	0	0	0	0
2 *Special* coverage of current events, *heavy*	0	0	1	0	0	0	0	1	0	0	0	0	0
3 *Special* coverage of current events, *light*	0	0	0	0	2	0	0	0	0	0	0	0	0
4 *Documentaries* on issues	0	0	0	0	1	0	0	0	0	0	0	0	0
5 Documentary, interview, emphasis on *people*	0	0	1	0	2	0	0	2	0	0	0	1	0
6 More *academic* issues or approach	1	0	1	0	1	0	0	0	0	1	0	1	1
7 Variety—information	0	0	0	0	0	0	0	0	0	0	0	0	0
8 Quiz shows—serious or general	4	3	4	6	8	4	5	3	6	4	2	5	3
9 Other information or "information general"	0	0	0	0	0	0	1	0	1	0	0	0	1
11/1 Religion	0	0	0	0	2	0	0	0	0	0	0	0	1
12/1 Movies, *heavy*	0	0	0	0	0	0	0	0	0	0	0	0	0
2 Movies, *medium*	0	0	0	0	0	0	1	2	0	1	0	0	0
3 Movies, *other*	4	4	4	4	4	4	4	2	5	3	5	3	5
4 Movies, other or general	1	1	1	2	2	1	0	3	1	1	1	1	1

TABLE 14

Q. 24B   Programs you'd like to see put back on the air?
(Those mentioned more frequently appear on page 151.)

Times Mentioned		Times Mentioned	
19	George Burns and Gracie Allen	9	Big Top
			Climax
18	Hit Parade		Hallmark Hall of Fame
	Medic		Nat "King" Cole
	Twenty-one		Sergeant Bilko
17	Bold Journey		Topper
	Dragnet	8	Art Carney
16	Jimmy Dean		Fibber McGee & Molly
	Our Miss Brooks		Meet Millie
15	Amos 'n' Andy		People's Choice
	Godfrey Talent Scouts		Queen for a Day
	Lowell Thomas		Red Buttons
	Treasure Hunt		Science Fiction Theater
14	Big Payoff		Steve Allen
	See It Now		Thin Man
	Tic Tac Dough		Victory at Sea
	Zorro	7	Cimarron City
13	Arlene Francis Home Show		House on High Street
	Bishop Sheen		I Married Joan
	Meet McGraw		Information Please
12	Grand Ole Opry		It's a Great Life
	I Remember Mama		Lawrence Welk
	My Little Margie		Noah's Ark
	Show of Shows		Person to Person
	You Asked for It		Two for the Money
11	Bob Cummings		Wagon Train
	Kraft Theater		Yancy Derringer
	Matinee Theater		Gisele Mackenzie
	Polka Go-Round		Phil Silvers
	$64,000 Challenge		Philip Marlow
10	Bell Telephone Hour		Richard Diamond
	Edward R. Murrow		Sam Levinson
	Five Fingers		Stop the Music
	Highway Patrol		Zoo Parade (Chicago)
	Ken Murray	5	Amateur Hour
	Life of Riley		Bob Crosby
	Mama		Bob Hope
	Strike It Rich		Broken Arrow
	You Are There		

NOTE: Those mentioned by fewer than 5 respondents not shown.

TABLE 15

Q. 25   Personalities or stars that you especially liked that aren't on any more?

(Those mentioned more frequently appear on page 154.)

Times Mentioned		Times Mentioned	
14	Eddie Fisher	7	Gene Autry
	George Burns and Gracie		Jack Wayne
	Allen		Jack Webb
	Gisele Mackenzie		Rosemary Clooney
	Hal March		Roy Rogers
	Kate Smith		Steve Allen
	Ken Murray	6	Amos 'n' Andy
	Patti Page		Arlene Francis
13	Jerry Lewis		Fred Allen
	Jimmy Dean		Guy Lombardo
11	Eve Arden		Jack Benny
	George Gobel		Joan Davis
	Nanette Fabray		Jonathan Winters
	Ted Mack		McGuire Sisters
10	Bishop Sheen		Phil Silvers
	Gracie Allen (*mentioned*		Robert Montgomery
	alone)	5	Art Linkletter
	Red Skelton		Bess Meyerson
9	Ed (Kookie) Burns		Dean Martin
8	Audrey Meadows		Elvis Presley
	Dave King		Fred Astaire
	Lowell Thomas		Jane Wyman
7	Bob Crosby		Perry Como
	Dennis Day		Spring Byington
	Dennis James		Victor Borge
	Gail Storm		Wally Cox

NOTE: Those mentioned by fewer than 5 respondents not shown.

TABLE 16

Q. 26A   Is there any single program or broadcast that you'd like to see again if it could be re-run? (Not a series, I mean one particular show—either part of a series or a separate show.) (Which one?)

(Those mentioned more frequently appear on page 155.)

Times Mentioned		Times Mentioned	
14	Frank Sinatra	7	Princess Margaret's wedding
13	Ed Sullivan		Rodeo
	Evening with Belafonte		Sinking of the Titanic
	Olympics		Spectaculars
	Walt Disney		Turn of the Screw
12	Ford		Victor Borge
	Operas	6	Basketball
11	Arthur Godfrey		Bells of St. Mary's
	Coronation of Queen Elizabeth		Bob Hope
	Leonard Bernstein		Crusade in Europe
	Loretta Young		Heart operation
	Wagon Train		Jack Paar
10	Hitler		Jerry Lewis
	Russian Revolution		Maurice Chevalier
	Untouchables		Perry Mason
9	Play of the Week		Project 20
	Shirley Temple		Red Skelton
8	Omnibus		Shakespeare
7	Abraham Lincoln		Sid Caesar
	Armstrong Circle Theatre		Twentieth Century
	Baseball games		U. S. Steel
	Bing Crosby		Voice of Firestone
	Boxing, fights		Wizard of Oz
	Bold Journey	5	The Bat
	Chevy Show (Dinah Shore)		Danny Kaye
	Football		Ed Murrow
	For Whom the Bell Tolls		Gene Kelly
	Lowell Thomas		Hallmark Hall of Fame
	Jackie Gleason		Medea
	Perry Como		Movies, general
			This Is Your Life

NOTE: Those mentioned by fewer than 5 respondents not shown.

TABLE 17

*Q. 27   Considering everything you've ever seen on television, is there
some highlight or special moment that stands out in your mind?
(It can be either a whole program, an event, or something that
happened during a program—just anything that impressed you.)
(What was it?)*

(News events not tabulated)

Incident occurred on:

51	Jack Paar
24	Ed Sullivan
13	Playhouse 90
9	Arthur Godfrey
8	Perry Como
	Tennessee Ernie Ford
	Green Pastures
	Play of the Week
7	Garry Moore
	Alcoa Presents
	Dinah Shore
6	Loretta Young
5	Leonard Bernstein
	Medea

NOTE: Those mentioned by fewer than 5 respondents not shown..

TABLE 18 — ARB PARTICULARS

1) From the cover of the *ARB Monthly National Report:*

THE UNITED STATES TELEVISION AUDIENCE

This is a comprehensive program-by-program report on the size and characteristics of audiences to commercial and sustaining network television programs. Its purpose is to furnish broadcasters and advertisers with accurate and reliable audience data for use in making decisions concerning the buying and selling of television time.

Measurement Method

The information in this report is secured through the use of special interviewer supervised family viewing diaries developed through many years of research and experimentation in television audience measurement. Special effort is made to obtain information from families in the sample who are away or not using their television set during the entire survey week. In this way, sets that were not in use can be taken into account in the measurement of audience size. ARB's method reflects all viewing by all members of the family at the time the viewing is being done.

Sampling

Sample homes are selected by means of probability sampling throughout the United States. Individual sample locations are chosen in such a way as to represent every rural and urban telephone home in the area having a television set regardless of location, type of set, or other factors. Careful controls are maintained to insure proper distribution of the tabulated sample by census regions and districts. The national sample for each of these network reports is composed of usable records obtained from approximately 1600 different television families. A new sample selection is made for each survey.

Measurement Periods

Surveys are scheduled throughout the year in such a way as to measure representative programming periods and also furnish reports to clients during the seasons when they are most needed. The schedule below lists survey dates for the 1960-1961 season:

November 10-16, 1960	March 2-8, 1961
December 7-13, 1960	May 15-21, 1961
January 13-19, 1961	May 8-14, 1961

2) Specimen Diary pages follow:

These instructions and the Sample Page (at right) will show you just how to fill in your diary. It should be a **complete** record of your set's use, whether or not this period is a typical week in your home.

WHO should keep the diary —

It is best for one member of the family to act as "head-diary-keeper" — **BUT,** everyone in the family should know about the diary and how to keep it, so they can help make it a complete record.

WHEN to fill in the diary —

(1) Each time the set is turned on

(2) Then, immediately after each program

(3) Each time the set is turned off

IF your set is not turned on for any full day — Write "Set not used today" across that day's page. This is **VERY** important.

Please do not let the fact that you are keeping a diary influence your viewing. Simply record in your diary what is actually turned on during this particular week.

SEE EXAMPLE

FOLD OUT PAGE AT RIGHT

We hope you will find it fun to take part in the survey. Your efforts in keeping this diary accurately will help improve TV for everyone.

POINTS TO REMEMBER:

The items below will help you keep the diary easily and correctly. Read them carefully:

① **YOUR FAMILY:** Fill in the members of your family in these columns. Use M for male, F for female, and put the exact age of each person underneath the code letter for male or female. (Example: A man aged 30 would be listed M 30.

② **TIME:** Fill in to the **nearest minute** the beginning and ending time for each program or part of a program turned on.

③ **STATION:** Fill in the Station Call letters. Do not use ditto marks.

If two stations are on for at least 5 minutes each, enter both stations.

④ Write in the "Name of Program" as given by the TV station. If you miss the title, fill in the **type** of program, such as drama, variety, news (including commentator's name) etc. This description, plus the **correct** station is more reliable than the printed schedule.

⑤ Place an X in the proper columns to indicate the persons who were paying attention to TV for 5 minutes or more. Count those who were either watching or listening. Also record the age and sex of all visitors, as for example: F 29.

⑥ If the set was on but **no one** was paying attention, write in the time and station and "O" under all columns.

This is a sample of a family's viewing for one day. (The stations and programs are fictitious.)

Time from	to	Station	Name of Program	M 30	F 28	F 4	VISITORS
A.M.							
10:00	10:15	KAAA	News-Jal Brown	X			
10:15	10:38	KBBB	Kiddieland		X	X	
10:38	11:00	KAAA	Songs of Today		X	X	
11:30	12:00	KAAA	Morning Theatre			X	
P.M.							
12:00	12:30	KAAA	Midday News	X	X	X	
12:30	12:35	KCCC	Countdown Theat.	X	X		
12:35	12:40	KBBB	Noon Melodies		X		
2:00	3:15	KCCC	Film Festival		X		
3:30	4:00	KBBB	(Quiz Show)	X	X		
6:00	6:15	KAAA	News-Ira Smith	X	X		F 9 F 9
8:00	8:30	KAAA	Mr. West Goes Home	X			F 29
8:30	9:00	KCCC	Battle of Sports	X	X		M 50
9:00	10:00	KBBB	Fights	X			M 32

Set turned off at ......10:00 P.M...... o'clock

Turn page to begin your Diary ➜

SUGGESTION: Keep your diary open on a flat surface near the TV set — you'll find it easier t[o] make your entries.

REMEMBER: **Before** you start, fill in the age and sex for each member of your family in th[e] columns at right. Check the instructions if you're not sure how to do this.

NOTICE THAT the headings for these columns do not have to be written in for each day. All y[ou] do is turn the page to the correct day of the week, and the columns should line [up] exactly.

— It's **Easy** to be accurate —

N 187

Time from A.M.	to	Station	Name of Program	M. 4½	F. 5½	F. 32					V I S I T O R S
8:30	9:30	WNEW	Sandy 6443 Becher	X	X						
9:30	10.00	WNEW	Topper	X	X						
11.00	11:30	C.B.S.	I Love Lucy	X	X	X					
11:30	12:30	WNEW	Romper Room (Kids)	X	X						
12:30	1:00 PM	WNEW	Cartoons—Fred Scott	X							
P.M. 1:00	1:30	WNEW	Cartoons Tom Gregory	X							
4:00	5:00	ABC	American Bandstand	X	X	X					
5:00	5:30	WPIX	Bozo Clown + Clutch Cargo	X	X						
5:30	6:00	WPIX	Three Stooges	X	X						
7:30	8:30	NBC	Laramie			X					
8:30	9:30	NBC	Startime (Drama)			X					
9:30	10:00	NBC	Arthur Murray Varsity			X					
10:00	10:30	NBC	M Squad (Police)			X					
10:30	11:00	NBC	Mike Hammer			X					

TUESDAY MARCH 1

Set turned off at _1:00 P.M_ o'clock

PLEASE REVIEW to check if you ~~have~~ written in every time your set was turned on today — whether anyone was paying attention or not.

TABLE 19: CONTENT ANALYSIS OF AVAILABLE PROGRAMS FOR WEEKS OF:

Sept. 20, 1959	Nov. 15, 1959	Feb. 23, 1960							
Oct. 18, 1959	Dec. 3, 1959	Mar. 1, 1960							
Nov. 8, 1959	Jan. 13, 1960								

Weekdays—6 p.m. to signoff
Sat. and Sun.—7 a.m. to signoff

		Programs	%	Minutes	%	Unduplicated Minutes	%
COMEDY-VARIETY	*Family situation comedy*	32	0.5	960	0.4	960	0.6
	Situation *comedy*	189	3.0	6190	2.6	5695	3.3
	Standup or *star comedian*	40	0.7	1200	0.5	1110	0.7
	Comedy—*variety regular*	97	1.6	7500	3.2	6190	3.6
	Comedy—*variety specials*	13	0.2	990	0.4	840	0.5
	Light musical *specials*	6	0.1	360	0.2	330	0.2
	Panel, games, light quiz	181	3.0	2251	1.0	2100	1.2
	Adult cartoons	14	0.2	420	0.2	420	0.3
	Comedy—variety	10	0.2	1140	0.5	1140	0.7
	Child cartoon	341	5.6	12,245	5.2	7270	4.3
DRAMA	*Light and medium* drama	435	7.2	14,880	6.3	11,905	7.0
	Heavy drama	79	1.3	7875	3.3	6285	3.7
	Daytime serials	2	0.0	60	0.03	60	0.4
	Personal, "real life" drama	14	0.2	475	0.2	415	0.2
	Courtroom enactments—crime or general	20	0.3	630	0.3	630	0.4
	Courtroom enactments—family relations	20	0.3	720	0.3	720	0.4
	Westerns, *adult*	32	0.5	1140	0.6	1380	0.8
	Westerns, other or general	333	5.5	10,560	4.5	8790	5.2
	Adventure—"other worlds"	150	2.5	4770	2.0	4170	2.5
	Child—non-cartoon	140	2.3	6825	2.9	5805	3.4
	Drama, stories—other or general						
CRIME	Crime *drama*	20	0.3	1090	0.5	1090	0.6
	Private-eye—sophisticated	36	0.6	1590	0.7	1560	0.9
	Police, detective, private-eye	404	6.7	12,070	5.1	9620	5.7

TABLE 19—*continued*

	Programs	%	Minutes	%	Unduplicated Minutes	%
MUSIC						
Star, *light* music	122	2.0	4735	2.0	4620	2.7
Medium music	7	0.1	420	0.2	420	0.3
Heavy music	7	0.1	450	0.2	420	0.3
Teen music or dance	53	0.9	3390	1.4	3180	1.9
Music, other or general						
SPORTS						
American sports, *regular*	130	2.1	9575	4.0	7155	4.2
Sports coverage, *special or unusual*	34	0.6	1875	0.8	1725	1.0
Boxing	14	0.2	630	0.3	630	0.4
Wrestling	47	0.8	4245	1.8	4245	2.5
Other sports	2	0.03	60	0.03	60	0.04
NEWS						
Regular news coverage	1207	20.0	12,760	5.4	8220	4.8
Special coverage of *current* events, *heavy*	25	0.4	735	0.3	665	0.4
Special coverage of *current* events, *light*	3	0.05	165	0.07	165	0.1
Documentaries on issues	104	1.7	3250	1.4	3175	1.9
Documentary, interview, emphasis on *people*	214	3.5	7935	3.4	6285	3.7
More *academic* issues or approach	68	1.1	1875	0.8	1740	1.0
Variety—information	8	0.1	240	0.1	240	0.1
Quiz shows—serious or general	—	—	—	—	—	—
Other information or "information general"	125	2.0	4020	1.7	3390	2.0
RELIGION Religion	336	5.5	4400	1.9	3710	2.2
MOVIES Movies, *heavy*	43	0.7	3985	1.7	3710	2.2
Movies, *medium*	745	12.3	63,770	27.0	28,740	16.9
Movies, *other*	146	2.4	10,465	4.4	7900	4.6
Movies, other or general	8	0.1	840	0.1	780	0.5

TABLE 20: The "Menu" vs. the "Diet" in Detail

	Available		Watched	
	Programs	%	Programs	%
Family situation comedy	32	0.5	128	1.7
Situation *comedy*	189	3.0	339	4.6
Standup or *star comedian*	40	0.7	92	1.1
Comedy—*variety regular*	97	1.6	342	4.6
Comedy—*variety specials*	13	0.2	142	1.9
Light musical *specials*	6	0.1	222	3.0
Panel, games, light quiz	181	3.0	246	3.3
Adult cartoons	14	0.2	14	0.2
Comedy—variety	10	0.2	5	0.1
Child cartoon	341	5.6	44	0.6
Light and medium drama	435	7.2	448	6.0
Heavy drama	79	1.3	269	3.6
Daytime serials	2	0.0	3	0.04
Personal, "real life" drama	14	0.2	35	0.5
Courtroom enactments—crime or general	20	0.3	11	0.1
Courtroom enactments—family relations	20	0.3	13	0.2
Westerns, *adult*	32	0.5	187	2.5
Westerns, other or general	333	5.5	541	7.3
Adventure—"other worlds"	150	2.5	191	2.6
Child—non-cartoon	140	2.3		
Drama, stories—other or general			52	0.7
Crime *drama*	20	0.3	161	2.2
Private-eye—sophisticated	36	0.6	148	2.0
Police, detective, private-eye	404	6.7	397	5.4

TABLE 20—*continued*: The "Menu" vs. the "Diet" in Detail

	Available Programs	%	Watched Programs	%
Star, *light* music	122	2.0	222	3.0
Medium music	7	0.1	55	0.7
Heavy music	7	0.1	8	0.1
Teen music or dance	53	0.9	48	0.6
Music, other or general				
American sports, *regular*	130	2.1	119	1.6
Sports coverage, *special or unusual*	34	0.6	41	0.6
Boxing	14	0.2	28	0.4
Wrestling	47	0.8	33	0.4
Other sports	2	0.03	5	0.07
Regular news coverage	1207	20.0	2184	30.0
Special coverage of *current events, heavy*	25	0.4	43	0.6
Special coverage of *current events, light*	3	0.05	3	0.04
Documentaries on issues	104	1.7	105	1.4
Documentary, interview, emphasis on *people*	214	3.5	129	1.7
More *academic* issues or approach	68	1.1	48	0.6
Variety—information	8	0.1	19	0.3
Quiz shows—serious or general			2	0.03
Other information or "information general"	125	2.0	15	0.2
Religion	336	5.5	17	0.2
Movies, *heavy*	43	0.7	39	0.5
Movies, *medium*	745	12.3	389	5.3
Movies, *other*	146	2.4	26	0.4
Movies, other or general	8	0.1		

TABLE 21

The Diet, by Parts of Q. 18A

	"Not enough laughs"	"Enough or too much"	"Not enough escape"	"Enough or too much"
Comedy-variety	15%	19%	13%	18%
Light drama	7	7	6	7
Action (western, crime, adventure)	26	22	27	22
Light music	4	4	3	4
Sports	3	3	3	3
Regular news	32	32	28	32
Information—public affairs	4	5	7	4
Heavy drama (including film "classics")	3	3	4	3
Heavy music	0	0	0	0
Religion	0	0	0	0
Movies (exclude "classics")	6	6	8	6
Summary				
Light entertainment	60%	60%	61%	60%
Heavy entertainment	4	3	4	3
News	32	32	28	32
Information—public affairs	4	5	7	4

TABLE 22

Examples of "Heavy Information" Programs

UN in Action
Johns Hopkins
Face the Nation
CBS Reports
Eye on New York
New Horizons
College News Conference
Agriculture, U.S.A.
Encyclopaedia Britannica
Ask Washington
Look at Congress

TABLE 23

Critical Hours : Heavy Information
Sundays Only—All Weeks

| | **ALL** | By Survey Response: | | | | By Viewer Characteristics: | | | | |
| | | QUESTION 18A THOSE WHO SAY: | | | | EDUCATION | | RELIGION | | |
		"Not enough food for thought"	*"Enough" or "too much"*	*"Not enough information"*	*"Enough" or "too much"*	High School and Below	College and Beyond	Protestants	Catholics	Jews
Number of Viewers	**237**	117	120	136	101	143	79	63	99	65
HEAVY INFORMATION Opportunities per Sunday, average	**20.3**	20.1	20.3	20.1	20.2	20.3	20.2	20.4	20.2	20.3
WATCHED DURING CRITICAL HOURS:										
HEAVY INFORMATION SELECTED										
Exposures	**173**	108	65	108	65	95	64	64	53	51
Per Viewer	**0.7**	0.9	0.5	0.8	0.6	0.7	0.8	1.0	0.5	0.8
MISSED OPPORTUNITIES saw something else										
Exposures	**898**	427	471	540	358	586	248	238	377	245
Per Viewer	**3.8**	3.6	3.9	4.0	3.5	4.1	3.1	3.8	3.8	3.8
HEAVY INFORMATION Selection Rate	**16%**	**20%**	**12%**	**17%**	**15%**	**14%**	**21%**	**21%**	**12%**	**17%**
CRITICAL HOURS NOT WATCHED:										
Per Viewer	**3728**	1821	1907	2100	1628	2218	1291	983	1570	1022
Number	**15.7**	15.6	15.9	15.4	16.1	15.5	16.3	15.6	15.9	15.7

Summary : On Sundays, Of All Possible
Heavy Information Exposures . . .

Watched	Missed	Not Watching
	saw something else	at all at the time

			Exposures	Viewers
			Base: 100% =	
ALL	4	19% 77%	**4799**	**237**
THOSE WHO SAY: *"Not enough food for thought"*	5	18 77	2356	117
"Enough" or "too much"	3	19 78	2443	120
THOSE WHO SAY: *"Not enough information"*	4	20 76	2748	136
"Enough" or "too much"	3	17 80	2051	101
High School and Below	3	20 77	2899	143
College and Beyond	4	15 81	1603	79
Protestants	5	19 76	1285	63
Catholics	3	19 78	2000	99
Jews	4	19 77	1318	65

TABLE 24

Q. 42C, Item C   *"I'd rather pay a small amount yearly, if I could, to have TV without commercials."*

By Income	Agree	By Education	Agree
Under $1,000	23%	0–6 G.S.	22%
$1000–$1999	22	7–8 G.S.	17
2000– 2999	24	1–3 H.S.	24
3000– 3999	17	4 H.S.	24
4000– 4999	22	1–2 Coll.	25
5000– 5999	22	3–4 Coll.	31
6000– 6999	24	Beyond Coll.	39
7000– 7999	27		
8000– 8999	32		
9000– 9999	23		
Over $10,000	36		

TABLE 25

Bases for Table on page 223
Analysis of Q. 45 A, B; 52 C, D

All	By Education			By Income			By Religion		
614	162	305	132	214	211	160	405	151	32
607	175	286	128	183	247	151	406	144	24
615	147	325	127	143	204	154	439	140	19
591	143	298	129	182	174	141	420	131	21

TABLE 26

Possible *advantages* of pay TV, cited by those who think it "should be tried out" and those who think it "should not."

(Q. 45, 53E)

	Should			Should Not		
	G.S.	H.S.	C.&B.	G.S.	H.S.	C.&B.
Base: 100%=	104	252	206	387	799	240
No interruptions	9%	12%	4%	2%	4%	5%
No commercials	25	16	14	9	11	15
Summary (commercials)	**34**	**27**	**18**	**11**	**14**	**20**
Improved programs—no program restrictions	20	32	43	5	10	14
More choice—new things to see—more special interest	12	21	29	3	7	6
First-class programs	3	7	3	1	2	1
Summary (programs)	**33**	**54**	**69**	**8**	**18**	**20**
Make audience more selective	6	8	10	2	4	4
Specific advantages—other	15	11	12	3	5	8
None	7	6	3	57	44	36
DK, NA, AO	15	6	5	20	18	16

TABLE 27

Possible *disadvantages* of pay TV, cited by those who think it "should be tried out" and those who think it "should not."

(Q. 45, 52F)

	Should			Should Not		
	G.S.	H.S.	C.&B.	G.S.	H.S.	C.&B.
Base: 100%=	104	252	206	387	799	240
Hardship to people—benefit those who have money	15%	14%	10%	17%	14%	15%
"Commitment"—must watch	2	7	7	2	4	3
Too expensive—shouldn't have to pay	24	25	26	45	43	40
Summary (cost)	**41**	**45**	**42**	**63**	**59**	**56**
No benefits—programs limited	6	4	11	4	6	9
Lack of sponsor's control of program content to protect his reputation	5	3	2	5	6	6
Danger of political control— loses information value	3	4	4	3	4	3
Eliminate or worsen free TV	6	9	8	5	6	7
Impractical—drive movies out of business	15	13	15	8	11	14
None	12	14	16	3	3	4
DK, NA, AO	19	13	8	13	12	11

TABLE 28

Content Analysis of Cartoons About TV

Manifest content of all TV cartoons in these magazines for the years listed

	The New Yorker 1950–'1	'59	The Saturday Evening Post '50	'59	Esquire '50	'59	Ladies' Home Journal '50	'59	All Magazines '50 No.	%	'59 No.	%
VIEWING AS AN ACTIVITY	43	7	31	15	0	4	3	5	77	57%	31	42%
"desocialization"—family	4		4	5			1	3	9	7	8	11
"desocialization"—guests	2		9				1		12	9	0	0
competes with reading, etc.	5	1	3	4					8	6	5	7
produces togetherness	5			1					5	4	2	3
competes with movies, radio	3					1	1		4	3	1	1
problems with children	5		10	2				1	15	11	3	4
other	19	6	4	3		3			23	17	12	16
Technical (screen size, color, etc.)	17	2	1	4	3	3			21	16	9	12
CONTENT												
Commercials	12	8	2	6		3			14	10	17	23
Programs	21	9	9	11	13	5			43	32	25	34
ALL	76	24	42	32	13	12	3	5	134	100%	73	100%

TABLE 29

Word List Analysis by Religion:

QUESTION 13C *"Most television programs are . . ."*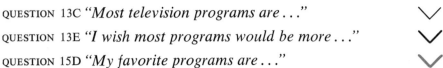

QUESTION 13E *"I wish most programs would be more . . ."*

QUESTION 15D *"My favorite programs are . . ."*

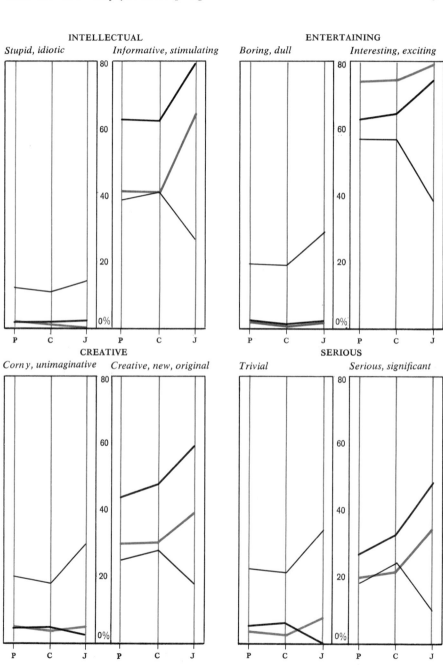

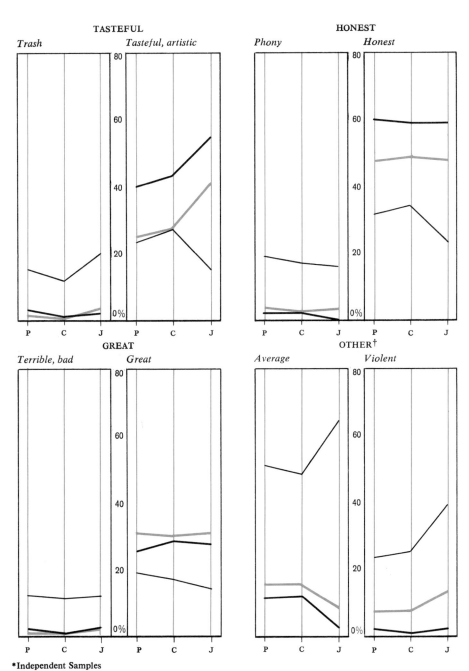

Respondents:	Q. 13 C & E*	Q. 15D*
Protestants	**829**	**841**
Catholics	**282**	**284**
Jews	**56**	**40**

TASTEFUL

Trash *Tasteful, artistic*

HONEST

Phony *Honest*

GREAT

Terrible, bad *Great*

OTHER†

Average *Violent*

*Independent Samples

†"Sinful" on next page

TABLE 29—*continued*

Q. 13 C&E, 15D "SINFUL" BY

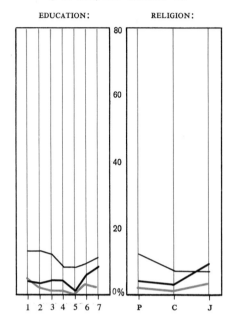

EDUCATION: RELIGION:

80

60

40

20

0%

1 2 3 4 5 6 7   P   C   J

TABLE 30

The DIET by Religion:

LIGHT ENTERTAINMENT

HEAVY ENTERTAINMENT

NEWS

INFORMATION & PUBLIC AFFAIRS

	Viewers	Programs	Programs per Viewer
		Base: 100% =	
Protestants	63	1963	31.2
Catholics	99	3282	33.2
Jews	65	1893	29.1

Proportion of all programs watched in various categories

ACTION	Protestants 20%	6.2
	Catholics 25%	8.3
	Jews 19%	5.4
COMEDY/VARIETY	18	5.7
	19	6.2
	19	5.5
LIGHT DRAMA	7	2.0
	7	2.4
	7	2.0
LIGHT MUSIC	5	1.4
	4	1.4
	4	1.3
SPORTS	4	1.1
	3	1.0
	3	1.0
REGULAR NEWS	34	10.5
	26	8.6
	31	9.1
INFORMATION & PUBLIC AFFAIRS	6	1.7
	4	1.3
	6	1.8
HEAVY DRAMA	4	1.1
	3	1.0
	5	1.5
RELIGION	0	
	0	
	0	
MOVIES	4	1.2
	7	2.5
	6	1.6
HEAVY MUSIC	0	
	0	
	0	

SUMMARY:

Base: 100% =

Protestants	57% 4 34% 6%	1963
Catholics	66 3 26 4	3282
Jews	57 5 31 6	1893

APPENDIX D

TECHNICAL NOTES ON STATISTICAL INFERENCE AND SAMPLE DESIGN

A TECHNICAL NOTE ON STATISTICAL INFERENCE

THE INTERPRETATIONS in this study are based directly on the point estimates in the tables. The method of sample selection is fully described on the following pages, and all sample and sub-sample sizes are stated in the individual analyses.

Treatment of sampling error has been almost wholly informal, based in part on the internal consistency of the findings and, most of all, on the remarkable similarity of two independent replications of the entire design, documented in the NORC-Roper comparisons.

More specifically, our reasons for not giving probabilistic interpretations are as follows: Our approach is one of estimation rather than testing of hypotheses. Within the framework of estimation, it has not seemed worthwhile to attempt to present confidence regions (in the traditional terminology) or posterior distributions (in Bayesian terminology). The reason is mainly that the cost of making the computations seemed far out of proportion to the possible benefits. First, the sampling designs are clustered probability samples and not simple random samples. Second, the statistical theory needed for even the simpler tables often does not exist as yet and, when it does, would lead to results that would be hard to assimilate.

The easy way out of these difficulties would be the common procedure of testing "null-hypotheses." But we have no "null-hypotheses" to test. And if we had, the conventional tests would be invalidated by the clustering and other restrictions of sample design and by the doubt that is cast on these procedures, in our minds, by the Bayesian criticisms of them.

Thus we have followed what we have always felt to be the best sample-survey practice in basing our interpretations on tables of (self-weighted) point estimates from carefully designed and executed samples. Indeed, one can make a strong Bayesian argument for point estimation rather than interval estimation for this kind of analysis, and we can regard our point estimates as rough certainty equivalents, or at least quasi-certainty equivalents. That is, they are the numbers that one will be able to carry away from the study for possible use in future analyses. (Consider, as an example, the analogous case of monthly unemployment percentages, where the point estimates are almost invariably, and with good reason, interpreted as certainty equivalents.)

If the reader is skeptical of our interpretations of point estimates, we have given him all the tables available to us and have described our methods fully. If any professional reader wishes to carry out statistical computations that cannot be made from the data in this book, we will be happy to make available upon request, at cost, the necessary tabulating cards.

SAMPLING PROCEDURE—NORC

CONVENTIONAL areal probability sampling procedures were employed in connection with the first three stages of selection. In order to select primary sampling units, each Standard Metropolitan Area (SMA) and each non-SMA county in the United States was allocated to one of sixty-eight strata on the basis of its geographic location and a number of its 1950 demographic, economic, and social characteristics. One SMA or one non-SMA county was then randomly selected with probability proportionate to its estimated 1953 population to represent each stratum.

Within each primary sampling unit thus selected, several secondary units (municipalities, "unincorporated places," or townships) were then drawn with probability proportionate to 1950 population. Stratification by size of incorporated place was employed at this stage of sampling. Within each locality, one or more third-stage units were selected, again with probability proportionate to 1950 population. These units were the ultimate sample segments. In cities and towns these segments were generally made up of four square blocks; in open-country areas, a segment was generally an area clearly demarcated by roads, streams, and other identifiable boundaries. An open-country segment generally contained several hundred dwelling units. A total of 293 segments were employed to obtain the 1250 interviews. Thus, approximately four interviews were assigned per segment.

A rather rigidly controlled quota sampling procedure was employed within the chosen segments. Both the particular dwelling units and the time of day at which the interviewer was to attempt to obtain interviews were predesignated, but generally only those people who were at home and were willing to be interviewed the first time a dwelling unit was approached were included in the survey. In other words, no call-backs were made to obtain interviews with respondents who either refused to be interviewed or were not at home at the time of the first approach. The interviewer was also allowed some latitude in choosing which of the individuals aged 18 or older in a particular household was to be interviewed. Quota controls, as described later, were superimposed on this procedure to prevent sample distortion with respect to certain demographic characteristics.

Quota rather than probability sampling was employed within segments for reasons of economy. Since an extremely high level of accuracy in the estimation of population parameters was not considered essential to the fulfillment of the research objectives, it was felt that the probable gains in precision to be had from using a procedure necessitating large numbers of call-backs were not sufficiently large to warrant the consequent substantial increase in data-collection costs.

As a first step in establishing the segment quotas, the total number of cases to be taken from each primary sampling unit was determined. The goal was to make the quota for each primary sampling unit proportionate to the total population aged 18 or older of the stratum it was to represent. Since up-to-date population statistics for the individual strata were not available, rough adjustments in the quotas were made on the basis of the general demographic trends revealed by census releases pertaining to the period from 1950 to late 1959.

The interviewer was instructed to obtain exactly a specified number of interviews in each of the segments to which she was assigned. Since the first three stages of sampling involved selection with probability proportionate to the estimated population residing in the sampling unit, approximately equal numbers of interviews were assigned to each segment within a given primary sampling unit. To the extent that the population distribution within the primary sampling unit had undergone recent changes, sample estimates could be somewhat biased.

The interviewer was given a random starting point for each segment and was instructed to call at each house in succession until her quota for a particular segment was filled. In order to avoid excessive clustering, the interviewer was instructed to take not more than one interview from any particular multiple-unit structure or from adjacent single-dwelling-unit structures. Thus, after completing an interview with a respondent residing in a multiple-unit structure, the interviewer discontinued her canvass in that structure and began the search for the next eligible respondent in the adjoining structure. When an interview was completed in a single-family structure, the adjacent structure was skipped, and the search began with the second structure following the one in which the interview was taken. (When a multiple-unit structure adjoined a single-unit structure, the interviewer began her canvass in the multiple-unit structure even if an interview was obtained in the preceding structure.)

In 23 segments, interviews were conducted only with Negroes. (Negro interviewers were assigned to these segments.) In the remaining 270 segments, interviews were conducted only with respondents of races other than Negro.

As a control against the tendency to obtain a disproportionately small number of employed men and women in quota samples, interviewing was restricted to evenings and weekends in three-quarters of the segments used in the present survey. Seventy-three segments were randomly selected for 9:00 a.m-5:00 p.m. weekday interviewing of females. These 73 segments constituted a stratified sample of the 293 segments used on the survey. Practically every one of the 68 primary sampling units had at least one segment set aside for daytime interviewing. In the remaining

220 segments, all interviews were conducted either on weekends or after 5:00 p.m. on a weekday.

Age quotas were imposed for each of the 73 segments assigned for weekday daytime interviewing of women. For the remaining 220 segments, age-sex quotas were imposed on each interviewer's total assignment of evening and weekend segments rather than on a segment-by-segment basis. Thus, a given interviewer might have been assigned one daytime segment, with a specific age quota for the women to be interviewed there, and three evening segments, with a single set of age-sex quotas covering the work in the three segments combined.

The age-sex quotas were set separately for Negroes and for those of other races on the basis of 1959 Census Bureau estimates. Five age-sex categories were used within each racial group. These were:

Males:	18-29
	30-54
	55+
Females:	18-34
	35+

In a number of prior studies, the combination of assignment to specific small areas and the imposition of sex-age-race quotas has proved to provide sufficient control to avoid appreciable biases with respect to almost any demographic variable for which comparable Census data were available. It is, of course, impossible to ascertain definitively whether or not serious sample biases have been similarly avoided in connection with the estimation of important substantive parameters from the present survey. Nevertheless, it is not unreasonable to suppose that the addition of the time-of-day, day-of-week restrictions on the interviewing has reduced the likelihood of marked unrepresentativeness to a level below that applicable to the usual survey employing a quota sample.

SAMPLING PROCEDURE—ELMO ROPER and ASSOCIATES

THE PROCEDURES used by Elmo Roper and Associates paralleled closely the procedures used by NORC. Both organizations used probability methods in determining interviewing locations; both organizations imposed controls for sex and age of respondents within specific interviewing locations; both organizations required that interviews be confined to specific hours of the day. As would be inevitable where two organizations are involved, however, there were some minor variations in procedures which should be noted.

For example, somewhat different probability selection procedures were used by the Roper organization in determining its sampling locations. After stratifying all the counties in the United States on the basis of geographical area and degree of urbanization, 100 counties were selected at random proportionate to the 1950 population. Within these counties, cities, towns, and open-country areas were selected, also at random, proportionate to the 1950 population. Within the cities of 50,-000 and over, blocks were selected from block statistics. In smaller cities and towns, blocks were selected at random and the number of interviews assigned to the town were distributed among the blocks in proportion to the number of dwelling units found on the blocks. In open-country areas, specific segments that could be clearly outlined on maps were selected at random. In all, 244 specific locations (blocks or open-country segments) for interviewing were assigned, the assignments averaging four interviews per block in towns and cities, twelve interviews in each open-country segment.

Similarly, there were slight variations in the implementation of the quota controls. Instead of confining daytime interviews with women to a random portion of the locations, a specific number of daytime interviews were assigned to each location. In addition, controls by age for each sex were imposed using three age levels for both men and women (18 to 29, 30 to 54, and 55 and over).

One variation in interviewing technique was used in order to minimize the number of people who might refuse at some point in the interview to go on and complete the full interview. At a point early in the questionnaire, respondents were given a choice between continuing at that time or making an appointment to complete the interview at some later date. About 4 per cent of the respondents chose to have the interview call back and complete the interview at a later date. These were presumably people who otherwise would not have been able to complete the interview at the time of the first call and would thus not have been included in the final sample. Interviews that were carried over in this manner were classified in the final results according to the time of original contact, and not at the time of the call-back.

Afterword

SOME REFLECTIONS ON PAST AND FUTURE RESEARCH ON BROADCASTING

BY

PAUL F. LAZARSFELD

The People Look at Television is the third general survey of public attitudes toward broadcasting to be analyzed by the Bureau of Applied Social Research. The first of these studies was *The People Look at Radio* (1946), which demonstrated the general satisfaction of the public with radio broadcasting as it then was, as an entertainment and news medium. The second survey, *Radio Listening in America* (1948), confirmed this general finding but provided more information on the criticisms of radio made particularly by the better-educated people. Dr. Steiner's study employs many new techniques and produces findings going well beyond our previous efforts in its exploration of the nature of satisfaction and discontent with television.

NOTE: Because this afterword reviews a whole tradition, acknowledgment cannot be made individually to all the men and women who contributed to it. I do want to acknowledge my long-standing debt to Frank Stanton, who helped to create the Bureau traditions in the first place, and who continues to support them. I am grateful to William McPhee, the author of the wide-ranging proposal to the Columbia Broadcasting System, from which stemmed the present study, as well as some of the ideas discussed in this afterword.

This study, like the earlier efforts, shares in the Bureau's belief that broad surveys of public attitudes constitute one essential part of research on the role of the mass media in society. At the same time we would all agree that this is not the only kind of research required if our society is to cope with the problems raised by modern means of mass communication. If research is to play a part in the "great debate" of which Dr. Berelson has written, the researchers themselves have a public responsibility to indicate the limitations of their own efforts and the range of questions which remain to be answered.

This afterword will therefore look at some problems which television research has not yet adequately explored; it will speculate as to why they have not been; and it will suggest some possible ways of studying them. It might be argued that such a discussion could be of interest only to my fellow researchers and to the sponsors of research, but I believe it is important for the general reader to "eavesdrop" on such discussions. Research is being done on the public every day, on behalf of all kinds of organizations—profit-making, non-profit, and governmental. The results of this research play a major role in shaping organizational policies and in justifying them to the public. It is only proper that the people be allowed to know what is being done to them and for them by researchers. I would even say that one cannot be a responsible citizen in an "age of social research" without some understanding of what research is all about, its uses, abuses, potentials, and limitations.

Some of the ideas presented here were raised in the early days of the Office of Radio Research, which later developed into our Bureau. Some were developed when the Bureau staff worked out a broad programmatic proposal for "Research on the Potentialities of Television" in 1956 under the direction of William McPhee, of which the Steiner study is an outgrowth; and some have been inspired by reading Dr. Steiner's report. The areas I have in mind can be briefly labeled:

(1) The detailed study of the audience's experience
(2) Experiments in changing public preferences
(3) Studies of the long-range effects of television
(4) Research on matters of taste
(5) Research on decision-making in the broadcasting industry.

In discussing each area, I will refer to early explorations by our own research group, which might form a starting point for new studies. Researchers must learn to look back occasionally on their "roads not taken" if valuable ideas are not to be lost. They would also do well to speculate as to why they took certain roads and not others if they are to gain more rational control over their scientific destinies. "Way leads on to way." Something inherent in the structure of any research organization leads its members to examine certain problems and not others of equal or greater intellectual merit. Availability of funds, access to people and documents to study, the "practicality" of certain research techniques, the desire to do studies that can be finished in a reasonable time, fear of entering a blind alley, the fact that an organization becomes known for certain kinds of studies and is asked to do more—all these affect the history of a field of research at least as much as does rational planning.

The Audience Experience

What does it mean for the average American to watch television for two and one half hours a day? When television first came upon the American scene we attributed the heavy use to a so-called novelty effect. Surely by now the novelty must have worn off, yet the usage rates show no signs of dropping. Could it be that television has acquired the character of an addiction whereby people hate themselves the next morning but cannot help starting all over again when evening comes?

Dr. Steiner, as a trained psychologist, designed the projective test described in his book to help answer this question. He found that a large number of respondents felt ambivalent about their amount of viewing. They were ready to say that television is both relaxing *and* a waste of time. Their other leisure activities were not surrounded by such a haze of doubt; reading is elevating, playing golf is wholesome, and sitting in a bar is clearly wrong. Among the better-educated, he found a number of respondents who stated frankly that they felt they watched more than they should.

Ambivalence is not necessarily the same as addiction, and the concept of addiction must itself be specified. Using the present findings as a start, intensive interviews with television viewers could be used to answer the following questions:

Do people make an effort to "break the habit," to watch less? Addicts try to.

Do they watch more when they are depressed than when they are vigorous and optimistic about themselves? Addiction seems to be used in this way.

Do they consider television as a problem, perhaps one which they discuss with friends? One sign of addiction is this self-awareness.

If they are ambivalent about television, is this a result of some intrinsic element of dissatisfaction with the television experience? (That is, do they watch in the hope that it will be better tonight than in the past?) Or is it more the result of a social norm: do they really like television, but express dissatisfaction because they think they ought to?

These illustrate the kinds of questions that are asked when researchers become introspective and probe more deeply into the audience experience. The interplay between research and theoretical concepts, such as addiction, is most successful if the indicators of concepts can be built from studies like the present one, and then tested in later research. The technique for obtaining detailed answers to questions such as the ones outlined above has been the detailed interview.

A good example of this technique is Herta Herzog's study on why people listen to *Professor Quiz,* which was published as a special pamphlet by CBS. At the time, the success of radio quiz programs had been attributed to the belief that people liked to watch competitive games. But Miss Herzog's detailed interviews made it clear that many thought that such programs increased their education, and were gratified to learn odd facts in this way. A more famous use of detailed interviews was in the analysis of Orson Welles's program, *The Invasion from Mars.* On the morning after the event, Frank Stanton asked Miss Herzog to make a series of detailed interviews. These showed, among other things, how it was possible for people to continue to believe in the "invasion" in spite of many opportunities to check the facts. Given initial acceptance, they became impervious to outside checks—those who looked in the streets and saw a lot of cars were convinced that everyone was fleeing; those who saw empty streets were sure that everyone else was dead.

Such research relied on detailed interviews—and on introspection. Such techniques and talents should be applied to the broader meaning of television.

There is also the enormous range of questions involving the experiences of the viewer while he watches a particular program. Detailed interviewing can produce valuable evidence here, as seen in the *Professor Quiz* example. Yet if you interview people while they are listening or watching, you disturb them; if you wait until later, some of their impressions will be forgotten. To resolve this dilemma, we developed the Lazarsfeld-Stanton program analyzer. Assembled test audiences were asked to push buttons minute by minute throughout the program, a green one if they liked what they saw, a red one if they disliked it. The reactions were recorded electrically and this record was used as the basis of a later interview. It provided a way to reduce interference with the experience of watching or listening but at the same time permitted us to match the interview with the content of the program and thus greatly reduce memory loss.

The peak utility of the Program Analyzer came during World War II, when we studied the effect of indoctrination films on American soldiers. Since then, use of such a technique by academic researchers has greatly decreased, perhaps because the method is an expensive one.

However, from a scientific point of view it has not lost its importance. What people feel about television programs is a question which deserves to be answered in great detail, not only to provide producers with criteria for evaluation of programs but also to give social scientists further knowledge about the audience experience, the sensations of watching television, and the kinds of gratifications, if any, that television brings minute by minute.

Perhaps such a device is most useful for finding out reactions to programs not yet on the air. With the proper research design it would provide one way of studying the detailed reactions of unsophisticated viewers to sophisticated programming, and can provide clues to the serious problem of raising the level of sophistication. Program analysis has been used primarily to change the content of programs, to edit or delete difficult parts, to avoid the so-called boomerang effect; however, it could as well play a role in helping to locate people's viewing difficulties. If we could learn something about the stumbling blocks less-educated people have when viewing, let us say, a serious play—and the program analyzer provides a useful technique for getting at this—we could then experiment to find out whether supplementary aids, such as program materials or an introductory discussion of the play, have any noticeable effect. This leads logically to the next area, experiments in changing public preferences.

Experiments in Changing Preferences

In 1937, the Rockefeller Foundation launched the first major attempt to study the effects of radio on American society, with the creation of the Office of Radio Research, staffed by Hadley Cantril, Frank Stanton, and myself. What did we decide to do with this opportunity? Most American radio research had consisted of laboratory experiments on the effects of this or that kind of presentation. Cantril had done experiments on the essential differences between people's response to the disembodied radio voice as compared with the live and visible speaker. But coming from a tradition of survey research in Europe, nothing in my past qualified me for such experimental work; and Stanton's experience was in measurement of the amount of listening by the public. Therefore we took a different direction: the use of surveys to study audience behavior as it went on in their homes.

Of course, we had too little money in those days to conduct our own national surveys. But even in 1937 there were already available large amounts of data on people's listening habits. These data existed because of the nature of the radio industry. Whereas printed communications media have always been able to count their audience by seeing how many copies were printed or sold, the broadcasters had to conduct surveys. Since the data were collected for commercial audience-measuring purposes, they were always presented as simple totals for the population as a whole. We suspected that by studying these materials more closely, significant differences in listening behavior would be found for men and women, older and younger people, better-educated and less-educated, and so on. Our early work focused on such differences, and is represented by the series of "Radio Research" studies. The present study of television is also heir to this tradition.

Yet all such studies are by their nature static; they report the status quo, the existing pattern of preferences as related to social background. Are these patterns immutable? To answer such questions requires the combination of surveys with experimental ideas. Such methods are neglected partly because of the division of skills which exists in research organizations and partly because such combined efforts are more expensive. Let me give an example of an experiment which we discussed but never carried out.

Regardless of whether or not one considers it the duty of television to be concerned with raising the level of taste, it would be important to find out whether a supply of better programs could actually succeed in doing this. There is a very simple experiment which we have discussed off and on in Bureau staff meetings for twenty years but have never actually done. This would be to "hire" a few hundred adults who had at most a high school education and ask them to watch in their own homes a program commonly considered "too sophisticated" for them, manifestly to keep track of how much time is given to commercials (or some other job for which they would get paid). This job would last for three months or so. Some months after their pay for listening ended, these former employees could be interviewed to find out how many of them kept on watching that program or similar programs—to see whether they had acquired the taste. In this way one would discover whether less-sophisticated people can learn to like more complex activities merely through repeated exposure alone. Detailed interviews with those who did not continue could find reasons for their lack of interest and might suggest means to help them enjoy such materials, which could be embodied in further experimentation. Such an experiment could help considerably in teaching us more about the potentialities of learning in television. Through continued exposure to television, the American people have learned to like certain forms of popular culture; they can understand complicated jokes in which one comedian attacks a colleague; they readily grasp complex baseball statistics and weather reports. The question answered by this kind of experiment is whether through similar repeated exposure, the area of "high" culture can be introduced. Once the initial hurdle of avoiding the unfamiliar is jumped, is there an acquired taste?

Studies of the Long-Run Effects of Television

So far I have talked about relatively short-range studies of effectiveness and effects. Yet perhaps the most important questions social scientists are asked cannot be answered by short-range studies of effectiveness and effects. A good example is the question of whether watching television has a bad effect on children. This question is ambiguous at both ends, so to speak. On the one hand, what is meant by "bad effects"? Criminal tendencies? Debased taste? Wasted time which would otherwise be spent creatively? On the other hand, what is meant by "television"? The amount of time spent viewing? The particular programs seen? The isolation from other children which might result?[1]

[1] I have dealt with these ambiguities in some detail elsewhere. "Communications Research and the Social Psychologist," in Wayne Dennis (ed.): *Current Trends in Social Psychology* (Pittsburgh: University of Pittsburgh Press, 1948), esp. pp. 249–57.

Both the form and the content of the medium may have significant effects. If one compares reading a story with seeing one on television, the differences in form are that the book reader must visualize for himself the characters, the setting, and the sounds, while for the viewer the sights and sounds are provided. On the other hand, the book explicitly reports inner thoughts and feelings, while the screen shows external cues, in expression and speech, to what is within. What are the effects of these differences on children growing up with mainly a print or mainly a screen diet? Do screen children become less, or more, visually creative than print children? Less, or more, insightful into people's thoughts and feelings? And are the effects different depending on the range of direct experiences which the child has? Recent research on child development stresses "creativity" and "emphatic ability," as well as the now traditional notion of "intelligence." All these are related to the social class and cultural style of parents; what is the role of the various media in helping the parents transmit their styles and skills to children?

The content of television is not unique; its themes of violence and counter-violence, of the value of beauty and the value of virtue, of what constitutes success and failure, appear in other media—comics, films, picture magazines, story magazines, and books. Still there may be wide differences in emphasis. One study proposed years ago was a comparison of the content of television with other media—popular magazines, popular books, or the entire contents of a magazine store or of a good small public library. We don't know what the results would be. Even if its content is like other media, the sheer amount of time spent on television may give it a qualitatively different impact. The question of the effects of exposure to television violence over a period of years remains on the research agenda of our society.

Whatever the answers may be, we cannot find them out without long-term studies in which groups of children are kept under observation for a number of years. We would start out with a cohort of children, say, three years old, recording in addition to the usual background factors, their mass communications diet. Such a simple factual survey might be repeated once or twice a year. As they grow older we would seek additional data as to the kind of relations they have with other children, how they perform in school, whether they engage in destructive or constructive behavior. Obviously many factors other than mass communications diet must be taken into account, such as the differences in cultural background of the family, other leisure experiences, the character of the neighborhood, and the quality of the school. What is required is the integration of mass communications data into general research on child development, in a way which has not yet been done. The mass communications industry might well take on responsibility for supporting basic research of this type.

Research on Matters of Taste

It is generally assumed that there is no sense arguing about taste and no justification for highbrows to enforce their standards on lowbrows, or vice versa. But we have known for some time that the argument is not so simple. In 1941 Arnheim made a careful content analysis of some forty daytime serials. He was able to show that some of these soap operas pandered to the mood of the female audience: it was usually the man who created the troubles and the woman who straightened them out. The problem to which Arnheim addressed himself was not whether the daytime serial pattern, that of families getting in and out of trouble, was great literature, but whether he could make distinctions within the pattern. The distinctions were based, it is true, on some normative criteria like honesty, credibility of motivation, and so on, but these were criteria on which one could quite easily agree. He found that some scripts were more realistic than others in terms of modern family life, without losing their dramatic impact. This type of study has not been seriously continued though the need is as great as ever.

Producers in recent years have talked about "mature" Westerns, and the term has been the object of some unjustified ridicule. Missing is a detailed content analysis on precisely the difference between a mature and a primitive Western so that programming decisions could be made on the basis of explicit content criteria. Another good object of study would be mystery and detective stories. In the European version of this genre, the crimes are highly varied: stolen documents, unexplained embezzlements, temporary disappearances of people, and so on. The American version concentrates much more on just one crime: "murder." Is suspense really heightened by the injection of murder, or could the range of topics be enlarged, and violence be reduced, if script writers tried themselves on such other topics? In other words, even if one accepts the current division of programming types—soap operas, family situation comedies, crime stories, and the like—one can through appropriate studies suggest ways to raise the standards within each grouping.

Content analysis is only one source of ideas. The same goal could also be reached by another kind of audience study. It is well known, and Dr. Steiner's book reminds us again, that American listeners make few concrete suggestions when asked what they would like to see on television that is not now available. This is often taken as evidence that people don't know what they would like until they can try it out.

One way of getting at this potential audience demand would be through the use of experimental juries. In several cities, an effort could be made to use social research and the public for developing new ideas for television. Panels of viewers from the population at large along with persons of special talents and competence would be brought together for a series of weekly meetings. In the course of such a meeting they would listen to talks by, or arguments among, television experts designed to stimulate their imagination about what television could do; this would form the basis of the first discussion. Later they might be shown experimental films or kinescopes that illustrate a wide range of program possibilities; these too would be discussed afterwards. Finally, the researchers would interview the panel members in detail on any ideas that emerged during the evening.

The researcher would then analyze his notes and interviews in preparation for the next meeting, and pull together the points of emerging focus—the reactions to good ideas that turned up, and points that still remain fuzzy. At the next meeting, he could then guide the group discussions at a somewhat higher level.

A venture like this—part field work, part group discussion, part experiment—could generate potentially useful ideas for programming materials. It is hard to anticipate what they might be, but the point is that it might lead us to think more intensively about ways to get around the dilemma that people don't know what they like until they are given concrete alternatives. In order to generate new ideas, radical departures such as this must probably be developed; they are effective to the extent that the panel is provided good alternative possibilities, active discussion and interaction (as through the staging of arguments by disagreeing television experts), and the extent that the researcher can successfully play the role of diagnostician concerning suggestions that emerge which are worth following up.

Another insufficiently explored area is the role of the television critic. One can find a reasonable number of good book reviews in American newspapers and some decent movie criticisms, but relatively few well-reasoned discussions of the major television offerings. Even in the best newspapers the television critics usually just say whether they did or did not like a new program. They don't back up their judgments and hardly ever discuss noticeable variations in the serious programs.

If television criticism were to be taken more seriously, it would have two beneficial effects. For one thing, the criteria of judgments would be made cumulatively more explicit. And secondly, the selectivity of the average viewer, which the present book documents so clearly, might be improved.

A Bureau study on the functions of radio once proposed that radio and perhaps educational television carry extensive criticism and discussion of television programs; based on the assumption that one subject that Americans are interested in is television, it was felt that a well-designed set of programs could stimulate audiences and at the same time help in the development of more critical faculties. A public debate or argument by intelligent and verbal critics on a program just seen, possibly including discussions by its producer, some of the cast, the script writers, and so on, might help establish more firmly the criteria by which television programs can be judged.

James Joyce is reported to have said once, in answer to the cliché that there's no arguing about taste, that in fact matters of taste are the only things worth arguing about. To a large extent, the merit of these plans is built on Joyce's contention; the problem is how to get the argument going and how to lead it in fruitful directions.

Decision-Making in the Broadcasting Industry

Probably the greatest gap in our knowledge about television pertains to the structure of the industry, its relations to the advertiser and to the Federal Communications Commission. To be sure, this is a difficult area to study. As in most other industries, broadcasters are understandably reluctant to let themselves be studied on a top managerial level. Each company feels that competitively valuable information will be disclosed or embarrassing situations revealed. But this might be a short-sighted view. From time to time, Congressional committees crash through this curtain of secrecy and when that happens the public gets not a balanced picture but a series of horror stories. What is so badly needed is various kinds of studies of the industry, such as detailed biographies of programs: Take a successful TV program; through what steps did it go from the moment when the idea was first conceived? Who had influence and in what direction did he exercise it? Here one should not just shrug off the controversial role of the advertiser. On aesthetic matters, who exercised the judgment which would correspond to, say, the Artists' Councils Incorporated in French broadcasting? It would be equally interesting to take a number of unsuccessful programs and attempt a similar biography.

Another area deserving study is the industry's relation to the Federal Communications Commission. Its present chairman is relatively active in the exercise of his office. He, the industry, and the public could learn a great deal if we knew what happened when Clifford Durr played a somewhat similar role fifteen years ago. But no history of his regime was ever written.

The relation between the networks and the affiliated stations was a topic recently explored by a Congressional committee, without clear results. One could dig up a considerable number of legal squabbles, but it would be much more instructive to compare situations where the affiliates take the good sustaining programs and situations where they don't. Is the difference due to the personality of the local managers or to a different objective structure in the market? How do communities actually react to the policy of their local stations? Studies of the kinds just mentioned have often been neglected because up to rather recently the social research institutes themselves stayed away from such institutional analysis. We were all fascinated by the opportunities which opened up three decades ago when sampling technique and attitude measurement became well-developed techniques.

Social institutions like broadcasting are slowly becoming amenable to research, and social scientists are slowly developing the proper techniques for studying institutions. Because of the complicated relationships among the various component parts—the networks, the sponsors, the FCC, and the audiences (as represented in part by the rating services, in part by other forms of "feedback")—a whole series of studies is required to give a rounded picture. However, ingenious ways to "cut into the system" can surely be devised—the suggestion to study biographies of successful and unsuccessful programs constitutes one example

—which would unfold these complexities. In the study of most organizations and institutions, one can find such critical points, and once they are understood, the other parts of the system are illuminated as well. One example from the Bureau files is an old study of the organization of radio. While several kinds of research were conducted, the organizational structure became best understood after we studied in detail the role of the disk jockeys. These turned out to be crucial links, at least in the area of music (which comprised the largest share of broadcasting activities), and played roles vis-à-vis the radio stations, the sponsors, the music industry, and the public, which, once we understood them, helped us to characterize the total organization of the industry.

One can hope for a convergence of the increased interest of the social scientists in business management and the structure of organizations with an increasing recognition by management itself of the value of such studies.

The theme touched on most frequently in the preceding pages concerns questions of taste—whether television can be utilized to raise levels of taste and cultural sophistication, whether it has in fact been doing this, and how the process might work. The program analyzer isolates the moments in which taste differences make themselves felt, the non-laboratory experiments help identify and characterize the groups in the population which have divergent tastes, long-range studies determine some of the good and bad effects of good and bad experiences with television, studies of the decision-making process can provide ways of finding out how the whole organization might be made more flexible, and how some good programs, now systematically excluded, might in the future be introduced.

Fifteen years ago I commented on the disappointment of liberals who for generations fought to give people more leisure time, only to find that "instead of going to Columbia University, they go to the Columbia Broadcasting System."[2] But now that the lectures of my colleagues at Columbia University are telecast daily, this separation is no longer so clear-cut. It would be satisfying indeed if such inroads could be ex-

[2] In a talk given at the National Association of Broadcasters 1947 meetings, cited in "The Role of Criticism in Management of Mass Communication," in Wilbur Schramm (ed.): *Communication in Modern Society* (Urbana: University of Illinois Press, 1948), p. 192.

tended; research which might help provide some of the direction is suggested here.

The present study of public attitudes toward television, along with Dr. Steiner's personal comments, should help to define some of the issues concerning the cultural role of television in our society. I hope that the other components of television as a social phenomenon, illustrated in the preceding pages, will be given a high place on the research agenda of our society, that they will attract the attention and ingenuity of the younger research generation, and be carried out on a scale appropriate to the importance of the problem.

A NOTE ON THE TYPE

THE TEXT of this book was set on the Linotype in a face called TIMES ROMAN, designed by Stanley Morison for *The Times* (London), and first introduced by that newspaper in 1932. Among typographers and designers of the twentieth century, Stanley Morison has been a strong forming influence, as typographical advisor to the English Monotype Corporation, as a director of two distinguished English publishing houses, and as a writer of sensibility, erudition, and keen practical sense.

Composed by Howard O. Bullard, Inc., New York.
Printed and bound by
American Book–Stratford Press, Inc., New York